PRAISE FOR *The Accidental President*

"The story of Truman's accession to the presidency is worthy of a Hollywood melodrama, and A. J. Baime's zippy, well-judged, and hugely readable book more than does it justice . . . although there are plenty of good biographies of Truman, few are as entertaining as Baime's."
—**Dominic Sandbrook,** *Sunday Times*

"An entertaining new history of Truman's first months in office . . . filled with events that are strikingly proportionate to what the Trump administration has weathered since January."
—**John Batchelor,** *Daily Beast*

"A well-written and interesting account."
—**Harry Levins,** *St. Louis Post-Dispatch*

"Baime . . . not only captures Truman's rise in popularity, but further analyzes why this unimposing senator from the nation's heartland has so captured the imaginations of two generations . . . Baime describes in exciting and highly charged prose four months of unrelenting activity that left everyone around the new president in awe of his energy . . ."
—**Edward Cuddihy,** *Buffalo News*

"A. J. Baime is a master. His reporting and storytelling are woven to hypnotic effect. Opening the first page of *The Accidental President* is like pulling up a chair to Truman's White House desk, where we sit engrossed as world events unfold in the most intimate manner, titanic in scale. Baime brings us as close as we are likely to get to this completely surprising, quirky, wily, and transformational president. This is history and humanity in lush, vivid color."
—**Doug Stanton,** author of *The Odyssey of Echo Company* and *Horse Soldiers*

"Intimate and absorbing, A. J. Baime's biography uses new sources to paint Harry Truman as a complex and thoroughly American figure. A sharply drawn portrait of an era as well as a man."
—**Stephan Talty,** author of *The Black Hand* and *Agent Garbo*

"A. J. Baime is a master storyteller, and *The Accidental President* contains everything a reader could ever want from a work of history: characters that jump off the page, tension that makes your pulse pound, and smooth, smart writing that makes you think. Amazing!"

—**Jonathan Eig**, author of *Ali: A Life* and *Luckiest Man*

"No president in history—particularly one who came in without having been briefed by his predecessor—has faced such monumental decisions. A. J. Baime has put a spotlight on those four months, recounting them faithfully and with heart, so that you come away with not only a sense of history, but a sense of the man, Harry Truman, as well. As Grandpa himself said a few years later, 'It's hell to be President of the Greatest Most Powerful Nation on Earth.'"

—**Clifton Truman Daniel**, Truman's grandson and author of *Growing Up with My Grandfather: Memories of Harry S. Truman*

"Baime is a master storyteller who appears to have invented a time machine. His carefully crafted narrative transports the reader back in time . . . Each sentence is carefully constructed and colorfully packed with details that makes Harry Truman and this period in history come alive. *The Accidental President* reads more like a captivating novel than nonfiction. The book is good history in that it simplifies events without being simple."

—**PresidentialHistory.com**

"A fast-paced, well-detailed chronology of Truman's transformation from an official with little administrative responsibility into a politically astute and ultimately beloved leader . . . A warmly human portrait of an unlikely president."

—*Kirkus Reviews*

"By relying mostly on primary sources, Baime allows for a better perspective of Truman, in which his political decisions are equally as significant as the correspondence with his beloved wife, daughter, and mother. He also adeptly manages to include nuanced U.S.-Russia relations and East Asian diplomacy."

—*Library Journal*, starred review

The Accidental President

BOOKS BY A. J. BAIME

*The Arsenal of Democracy: FDR, Detroit, and an
Epic Quest to Arm an America at War*

*Go Like Hell: Ford, Ferrari, and
Their Battle for Speed and Glory at Le Mans*

Big Shots: The Men Behind the Booze

THE
ACCIDENTAL
PRESIDENT

Harry S. Truman

AND THE

Four Months

THAT

Changed the World

A. J. Baime

Mariner Books
Houghton Mifflin Harcourt
Boston New York

First Mariner Books edition 2018

Library of Congress Cataloging-in-Publication Data
Names: Baime, A. J. (Albert J.), author.
Title: The accidental president : Harry S. Truman and the four months that
changed the world / A.J. Baime.
Description: Boston : Houghton Mifflin Harcourt, 2017.
Identifiers: LCCN 2017045178 (print) | LCCN 2017044086 (ebook) |
ISBN 9780544618480 (ebook) | ISBN 9780544617346 (hardcover)
ISBN 9781328505682 (paperback) |
Subjects: LCSH: Truman, Harry S., 1884–1972. | Presidents – United
States – Biography. | United States – Politics and government – 1945–1953. |
World War, 1939–1945.
Classification: LCC E814 (print) | LCC E814 .B35 2017 (ebook) |
DDC 973.918092 [B] – dc23
LC record available at https://lccn.loc.gov/2017045178

Book design by Greta D. Sibley

Printed in the United States of America
DOC 10 9 8 7
4500799788

For Judge David S. Baime,
my father,
who has kept a portrait of
Harry S. Truman on his office wall
for more than forty years

Contents

Part V

Little Boy, Fat Man, and Potsdam

293

Introduction

FEW AMERICAN PRESIDENTS have left such a polarizing legacy as Harry Truman. Perhaps none have. Historians have ranked him among the greatest and among the worst chief executives. His administration was deeply frowned upon when he left office in January 1953. Less than ten years later, a poll conducted by the prominent historian Arthur Schlesinger ranked Truman ninth among American presidents. As recently as 2014, a *Washington Post* poll ranked him sixth. At the same time, others have labeled him a war criminal, for it was Truman who gave the go-ahead to drop the atomic bombs on Japan — Little Boy and Fat Man, August 6 and 9, 1945.

This book poses a new thesis. Regardless of Truman's legacy, the first four months of his administration should rank as the most challenging and action-packed of any four-month period in any American presidency. Through declassified war documents, personal diaries, international communications of the highest diplomacy, and other primary sources, the figures who appear in this book will tell you that themselves. Arguably, no other four-month period has had so much import in shaping the world we live in today.

Truman's presidential odyssey began on April 12, 1945, the day Franklin Roosevelt died. It is impossible to overstate the shock to the world FDR's death caused. "The Romans must have felt this way when word came that Caesar Augustus was dead," the columnist I. F. Stone wrote at the time. "Perhaps not since the dawn of history," State Department veteran Joseph Davies wrote in his diary, "has the passing of a great man been mourned contemporaneously by so many different nations, so many different religions and races, spread over the earth."

Roosevelt had played the role of chief executive as if history had written it for him. Prestige was his defining characteristic, in an age when Victorian values and class structure still dictated so much of people's lives. He served as president longer than any other man, and was the first to be widely considered one of the all-time great American presidents during his administration. (Washington, Jefferson, and Lincoln all found their places in the canon of greats after their deaths.) In a 1945 Gallup poll, in which Americans were asked to name world history's greatest figure, the country put Roosevelt first, ahead of Abraham Lincoln and Jesus Christ.

The man forced to fill his shoes — Truman, the vice president — was the prototypical ordinary man, in contrast. He had no college degree. He had never had enough money to own his own home. He had never governed a state or served as mayor of a city. He became president "by accident" (his words). His ascendancy to the most powerful office in existence was the result of a confluence of almost bizarre events, and his obscurity confounded the world.

"Here was a man who came into the White House almost as though he had been picked at random off the street," recalled Robert Nixon, a Truman White House correspondent, "with absolutely no useable background and no useable information." "Here was a guy like you, or your next door neighbor," one of Truman's closest friends, Harry Vaughan, said, "and he got into a job that was too big for him." When Truman took office, a *Chicago Tribune* columnist spoke for all of civilized humanity when he wrote: "All the world is asking two questions. 'What sort of man is Harry S. Truman?' and 'What kind of president will he make?'"

The first four months of Truman's presidency saw the collapse of Nazi Germany, the founding of the United Nations, firebombings of Japanese cities that killed many thousands of civilians, the liberation of Nazi death camps, the suicide of Adolf Hitler, the execution of Benito Mussolini, and the capture of arch war criminals from Hitler's number two, Hermann Göring, to the Nazi "chief werewolf" Ernst Kaltenbrunner. There was the fall of Berlin, victory at Okinawa (which the historian Bill Sloan has called "the deadliest campaign of conquest ever undertaken by American arms"), and the Potsdam Conference, during which the new president sat at the negotiating table with Winston Churchill and Joseph Stalin in Soviet-occupied Germany, in an attempt to map out a new world. Humanity saw the first atomic explosion, the nuclear destruction of Hiroshima and Nagasaki, the dawn of the Cold War, and the beginning of the nuclear arms race.

Never had fate shoehorned so much history into such a short period. "The four months that have elapsed since the death of President Roosevelt on April 12 have been one of the most momentous periods in man's history," wrote a *New York Times* columnist at the time. "They have hardly any parallel throughout the ages."

This book is not a full-length biography of Truman, nor is it a study of the decision to drop the atomic bomb, for those books have been written. It is rather an intimate biographical portrait of Truman during the first four months of his administration — the climactic months of World War II. It was a time when Americans achieved a sense of unity that seems unimaginable today. It was also a time of massacre, when the U.S. military committed acts it still struggles to justify more than seventy years later. New documents have appeared for research since the wave of Truman biographies was published nearly a quarter century ago. Also, the early days of the Truman administration seem particularly relevant given the global political picture today and all the debate about what the American presidency has or should become.

Whether or not the reader accepts my thesis is obviously subjective. Each can decide at the end. But first, there must be a beginning: April 12, 1945.

Timeline

The Rise of Truman

MAY 8, 1884: Harry S. Truman is born in rural Lamar, Missouri.

1901: Truman graduates high school. Due to lack of funds, he does not go to college. He works through a series of jobs, on a railroad and then as a clerk at Kansas City banks.

1906–1917: Truman returns to the family farm in Grandview, Missouri, where he will toil obscurely for eleven years. Get-rich-quick schemes – from oil wells to mining operations – all end in failure.

1918: APRIL 13: Truman lands in France as a thirty-three-year-old captain in the U.S. Army during World War I.

JULY 11: He takes command of Battery D.

NOVEMBER 11: World War I ends. While more than 5 million Allied soldiers have been killed, including roughly 117,000 Americans, Truman's Battery D does not lose a single man.

JUNE 28, 1919: Truman marries Elizabeth "Bess" Wallace and moves into her family home in Independence, Missouri.

1922: Truman and Jacobson, a Kansas City haberdashery, fails, leaving Truman financially devastated.

– With virtually no qualifications, Truman wins an election for a judgeship in rural Jackson County, due to the backing of Tom Pendergast – the corrupt "boss" of Kansas City's Democratic machine.

1924: Truman fails in his bid for reelection. It is the only election he will ever lose.

1926: Truman wins election for presiding judge of Jackson County, again due to the patronage of Boss Tom Pendergast.

OCTOBER 24, 1929: Black Thursday. The Great Depression begins.

1933: JANUARY 30: Adolf Hitler becomes chancellor of Germany.

MARCH 4: Franklin Roosevelt is inaugurated the thirty-second president of the United States.

NOVEMBER 6, 1934: Truman is elected a U.S. senator under dubious circumstances, due to the patronage of the corrupt Kansas City machine. Critics label him "the Senator from Pendergast."

1939: APRIL: Boss Tom Pendergast is indicted on tax evasion charges and is later imprisoned at Leavenworth. Dozens of Pendergast machine operatives are jailed on charges of rigging elections.

SEPTEMBER 1: Nazi Germany invades Poland.

1940: OCTOBER: Truman's mother and sister are evicted from their farm in Grandview, due to bank foreclosure.

NOVEMBER 5: Stained by his Pendergast alliance, Truman is given almost no chance of reelection. But against all odds, he wins a second term in the U.S. Senate.

1941: MARCH 1: Truman founds the Senate Special Committee to Investigate the National Defense Program — the Truman Committee.

DECEMBER 7: Japan attacks the United States at Pearl Harbor, forcing America into World War II.

1941–1944: The Truman Committee's investigations of waste and corruption in the national defense effort gain the senator from Missouri his first national recognition.

1944: JULY: Truman stuns the Democratic National Convention in Chicago when he is nominated as the vice presidential candidate on the 1944 ticket with FDR.

NOVEMBER 7: Roosevelt becomes the first four-term president, with Truman as his VP.

1945: APRIL 1: U.S. forces land on Okinawa on Easter Sunday.

APRIL 12: Roosevelt dies. Truman becomes the thirty-third president of the United States. The night he takes the oath, he is told of a secret weapon the U.S. military is working on, an "atomic bomb."

The Accidental Presidency and World War II

1945: Truman's First Four Months

APRIL 13: Truman's first full day in office. He meets with his cabinet for the first time.

— Major General Curtis LeMay's Twenty-First Bomber Command firebombs Japan. Thousands of civilians are killed.

APRIL 14: Roosevelt's funeral procession winds through Washington, DC. A service is held in the White House East Room.

APRIL 15: Truman attends Roosevelt's burial in Hyde Park, New York.

— Allied troops liberate the Nazi death camp at Bergen-Belsen.

APRIL 16: Truman addresses Congress for the first time as president, vowing to force Japan to surrender unconditionally.

APRIL 23: Truman meets with Vyacheslav Molotov, Joseph Stalin's number two, to discuss deteriorating relations between the United States and the Soviet Union.

APRIL 25: The United Nations Conference begins in San Francisco. Delegates from nearly fifty nations begin to map out the new peace organization.

— Truman meets with General Leslie Groves and Secretary of War Henry Stimson. The president learns in-depth details of the atomic bomb for the first time.

— "Elbe Day." American and Soviet forces meet at the Elbe River, joining the eastern and western fronts and severing Nazi Germany in half.

APRIL 28: Partisans execute Italian Fascist leader Benito Mussolini, along with his mistress, by gunfire. Mussolini's last words are reportedly, "No! No!"

APRIL 29: American forces liberate more than thirty thousand prisoners at the Dachau concentration camp.

— Nazi forces in Italy surrender.

APRIL 30: As Russia's Red Army closes in on Hitler's Berlin bunker, Hitler and his newlywed bride, Eva Braun, commit suicide.

MAY 2: The Soviet Union announces the fall of Berlin to the Red Army.

MAY 4: German forces in the Netherlands and Denmark agree to surrender.

MAY 5: American troops liberate the Mauthausen death camp.

MAY 7: The Trumans move into the White House.

MAY 8: VE-day. Following the surrender of Nazi forces to General Eisenhower in Reims, France, World War II in Europe ends. Harry Truman celebrates his sixty-first birthday.

MAY 11: As the battle for Okinawa rages, a Japanese suicide plane crashes into the USS *Bunker Hill*, killing nearly four hundred American sailors.

MAY 24–26: Under orders from Major General Curtis LeMay, the Twenty-First Bomber Command firebombs Tokyo again, this time striking the emperor's palace. Scores of civilians are killed.

MAY 28: Truman hosts his first White House state dinner, for the regent of Iraq, Prince Abd al-Ilah.

JUNE 1: The top advisory committee on the Manhattan Project advises Truman to employ the bomb against Japan "as soon as possible . . . without prior warning."

JUNE 5: Military leaders from the United States, the USSR, Britain, and France meet in Berlin to begin the process of occupying Germany, which is to be sliced into occupation zones, one for each of those four nations.

JUNE 18: Truman meets with his top military advisors to strategize the end of the war with Japan. The leaders agree on plans to invade Japan with nearly 800,000 ground troops. General George C. Marshall sets D-day at November 1.
— General Eisenhower makes his triumphant return to Washington. Truman fetes him at a White House "stag party."

JUNE 22: Allied victory is declared in Okinawa. Before the final bullets are fired, Japanese soldiers hand out grenades to civilians on the island, ordering them to kill themselves. Many do.

JUNE 26: Fifty delegations sign the UN Charter in San Francisco. President Truman addresses the delegations at the city's War Memorial Veterans Building.

JUNE 27: Truman returns to his hometown of Independence, Missouri, as president for the first time. The biggest crowds in the history of Jackson County turn out to welcome him.

JULY 3: James F. Byrnes is sworn in as the new secretary of state, becoming Truman's most important advisor.

JULY 6: Truman leaves the White House by car at night, bound for ship passage to the Potsdam Conference in Soviet-occupied Germany. His approval rating in the United States is 87 percent — higher than Roosevelt's ever was.

JULY 16: The Trinity shot is successfully fired in the New Mexico desert — the first test of an atomic bomb.

— In Babelsberg, Germany, Truman meets Winston Churchill face-to-face for the first time.

JULY 17: Truman meets Joseph Stalin for the first time. They discuss the startling deterioration of American-Soviet relations.

— The Potsdam Conference officially begins. Truman is named the historic conference's chairman.

JULY 24: At Potsdam, Truman tells Stalin that the Americans have an atomic bomb.

JULY 26: The United States, Britain, and China issue the Potsdam Declaration, demanding unconditional surrender of Japan. "The alternative for Japan is prompt and utter destruction."

JULY 28: The U.S. Senate ratifies the United Nations Charter.

AUGUST 2: The Potsdam Conference ends.

— Truman meets with Britain's King George VI. Much of their conversation is devoted to the secret atomic weapon.

AUGUST 6: While Truman is aboard the USS *Augusta* bound for Newport News, Virginia, the *Enola Gay* delivers the "Little Boy" bomb over Hiroshima — mankind's first atomic attack.

AUGUST 8: Back in the White House, Truman signs the United Nations Charter.

— The Soviet Union declares war on Japan.

AUGUST 9: The "Fat Man" atomic bomb explodes over Nagasaki.

AUGUST 14: Truman announces the surrender of Japan. World War II ends.

Part I

April 12, 1945

If ever I felt the awesome dimensions of
history, it was in that room, that night.

— Truman's only child, Margaret,
on her father's swearing in

1

IN THE FUTURE, Harry Truman would remember April 12 as the day "the whole weight of the moon and the stars fell on me." He would recall the phone conversation that started it all, and the drive to the White House in the rain. He would recall standing in the Cabinet Room feeling utterly alone, while surrounded by men long accustomed to wielding extraordinary power, their faces stained with tears. He would recall how the thirty-five-word presidential oath — which saw "a transfer of power . . . unparalleled in history," in his words — took hardly more than a minute to recite.

When the day began, however, there was little hint that the events of April 12 would shock the world. It began as an ordinary day, if such a thing could exist in America's capital city during the fourth full year of world war.

Truman awoke on his eighty-second day as vice president in his second-floor apartment at 4701 Connecticut Avenue. He was a man of precise routine, beginning with sunrise. He did not just get up at the crack of dawn, his friend and military aide Harry Vaughan liked to joke. "He's the man who *cracks* the dawn." Truman had spent much of the previous four years moving from hotel room to hotel room, train car to train car, and there were many solitary nights in Washington. He was a man who suffered loneliness with intensity, so he fancied the days when he woke with his wife next to him (they kept separate beds, as was custom at the time), and his daughter in the next room.

Here was his living room, with his familiar chair in the corner next to his piano, his phonograph and favorite records. ("Mozart, Beethoven, Bach, Mendelssohn . . . beautiful harmonies that make you love them," he described this music.) Here was his reading lamp and bookshelf full of favorites — a biography of his hero Andrew Jackson by Marquis James and a study of the ancient world called *Plutarch's Lives,* among others.

In the small kitchen, bare white walls framed a back door, which held a hook where Mrs. Truman hung her apron.

The Trumans' five-room apartment cost $120 a month. Harry and his wife of twenty-five years, Elizabeth "Bess" Wallace, shared one bedroom, while their only child, twenty-one-year-old Margaret, shared the other with Bess's mother, Mrs. Madge Wallace, who had never liked Harry very much. In a town full of East Coast money and stuffed pinstriped suits, guests of the Trumans gathered quickly that the family had little means. The press made colorful headlines of the fact that Bess Truman had no maid; the VP's wife did her own cooking and washing. (The Trumans' bank account measured $4,251.12 on this day, though more than $3,000 was owed to the Hamilton National Bank of Washington, from a loan.)

Truman chose a double-breasted gray suit with wide lapels, a white shirt, a spotted dark bow tie, and a pocket square folded so three corners poked out in perfectly pressed edges. He was unaware of the importance of this day's sartorial choices, that photographers would capture him in these clothes at the most important moment of his life. He liked a morning walk — 120 paces a minute, "regular Army marching speed," as he said, every step like a hammer driving in a nail. He was the first VP assigned secret service detail. "You had to get up early," recalled one secret service man, "because he came out at six o'clock or six-fifteen a.m." On this morning, it was humid and misty, the thermometer headed up to 87 degrees F. Truman had come of age long before the first motorcar's engine had cracked the silence of his midwestern plains, and the modernity that met his eye during his morning walks never ceased to fascinate him.

"Look at that thing lift up!" he shouted once while walking through Washington just after sunrise, pointing at an airplane roaring overhead. "It's one of the miracles of our age how a big, heavy thing like that will lift up off the ground . . . I can hardly believe my eyes when I see it."

His wife made him breakfast most mornings (he liked toast and bacon, sometimes an egg, with an occasional medicinal shot of bourbon and rarely any coffee). Then he made for the black Mercury state car idling out front, where his driver, Tom Harty, and a secret service man awaited. The car routinely swung by George Washington University, where Truman dropped his daughter off. Margaret — whom he called Margie with a hard *g* — was a junior majoring in history, though her great passion, like her father's, was for music. On this morning she was feeling nerves, for she had an exam in her History of Philosophy course (she would score a B–). Then Truman's driver motored on to the Senate Office Building, which sprawled stark white and regal along Constitution Avenue, just north of the Capitol.

Truman had walked the Senate Office Building's hallways happily for nearly a decade now. The building's striking symbols of power were quotidian to his eye: the Corinthian rotunda with its coffered dome, the nearby twin marble staircases that led to the Caucus Room, inside which the hearings over the sinking of the RMS *Titanic* had been held years earlier. Tourists came from all over to walk this building's corridors and to taste the famous bean soup in the cafeteria, which lived up to the billing.

On the second floor the sign on the door to suite 240 greeted Truman each morning: THE VICE PRESIDENT.

///

"I used to get down here to the office at 7 o'clock," Truman had written of his routine just the day before, on April 11. "But now I have to take Margaret to school every morning and I don't get here until 8:30 . . . By that time I have to see people one at a time just as fast as they can go through the office without seeming to hurry through." There were always "curiosity seekers" aiming to "see what a V.P. looks like and if he walks and talks and has teeth."

The vice president's staff included four stenographers and one secretary, Reathel Odum, who was at the ready on the morning of April 12. Truman dictated a letter to his sister-in-law May Wallace about her dog. "I imagine Spot is getting fatter and fatter. I have gained nine pounds myself." And another letter to an old friend, James Pendergast in Kansas City, who was asking for help with a small matter involving the War Production Board. "They are a contrary outfit," Truman dictated. "We will see what we can do right away." (This latter letter would not be mailed until the following morning, and Truman would write in longhand at the bottom: "Since this was dictated I'm Pres. of the U.S. . . . Pray for me with all you have.")

Truman had not gotten used to the fact that, as vice president, he had almost nothing to do, and whatever string he pulled in Washington left him open to political attacks. He held the second-highest elected office in government, and yet his only official duty was to serve as president of the Senate. He was to monitor proceedings in the Senate Chamber in the Capitol; his most important job on most days was to crack his gavel to signal the recess. In the rare case that senators voted to a tie on an issue, the VP would cast the deciding vote. For Truman, this had happened only once, two days earlier. He had voted against a bill amendment "with all the brisk eagerness of someone who is bored to death," recalled one reporter present. It was custom for a senator to sit in the VP's place on the dais in the chamber, so there was no urgency for Truman to get there at any particular hour.

An old army buddy of Truman's — Eddie McKim, an Omaha insurance salesman — showed up at the VP's office on this morning. McKim was in town on business, staying at the Statler Hotel. Truman took him to lunch around noon in the office of the secretary of the Senate, Leslie Biffle of tiny Piggott, Arkansas. Biffle's office was affectionately called "Biffle's Tavern," where the bar was stocked and congressional chatter was always on the menu. Afterward Truman and McKim drummed up an evening plan.

"Don't you think we ought to have a little game tonight?" Truman said, referring to his favorite pastime, poker.

"Yes, I think so. Where do you want to play?"

Truman suggested McKim's hotel. The Statler was one of the first chain hotels, and the first to advertise a bathroom in every room. Truman jotted down a list of players he wanted McKim to gather. The conversation, as McKim remembered it:

"How's your whiskey supply?" the VP asked.

"Well, it's nonexistent," McKim said.

"I've got some new whiskey over in the Senate Office Building office," Truman said. "You go over there and get what you think we'll need."

The VP turned and headed for the Senate Chamber, where he would make an afternoon appearance. McKim headed off to stock the liquor and ready the game — a game that would never be played.

///

Around the globe, extraordinary developments were unfolding on April 12. The U.S. Ninth Army reached the Elbe River on the western front, fifty-seven miles from Berlin. As the Allies were soon to find out, the Elbe was to play a strange and important role in shaping the future of Europe. Soviet forces had surrounded the Nazis at Vienna and were closing in on Berlin from the east. A simple read of the newspaper gave enough information for most Americans to understand that Nazi Germany was nearing collapse. The conquering Allied armies had made shocking discoveries as they marched toward Hitler's bunker in Berlin.

Eighty miles northeast of Frankfurt on the morning of April 12, the supreme commander of the Allied Expeditionary Force, General Dwight Eisenhower, stepped through the gates of the Ohrdruf death camp, witnessing for the first time the horrors of the Nazi Final Solution. Flanked by Generals George Patton and Omar Bradley, with dozens of military police, army officers, and infantrymen trailing behind, Eisenhower took it all in – the visions and odors of death and torture assaulting his senses.

Ohrdruf spread out across the flat landscape under an iron-gray sky, with crude wooden barracks standing near the camp's perimeter, which was lined by gunner towers and barbed wire fences. It was the first concentration camp liberated by the Allies that had prisoners still living onsite. Like innumerable other Americans, Eisenhower had read of these death camps; now the general was seeing the evidence with his own eyes. He felt it his "duty" to witness the camp's "every nook and cranny."

In the camp's center courtyard, dozens of human bodies lay where they had fallen, victims of point-blank gunshots less than two weeks earlier. The Nazis had done this work as they fled Ohrdruf. As Eisenhower would later learn, some twelve thousand prisoners from Ohrdruf had been forced on a death march to Buchenwald, some forty-five miles away, as the Allied troops closed in. In one section of the camp, Eisenhower saw a makeshift crematorium with piles of charred remains. Living inmates with the strength to move demonstrated for the fifty-four-year-old Texas-born general how they had been tortured by the Nazis. Others stared at Eisenhower silently, too fatigued to move the muscles in their faces. The experience, as the general would later recall, strengthened the sense of justice that had been the driving force of his work.

After Eisenhower's visit he and his fellow generals reconvened at Patton's nearby field headquarters. Eisenhower cabled the army chief of staff in the Pentagon, General George C. Marshall.

"The things I saw beggar description," he wrote on April 12. "The visual evidence and verbal testimony of starvation, cruelty and bestiality were so overpowering as to leave me a bit sick."

He urged Washington to organize a group of American journalists to come to Europe to begin documenting these horrors at once. There were still those who claimed "the stories of Nazi brutality were just propaganda," Eisenhower believed. "I felt that the evidence should be immediately placed before the American and British publics in a fashion that would leave no room for cynical debate."

In the Far East, the war was raging on Okinawa – a Pacific atoll less than half the size of Rhode Island. Tens of thousands of U.S. troops had landed there eleven days earlier, on Easter Sunday, April 1. In time this battle would pit some 541,000 troops from the U.S. Tenth Army against the 110,000-man Japanese Thirty-Second Army. Through history's looking glass, Okinawa would become known as the last massive human combat maelstrom of its kind on earth. The *Washington Post* on this morning, April 12, reported "furious ground fighting . . . the hottest of any Pacific campaign."

At the headquarters for the Twenty-First Bomber Command on the island of Guam in the South Pacific, Major General Curtis LeMay was preparing to unleash a mission of B-29s over mainland Japan, to strike the heart of Tokyo with incendiary bombs. The night before (April 11 in Washington, April 12 in the South Pacific), LeMay's Mission 63 had laid waste to the Nakajima aircraft factory in Tokyo. According to LeMay's official report: "Total roof area damaged or destroyed amounted to approximately 886,900 sq. feet. Or 48.2% of the total roof area." That mission had used conventional bombs. However, the mission of April 13 (April 12 in Washington) would use incendiaries – firebombs.

LeMay had recently emerged as the American military's most controversial man, due to his March 1945 firebombing campaigns – the destruction of Japanese urban areas with bombs that spewed sheets of unquenchable flames. He was known for sending men on missions that seemed impossible. "My idea of what was humanly possible," he later wrote, "sometimes did not coincide with the opinions of others." His B-29 Superfortresses – 327 four-engine bombers loaded with incendiaries – would take off at roughly 6 p.m. Guam time. As Harry Truman was going about his day on April 12, Curtis LeMay was preparing to burn miles of Tokyo to the ground.

///

In Washington, DC, on this morning of April 12, armies of workers were shuffling through the offices of innumerable federal buildings, fighting their own private wars. This was "Washington Wonderland," a wartime boomtown where jobs were easy to find and apartments nearly impossible.

The city had changed vastly during the war years. More than 280,000 Americans had moved into the district seeking work. Well more than half were women hunting jobs as clerks and typists, for paychecks hard to match in their hometowns as far off as Texas and California. In one year during the war twenty-seven new office buildings went up in the nation's capital. The federal government employed 3.4 million civilians, with enough committees and organizations to fill seventeen pages in fine print in the *Congressional Directory*. Washington was a city of bureaucratic madness, ruthless ambition, and tried-and-true patriotism, a city stretched to its limit with every kind of tension — overworked, overcrowded, under-slept, racially charged.

"If you want a friend in Washington," Harry Truman once said, "get a dog."

The city appeared different from other capitals in warring nations, from London to Berlin to Tokyo. Washington had not been bombed. There were no scars of war, with the exception of the wearied faces of men and women who had lost their sons and husbands, and the wounded soldiers struggling by in wheelchairs and on crutches.

Washington was a uniquely American metropolis, in that it was dreamed up on paper before its first brick had been laid. The founding fathers wrote in article 1, section 8 of the U.S. Constitution of a "District (not exceeding ten Miles square) as may ... become the Seat of the Government of the United States." The "federal city" rose out of the rural banks of the Potomac River starting in the days of George Washington's administration, with edifices meant to project all the magnificence of ancient Rome (the Supreme Court Building, the United States Capitol), buildings that had in fact no ancient history at all.

"It abounds in phonies," White House press secretary Jonathan Daniels wrote of the city. "There are Negro messengers, Irish politicians, Jewish lawyers, demagogues who sometimes look like statesmen, and statesmen who often act like demagogues ... Frustration is often normal. Ambition is standard. Envy can be malignant in a town in which everybody can know everybody else's pay."

Nothing symbolized the federal government's wartime work frenzy more than the new Pentagon, the largest office building on earth, situated on the other side of the Potomac River from the White House next to the Arlington National Cemetery. Completed in 1942, it stood five stories high, with 6.5 million square feet of offices, enough space to keep an army of janitors waxing the floors all year long. But Washington's greatest symbol had long since become its current president – the first "four termer." As the Washington writer W. M. Kiplinger put it: "I've never known any President who was as omnipresent as this Roosevelt."

///

Like most Americans, Harry Truman was mystified by his rise to number two in Roosevelt's administration. Most Americans knew little about the vice president. Those who did know some things smelled a strong whiff of American mythology. Truman had first come to Washington under dubious circumstances in 1934, elected to the U.S. Senate thanks to the support of a Kansas City political machine widely known to be corrupt. Truman had served as an obscure senator for the most part, until he burst onto the national scene by complete surprise – to America, and to himself – less than a year earlier at the 1944 Democratic National Convention in Chicago. There he was chosen as Roosevelt's running mate on the Democratic ticket, against Thomas Dewey of New York/John W. Bricker of Ohio.

Even the most connected politicos could not agree as to how this had happened. According to Democratic National Committee secretary George Allen, one of the organizers of the convention in Chicago: "It is one of the episodes in American history that will baffle scholars of the future because no two accounts of it agree completely and some vary widely."

According to a national poll published just as the Chicago convention was set to start in July 1944, only 2 percent of Democratic voters hoped to see Truman as the VP nominee on the ticket with Roosevelt, with five other names ahead of him on the list. Not long before Truman was chosen, Roosevelt had said of the senator from Missouri, "I hardly know Truman."

"I knew almost nothing about him," Admiral William Leahy, FDR's chief of staff, said of Truman. Even at the height of the 1944 campaign, as the VP nominee toured the nation stumping for Roosevelt, "Truman [was] still unknown to millions despite [the] fanfare," according to the *Washington Post*. Only 55 percent of Americans could name Roosevelt's running mate, according to a national poll.

Through the reams of press coverage that emerged during the campaign, Americans learned in 1944 that Truman had spent much of his life farming in obscurity, and that he had once been a haberdasher in Kansas City, selling hats and socks to well-to-do customers before going out of business, suffering lawsuits in the process from which it took several years to recover financially. He had served commanding troops in the field in Europe during World War I. His middle initial – S. – stood for nothing, exactly. His parents could not agree on his middle name when he was born in rural Missouri, except that it should begin with an *S* (referring to the names of Truman's grandfathers, Solomon Young and Anderson Shipp Truman). Americans also were well acquainted with the story of how Harry Truman's political patron – "Boss" Tom Pendergast, who was much responsible for the Missourian's rise to national politics – had been imprisoned, and was now serving time in the federal penitentiary at Leavenworth, Kansas, for fraud.

Truman played a small role in the 1944 election. "In the scheme of American politics there is nothing less important than a Vice-President unless it is a Vice-Presidential nominee," noted George Allen, who wrote many of Truman's campaign speeches. "He was nobody's darling." The focus of the election was the towering figure of Franklin Roosevelt, who defeated Republican Thomas Dewey to win an unprecedented fourth term. And so Harry Truman had become the vice president.

The job was "a graveyard of politicians" in Washington parlance, traditionally disparaged by the men who held it. The VP before Truman, Henry Wallace, bragged that he had never had so much time to work on his tennis game. "The Vice President has not much to do," Truman said, referring to himself as a "political Eunuch." When asked what he would do with his "spare time," he answered: "Study history."

But he did more than that. To keep busy, he attended ball games, teas, banquets. When Rocky Graziano knocked out Philadelphia's Billy Arnold in the third round at Madison Square Garden, Truman was ringside. At a National Press Club party in Washington, the vice president regaled guests with his talent on the piano keys, while sitting atop the piano itself was Hollywood's latest sensation, Lauren Bacall, bearing down on the VP with a most suggestive gaze. A soldier standing nearby could not believe his eyes, muttering: "Anything can happen in this country!"

Only the vice president's most inner circle knew that Truman suffered acute anxiety. He had failed to crack the inner circle of Roosevelt's trusted advisors and in fact knew almost nothing about what was going on in the Oval Office. During his eighty-two days as VP leading up to April 12, 1945, Truman had visited the president on official business just twice. He was terrified by what he saw. According to the Washington rumor mill, Roosevelt had suffered a stroke, a heart attack, cancer of the prostate, a nervous breakdown – the story changed every day. Truman had seen little of the president, but he had seen enough to know that the rumors about FDR's ill health were rooted in fact. When a reporter reminded Truman that just one heartbeat separated him from the White House, he squirmed and said, "Don't say that. I don't let myself think of it."

One day not long after his vice presidential inauguration in January 1945, Truman was at the White House for a tea, and he'd brought along his friend Eddie McKim. On the way out, McKim stopped Truman at the White House gate. "[I] told him to turn around and take a look at that place," McKim recalled. "That was where he was going to be living."

Truman stared at the stately building. Here was where the very essence of world power was wielded. "I'm afraid you're right, Eddie," he responded. "And it scares the hell out of me."

"He knew that . . . he would be president before the term was out," recalled close confidant and political advisor Harry Easley. "He said he was going to have to depend on his friends . . . He knew that he was going to be the president of the United States, and I think it just scared the devil out of him. I think it frightened him, even the thought of it."

///

At roughly 3 p.m. on April 12, Truman entered the Senate Chamber. Since 1859, senators had gathered in this room to debate policies that shaped American law. Ugly steel girders had been erected to hold up pieces of cracked ceiling four years earlier, and due to the war emergency, they were still there. The chamber held ninety-six desks for the ninety-six senators, two from each of the forty-eight states, all facing the dais where the president of the Senate (the VP) presided. Freshman senator Leverett Saltonstall of Massachusetts had been sitting in for the VP on the dais.

One reporter present watched Truman enter that afternoon: "We saw Harry Truman come in, cross to the Republican side and go into an obviously friendly huddle with Alexander Wiley [senator of Wisconsin] and

Ken Wherry [Nebraska]. We watched him for a moment, enjoying as always his enjoyment of other people and theirs of him . . . [Truman] is a fine fellow, presiding like some trim, efficient, keen-minded businessman, which is just what he looks like, with his neat appearance, heavy-lensed glasses, and quick, good-humored smile."

The Senate was pitched in an argument over a Mexican water treaty. Senator Wiley took the floor. "I feel somewhat hesitant to speak on the subject of the treaty now before the Senate," he said, before launching into an endless font of words, which drifted into the tobacco cloud that hung over the chamber with all the relevance of the ashes in the ashtrays. Sitting on the dais, Truman seized the moment to write a letter to his mother and his sister.

"Dear Mamma and Mary," he began, "I am trying to write you a letter today from the desk of the president of the Senate while a windy Senator from Wisconsin is making a speech on a subject which he is in no way familiar . . . We've had a week of beautiful weather but it is raining and misting today."

A reporter named Allen Drury, the Senate correspondent for the United Press, was sitting in the Senate gallery observing. He leaned over to a colleague, Tony Vaccaro, who held the same position for the Associated Press. "You know," Drury said, "Roosevelt has an awfully good man in that Truman when it comes to dealing with the Senate, if he'll only make use of him."

"He doesn't make use of him though," came the reply. "Truman doesn't know what's going on. Roosevelt won't tell him anything."

2

AT 9:30 A.M. on April 12, Franklin Roosevelt lay in his bed in his vacation cottage in rural Warm Springs, Georgia, with a breakfast tray and a copy of the morning's *Atlanta Constitution*, the area's local paper. His usual newspapers – the *New York Times*, the *New York Herald Tribune*, the *Baltimore Sun*, and the *Washington Post* – had been held up in the mail pouch from Washington. And so he was perusing the Atlanta paper when, outside his bedroom door, he heard loud laughter. He recognized the voice of his maid Lizzie McDuffie and called out her name. She appeared shyly in his doorway, apologizing for making so much noise.

"Oh no, no," said the president. "But what in the world were you laughing about?" With his back propped up on a pillow, Roosevelt tilted his head and looked down his nose through his round spectacles, his familiar conversational gaze.

"Well, Mr. Roosevelt," Lizzie said, "do you believe in reincarnation?"

"Do I believe in *what?*"

"Reincarnation."

The president thought for a moment, quietly considering the afterlife. Then he did what he so often did in his press conferences: turned the question on its asker, without revealing his feelings on the matter. "Well tell me, do *you* believe in reincarnation?"

"I don't know if I do or not," the maid said. "But in case there is such a thing, when I come back I want to be a canary bird."

McDuffie remembered this moment vividly. "He looked at me from head to foot – I weighed about two hundred pounds then – and he burst out into *peals* of laughter . . . He looked at how fat I was and said, 'A canary bird!'"

The maid thought Roosevelt was looking healthier on the morning of April 12 than he had of late. But then, she thought, he always looked his best in the morning. He seemed to age impossibly quickly as each day passed, as if the clock inside him was moving too fast.

Roosevelt had arrived in Warm Springs two weeks earlier, on March 29, for a long rest. His cottage was situated near pools of natural spring water where victims of paralysis had come for years to bathe in hopes of soothing the symptoms of polio and other diseases, and there was a hospital nearby where patients received medical care. This hospital was one of the few places where Roosevelt would allow the public to see him in his wheelchair, for he believed he could lift these patients' spirits by rolling out from behind the façade that hid his disability from the rest of the world. He had first come to Warm Springs in 1924, hoping for some miracle cure for his polio, a miracle that had never come. But he loved the place, so he built a six-room white cottage with four colonnades out front in 1933 (the year he took office) and visited often with his dog, Fala, to recuperate from the stress of his job. All the rooms were on one floor, easily maneuvered by wheelchair. Due to the white paint and the colonnades out front, the cottage became known as "the Little White House."

Now sixty-three years old, Roosevelt had led the nation through the Great Depression and World War II, achieving a new kind of presidential iconography. He had become almost a paternal figure for the American public; he had served as chief executive for so long, many soldiers fighting in the military could not remember any other president during their lifetimes. "There were times," White House chief of staff Admiral William Leahy wrote, "when I felt that if I could find anybody except Roosevelt who knew what America wanted, it would be an astonishing discovery."

The responsibilities of the presidency were crushing. After 4,422 days in office, Roosevelt had found it difficult to maintain his energy. He suffered hypertension and heart disease, not to mention chronic sinus pain. He was losing weight alarmingly. Privately, the president's doctor, Admiral Ross McIntire, had described his condition as "God-awful." On the night before his chat about reincarnation with his maid Lizzie, Roosevelt had dined with Secretary of the Treasury Henry Morgenthau in the Little White House. Morgenthau and Roosevelt had been friends for years.

"I was terribly shocked when I saw him," Morgenthau described that dinner. "I found he had aged terrifically and looked very haggard. His hands shook so that he started to knock over glasses. I had to hold each glass as he poured out the cocktail . . . I have never seen him have so much difficulty transferring himself from his wheelchair to his regular chair, and I was in agony watching him."

The president's martinis – an alchemy for which he took great pride – revived him, and Morgenthau noted that FDR had partaken of the caviar with zest.

Now, the next morning, Roosevelt lay in his bed awaiting the mail pouch to come in from the White House, so the day's business could get under way. In the afternoon he planned to attend a barbecue that locals and White House correspondents were throwing for him, in the village of Warm Springs. Already, suckling pigs were sizzling over an open fire, and secret service agents were scoping out the terrain. It was just the kind of thing the president needed to boost his spirits.

"Oh, I don't feel any too good this morning, Lizzie," the president told his maid. He touched the back of his head, complaining of a headache.

///

An alarming entanglement in world affairs confronted the president during his stay at Warm Springs – a development he had kept secret from the American people. Relations between the Soviet Union and the United States had taken an abrupt and dangerous turn.

For the past four years, Soviet dictator Joseph Stalin, British prime minister Winston Churchill, and Roosevelt had forged a most unlikely partnership, waging war together to defeat the Axis powers. Churchill had famously named this partnership "the Grand Alliance." As grand as it was, it joined as allies the Soviets and Americans, two nations with gravely contrasting political ideologies. The relationship between the United States and the USSR was so complex, the State Department's filing cabinets were jammed tightly with position papers, few in agreement.

The United States, under Roosevelt's direction, had opened its first embassy in Moscow in 1934, establishing diplomatic relations with the Soviet Union for the first time. In the next few years State Department staff in Moscow had witnessed the Great Purge – the bizarre disappearance and subsequent murder of so-called dissidents in the Soviet Union under Stalin's orders. Many of these victims, it seemed, were innocent of any crime. The Soviet dictator was intent on rooting out the slightest hint of political challenge, and paranoia gripped a populace of some 170 million people. "The purge was everywhere," remembered the Moscow embassy's Charles Bohlen. "The number of arrests, exiles, and executions would eventually reach 9 to 10 million – the figure now generally accepted . . . I found no evidence for a conclusion that [Stalin] was mentally unbalanced in the usual sense of the term, although obviously there must have been something wrong with a man who would send millions of people to senseless deaths."

George Kennan, another young diplomat among the first wave of Americans at the Moscow embassy, came to the following conclusion: "Never – neither then nor at any later date – did I consider the Soviet Union a fit ally or associate, actual or potential, for this country."*

When the United States entered World War II, however, the Allies had accepted Stalin's partnership, as he supplied millions of Red Army troops to fight the Nazis – far more, in fact, than the United States or Britain. The U.S. State Department's first official memo on this subject shot straight to the heart of the matter: "In the opinion of this Government . . . any defense against Hitlerism, any rallying of the forces opposing Hitlerism, from whatever source these forces may spring, will hasten the eventual downfall of the present German leaders, and will therefore redound to the benefit of our own defense and security." Or, as Churchill put it, "If Hitler invaded Hell, I would make at least a favorable reference to the Devil in the House of Commons."

The first U.S. ambassador to Moscow, William Bullitt, had warned that Stalin's intentions would ultimately conflict with the Americans'. "Stalin's aim is to spread the power of communists to the end of the earth," Bullitt cabled Roosevelt in August 1943. "Stalin, like Hitler, will not stop. He can only be stopped."

Roosevelt believed that the United States and the Soviet Union would emerge from the war as close allies. "I just have a hunch that Stalin is not that kind of man . . . He won't try to annex anything and will work with me for a world of democracy and peace," Roosevelt had told Bullitt. "It's my responsibility and not yours, and I'm going to play my hunch."

Now, in April 1945, with victory in Europe in sight, a disagreement had caused a potential break between the Americans and Soviets. It appeared that the president had been wrong about Stalin. A ping-pong of cables across the Atlantic between Roosevelt and Stalin formulated the first direct wartime confrontation between the two leaders and the two nations.

---

* The Soviet government had also signed the Nazi-Soviet Pact of 1939, further offending American officials. This pact was of course broken by the surprise Nazi attack on the Soviet Union, in 1941.

The problems began just after the last meeting of the Big Three — Roosevelt, Churchill, and Stalin, at Yalta in February 1945 — where the three leaders formulated military strategy to end Nazi resistance and to map out postwar Europe. FDR had returned from that conference reporting terrific optimism. "The far reaching decisions we took at Yalta," he cabled Stalin, "will hasten victory and the establishment of a firm foundation for a lasting peace." Right after Yalta, however, the new ambassador to the Soviet Union, Averell Harriman, began to raise red flags in his Washington communiqués. The mood in Moscow had shifted suddenly and darkly, as if by a switch.

The most immediate issue was the fate of Poland. The Soviets had installed a puppet regime in Poland, which the Red Army had recently liberated from the Nazis. At Yalta the Soviets had agreed that Poland would hold free elections "in about one month" to create its own democratic government representative of the people — according to the rules governed by Yalta's Declaration on Liberated Europe, which Joseph Stalin had signed. Those elections never occurred. In fact, Poland's government was a thinly veiled Sovietized regime controlled by Stalin himself. Moscow ambassador Harriman believed that hundreds if not thousands of American war prisoners were stranded in Poland, and U.S. officials were barred from getting inside to inquire about their condition. The Soviets would not allow it.

"I am outraged," Harriman cabled Roosevelt on March 14, 1945, two weeks before the president arrived at the Little White House in Warm Springs.

Two days later Churchill cabled the president: "At present, all entry into Poland is barred to our representatives . . . An impenetrable veil has been drawn across the scene . . . There is no doubt in my mind that the Soviets fear very much our seeing what is going on in Poland."

Stalin had agreed at Yalta to allow the United States to set up military bases in Hungary. Now he went back on his promise and was refusing to allow American representatives into the territory. Then came news that two of Stalin's deputies had entered Romania and had ousted Romania's leader. King Michael was given two hours and five minutes to inform the Romanian people that their political leader, General Rădescu, would be replaced by a man more friendly to the Russian government, Petru Groza. Meanwhile, all American planes in Soviet-controlled territory had been grounded.

The Soviets' domination of eastern European countries threatened the very ideology that American and British soldiers had fought and died for during this war. "I feel certain that unless we do take action in cases of this kind," Ambassador Harriman cabled Roosevelt, "the Soviet Government will become convinced that they can force us to accept any of their decisions on all matters and it will be increasingly difficult to stop their aggressive policy."

On March 29, the day Roosevelt arrived at Warm Springs, he cabled Stalin. "I cannot conceal from you the concern with which I view the developments of mutual interest since our fruitful meetings at Yalta," Roosevelt communicated. "I must make it quite plain to you that any so-lution which would result in a thinly disguised continuance of the pres-ent Warsaw regime would be unacceptable and would cause the people of the United States to regard the Yalta agreements as having failed."

The Soviet dictator refused any compromise. His puppet government in Poland would remain. "Matters on the Polish question," Stalin cabled Roosevelt, "have really reached a dead end." Then Stalin made a stun-ning allegation, that the Anglo-American forces had attempted to ne-gotiate a surrender with the Nazis without Russian participation, at a meeting Stalin claimed had occurred in Berne, Switzerland. This would enable, he claimed, Anglo-American forces to march into Nazi-occupied territory unharmed on the western front, while the Nazis continued to fight and kill Soviet troops on the eastern front. The Americans, Stalin believed, had betrayed their Russian allies.

Roosevelt assured Stalin that no such negotiations had taken place, but Stalin refused to believe it.[*] "It may be assumed that you have not been fully informed," Stalin cabled Roosevelt on April 3. "As a result of this at the present moment the Germans on the Western front in fact have ceased the war against England and the United States. At the same time they continue the war with Russia." (This claim was obviously false.) The situation, Stalin wrote, had caused "an atmosphere of fear and distrust" between the Soviets and the Americans.

The president responded with a furious cable two days later. "I have

---

[*] In fact, negotiations had taken place at Berne, regarding the surrender of Ger-man forces in Italy. But these were purely military and not political negotiations, and the American officials present had no authority to speak for the president of the United States.

received with astonishment your message of April 3," he communicated. "I have told you that . . . no negotiations were held at Berne . . . It is astonishing that a belief seems to have reached the Soviet Government that I have entered into an agreement with the enemy without first obtaining your full agreement . . . Frankly I cannot avoid a feeling of bitter resentment toward your informers, whoever they are, for such vile misrepresentations of my actions or those of my trusted subordinates."

Over the next few days the tension softened. Roosevelt attempted to end the feud graciously. "There must not, in any event, be mutual distrust and minor misunderstandings of this character . . . in the future," he wrote Stalin. Privately, he had come to a grave conclusion. "Averell [Harriman] is right," Roosevelt said of his Moscow ambassador. "We can't do business with Stalin. He has broken every one of the promises he made at Yalta."

///

Nothing like this had ever occurred — such outspoken vitriol between the leaders of the Soviet Union and the United States. And the turning of events had occurred with frightening alacrity. Two months earlier, at the end of the Yalta Conference, America felt a glow of optimism, specifically with regard to United States–Soviet relations. "We really believed in our hearts that this was the dawn of the new day we had all been praying for and talking about for so many years," professed Harry Hopkins, arguably Roosevelt's closest friend and aide. "We were absolutely certain that we had won the first great victory of the peace — and by 'we,' I mean *all* of us, the whole civilized human race."

Just two months later, all the security that American and British officials felt regarding the Soviets had vanished. Stalin's victories over the Nazis in eastern Europe had empowered him as never before. As Churchill described the mood in April 1945: "The two months that had passed since then [Yalta] had seen tremendous changes cutting to the very roots of thought . . . The whole relationship of Russia with the western Allies was in flux. Every question about the future was unsettled between us. The agreements and understandings at Yalta, such as they were, had already been broken or brushed aside by the triumphant Kremlin. New perils, perhaps as terrible as those we had surmounted, loomed and glared upon the torn and harassed world."

Americans were aware of this turning of events, but only of the surface details reported in their newspapers. A majority of them had long since placed their faith in their president to surmount such problems. In the future, many historians would look back on the Roosevelt presidency and find his greatest fault to be his failure to brief his vice president on the critical shift in global affairs, for Roosevelt would not live to see this narrative play out.

Just before noon on April 12, crusty and bespectacled Bill Hassett, the president's correspondence secretary, arrived at Roosevelt's cottage with the White House mail pouch. By this time Roosevelt was sitting in his wheelchair by a crackling fire. He was cold, even though the morning had ushered in an unseasonably warm Georgia spring day. He wore a gray blazer and a vest over his red Harvard tie, and he was holding court with three women. There were his cousins Margaret "Daisy" Suckley and Laura Delano. The third was Lucy Mercer Rutherfurd, a widow and an old flame of FDR's (Mrs. Roosevelt was unaware of Rutherfurd's presence in the cottage).

Hassett began to pass Roosevelt papers from the pouch. Here was a State Department document that required his signature. "A typical State Department letter," Roosevelt said mockingly. "It says nothing at all." When Hassett handed the president Senate Bill 298 (which would increase the borrowing power of the Commodity Credit Corporation), Roosevelt smiled at his female guests. "Here's where I make law," he said. He placed the document on a card table and wrote "Approved" along with the date and his signature.

As he signed documents, Hassett spread them out on a table so the ink would dry. Roosevelt's transportation secretary, Dewey Long, appeared, attempting to get the president's attention regarding travel logistics for an upcoming conference in San Francisco. The conference was to be a crowning moment for Roosevelt, as dignitaries from all over the globe would soon be arriving to try to hammer out agreements for a new world peace organization called the United Nations. The conference was set to open in thirteen days, on April 25, and Roosevelt had already begun work on the speech he intended to give. FDR had no patience for travel logistics, focusing instead on the pile of documents requiring his attention.

Among these documents was a top-secret cable from his Moscow ambassador, Averell Harriman, regarding the president's communiqué to Stalin from the day before. Harriman had held up this cable to Stalin and was now suggesting a rewording. He objected to the word *minor* in the following statement: "There must not, in any event, be mutual distrust and minor misunderstandings of this character . . . in the future."

"May I respectfully suggest that the word 'minor' as a qualification of 'misunderstandings' be eliminated," Harriman wrote Roosevelt. "I must confess that the misunderstanding appeared to me of major character and the use of the word 'minor' might well be misinterpreted here."

Harriman's cable had arrived in Roosevelt's hands with a suggested reply written by White House chief of staff Admiral Leahy, which was normal procedure. Leahy had grown adept at speaking for the president, after years of close service and friendship. His suggested reply read: "I do not wish to delete the word 'minor' as it is my desire to consider the misunderstanding a minor matter." Roosevelt wrote the word "Approved" on the suggested reply to Stalin and handed the cable off to be sent.

At around twelve thirty a portrait artist appeared at the cottage's front door. Elizabeth Shoumatoff, a tall fifty-six-year-old Ukraine-born artist with striking brown eyes and hair, had been invited to paint FDR. The president moved himself from his wheelchair to a high-backed leather chair for the sake of the portrait. Shoumatoff set up her easel. As she began to sketch, she engaged the president in light conversation, so she could study the contours of his moving face. Some servants were setting a nearby table for the president's lunch service. Roosevelt turned to Shoumatoff and said (as she recalled), "Now we've got just about fifteen more minutes to work," after which the artist would be asked to leave.

Roosevelt's eyes remained focused on his paperwork. In the chair next to him, his cousin Daisy Suckley was crocheting. His other cousin Laura Delano was filling vases with flowers. The portrait artist observed the president closely: "He was so absorbed in the material before him that I didn't dare ask him to look up." FDR slipped a cigarette into his cigarette holder and lit it, then he lifted his left hand to his temple and began rubbing his forehead. He uttered a sentence so quietly, no one but Miss Suckley heard it, not even the artist Shoumatoff, sitting about six feet away.

"I have a terrific headache," he said.

Then he lost consciousness, his head tipping lifelessly forward. Panicked, Suckley turned to Shoumatoff: "Ask the Secret Service man to call a doctor immediately."

OUTSIDE ROOSEVELT'S LITTLE WHITE HOUSE, secret service agents spotted the car of Dr. Howard Bruenn, the president's physician on call at Warm Springs, as it skidded to a stop at the front door. Dr. Bruenn rushed into the cottage and found Roosevelt unconscious in his bedroom (his butler and valet had moved him). The president's maids, secretaries, and cousins were all in the house. "It was a stricken and tense little crowd," remembered the head of the secret service detail, Mike Reilly. Bruenn began quick observations.

Pulse: 104. The president's blood pressure measured over the indicator's limit of 300. His left eye appeared widely dilated. Bruenn made an immediate diagnosis: cerebral hemorrhage. He injected the president with nitroglycerin. Then he called Washington.

FDR's chief physician, Admiral Ross McIntire, took the call in Washington at 3:05 p.m. (2:05 in Warm Springs).* For months McIntire had been giving the president routine examinations, and White House staffers had grown accustomed to seeing medical equipment in the hallway outside Roosevelt's bedroom in the morning. McIntire was not altogether surprised by this phone call. "Dr. Bruenn told me it was a very serious thing – undoubtedly a cerebral hemorrhage," McIntire recalled. He made an immediate call to a prominent heart specialist in Atlanta, Dr. James Paullin, and urged him to speed to Roosevelt's cottage. McIntire's next call was to Stephen Early, Roosevelt's longtime secretary and personal confidant. They discussed in grim tones how to handle the situation, and agreed that they needed to find the First Lady at once. They were able to determine that Eleanor Roosevelt was at the Sulgrave Club in Dupont Circle, less than a mile north of the White House, delivering

---

* In 1941 the Georgia legislature voted not to use daylight saving time, so Georgia's clocks were an hour behind Washington's.

a speech. They declined to contact her at that moment, waiting to see what would happen.

In Warm Springs, secret service agents began patrolling the roads, knowing that the heart specialist Dr. Paullin would be driving in at furious speeds from Atlanta, violating the wartime speed limit of 35 miles per hour. The agents did not want local police interfering with the physician's quick arrival. When Paullin made it to the Little White House, he found the situation critical.

"The President was *in extremis* when I reached him," Paullin's report read. "He was in a cold sweat, ash gray, and breathing with difficulty . . . On examination his pulse was barely perceptible."

At three thirty Warm Springs time, Dr. Bruenn called Admiral McIntire in Washington again. "Dr. Bruenn told me things were about the same," McIntire recalled. "Then he asked me to hold the phone as he was called away." McIntire could hear loud voices through the phone line, then there was silence. In that same moment, at the cottage in Warm Springs, Paullin and Bruenn were standing over the president's body. Roosevelt was pronounced dead at 3:35 p.m. (4:35 in Washington).

///

In the White House the president's longtime secretary Stephen Early and Admiral McIntire had decisions to make. It was a moment of strange despair, for so much had to be done, and it all had to be handled very carefully. There was no time for personal grief.

Early called Mrs. Roosevelt at the Sulgrave Club. "[I] asked her to come to the White House as soon as she possibly could," he recalled. As she herself remembered: "I got into the car and sat with clenched hands all the way to the White House. In my heart of hearts, I knew what had happened." Early brought the First Lady to her sitting room on the second floor and informed her of her husband's death. As he would recall, her reaction was to say: "I am more sorry for the people of this country and the world than I am for us."

Early then had to find the vice president — and quickly.

At the moment of Roosevelt's death, Truman was presiding over the Senate. Twenty-two minutes after, at 4:57 p.m., the Senate adjourned. Truman headed for what he called his "gold-plated office" — his second office, the traditional office of the vice president (which he rarely used), near the Senate Chamber in the Capitol. When he arrived a phone call was waiting for him from Sam Rayburn, the Speaker of the House.

"Sam wanted me to come over to the House side of the Capitol and talk to him about policy and procedure," Truman later wrote. In other words, they were to have a drink together. Truman sent word to his main office in the Senate building, and also to his buddy Eddie McKim at the Statler Hotel, explaining where he would be. By that time McKim had a suite all set for the night's poker game.

In the Capitol, Truman headed through the long hallways, past the eight-foot statue of Benjamin Franklin, and down a marble staircase to Rayburn's office, which was affectionately nicknamed "the Board of Education." Truman arrived at about 5:05 p.m. There the Speaker of the House, "Mr. Sam," was chatting with a couple of other guests. Here in this office, congressmen gathered to "strike a blow for liberty" — to drink whiskey. When asked why the room was called the Board of Education, Rayburn liked to say: "I guess some fellahs have been educated down there."

Rayburn handed Truman his drink of choice — bourbon and water — then told him that a call had just come in for him, from Steve Early in the White House. Truman picked up the phone and dialed.

"This is the VP," he said.

In a strained voice, Early ordered Truman to come to the White House "as quickly and quietly" as possible, and to use the main Pennsylvania Avenue entrance. Rayburn was watching Truman at this moment. "He is kind of a pale fellow . . . and he got a little paler," Rayburn recalled.

Truman hung up. "Jesus Christ and General Jackson!" he said. He turned to Sam Rayburn. "Steve Early wants me at the White House immediately," he said. He made for the door, and with his hand on the knob, he turned and said, "Boys, this is in this room. Something must have happened."

The vice president walked out the door, then broke into a run. The Capitol hallways were nearly empty by this time, and Truman's footsteps on the marble floor echoed through the corridors. He made it to his office in the Senate building quickly and out of breath. He grabbed his hat. "[I] told my office force that I'd been summoned to the White House and to say nothing about it," he later wrote.

Outside it had begun to rain again. Truman found his chauffeur, Tom

Harty, and off they went in the Mercury state car with no secret service detail. They arrived at the White House "in almost nothing flat," Truman recalled, motoring through the Northwest Gate. Ushers greeted the vice president at the door, bowing and taking his hat. They led him upstairs via an elevator to the First Lady's private study, where Truman found Mrs. Roosevelt, her daughter and son-in-law Anna and John Boettiger, and Stephen Early, sitting quietly. The First Lady approached Truman and put her arm around his shoulder.

"Harry," she said, "the president is dead."

Four words raced through Truman's mind: *The lightning has struck!* "I was fighting off tears," he later recalled. "It was the only time in my life I think that I ever felt like I'd had a real shock. I had hurried to the White House to see the president and when I arrived I found I *was* the president. No one in the history of our country ever had it happen to him just that way."

He gathered himself. "Is there anything I can do for you?" he asked the First Lady.

"Is there anything *we* can do for *you*," Eleanor Roosevelt answered. "For you are the one in trouble now."

///

From Warm Springs, news of Roosevelt's death began to spread in whispers and hurried phone calls. Chief secret service agent Mike Reilly dialed his underling James Rowley, who had been casing the location where the president was to attend the barbecue that afternoon in the village.

"I want to see you," Reilly said. "Come over to the cottage." Rowley pulled up in his car minutes later. "Come on, walk up the path with me," Reilly said. They started away from the cottage. "Don't say anything, but the president is gone."

"What do you mean, gone?" Rowley said.

"He's dead."

"What?"

At the picnic area in town, Georgia fiddlers and newspaper reporters had arrived, and so had everyone else who was supposed to attend the president's barbecue — except the president himself. Smelling a story, some reporters jumped into a car and made for the Little White House. "During the drive, none of us said a word because we were all thinking," recalled White House correspondent Robert Nixon. "Oddly enough the possibility of Roosevelt having died came right to my mind."

When the reporters arrived, they saw Grace Tully, the president's personal secretary, sitting on the porch crying. They entered the cottage, where they found correspondence secretary Bill Hassett standing in the living room by the fireplace. A moment of awkwardness passed, after which Hassett said in simple, sober words: "It is my sad duty to tell you that the president has had a stroke and is dead."

At the White House, Secretary of State Edward Stettinius – "Brother Ed," as many in Washington called him – was the first cabinet officer to arrive. He had been in a meeting in the State Department building across the street when he received a phone call at 5:10 p.m. from Steve Early, telling him to come immediately, without being noticed. It was "an order," Early had told him. An usher brought Stettinius to Mrs. Roosevelt's second-floor study, where she sat with Truman and Early. Stettinius had stark ivory-white hair and glaring black eyebrows, his face oddly reminiscent of piano keys. When the First Lady delivered the news to him, he was stunned. Conversation turned to procedure. What was to be done? "Everything was completely disorganized and nobody knew exactly where to turn," Stettinius recalled.

He advised that the rest of the president's cabinet be called to the White House at once. Truman agreed. Truman also wanted Secretary of the Senate Les Biffle, Senate majority leader Alben Barkley, minority leader Wallace White, Speaker of the House Sam Rayburn, Attorney General Francis Biddle, and a handful of others. He asked if Stettinius would make the arrangements, and the secretary of state quickly delegated the orders. The time was set for a cabinet meeting – 6:15 p.m., in less than an hour.

The First Lady and Early were now planning to fly to Warm Springs that night. Mrs. Roosevelt asked Truman if it would be "proper" to use a government airplane. "I told her as soon as I was sworn in I would order that all the facilities of the government should be at her command until the funeral was over," Truman recalled.

Early left the room and headed for the office of Jonathan Daniels, the White House press secretary, near the West Wing lobby. (Early had held this job for years and had recently resigned, yet he was so close with Roosevelt that he was still a White House fixture.) Early inquired as to whether there were any newsmen in the press gallery. There were not; they'd been told that there would be no more news from the White House that day, so they had departed. Early initiated a phone call to the three wire services – the Associated Press, the United Press, and the International News Service. When the three were on the line, Early said into the telephone, "I have a flash for you . . . The President died suddenly this afternoon."

"From then on there was no letup," assistant press secretary Eben Ayers recorded in his diary. "Time ceased to mean anything."

///

The phone in the Truman residence at 4701 Connecticut Avenue rang at approximately 6 p.m. Margaret Truman picked up. She had been getting ready for a date and was wearing a new party dress with white gloves and dancing shoes. It was her father on the line. "In an odd, tight voice," Margaret recalled, "Dad asked to speak to Mother. When I tried to kid with him in our usual way, he cut me off and ordered me to put Mother on the line."

Mrs. Truman took the phone. "Bess," Harry told her, "I'm at the White House. President Roosevelt died about two hours ago in Warm Springs. I'm sending a car for you and Margaret. I want you here when I'm sworn in."

Bess Truman fell to pieces. This was exactly what she had feared the most – for her husband and for their family. They had never wanted this – she most of all. She walked the short hallway to the bedroom shared by her mother, Mrs. Wallace, and her daughter, Margaret. Margaret rushed to her mother and put her arm around her. "Mother," Margaret said, "what's the matter, what is it?"

"President Roosevelt is dead," Bess said.

"Dead?"

Margaret Truman watched her mother straighten her back and compose herself; from that moment forward, she never looked at her mother the same way again.

"You'd better change your clothes," Bess said to Margaret. "Pick out something dark. A car will be here in a few minutes to take us to the White House."

///

At almost the exact time Truman was on the phone with his wife, news of the president's death hit the airwaves. At the New York headquarters of CBS Radio, John Charles Daly – the thirty-one-year-old reporter from *The World Today* – sat in the newsroom preparing for his 6:15 newscast as a children's program called *Wilderness Road* piped into living rooms across the country. One of Daly's assistants passed him a news flash from the teletype: FLASH WASHN — FDR DEAD.

Breathlessly, Daly waited for confirmation, which quickly arrived, so he leaned over to the station's engineer and said, "Cut! Give me the network." Then he spoke firmly into a microphone, his words broadcast across the nation.

"We interrupt this program to bring you a special bulletin from CBS World News. A press association has just announced that President Roosevelt is dead. All that has been received is just that bare announcement. There are no further details as yet, but CBS World News will return to the air in just a few moments with more information as it is received in our New York headquarters. We return you now to our regularly scheduled program."

Two minutes later NBC made a similar announcement, and ABC followed seconds after that.

///

Minutes after 6 p.m., Truman walked along a hallway that led from the residential part of the White House, where Mrs. Roosevelt's study was, to the executive offices. When he arrived at the Cabinet Room in the West Wing, he was the first one there. He had been in this room before, but only a few times. Upstairs in her private study, Mrs. Roosevelt remained secluded. She was scheduled to leave for Warm Springs at 7 p.m.

Labor secretary Frances Perkins was the next to arrive in the Cabinet Room. Perkins was a legend among American women, as she was the only female ever to serve in the cabinet, and had held her position since 1933. No one had ever served as labor secretary longer. Perkins had no idea yet why she had been summoned, but she could sense tragedy the moment she stepped into the room.

Soon others arrived: Secretary of Commerce Henry Wallace of Iowa, who had been in a dentist's chair when he learned of FDR's death, and White House chief of staff Admiral William Leahy, who had been sitting in his bedroom at his Florida Avenue apartment when he heard the radio announcement. Secretary of War Henry Stimson, Secretary of the Navy James Forrestal, Secretary of the Treasury Henry Morgenthau, Speaker of the House Rayburn and the attorney general, Frances Biddle — one by one they appeared. Amidst the crowd, Steve Early stood with tears streaking down his clenched jaw. One present remembered seeing Roosevelt's daughter Anna Boettiger: "Her face was a study — grim. Her chin was up, but it was all she could do to hold herself together."

Sitting at the conference table was Harry Truman. "In the long Cabinet Room," remembered press secretary Jonathan Daniels, "[Truman] looked like a little man as he sat waiting in a huge leather chair."

Most of the cabinet officers who were in town had arrived by 6:10, along with numerous members of the press. "The Cabinet was assembling," recalled State Department official Joseph Davies, who had just arrived himself. "All was confusion . . . The shock of the tragedy was very evident. Everyone seemed more or less numb. There was one fact which impressed me very much, and that was the grief which could be found in the faces of even the hard-boiled news and radio men. Their faces were set. In some instances, tears streamed down the faces of men who obviously were exercising all of their will to maintain self-control."

Truman stood and called the meeting to order. "It is my sad duty to report that the president died [at] 5:48," he said. "Mrs. Roosevelt gave me this news, and in saying so she remarked that 'he died like a soldier.'" He continued, "I want every one of you to stay and carry on, and I want to do everything just the way President Roosevelt wanted it."

Nobody said anything, so Truman nodded to the secretary of state. Stettinius stumbled through a statement, saying that all the cabinet members would be behind Truman. Treasury secretary Henry Morgenthau spoke up: "Mr. Truman, I will do all I can to help, but I want you to be free to call on any one else in my place." The secretary of agriculture, Claude Raymond Wickard, seconded Morgenthau's sentiment.

The attorney general had already summoned Chief Justice of the Supreme Court Harlan F. Stone to administer the presidential oath, but Stone had not yet arrived. The founding fathers had written the thirty-five-word oath in article 2, section 1 of the Constitution. Once those words were recited, the new president would assume his duties. Awkward moments passed while various people went hunting through the White House for a Bible. Truman preferred to use the Bible his grandfather had given him, which was sitting at that moment on a shelf in his Senate office. There was no time to fetch it. The one produced was an inexpensive Gideon edition found in the desk drawer of White House head usher Howell Crim. As the group awaited Chief Justice Stone, Truman approached the secretary of war, Henry Stimson, and asked that he arrange for the top military advisors to report to the White House for a morning meeting the following day. "He spoke very warmly of the work we were doing," Stimson recorded.

The chief justice arrived at about six thirty. A few minutes after that, Bess and Margaret Truman appeared. Their journey had been a strange one; by the time they had readied themselves to leave the Connecticut Avenue apartment building, a crowd had gathered out front. Secret service had led them out the back door, and even there, newsmen barraged them with camera flashes. As Bess entered the Cabinet Room, she looked "sad and a little frightened," according to press secretary Jonathan Daniels.

As the crowd assembled, Truman pulled Secretary of State Stettinius aside and asked him if he thought it appropriate for a photographer to capture the moment when he took the oath. Truman's ninety-two-year-old mother was at home in Grandview, Missouri, and he was wishing she could be there. Stettinius agreed it would be fine. Truman admitted he was bewildered, and Stettinius eyed him sadly. As the secretary of state wrote in his diary: "I told him that he had a job with the greatest responsibility of any one man in the world . . . I said somehow a person is given an inner strength to arise to any occasion and said that I had full confidence that the American people would rally around and see us through."

Truman responded that he would do his best.

///

At the gates of the White House, crowds began to gather. Many would remember this moment for the manner in which blacks and whites stood grieving next to one another, the color of their skin suddenly irrelevant. Rain clouds had moved on and the evening had turned dark and balmy. From behind the White House gates, the crowds could see the mansion's crystal candelabra flickering in the window in the main entrance hallway. They were left to wonder how the drama was unfolding inside. Across the street from the White House, in Lafayette Square, where Roosevelt used to light the national Christmas tree in the years before the war, some two thousand more had gathered. Newsboys darted through the crowds like minnows, handing out extras, moving people to huddle under streetlights so they could read the fine print.

Inside the White House, at 7:08 p.m., Chief Justice Stone and Harry Truman took their places facing each other by the Cabinet Room's mantel, underneath a clock that marked the time. The twenty-eighth president of the United States, Woodrow Wilson, looked on, from within his portrait on the wall. Truman held an index card with the oath printed on it, to make sure he spoke the thirty-five words exactly as the founding fathers had written them. Others in the room formed a semicircle behind the vice president and Chief Justice Stone. Standing inches to Truman's left was his wife, Bess. She looked as if her husband were stepping not into the office of the presidency but to the gallows. Directly behind her was Margaret. Along with the secretary of labor, they were the only three women present. Truman held the Bible in his left hand and placed his right hand on top of it. The index card with the oath was also atop the Bible, where Truman could see it. A silence fell over the room, and Chief Justice Stone began.

"I, Harry Shipp Truman," he said, thinking wrongly that the S. stood for Truman's mother's maiden name, which it did not.

"I, Harry S. Truman," the vice president said, correcting the judge.

"Do solemnly swear that I will faithfully execute the office of the president of the United States . . ."

As Truman uttered these words, the others looked on. "In that moment of actual succession, he seemed almost sacrilegiously small," press secretary Daniels said of Truman. A photographer captured the scene, but when it was over the chief justice told Truman that he had failed to raise his right hand while he held the Bible. And so the oath was repeated. Truman uttered the final words "firmly and clearly," as one in the room remembered.

"So help you God," Justice Stone said.

"So help me God," Truman responded.

He kissed the Bible, then he turned to Bess and Margaret and kissed them both. He was no longer Harry. He would never be just Harry again.

Following an exhausting amount of solemn hand shaking, Truman felt a tug on his arm. "Mr. President, will you come with me." It was a White House aide he did not know (assistant press secretary Eben Ayers), and along with Steve Early, Truman left the Cabinet Room. His wife and

daughter followed, along with the secretary of state. In the quiet con-
fines of the White House Red Room, Truman had a moment to gather his
thoughts. Stettinius asked him if the San Francisco conference should
be called off. This was the international meeting in which representatives of governments from all over the world were set to gather in less
than two weeks, to attempt to form a charter for the new United Nations
peace organization. Truman was emphatic: the conference should go on.
And with that, he had made his first decision as president. Soon afterward, he delivered his first statement as president, which was handed to
members of the press at 8:10 p.m.: "The world may be sure that we will
prosecute the war on both fronts, east and west, with all the vigor we
possess to a successful conclusion."

Bess and Margaret headed home in a secret service car, and Truman
remained behind. It was then that the secretary of war, Henry Stimson,
asked to speak to him alone "about a most urgent matter," as Truman
would later recall.

Stimson was a towering figure in Washington. Statesman, former Wall
Street lawyer, the only Republican serving in FDR's cabinet, he was well
into his seventy-seventh year. A member of the old moneyed East Coast
establishment, he was a Victorian throwback who spoke as if he had
walked out of a Henry James novel. There was a matter of terrific importance to discuss, Stimson told Truman, a matter of grave secrecy. "He
wanted me to know about an immense project that was under way," Truman later recalled, "a project looking to the development of a new explosive of almost unbelievable destructive power." Truman had heard
whispers of some strange military program that was costing taxpayers
millions. But he had no knowledge of the details.

In fact, the matter was so top secret, Stimson explained, he could reveal nothing more as of yet. "That was all he felt free to say at the time,"
Truman recalled, "and his statement left me puzzled."

After this brief meeting with Stimson, Truman had a moment to sit
alone and think. He wrote in a diary of this moment:

> I was very much shocked . . . I did not know what reaction the
> country would have to the death of a man whom they all prac-
> tically worshiped. I was worried about reaction of the Armed
> Forces. I did not know what affect the situation would have on
> the war effort, price control, war production and everything

that entered into the emergency that then existed. I knew the President had a great many meetings with Churchill and Stalin. I was not familiar with any of these things and it was really something to think about but I decided the best thing to do was to go home and get as much rest as possible and face the music.

When Truman walked out the White House door to the motorcade awaiting him, he heard the traditional reception clerk's bark for the first time: "The President has left his office." The motorcade left the Executive Mansion's grounds, through the South Gate.

4

ALL OVER THE GLOBE THAT NIGHT, world leaders and humble citizens alike attempted to digest the news — the most revered of all men was gone.

"It finally crushed him," one of FDR's top speechwriters, the playwright Robert Sherwood, wrote. "The 'it' was the awful responsibility that had been piling up and piling up for so many years. The fears and the hopes of hundreds of millions of human beings throughout the world had been bearing down on the mind of one man."

Part of the shock was the idea of the person who had now taken FDR's place. "Good God!" it could be heard in taverns, on buses, and in living rooms around the country. "Truman will be President!"

Already, radio stations by the hundreds were airing tributes to the fallen leader. In Truman's home state of Missouri, a close friend by the name of Tom Evans had gone on the air. "I realize," he told listeners, "that because of [Truman's] humble beginnings . . . there may be some apprehension today about our country's future. I wish I could speak personally to every man who feels that apprehension and say to him: *You have no cause to fear.*"

Senators and statesmen sat with strong drinks distilling the world's anxiety into the ink in their diaries. "The gravest question-mark in every American heart is about Truman," Michigan senator Arthur Vandenberg wrote that night. "Can he swing the job?"

In Moscow, Ambassador Harriman phoned Stalin's number two in the Kremlin, Vyacheslav Molotov, at 1 a.m. Surprised by the call, Molotov insisted on coming straight over to confer with the ambassador in person at the U.S. Embassy. "He seemed deeply moved and disturbed," Harriman recorded in a cable sent to the White House the next morning. "He remained for some time talking about the part President Roosevelt had played in the war and in the plans for peace . . . I have never heard Molotov talk so earnestly."

Molotov expressed consternation over the new American president. "Do you know this new President Truman?" he nervously queried Ambassador Harriman. "What is he like?"

In Berlin, in his secret bunker, Adolf Hitler had spent the previous few days in desperate straits. The Nazi empire was all but crushed by the Allies, and Hitler was on the brink of nervous collapse, his hands shaking so violently, he found it difficult to sign his name on official documents. When he heard the news of Roosevelt's death, he rushed at once to his production chief, Albert Speer. "We have the miracle I always predicted!" the führer ranted. "The war isn't lost . . . Roosevelt is dead!"

When Prime Minister Churchill received the news, he felt "as if I had been struck a physical blow." "Indeed, it may be said," Churchill later wrote, "that Roosevelt died at the supreme climax of the war, and at the moment when his authority was most needed to guide the policy of the United States."

In Germany, the supreme commander of the Allied Expeditionary Force, General Dwight Eisenhower, sat with Generals George Patton and Omar Bradley at Patton's field headquarters that night, rifling through packages of cigarettes. "We pondered over the effect the president's death might have upon the future peace," Eisenhower recalled. "It seemed to us, from the international viewpoint, to be a most critical time to be forced to change leaders." General Bradley recalled: "We talked for nearly three hours [in the middle of the night]. It seemed an irreplaceable loss . . . None of us knew Truman or much about him. He came from my home state, Missouri, but I had to confess almost complete ignorance."

Patton was more explicit, expressing in his diary his disgust with the idea of Truman as president, a feeling millions in America were experiencing too: "It seems very unfortunate that in order to secure political preference, people are made Vice President who are never intended, neither by Party nor by the Lord, to be President."

At the home where Truman's mother and sister lived in Grandview, Missouri, reporters came calling in the dark of the night. This was perhaps what worried Harry Truman the most: that his family would suffer the consequences of his career. He had always looked after them with fierce devotion. "As long as he lived he always seemed to think that I was his special care," his younger sister, Mary Jane, once said, "and no matter how busy he was he always had time to talk to me." But Harry was not there to protect his sister and mother from the hungry reporters who would do anything for a story that night.

"Mother is terribly, terribly distressed," Mary Jane Truman told them. "The news came as such a shock; we have been unable to adjust ourselves to it."

Meanwhile, at a laboratory called Los Alamos, hidden in plain sight by the stark emptiness of the New Mexico desert, word spread around a collection of the world's brightest scientists, who were at work on a project so secret, not even Harry Truman — now the president of the United States — had any in-depth knowledge of it. The chief scientist at this secret lab, forty-year-old J. Robert Oppenheimer, summoned his colleagues to a flagpole near the lab's administrative building. In his high-pitched voice, the skeletal-thin Oppenheimer made a formal announcement of the death of Franklin Roosevelt. He too feared for the competence of the new president.

"Roosevelt was a great architect," Oppenheimer figured. "Perhaps Truman will be a good carpenter."

///

When Truman arrived at his apartment building that night it was after nine o'clock. Crowds had formed out front to glimpse the new president, who lived here in this humble, tree-lined neighborhood. Truman was able to enter once again the privacy of his quiet second-floor domicile. He felt as if the globe had flipped on its axis, but here at 4701 Connecticut Avenue everything was situated where it had been when he had left for work that morning — his reading chair and lamp, his phonograph and records.

Some neighbors, the Davises, had come over and had brought cake and some turkey. "He did not say much to us," Margaret said of her father. "I realize now that he did not feel he could talk freely with the Davises in the apartment." Truman said he was hungry, that he had not eaten since noon, so his neighbor Mrs. Davis made the president of the United States a turkey sandwich. He ate it, then retired to a bedroom to call his mother, who was awake. He was going to be very busy for a while, he told her, so he would not be able to call her often in the next few days.

"Be good, Harry," ninety-two-year-old Mamma Truman said. "But be game, too."

Minutes later Truman was asleep. He had a peculiar talent in this regard, to sleep when he needed to, in moments of terrific emotional strain. In the middle of the night, however, he awoke to find his wife sobbing in the bed beside his. He tried to comfort her, but there was little chance of that. What could he say? So he went back to sleep, knowing that when he awoke, millions all over the world would be asking a single question. It was the same question FDR's chief of staff, William Leahy, had asked less than nine months earlier, when Truman's name had suddenly and inexplicably been placed on the 1944 presidential ticket as VP, beside Roosevelt's own.

"Who the hell is Harry Truman?"

Part II

The Political Education
of Harry S. Truman

I've always had a sneakin' notion that
someday maybe I'd amount to something.
I doubt it now though like everything.

— Harry Truman, farmer,
age twenty-seven, 1911

5

HARRY TRUMAN was born on May 8, 1884, in Lamar, Missouri, the first child of John Anderson Truman and Martha Ellen Truman, two not-so-young parents who had grown up under the grating realities of pioneering life in rural America. The doctor who delivered the boy was paid $15 for the job. The world Harry was born into made the year 1945 seem like the wildest imaginings of the most apocalyptic philosophers. There were no machines in 1884 — no airplanes, no motorcars. When Harry was a child, the loudest noises he would hear were the occasional thunder crack and the smack of an ax blade.

America was still an agrarian experiment. The nation was a loose partnership of thirty-eight states (six more would join by the time Harry was six). The population of New York City had just surpassed 1 million when Harry was born, with Chicago and Philadelphia soon to follow. The rest of the country's 50-plus million citizens (compared with 325 million today) lived rurally, as the Trumans did.

By the time he could recall, his family had moved to a farm of many hundreds of acres in Grandview, the family plot where his mother, Martha Ellen Truman, had grown up. He had a little brother (John Vivian, born April 25, 1886) and a sister (Mary Jane, August 12, 1889). The farm was a whole world unto itself. Kids were free to roam, often followed by a gray Maltese cat named Bob and a dog named Tandy. "We would hunt birds' nests in the tall prairie grass," Truman recalled, "and gather daisies, prairie wild flowers, and wild strawberries."

Almost all the resources needed were reachable upon horseback, which made faraway places seem like fantastical lands that would never be seen, only imagined. Life moved in a cadence, according to the seasons. Autumn brought harvest, when work hours knew no end. Winter meant "hog-killing time"; slabs of meat were kept cool using blocks of ice sawed out of riverbeds. The farmhouse had no electricity, nor running water, and cooking was done over a wood-fired stove, as in all the other homes in rural Jackson County.

The family was far from rich. "You know," said a Grandview neighbor, Stephen Slaughter, "they didn't have much spare money. The Trumans were always strapped." They were "light-foot Baptist," in Harry's words — not terribly religious. Politically, the Trumans considered themselves "Rebel Democrats." Their party affiliation had come about during the Civil War. Missouri had been a hotbed of secessionist violence; families supported both sides, sometimes neighbors against one another, to the death. Both of Harry's parents came from slave-owning families that sided with the South, in bitter opposition to Abraham Lincoln's Republican Party and its Union Army. As Rebel Democrats, they thought of themselves as Confederate soldiers, politically. It was not simply a party affiliation but a deep passion born from the bruises of a lost war.

Harry's father, John Anderson Truman, was a reticent and diminutive man with a dangerous temper, who had no education beyond rural elementary school. He taught his children the only way he could, by example. First, women were sacrosanct. "No one could make remarks about my aunts or my mother in my father's presence without getting into serious trouble," Harry later wrote. And then there was work and honor. "He was one of the hardest working men that ever lived," Harry said of his father. "He raised my brother and myself to believe that honor is worth more than money. And that's the reason we never got rich."

Mamma Truman was the more influential parent in Harry's case. She was no ordinary Jackson County woman. At five feet six, she was taller than her husband, and skilled with a shotgun. She had spent two years at Lexington Baptist Female College, where she studied poetry and piano, which made her remarkably educated for a farm woman. She taught Harry to read by the time he was five. When she noticed Harry having trouble with small print, she took him to a Chinese doctor in Kansas City (an all-day horse-and-buggy round trip), who diagnosed him with "flat eyeballs" and fitted him with glasses. The spectacles were expensive, so Harry was forbidden from playing sports.

"It was very unusual for children to wear glasses then," recalled Mize Peters, a schoolmate of Harry's. "Kids had a tendency to make fun of people who wore glasses. They'd call him four-eyes. But it didn't seem to bother him to be called that."

Martha Ellen was also the driving force behind moving the family off the farm and into town – so Harry, her oldest, could get a good education. In December 1890, when Harry was six, the Trumans relocated to a house on South Crysler Avenue in Independence, Missouri. A Missouri Pacific depot stood a couple hundred yards behind the house, close enough that the floor rattled every time a steam train chugged by.

Independence was a different world, and an extraordinary one. Ten miles outside Kansas City, the town was known as "the Queen City of the Trails," as it was the point of departure for the Santa Fe, Oregon, and California Trails. For much of the nineteenth century, pioneers heading west gathered in the spring in Independence to prepare for their journeys. All were seeking a better life in an untamed land, the West offering "a new consciousness of the country," as Willa Cather wrote in her novel *O Pioneers!* Independence was the last stop before "the jumping off." Even the town's name embodied the spirit of a youthful America.

By the time the Trumans showed up, Independence had become a thriving town, with a southern air. Electricity had arrived three years before the Trumans. Downtown, wooden ramps formed sidewalks around rows of storefront businesses: H. W. Rummel's harness and saddle shop, the Hotel Metropolitan, Bundschu's Dry Goods, a Western Union office, banks and saloons. ("There were quite a few saloons," remembered Harry's sister, Mary Jane.) Harry's father opened a business trading horses and mules. "Work Mules for Sale!" read his advertisement. "Parties Wanting Teams! I have 20 Head! Of Work Mules. Go to the White Barn, on Kentucky Ave., near Missouri Pacific Depot, see my stock and get prices."

One morning Harry's mother took him to a new church school. "When I was about six or seven years old," he later wrote in a diary, "my mother took me to Sunday School and I saw there the prettiest sweetheart little girl I'd ever seen . . . She had tanned skin, blond hair, golden as sunshine, and the most beautiful blue eyes."

Her name was Elizabeth "Bess" Wallace. Her family lived at 608 North Delaware, in a fashionable house with a cupola and a broad porch. The Wallaces were different from the Trumans, who were farm people. Bess Wallace's father, David, was a prominent town figure, "the most popular man in the county at that time," according to a schoolmate of Harry and Bess's, Henry Chiles. David Wallace had a dark secret, one that would soon become known in the most horrific way. But at the time he was a man who commanded respect in town.

Bess Wallace was everything Harry was not. She was fashionable, ath-
letic, and popular. Harry, in his own words, "was never popular. The popular boys were the ones who were good at games and had big, tight fists.
I was never like that. Without my glasses I was blind as a bat, and to tell
the truth, I was kind of a sissy. If there was any danger of getting into a
fight, I always ran."

Harry sat next to Bess Wallace in church school. Somehow he knew
already that he would devote his whole life to this one person. It took
him five years to get up the courage to say hello.

///

While in first grade, Harry came down with a high fever. "At one time,"
according to his cousin Ethel Noland, "he was so low that they thought
he might not live." The family physician, Dr. G. T. Twyman, diagnosed
him with the infectious disease diphtheria. In the days before aspirin,
children with high fevers were placed in ice to cool them, but the family
had no ice. It was winter, so Harry's mother packed him in snow. "He
ended up being paralyzed for about a year," recalled Harry's younger sister, Mary Jane. "So, that's when he started reading so much. He couldn't
do anything else and he couldn't get up without help, and so he'd lie on
the floor and put the books down on the floor in front of him and read
the book that way."

Harry had begun his political education, without knowing it.

His mother had purchased a set of books for him called Heroes of
History, and he also liked to read the Bible, particularly Exodus and Matthew's Gospel. He consumed the stories of Moses, Cyrus the Great, Cin-
cinnatus, and Hannibal. There was the Duke of Wellington, and Ulysses
S. Grant. In the stories of great men and women lay the answers to all
the questions that were forming in the young boy's mind, and as he
learned, their triumphs and mistakes had shaped history's path.

"In reading the lives of great men," he later wrote in a diary, "I found
that the first victory they won was over themselves . . . Self-discipline
with all of them came first." On another occasion, he wrote of his early
reading:

> History showed me that Greece, which was not as big as the
> state of Missouri, left us ideas of government that are imperish-
> able and fundamental to any society of people living together

and governing themselves. It revealed to me that what came about in Philadelphia in 1776 really had its beginnings in Hebrew times. In other words, I began to see that the history of the world has moved in cycles and that very often we find ourselves in the midst of political circumstances which appear to be new but which might have existed in almost identical form at various times during the past six thousand years.

When Harry recovered from diphtheria, he returned to school in summertime to catch up. The town of Independence had built a new school called Columbian – for Caucasian children, as the schools were segregated – and it was here where he continued his education. He was a natural lefty trained to write with his right hand. He was a good student but not extraordinary, his focus often drifting from his work to the girl who sat near him, Bess Wallace. "If I succeeded in carrying her books to school or back home for her, I had a big day," he recorded.

On August 23, 1898, upon Mamma Truman's suggestion, Harry's father made his first fifty-dollar payment on a piano. It was a W. W. Kimball purchased on credit from a music store in Kansas City, and getting it home to Independence was a chore. Harry was drawn to the instrument. He began traveling into Kansas City twice a week for lessons. Most days his brother and sister would awake before sunrise to the sound of his fingers on the keys.

He had become something of an oddball teenager, with thick spectacles, an obsession for a girl who paid him no attention, and dreams of a future regaling crowds with his music. There was an air of loneliness about him, but an affability too that drew his teachers to him. "He didn't get to play and have games with the other boys because he wore such heavy glasses," recalled one of his teachers, W.L.C. Palmer. "I can remember going through [the library], and many times I would see Harry in there reading." He was "a very, very genteel and polite human being," recalled family friend Pansy Perkins. "He was the type of person that you just felt so at ease when you met him. He was so down-to-earth, and yet he was something else, too, even then."

Harry ended his high school education at the turn of the new century. He had already lived through economic turmoil (the Panic of 1893) and war (the Spanish-American War had been fought and won). And yet, world events seemed to exist only in the form of newspaper ink. Citizens of Independence felt the tug of modernity from nearby Kansas City, but most were focused on their everyday commerce. The century was ending on a drumbeat of optimism – a high point to the Gilded Age (a term of slight sarcasm coined by Missouri's own Mark Twain). The nation was still young, not yet 150 years old, self-sufficient and full of promise.

On graduation day at Independence High School, Harry's fellow student Charlie Ross was named valedictorian. Ross had a gifted pen, and had proclaimed a future as a journalist. Onstage at the graduation ceremony, Harry watched as English teacher Matilda Brown gave Charlie Ross a kiss and congratulated him. Standing next to Charlie, Harry asked his teacher, "Well, don't I get one, too?"

"Not until you have done something worthwhile," she answered.

Decades later, Truman would sit with Charlie Ross remembering this moment poignantly, in the White House.

When Independence High School's graduating class of 1901 posed for a picture, twenty-four girls and nine boys stared into the camera lens, all gathered on the stairs in front of the school's doors. Among these students was a future president, a First Lady, and a presidential press secretary. Behind the group, looming above, was a stained glass window with a Latin phrase displayed prominently: JUVENTUS SPES MUNDI.

"Youth, the hope of the world."

6

FINANCIAL TRAGEDY STRUCK the Trumans just after Harry's graduation. "My father's finances became entangled," as he put it. John Anderson Truman gambled on wheat futures, and the market bit him. At fifty-one years of age, he was wiped out. Harry had dreamed of West Point, of becoming a professional soldier like the heroes in his books, but his eyes were so bad, the school would not have him, and he could not afford regular college. As many of his schoolmates went off to the University of Missouri, seventeen-year-old Harry began working his way through a series of jobs. "It took all I received to help pay family expenses," he later wrote, "and keep my brother and sister in school."

He worked as a timekeeper on the Santa Fe Railroad, sleeping at night in makeshift camps along the tracks with the itinerant men who did odd jobs on the trains. "I became very familiar with hobos and their viewpoints," he recalled. "I learned what it meant to work ten hours a day for $1.50." He got a job in the mailroom at the *Kansas City Star*, then moved to a Kansas City bank as a clerk. In 1906, at his father's request, Truman moved back to the Grandview farm. He was twenty-two years old, and family members wagered how long he would stay. The six-hundred-acre plot in Grandview became "J. A. Truman & Son," and Harry was strapped with long days, which turned into weeks and months, and then years.

The farm was worth quite a bit — $58,000 according to the Truman family's 1910 tax return — but it was mortgaged to the hilt. There was a herd of about four dozen cows, about 50 pigs, 14 horses, 65 chickens, 40 acres of oats, 100 acres of corn, 60 acres of wheat, 40 acres of clover, 3 acres of alfalfa, and an acre of potatoes. Work began before sunrise, often in bitter cold, and ended with sunset, the heat seething in summer. In letters, Harry described the loneliness of his days on the farm. "I have memorized a whole book while plowing forty acres," he wrote. "When I run out of something to think of I count the revolutions of the plow wheel and figure how many acres there are left." Meanwhile the family continued to struggle. "We are living on bread and bacon with some canned goods thrown in," Harry wrote. The farm, he recorded, was "a total failure." Gone were the dreams of piano stardom. There was no inclination that the future held anything else for him — until the cake-plate incident.

One day in 1910, twenty-six-year-old Harry was visiting his cousins Ethel and Nellie Noland. Across the street lived Bess Wallace with her mother, Mrs. Madge Wallace. (Bess and her mother had moved to this house, at 219 North Delaware — the home of Bess's maternal grandparents, which the family had purchased back in 1867.) On this day, there was a cake plate at the Nolands' that needed returning to the Wallaces. Harry saw opportunity. He walked the plate across the street and knocked on the door, and there appeared Bess Wallace.

She was twenty-five now — the oldest Wallace child. Her mother was alone, so Bess was staring down a future of spinsterhood, taking care of Mrs. Wallace. The family had suffered terribly since Harry had last seen Bess. Everyone in town knew that Bess's father, David Wallace, had taken his own life while lying in the family's bathtub. No one knew why, though it was clear he suffered from alcoholism and financial problems. Bess was home and heard the gunshot. She was found minutes later pacing behind the house with clenched fists. The Wallaces had left Independence for Colorado for some years, to recover in privacy. Now, seven years after her father's death, Bess found Harry Truman at her door — tan-faced, with the lithe body of a hardworking farmer.

"Aunt Ella [Harry's aunt Ella Noland] told me to thank your mother for the cake," Harry said. "I guess I ought to thank her too. I had a big piece."

Bess smiled. "Come in," she said.

On that evening, Harry and Bess began a relationship that was not to end until Harry passed away sixty-two years later.

///

Not that Bess was easy to get. Harry had to work hard for her. In the days before cars, it took several hours to travel from the Grandview farm to Independence by train. The exciting new technology — telephones — did not often function as advertised. So Harry's courtship unfolded through letters, hundreds of them, in which he poured out his affection along with depths of self-doubt.

He was awkward socially, he admitted. "It seems to me," he wrote her, "that I never manage to say the proper thing in the proper place." He confessed his dim financial prospects: "It is a family failing of ours to be poor financiers." To get her to come to Grandview on Labor Day in 1911, he promised to build her a tennis court on the farm, since she was an ace player. He spent hours rolling out a court. His mother butchered chickens for a special dinner and even wallpapered some rooms to make the house look nicer. But Bess failed to show up, due to bad weather, she claimed. When Harry asked her to marry him, she said no.

Truman was nearing his sixth year as a farmer. With the exception of his father, all the most important people in his life were women. Mamma Truman was still central to his everyday life. His best friends were his cousins Ethel and Nellie Noland. And then there was "Bessie." Harry and his father, John Anderson, were business partners who had little in common. "He thought I was about right," Harry recalled, "and I know he was." Outside of farm work, they connected on one subject: politics.

For years, John Anderson Truman had taken his family to Jackson County town picnics to hear local politicians speak. "Politics is all he ever advises me to neglect the farm for," Harry wrote Bess. Harry had studied the lives of all the American presidents. His hero was Andrew Jackson, the seventh president of the United States (1829–1837) and the founder of the Democratic Party, for whom Jackson County, Missouri, was named. Jackson's adventures in war and politics made his life story read like an adventure novel. "I have been tossed upon the waves of fortune," Jackson famously said. He was the first American president to come from the common people – people like the Trumans. "If Andrew Jackson can be President, anybody can!" was a common quip of Jackson's day.

In the fall of 1912 the presidential election was the talk of the Truman dinner table for weeks. Not in Truman's lifetime had an election been so bitterly fought. A schism tore apart the Republican Party. The incumbent president, William Howard Taft, had won the nomination, leading a humiliated Republican opponent, Theodore Roosevelt, to strike out independently. With his newly created Bull Moose Party, his magnanimity, and his wild oratory style, Theodore Roosevelt riveted Americans. The Democrat Woodrow Wilson had only two years of political experience, and none in national politics. Less than a month before the election, a would-be assassin fired a gunshot into Theodore Roosevelt's chest, the bullet passing through the pages of a speech he was about to give. With the bullet lodged less than an inch from his heart, he delivered the speech, then went to the hospital and survived. Two weeks later Vice President James Sherman died, leaving the Republican Taft with no running mate.

"Nobody talks anything but election," Harry wrote Bess on November 6, the day after the contest, which Wilson won, becoming the twenty-eighth president of the United States. The brutality of this election made Truman philosophical about his future and politics itself, especially when his father threw his hat in the ring, running and winning the local office of road overseer.

"Politics sure is the ruination of many a good man," Harry wrote Bess. "Between hot air and graft he usually loses not only his head but his money and friends as well. Still, if I were rich I'd just as soon spend my money buying votes and offices as yachts and autos. Success seems to me to be merely a point of view anyway . . .

"To succeed financially," Harry concluded, "a man can't have any heart. To succeed politically he must be an egotist or a fool or a ward boss tool."

///

By Truman's thirtieth birthday, America was speeding toward its destiny as the world's first modern global superpower. All the ingredients needed to become the wellspring of modernity were at the ready: coal, oil, gold, vast lands of fertile soil, endless human ingenuity, and the political freedom to put that ingenuity to work. In 1914, America's movie industry was booming for the first time. Charlie Chaplin starred in his first thirty Hollywood films that year. Wall Street had become the world's most important economic center, while Detroit's motorcar industry was revolutionizing human life as nothing ever had. Henry Ford's Model T had become an unprecedented consumer phenomenon, spreading the gospel of motoring and Americanism everywhere it went. Overseas, cars were still toys for the wealthy. In America, they were fueling the rise of a new middle class.

In Europe in 1914, the outlook appeared vastly different. Europe's societies were centuries older, and tensions had been building for years. Imperial rivalries and competition for resources were about to turn violent. When assassins shot dead the archduke Franz Ferdinand – heir to the throne of the Austro-Hungarian Empire – in broad daylight on a Sarajevo street on June 28, 1914, Americans took little notice. When huge armies mobilized, empowered as never before by the industrial revolution, few in the United States felt the danger. During the first two weeks in August, Germany declared war on Russia, France, and Belgium; Austria-Hungary declared war on Russia; and Britain and France declared war on Austria-Hungary and Germany. Still, Americans believed the oceans protected them, like a giant moat.

Truman spent 1914 farming in obscurity, and chasing the love of his life. Two things happened that year that altered his situation considerably. His mother surprised him with a wad of money, cash she had squirreled away so that her oldest son could buy the family's first automobile. For $650, Harry purchased a used 1911 Stafford, built right in Kansas City. The car put his ambitions on wheels, especially when it came to Bess Wallace. (In 1914 nothing worked to woo a woman like a sixty-mile-per-hour motorcar.) Harry became a regular guest at the Wallaces' on Sundays. Bess's brothers George and Frank took to him, with his easygoing charm, but Bess's mother, Mrs. Wallace, was ice cold. "Mrs. Wallace wasn't a bit in favor of Harry," recalled one of the Noland family. "And she says, 'You don't want to marry that farm boy, he is not going to make it anywhere.'"

Also in 1914, Truman's father died. John Anderson Truman had been convalescing from a dangerous intestinal surgery, at the farmhouse, with his son by his side. "I had been sitting with him and watching a long time," Harry recalled. "I nodded off. When I woke up, he was dead." Harry was devastated. He now had the full responsibility of the farm to himself – a farm deep in debt.

He was desperate for money, as without it, there would be no marriage, nor any escape from the monotony of the farm. So he entered into a series of get-rich-quick investments. He traveled to Texas in 1916 because, as he wrote, "I am convinced that I can make some money down here." He did not. Later that year he invested more than he could afford to lose in a zinc and copper mine in Commerce, just over the Missouri border in Oklahoma. "My money is in now and I am feeling better over it every minute," he wrote Bess. "After next week the money will begin to return . . . If the bloomin' thing fails to connect I'll be so disappointed I won't know straight up from crossways." The mine failed to turn any profit, but still, Harry entertained his visions of grandeur. "My ship's going to come in yet," he wrote Bess. "I've been crazy about you since the day I met you . . . Who knows, I may be His Excellency the Governor of Montana someday (hee haw). How would you like to be Mrs. Governor?"

In 1916 he set his sights on an oil-drilling operation, and with some partners he formed a company that became Morgan Oil. The company leased well sites across four states, then offered investors shares of these leases, hoping that the drills would strike black gold. He was determined to change the course of his life, but events overseas were about to change it for him.

On May 7, 1915, the German submarine *U-20* fired a torpedo into the hull of the RMS *Lusitania* as the ship was steaming past the Irish coast, bound for Liverpool. The *Lusitania* was the world's grandest passenger ship. Like the *Titanic* before it (the *Titanic* sank in 1912), the *Lusitania* had captured the imagination of millions when it first launched. The *Washington Post* called the ship "Queen of the Waves," "the wonder of the maritime world." The German navy sent it to the bottom of the sea, killing 1,198 passengers. There were no soldiers aboard, but there were 128 American citizens. German officials claimed that the ship was carrying munitions from New York to British troops, and thus the killings were permissible according to international law. (While the British denied this claim, evidence in recent years suggests the Germans were correct – the *Lusitania* was apparently carrying munitions.)

Americans were repulsed. "The country was horrified," recalled Senator Henry Cabot Lodge of Massachusetts. If President Wilson asked for war, Lodge said, "he would have had behind him . . . the enthusiastic support of the whole American people." When German leaders announced unrestricted naval warfare – the right to sink American merchant ships – anti-German fervor swept across the United States. At countless lunch counters, sauerkraut became liberty cabbage, and frankfurters – named for the German city Frankfurt – became hot dogs.

As a novice oil speculator, Truman saw a striking opportunity. The war was going to make oil prices skyrocket. If his Morgan Oil drills would only strike . . . "I am simply on needle points," he wrote Bess. He convinced her to invest in Morgan Oil, and he convinced his mother too. When the wells failed to produce, the investment went south; Bess lost her money, Mamma Truman was forced to take another mortgage on the farm, and Harry was left with near worthless shares of a company hanging on by a thread.

He was overcome with gloom. "My luck should surely change," he wrote Bess on January 23, 1917. "Sometime I should win. I have tried to stick. Worked, really did, like thunder for ten years to get that old farm in line for some big production. Have it in shape and have had a crop failure every year. Thought I'd change my luck, got a mine, and see what I did get. Tried again in the other long chance, oil.

"If I can't win straight," Harry concluded, "I'll continue to lose."

///

In March 1917, German submarines sank three unarmed American merchant ships — the *Vigilancia,* the *City of Memphis,* and the *Illinois* — killing many aboard. Reaction in America was violent. "[Germany] is firing upon our ships, sinking them, destroying or endangering the lives of our citizens," the *New York Times* responded. "This is the very essence of war." When President Wilson polled his cabinet, all ten men voted for war, some with tears streaming down their faces. On April 6, Wilson stood before Congress in the United States Capitol and asked for a declaration of war against Germany. Wilson's speech would be remembered as one of the century's milestones.

"I advise that the Congress declare the recent course of the Imperial German government to be in fact nothing less than war against the government and people of the United States," he said. It would be "a war to end all wars," he declared, to "make the world safe for democracy."

"I was stirred in heart and soul by the war messages of Woodrow Wilson," Harry later said. "I thought I ought to go." He decided to abandon his oil investment. (Months later, when he would be fighting in Europe, a well called the Teeter Oil Pool would strike it big, right next to one of his own. To quote one of Harry's future friends and political advisors, George Allen: "The difference between a bold enterpriser and a sucker is no more than the thickness of a cigarette paper.") At thirty-three, Harry was well beyond draft age, but he ventured to the National Guard office in Kansas City and enlisted. On June 22, 1917, he signed papers accepting a commission as a first lieutenant in the 129th Field Artillery Regiment. On his enlistment papers he scribbled his occupation as "farmer, oil." He cheated on his eye exam to pass his medical by memorizing the letters on the chart before he was asked to take his glasses off. On the Fourth of July, 1917, he showed up at Bess's house in his new uniform. She wept on his shoulder and asked that they get married. After all those years of courtship, he refused: "I don't think it would be right for me, to ask you to tie yourself to a prospective cripple – or a sentiment."

Millions of young men had registered for the country's first military draft since the Civil War. Truman put his sister, Mary Jane, in charge of the family farm. In September 1917 he jumped into the Stafford and pulled out of town, headed for an army camp in Oklahoma. Wars had a way of making heroes of ordinary men. For Truman, the war was also an escape from a life that seemed doomed to failure.

7

MOTORING THROUGH THE FLATLANDS of Oklahoma in the Stafford, Truman spotted Camp Doniphan through his windshield. It was a tent city spread over hundreds of acres of Comanche Indian reservation, outside the town of Lawton, on land so flat it looked like it had been shaped by a scythe. Soldiers came from all over to pass basic training at Doniphan. Truman would remember his six months there in the winter of 1917–1918 as brutal.

Drought had ravaged Oklahoma, and wind blew dust into everything. "Dust in my teeth, eyes, hair, nose, and down my neck," he wrote of life at the camp. Winter moved in and unleashed a furious blizzard. "It was the coldest winter they ever experienced in the Midwest," recalled one of Harry's fellow soldiers at Doniphan, Floyd Ricketts. "We were in what were actually tents, and we had what they called Sibley stoves. We kept that thing going red hot all night long."

Each unit at Doniphan had to organize a canteen (a supply shop), and Harry was put in charge of his battery's. He partnered with Eddie Jacobson of Kansas City — "a fine Jewish boy," Truman called him — who had been in the mercantile business and was experienced in handling cash. They staffed a tailor and a barber, and their canteen was quickly doing a booming business. Meanwhile, Harry was learning to soldier. The British, French, and Germans were employing chemical weapons — chlorine gas shells — on battlefields in Europe. At Doniphan, soldiers in training feared the gashouse, where they learned to put gas masks on their faces and on their horses while being exposed to the poison. If the gashouse inspired fear, these soldiers could only imagine what real combat would entail.

Due to the success of his canteen, Truman's superiors gave him the opportunity to test for a captain's position, and he passed. He received orders to ship out ahead of his unit to attend Overseas School Detail in France, so he closed out the canteen and sold his Stafford for $200. On March 20, 1918, he boarded a train. In New York he loaded up on a half dozen pairs of glasses, all pince-nez – the kind that pinch the nose, with no arms, since the arms would get in the way of the seal when he donned his gas mask on the battlefield. On March 28 he penned a last letter to Bess before he set sail. "It is eleven o'clock," he wrote, "and I've got to arise at three in order to get my goods and chattels in readiness to go on the boat, but I am going to write you one last letter on this side on the last day I can . . . Remember that I've always loved you and shall continue to no matter what happens."

On the day before Easter Sunday, 1918, Truman stood aboard the ship *George Washington* as it steamed from New York Harbor's choppy tide. He was nearing his thirty-fourth birthday, standing shoulder to shoulder with American soldiers, most of them far younger than he, many by more than fifteen years. He had a picture of his mother and his sister in his right pocket, and one of Bess in his left, the latter inscribed: "Dear Harry, May this photograph bring you safely home again from France."

Seven thousand men were aboard the *George Washington.* "There we were watching New York's skyline diminish," Harry recorded, "and wondering if we'd be heroes or corpses."

///

To a Missouri farm boy, wartime Paris was a wild scene. Bars and hotels spilled fresh-faced American soldiers into the streets. Few had ever left the county where they were born, and their pockets were full of army pay. France had an inexhaustible supply of wine and cognac, and American soldiers were "trying to drink all there is here," Harry wrote Bess. He went to the Grand Opera, and strolled the Champs-Élysées. "The country is very pretty," he wrote, "and I don't blame the French for wanting to keep it."

The first 100,000 U.S. troops under General Pershing were headed to the front lines as Harry spent his first days in France. Here he learned to fire the "French 75" – World War I's most heralded gun. It could blast a 75-millimeter shell 4.25 miles, at a rate of fifteen rounds per minute. The gun weighed more than three thousand pounds, and rolled on pneumatic tires, so it could be towed into position by car or horse from one battlefield to the next. It required an understanding of trajectory theory as well as mechanics. Harry barely slipped through artillery school, and soon joined his unit from Missouri at Camp Coetquidan in Brittany, France.

July 10 was one of the most momentous days of his life. He was called in to see a colonel and was sure he had done something wrong. In fact, the opposite was true. His superiors saw leadership qualities in him that he did not yet know existed. When he arrived at the colonel's office, he saluted and braced himself.

"Harry," the colonel said, "how would you like to command a battery?"

"Well, sir," he responded, "I hope to be able to do that someday."

"All right, you'll take command of D Battery in the morning."

Truman saluted, about-faced, and marched out of the office. Outside he told a major that his tour of duty in France would be short. He had just been given command of Battery D, the most incorrigible doughboys in the service.

"I think of Battery D as the most mischievous, unpredictable, and diffi-cult-to-handle unit in the whole AEF [American Expeditionary Forces]," recalled one member, Harry Murphy. "Most of the young fellows were athletes of some kind," recalled Battery D soldier Floyd Ricketts. "I was a semipro ballplayer around Kansas City, and there were fighters, and football players, and basketball players." Harry was no athlete. Battery D soldiers were predominantly Irish and German Catholics, and Harry was no Catholic, either. He had heard that four other commanders had tried to browbeat Battery D into line, and all had failed.

The next morning, at six thirty, he stepped in front of Battery D's 194 soldiers. He had never been so nervous in his life.

"He took command of the battery on a cold, frosty morning at Camp Coetquidon [*sic*]," recalled Battery D's Eddie McKim, who was about to become one of Truman's lifelong friends. "My recollection of him was that his knees were knocking together . . . Yes, you could see that he was scared to death . . . I didn't care much for him. I didn't care much for the idea of going through a war with a man I considered a 'sissy.'"

"He was kind of a rather short fellow — compact, serious face, wearing glasses," recalled another Battery D soldier, Vere Leigh.

Harry got straight to the point: When he gave an order, he wanted it carried out. "I didn't come over here to get along with you fellows," he barked. "You're going to get along with me. And if I hear there are any of you who can't, speak up right now and I'll bust you right back."

"He let us know he was Boss!" McKim concluded. "There was no trou-ble whatever when Truman took command."

"I am a Battery commander now," Truman wrote Bess on July 14, 1918.

"You've no idea the experience I'm getting . . . I have attained my one ambition, to be a Battery commander. If I can only make good at it, I can hold my head up anyway the rest of my days."

On August 17, the 129th Field Artillery moved out to the front. Battery D soldiers boarded train cars with all their gear, 105 horses, and 6 French 75 cannons. The trip to the front would take two days, and as the train clattered along the tracks, Captain Truman was suffering the same emotions the rest of the men were. "I have my doubts about my bravery when heavy-explosive shells and gas attacks begin," he wrote. They were headed for France's Vosges Mountains, the only mountainous battlefield on the western front.

Behind the lines, the battery found chaos waiting. "The roads [that led to the front] were literally blocked, jammed and packed with men, caissons, limbers, trucks, field guns, heavy artillery, autos, ambulances, motorcycles, field kitchens, thousands of horses and mules and men fighting with them," remembered Battery D soldier Verne Chaney. "Add to this two or three thousand tanks, a night dark as Hades itself, and over all a drizzling rain creating a mud hole the likes of which the world has never seen."

Truman moved his men deep into the Vosges. On the morning of September 6, "we pulled over the crest of [a] mountain in view of the lines," Chaney recalled. On this terrain, huge dugouts had to be shoveled to situate the French 75s on level ground. Across the valley, Truman could see smoke from enemy encampments, and as the sun began to set, he ordered his sleepless men to fire the guns at 7:45 p.m. "It was our first taste of war," recalled Battery D's Floyd Ricketts. From atop his horse, Truman gave the order.

"Then all hell broke loose," according to Chaney, "not only where we were but in the woods all around us [from other American batteries]."

The gunners fired the French 75s as fast as they could, as many as forty rounds of gas shells in three minutes' time. Between shots, soldiers dumped buckets of water down the sizzling cannon barrels to cool them. After forty-five minutes the barrage ended. A moment of silence passed, then suddenly shells and bullets came whistling through the forest — enemy fire, returning.

"My battery became panic-stricken," Truman recorded. The men dashed for cover in trenches, some sprinting through the woods. Spooked horses darted in every direction. "The first sergeant got so scared," recalled Battery D's Walter Menefee, "that he ran back eight miles to the echelon and I've never seen him to this day." Truman stayed on his mount, but a shell hit some fifteen feet away, tumbling him from his horse and pinning him beneath. One soldier recalled Truman fighting to get out and "gasping like a catfish out of water."

When he was later able to collect his men and retreat, Truman found that not one Battery D soldier had been killed. Four horses perished in the shelling, and two more were wounded and had to be shot. Battery D members would name the night's fight the Battle of Who Run, for some had fled at the first sign of enemy fire. Captain Harry Truman was not one of them.

///

For the next two months, Battery D moved from one position to the next along the western front, firing barrages at the Germans. Night marches left the horses near death from exhaustion and malnutrition, while the soldiers grew so tired, they slept as they walked, forced to eat rotten meat at times for sustenance. One soldier recalled marching all night, so weary that he hallucinated: "I would make an effort to see something ahead and all I could make out was tall office buildings and large residences. I knew then I was seeing things, optical illusions."

The battery landed in the Argonne Forest, in mid-September. For days the American forces prepared for a push at the Germans, what would later be known as the Meuse-Argonne drive – the largest American military operation in history up to that time.

On the morning of September 26, the drive began. At 4 a.m. Truman's battery unleashed some three thousand rounds of 75-millimeter ammunition. "The fireworks started," recalled Battery D soldier McKinley Wooden. "It was the greatest artillery battle the world had ever seen up until that time. You never saw anything like it. I mean to tell you, for seven days after that, our guns were still warm, all the time." At 8 a.m., four hours after the artillery barrage started, some 140,000 American troops drove forward into a fog and light rain. Many were cut down by enemy fire. "I saw bodies without heads," recalled one soldier, "some without arms or legs, some cut in two at the waist and parts lying several feet apart." The drive continued, and the German lines faltered.

By this time, Truman had gained an affection for his men that he struggled to put into words, a respect particular to brothers in arms. He was "plumb crazy" about them, he said. They felt the same way about him; they would call him their captain for the rest of their lives. He had yet to lose a single soldier in his command. Curiously, his men noticed, he always seemed neat and trimmed, even after long marches. "The rest of us would look like bums with mud sticking all over us," remembered another soldier, Harry Vaughan. "He always looked immaculate. And I was never able to understand why."

When Truman finally found the time to write Bess, the Meuse-Argonne drive was nearly two weeks old. "The great drive has taken place," he wrote on October 6, 1918, "and I had a part in it, a very small one but nevertheless a part. The experience has been one that I can never forget, one that I don't want to go through again unless the Lord wills but one I'd never have missed for anything. The papers are in the street now saying that the Central Powers have asked for peace, and I was in the drive that did it!"

On November 11, Truman was awoken by a field telephone ringing in his tent at 5 a.m. Cease-fire orders had come in, for 11 a.m. He gathered his men and set them to work, firing 164 more rounds that morning, stopping at 10:45, when Battery D fired its last shot at a village northeast of Verdun. On this day — in Independence, Missouri, as in cities and towns around the United States — sound is what most people would remember: the booming clang of church bells, the pouring of frenzied citizens into the streets. For Truman it was silence that symbolized American victory. "The silence that followed almost made one's head ache," he recalled. That night he was desperate for sleep, but a unit of French soldiers — many of them drunk — insisted on filing by and saluting him one at a time. They slurred: "Vive President Wilson! Vive le capitaine d'artillerie Americaine!"

For weeks Truman was stuck in Europe, awaiting his ticket home. He was bursting with anticipation. Bess wrote him, "You may invite the entire 35th Division to your wedding if you want to. I guess it's going to be yours as well as mine."

///

"You've just never seen such a radiant, happy look on a man's face," Truman's cousin Ethel Noland recalled. Truman was standing at the altar at Trinity Episcopal Church in Independence, watching his bride walk down the aisle toward him. Since Bess's father was dead, her brother

Frank held her arm as she walked. Even on Truman's wedding day, destiny was at work. On this same day — June 28, 1919 — President Wilson signed the Treaty of Versailles in France, a treaty that was meant to bring on lasting peace but was in fact ill constructed and destined to fail.

For her wedding day Bess wore a gown of ivory chiffon, a white faille hat, and pointed white leather shoes with Louis XV heels. The groom wore a single-breasted cream and black houndstooth suit freshly stitched by his best man, Ted Marks, a fellow captain in the 129th Field Artillery, who had just opened a tailor shop in Kansas City. The suit cost Harry $65, and his best man let him have it on credit, since Truman had spent quite a bit on a wedding ring, purchased in New York on his way home from Europe. The reception was at Bess's home, and if there was one awkward element, it was the mothers. Bess's mother, Mrs. Wallace, had never been fond of the "farm boy" from Grandview. As for Mamma Truman, she was escorted from the affair at the end by best man Ted Marks. "Well, now, Mrs. Truman," Marks said, "you've lost Harry." She looked at him with fierce blue eyes ("I can see her face to this day," Marks remarked decades later). "Indeed I haven't," Mamma Truman said.

Harry and Bess departed for Chicago, where their honeymoon began. When they returned, Truman moved into the Wallace home at 219 North Delaware. It was not a comfortable fit. Bess's grandmother Mrs. Gates slept in a room on the first floor, while Bess's mother occupied the master bedroom on the second floor, a few feet from where Harry and Bess began their marriage, in separate beds in their own small room. Harry brought his belongings — nothing but a stack of books, some clothes, and some souvenirs from the army. Bess's mother endured Harry's presence. "The Wallaces . . . rather ignored Mr. Truman," a friend and future secretary of Harry's later said. "Not blatantly, rudely. But it was there."

Truman set out to make some money. "I finally decided to sell all my farm equipment, hogs, horses, cows, harnesses and whatnot," he wrote in a diary, "and go into business with my Jewish friend, my canteen Sergeant, Edward Jacobson."

Thus began the next of Harry Truman's business debacles.

8

ON NOVEMBER 28, 1919, Truman & Jacobson held its grand opening. It was a haberdashery on Twelfth Street and Baltimore, in the heart of downtown Kansas City. Upon entering the store, customers saw a menagerie of luxury products, from neckties to silk underwear. They also found thirty-five-year-old Harry Truman behind the counter. Truman & Jacobson had twenty feet of storefront, with broad windows and a sign advertising SHIRTS, COLLARS, HOSIERY, GLOVES, BELTS, HATS.

Eddie Jacobson had been Truman's partner running the canteen at Camp Doniphan and had served in Battery D. Legend has it that the pair concocted their haberdashery while playing poker and fighting seasickness aboard the ship home from Europe. Harry put all his money in from sales of his share of the family farm, plus thousands more in borrowed funds. The partners paid for the store's build-out, and the lease called for $350 a month for five years, according to lawsuit papers later filed. The location offered a steady stream of foot traffic. "Twelfth Street was in its heyday then," Jacobson recalled. "It was the fastest place in America. Gambling houses right around the corner from the store. Four hotels and a lot of night clubs, all full of a sporting crowd."

In January 1920 (the same month that Prohibition went into effect), a sharp decline in the economy jolted the business. For the next eighteen months a recession lingered, and by the spring of 1922 the store was shuttered. Jacobson had to declare legal bankruptcy, but Truman avoided that route. Still, their lease ran for many more months, and bank loans were unpayable. Of all Harry's financial setbacks, this one hurt the most. "I am still paying on those debts," he wrote in his diary twelve years later.

Nightly suppers at home with Bess and her mother grew all the more strained. Harry was broke. One day, just before the haberdashery closed for good, he was inside his store pacing the floor tiles he had spent so much money on. He would remember feeling exceptionally blue, when an old pal burst through the shop's door — Mike Pendergast, one of Jackson County's more influential political figures. Harry had served in the army with Mike's son Jim, and Mike had taken a liking to the haberdasher.

"How'd you like to be county judge?" Mike Pendergast asked.

Harry must have laughed the notion off at first. "I don't know," he said.

"If you would like," Pendergast said, "you can have it."

In Jackson County, judges were not arbiters of jurisprudence but rather county commissioners. They ran things, and every two years they came up for reelection. Not until after the haberdashery was closed for good did Harry start to take Mike Pendergast's idea seriously. His wife thought it a terrible idea, and his friends found it odd, as if fetched out of thin air. Truman was known to be an avid reader of political history, but he had never seriously entertained the idea of actually becoming a politician. "Funny thing," Eddie Jacobson remembered about his months at Truman & Jacobson. "Harry never talked much about politics."

In the spring of 1922 a small notice appeared in the local *Independence Examiner*, announcing the candidacy of Harry S. Truman for eastern county judge. Truman made his first attempt at a political speech at an American Legion post meeting in Lee's Summit, a farming town directly south of Independence. He rallied the Battery D boys, and Bess sat near the front row, joining some 360 locals, many of whom had come for the free cigars. "I never will forget the first speech he made," recalled war buddy Edgar Hinde. "Boy, it was about the poorest effort of a speech I ever heard in my life. I suffered for him." "He kind of stammered and hummed around," said another Independence local, Henry Chiles. "But he got through it."

Jackson County judges controlled the salaries of about seven hundred municipal employees. Traditionally, a portion of the county income ended up in the judges' pockets, through illegal kickbacks. Road, oil, and cement contractors got jobs oftentimes not by promising the best work or the cheapest price but by promising to slide money back to the judges under the table. It was an easy scam. As one powerful Jackson County newspaper editor put it around this time: "The purse strings of the county are therefore the prize."

The county employed three elected judges: a western judge, who handled Kansas City; an eastern judge, who handled the rural communities east of the city; and a presiding judge, the county's chief executive.

Harry was running for eastern judge. In May 1922 he drove his Dodge all over the county, knocking on doors. His platform had two major selling points: (1) Honesty. Truman promised not to filch county purses, as was custom in the past. His family had lived in this rural community for years, and people knew the Trumans to be trustworthy and true to their word; and (2) Roads. Henry Ford's Model Ts had swarmed the county, and Truman believed that a new arterial system of paved roads would usher Jackson County into the future.

He had no qualifications outside of his army and some National Guard service. He did, however, have the backing of Mike Pendergast, who had first approached him about the eastern judgeship. Mike's brother, "Boss" Tom Pendergast, ran Kansas City's Democratic political machine from his office above his saloon at 1908 Main Street, while Mike ran the machine in Jackson County's rural areas. Tom Pendergast in particular had emerged as one of the most powerful figures in the state, and he defined machine politics in the simplest terms.

"It's a very simple thing when you come down to it," Boss Tom Pendergast said. "There's people that need things, lots of 'em, and I see to it that they get 'em. I go to my office on South Main Street in Kansas City at seven o'clock in the morning and I stay there when I'm in town till about six o'clock at night and during that time I see maybe 200, maybe 300 people. One needs a half a ton of coal. Another woman's gotta get a job for her boy. I see to it that they get those things. That's all there is to it."

He left out one piece of information, the key to machine politics: in return for favors, people would be in Pendergast's debt. Which meant he told them how to vote, so he controlled elections throughout Jackson County. It was Boss Tom Pendergast – racehorse gambler, saloon owner, the "Big Fellow" and "Democratic Czar" of Kansas City – who really had his fingers on the county purse strings.

The Pendergasts were fending off a challenge from a rival machine run by a Democratic politician named Joe Shannon. Pendergast's faction of the Democratic Party was called the Goats, while Shannon controlled the Rabbits. The race for eastern judge in Jackson County in 1922 became a contest between the two, and inexperienced Harry Truman found himself a cog in a heated battle of the machines. On August 1, 1922, voters turned out in unprecedented numbers, due to the Pendergast versus Shannon showdown. Truman won by fewer than 300 votes

(4,230 to 3,951 for the top Rabbit candidate), and so at age thirty-eight he began a new career as a rural politician.

It is highly likely that the Pendergasts had engineered the win. As Truman scholar Robert H. Ferrell once wrote: "Certainly Mike and Tom Pendergast used repeaters [repeat voters] . . . They not only took care that absent voters had ballots cast for them, they even voted the dead – a well-known quip on election day was, 'Now is the time for all good cemeteries to come to the aid of the party.'"

Still, Truman emerged victorious and unscathed. Despite what may have occurred behind the scenes, he himself had proven a rare breed – an honest politician – and he had run a campaign that would have made his father proud. As he wrote his cousin Ralph Truman at the time: "I won the dirtiest and hardest fought campaign Eastern Jackson Co. has ever seen without money or promises."

///

Mornings in Independence found Truman striding the cobbles of Independence Square, greeting locals with his affable smile. Two words – "Morning, Judge" – became part of his daily routine and his identity. He carried a badge now, the badge of a Jackson County judge, and he also started taking classes at Kansas City Law School (though he never got any degree).

In 1924, after his first two-year term, he lost his bid for reelection (it would be the only election he would ever lose). But he won again in 1926 – not as eastern judge but as presiding judge, the county's chief executive. By this time, Boss Tom Pendergast had become Missouri's political kingmaker. His Kansas City machine was known to be corrupt, all the more reason why Truman became a preferred face of the organization in Jackson County. "Old Tom Pendergast wanted to have some window dressing," said Harry Vaughan, one of Truman's closest friends. "And Truman was really window dressing for him because he could say, 'Well, there's my boy Truman. Nobody can ever say anything about Truman. Everybody thinks he's okay.'"

On February 17, 1924, Harry and Bess had a baby daughter, Mary Margaret. The Trumans had married later in life, and Bess had suffered two miscarriages, so the arrival of Margaret was the most important moment of their lives. The baby was born four days after Bess's thirty-ninth birthday. At home, financial troubles continued. Harry was sued by a landlord for the remaining $2,950 rent due from the Truman & Jacobson store, and he owed banks too. His $6,000 salary got the family by but was not enough to pay off debts.

The judgeship served as on-the-job political training. The 1920s economy was roaring indeed – a strong wind at Truman's back. Jackson County was still mostly rural, with 610 square miles and roughly 470,000 citizens (almost 400,000 of those living in Kansas City). The county judges employed the sheriff and police, health officials, civil engineers, jailhouse personnel, a treasurer, and a coroner. Truman ran the county's finances "as if I were the president of a private corporation," he said. Or, as he put it, he tried "to live up to my good mother's teachings."

As he had promised in his first campaign, paved roads would be the focus of his tenure. The county's roads were what was commonly called "piecrust," oiled-dirt thoroughfares that turned to pools of mud in spring rains and then froze in winter. Truman wanted every farm to be within 2.5 miles of a paved road, and a road system that could handle not just the 100,000 autos in Jackson County at the time but exponentially more in the future. This meant 250 miles of new, paved roadways – and a big bill for county taxpayers. "Everybody thought Mr. Truman was crazy," recalled a local, Mize Peters, "because he was advocating paved roads."

Truman convinced county officials and citizens to issue a $6.5 million bond (there was a hard-fought referendum, which Truman won), and soon construction crews were at work. But the project forced a hard lesson on him. In politics, issues do not always pit right against wrong. Sometimes a politician is forced to choose the lesser of two evils. Truman discovered that one of the two judges working under him was collecting kickback money in the road-building program. He was forced to look the other way in order to prevent more injurious crimes from occurring and to keep on the good side of Boss Pendergast, who had given him his career.

Harry wrote bitterly of this crooked judge, in a diary entry: "This sweet associate of mine, my friend, who was supposed to back me, had already made a deal with a former crooked contractor, a friend of the Boss's . . . I had to compromise in order to get the voted road system carried out . . . I had to let . . . a friend of the Boss's steal about $10,000 from the general revenues of the county to satisfy my ideal associate and keep the crooks from getting a million or more out of the bond issue. Was I right or did I compound a felony? I don't know."

As far as the public knew, Truman had come through on his word – spent $6.5 million, every penny honestly. "We never had to do a thing that wasn't right through that whole job," recalled Tom Veatch, one of the road program's chief engineers. "And it is one of the miracles that I have been through in my life."

Truman set his sights on another ambitious plan: a new courthouse for Kansas City and a complete remodel of the Independence courthouse. He hit the road, driving for days to examine courthouses so he could hire the best architect. He crossed the borders of Oklahoma, Arkansas, Texas, and Louisiana, all at his own expense. In these travels, a man named Fred Canfil did most of the driving. It was Canfil's first appearance in a partnership with Truman that would last for years. Canfil was a heavily muscled associate of Tom Pendergast, with an oversized head and a hero-worshipping dedication to Truman. He carried a strong odor of garlic and was so unusual-looking, one Independence local said of him, "If I were to choose the five or ten most memorable people I have ever known, I would say that Fred Canfil was one of them." In Shreveport, Louisiana, Truman and Canfil found a courthouse on which to model their own, and soon construction in Kansas City was under way. Truman also hired a sculptor to build a statue out front – his hero and the namesake of Jackson County, Andrew Jackson, on horseback.

Truman's tenure as presiding judge was going surprisingly well. "Mr. Truman had a natural, human instinct of understanding the man in the street," said Oscar Chapman, who would later serve with Truman in Washington. "He really had a gift for interpreting the thinking of the problems that that man had . . . and he seemed to understand them so well that he got along with people very well." The *Kansas City Star* called him "extraordinarily efficient"; his plans were achieved with "not a suspicion of graft."

Everywhere one looked in Jackson County in 1929 there were signs of prosperity. There was money in the coffers, and plenty of jobs. What could go wrong?

///

In August 1929, the New York Stock Exchange soared to a series of record highs. The market cracked 350 for the first time on August 1. It launched past 360 on the sixteenth, past 370 one week later, and set another record high on August 30, of 380.33.

The small savings of ordinary citizens fueled the hot marketplace, the hard earnings of the new American middle class. To most it was a wholly new idea – to invest money and watch it grow, as if dollars were seeds planted in the soil. Much of the stock-buying frenzy was on margin; small-town investors put up a quarter of the price, while stockbrokers (there were 70,950 of them in the United States in 1929, up from 29,609 at the start of the decade) put up the rest by borrowing from banks. As the market grew, a hunger for easy capital began to spread like a contagion. As one financial columnist wrote of Wall Street investing: "I am firm in my belief that anyone not only can be rich, but ought to be rich." There seemed no end to the pyramiding profits – until October 1929, when sharp declines sent shock waves of panic across the globe.

On October 24, in a single trading day, $5 billion evaporated from the stock market. President Herbert Hoover tried to assuage the nation's nerves, issuing a statement the following morning: "The fundamental business of the country, that is the production and distribution of commodities, is on a sound and prosperous basis." The week following this unfortunate utterance, real panic set in, resulting in what the *Christian Science Monitor* called "one of the most uncontrollable selling stampedes ever witnessed on the floor of the New York Stock Exchange," with "billions of quoted values erased as by the sweep of a sponge."

In Jackson County, Truman entered 1930 facing reelection. He breezed through on the strength of his road program, with the backing of Tom Pendergast. But now the job of presiding judge became a nightmare. In 1931, weighed down by skyrocketing unemployment, Jackson County revenues sank tens of thousands of dollars. That same year, the Jackson County Bank of Independence failed, along with two other banks outside Kansas City. In Truman's hometown the signs of prosperity disappeared. As the man who controlled the county's purse strings, he was forced to cut jobs and order pay cuts to people he knew well, whose wives and children he knew well. The county sliced huge numbers from its workforce, cut salaries of others, and sent two hundred patients home from mental asylums.

It was all "pretty hard on head and nerves," Truman wrote, and he began to suffer insomnia and headaches. On one short business trip to Little Rock, Arkansas, in February 1931, a trip he engineered just to get away, he wrote Bess, "The finances of the county were never in such shape since [the previous presiding judge] Miles Bulger handled them, and every person I've ever had any association with since birth has wanted me to take pity and furnish him some county money without much return. On top of that, the refinancing on the farm at home [the Truman family farm in Grandview, where Harry's mother and sister were living] has been getting deeper and deeper into difficulties . . . I was becoming so keyed up that I either had to run away or go on a big drunk."

As the county sunk deeper into the Depression, two shocking crimes drew the nation's attention to Kansas City. On June 17, 1933, a convicted murderer named Frank Nash was being transported through Union Station when a gang led by Charles "Pretty Boy" Floyd opened fire on law enforcement officials with machine guns. Six county employees were gunned down in the "Kansas City massacre," and Nash and his gang made a getaway. (All were later believed to be caught or killed, including Pretty Boy Floyd, shot dead in a hail of FBI gunfire in Ohio on October 22, 1934.)

The second crime hit closer to home for Truman. A city election held on March 27, 1934, pit candidates of Tom Pendergast against a reformist party struggling to dismantle the Kansas City machine. Pendergast won big, but the election was marred by a fury of violence. Two election workers were shot dead, and numerous others were injured. Reporters investigating whether Pendergast's operatives were "running repeaters" (repeat voters) were assaulted by hoodlums from one precinct to another. The *Washington Post* reported "outbreaks of gunplay, kidnapping, slugging and fist-fights . . . Tom Pendergast's Democratic organization tonight moved like a steam roller."

Jackson County politics had always been crooked; now the scene had grown sinister. It was during these anxious days that Truman began a new ritual. He checked into a room at the Pickwick Hotel on McGee Street in Kansas City, where he would stay up all night — likely with a bottle of bourbon — trying to sort through his thoughts. "The manager gave me a room without registering," Truman noted in a letter to Bess, so no one would be able to "see or phone me." He was now forty-nine, and he had served as a county judge for nearly ten years. He sat scribbling in the middle of the night on hotel stationery with a fountain pen, spelling out a political philosophy that was to guide him for the rest of his life.

On ethics: "Since childhood at my mother's knee, I have believed in honor, ethics and right living as its own reward. I find a very small minority who agree with me on that premise."

On money and the cost of integrity: "We've spent $7,000,000 in bonds and $7,000,000 in revenue in my administration. I could have had $1,500,000; I haven't $150."

On the ambiguity of political compromises: "I wonder if I did the right thing to put a lot of no account sons of bitches on the payroll and pay other sons of bitches more money for supplies than they were worth in order to satisfy the political powers and save $3,500,000. I believe I did do right."

He wrote pages on his war experiences – for in war, he believed, unlike politics, there was a clear sense of right and wrong. He wrote of love – how like war, it meant always doing the right thing, of putting the cause before oneself. Most of all he wrote of the confounding nature of politics. "Maybe I can put the County where none of the crooks can profit," he wrote. "I wonder if I can. All this gives me headaches and my private business has gone to pat so that I'll be worse than a pauper when I'm done."

Even at that moment as he sat scribbling in the Pickwick Hotel, a number of narratives around the globe had begun to unfold, plot lines that in the years to come would converge upon this obscure county judge in their climactic moments. Franklin Roosevelt had been inaugurated the thirty-second president of the United States, on March 4, 1933, uttering the famous words on that day: "The only thing we have to fear is fear itself." Adolf Hitler had also taken power, and had been photographed waving from the window of Berlin's Reich Chancellery as 25,000 Nazi followers marched past saluting him. "No power on earth will ever get me out of here alive," Hitler was overheard saying. On the other side of the globe, Japanese troops had charged over the border into Chinese Manchuria on the night of September 18, 1931, starting an armed conflict in the East not to end until August 1945. In a small laboratory on the second floor of the Physics Institute at the University of Rome, a brilliant thirty-two-year-old scientist named Enrico Fermi had made a startling discovery. By bombarding atoms with neutrons, he could transform elements – a key revelation that would eventually lead to the discovery of nuclear fission and ultimately to the bomb.

In Kansas City, a more immediate situation was about to confront Truman. In the office of Boss Tom Pendergast, above Pendergast's saloon at 1908 Main Street, conversation in the spring of 1934 turned to the upcoming elections for the United States Senate. Pendergast had approached three potential candidates, but none of them was in a position to run.

The Boss was nearing the peak of his power. The Great Depression had only served to strengthen him, for it put voters in need of his help. He had become extraordinarily rich and had built a $175,000 mansion for himself and his platinum-blond wife. He was "the Mussolini of Missouri," "the last of the political bosses," as the *Washington Post* put it. "In almost every block of Kansas City is someone who is looking after the interests of the machine." He fed Thanksgiving turkeys to prison populations, gave out ball game tickets by the dozens, and had big money in the rackets, too — prostitution and gambling, which thrived in Kansas City, protected by paid-off police. Pendergast played all the strings like a virtuoso. "He was an able clear thinker and he understood political situations and how to handle them better than any man I have ever known," Truman said of Pendergast.

In a meeting with the chairman of the Jackson County Democratic Committee, James P. Aylward, in the spring of 1934, Pendergast found himself shuffling through names, unable to come up with the right one to run for the U.S. Senate seat. Time was short, and the situation was getting critical. As powerful as he was, Pendergast found himself in a precarious situation. The senior senator from Missouri, Bennett "Champ" Clark, was based in St. Louis, and he was backing another St. Louis candidate for the second seat. If St. Louis was to win both Senate seats, the Kansas City machine would crumble. "If you don't have a candidate for the Senate," Aylward warned Pendergast, "you'll be out of state politics. You'll be finished."

Aylward made a suggestion: "Well, why don't you run Harry S. Truman for the United States Senate? He's a former soldier . . . He's a member of the Masonic order; he's a Baptist; he's been active in affairs around here."

"Nobody knows him," Pendergast came back. "He's an ordinary county judge and not known outside Jackson County." After further thought, Pendergast asked incredulously: "Do you mean seriously to tell me that you actually believe that Truman can be nominated and elected to the United States Senate?"

9

TRUMAN WAS ON BUSINESS in the town of Warsaw, Missouri, in early May 1934 when he got a phone call at his hotel. It was Jackson County Democratic Committee chairman James Aylward. The conversation, as remembered by Aylward:

"Judge," Aylward said, "Jim Pendergast and I are in Jefferson City, and it's very important and imperative that we see you almost immediately."

Truman smelled trouble. "Why do you want to see me?"

"We can't discuss it on the phone."

Truman, Aylward, and Jim Pendergast — Boss Tom Pendergast's nephew and Harry's war buddy — met that night in the lobby of the Terry Hotel in the small farming town of Sedalia. Pendergast laid it on the line: the boss wanted to run Truman for senator.

"I can't win as a candidate for the United States Senate," Truman argued. "Nobody knows me and I haven't got any money. I'm not equipped to make a campaign."

Aylward said, "We'll help you financially . . . We're in a position to have all of the politicians — Democrats of any influence throughout this state — to support you, but we've got to do something now. We've got to start a campaign."

Truman knew a Senate campaign would hurl his life into chaos. He also knew that, with Pendergast behind him, he did have a shot at winning, no matter how obscure he was, or how ill-equipped he would be to perform in Washington. In fact, the story of the 1934 senatorial election was about to become, in the words of Tom Pendergast biographer Lyle W. Dorsett, "one of the most fascinating in the annals of Missouri politics."

On the night of May 14, 1934, Truman booked his familiar room at the Pickwick Hotel. It was 4 a.m. as he sat at a desk writing on hotel stationery. "Tomorrow I am to make the most momentous announcement of my life. I have come to the place where all men strive to be at my age and I thought two weeks ago that retirement on a virtual pension in some minor county office was all that was in store for me . . . Now I am candidate for the United States Senate. If the Almighty God decides that I go there, I am going to pray as King Solomon did, for wisdom to do the job."

A few hours later, sleepless Harry Truman stood among a crowd of four thousand in front of the Boone County Courthouse in Columbia, Missouri, a 125-mile drive from the Pickwick Hotel. The machine was showing its muscle. Buses full of state workers — Pendergast backers — had made the journey to Columbia. An American Legion band honked out crowd pleasers as a Harry Truman sound truck made rounds. Speakers warmed up the crowd, then Truman took the stage, delivering a speech short on words and even shorter on charisma. He could sum up his campaign in two words: "Back Roosevelt."

"Two words are all any Democratic candidate for the Senate or Congress needs," Truman said.

Franklin Roosevelt had been in office for less than two years, and for Democratic voters, his New Deal politics had proved a beacon in the Depression's storm. Truman promised, if he were senator, to vote as Roosevelt would vote.

By the next morning, Truman knew he had a fight on his hands. His rival in the primary, Jacob "Tuck" Milligan, announced his candidacy on the same day. Milligan had more than ten years of experience in Washington as a U.S. congressman from Missouri, and he was backed by the state's senior U.S. senator, Champ Clark. Clark had the St. Louis newspapers behind Tuck Milligan. Thus the Senate seat would pit Kansas City against the larger metropolis of St. Louis, and Harry Truman against a significantly more qualified candidate. To complicate matters, a third candidate joined the race — John J. Cochran, a St. Louis lawyer who had nine years' experience as a congressman in Washington. Whichever Democrat won the primary was almost sure to win the general election.

Truman set off on a Missouri odyssey, making between six and sixteen speeches a day. Trusty Fred Canfil did much of the driving. A historic heat wave baked Missouri in the summer of 1934; the mercury shot past 100 degrees F. for twenty-one days in a row, while a drought desiccated the Midwest. Truman and Canfil drove through the dust bowl from town to town, meeting voters hard hit by the Depression and thirsty for hope. In July 1934, at the height of Harry's campaign, six more Missouri banks were liquidated.

The opposition brutalized Truman, who was an easy target. "For this bellhop of Pendergast's to aspire to make a jump from the obscure bench of a county judge to the United States Senate is without precedent," one Cochran campaigner said. "When one contemplates the giants of the past who have represented Missouri, this spectacle is not only grotesque, it is sheer buffoonery." Even the *New York Times* pointed out that "Truman is little known and his only strength is that given him by Pendergast in Kansas City."

Money was tight. "I'll tell you we had plenty of trouble keeping the contest moving," James Aylward admitted. But the machine brought voters in line.

That summer, another killing shocked the state and drew more national attention to the brutality of Kansas City politics. "Brother John" Lazia, the Kansas City–born son of an Italian immigrant family, emerged as a power player in the city's Democratic machine — "the swarthy, right-hand man of Tom Pendergast," according to the *Washington Post*. Lazia was also an underground mobster who controlled gambling rackets run out of Kansas City hotels. On July 10, 1934, at 4 a.m., two gunmen shot him at close range as he exited a car on a city street. A rival gangster was fingered for the murder — Michael "Jimmy Needles" LaCapra, later assassinated in retaliation. Before his killing, Lazia had told an associate: "If anything happens, notify Pendergast . . . my best friend, and tell him I love him."

On election day, nervous voters headed to their polling stations. No violence was reported. Pendergast's man pulled off a stunning victory: Truman (276,850), then Cochran (236,105), then Milligan (147,614). The reaction from St. Louis was predictable: Truman was "Boss Pendergast's Errand Boy," according to the *St. Louis Post-Dispatch*. Even Truman's hometown papers could not hide from the truth. The *Kansas City Star*: "County Judge Truman is the nominee of the Democratic Party because Tom Pendergast willed it so."

In November, Truman won the general election; no Republican stood a chance against Tom Pendergast in Depression-era Missouri. Throughout Truman's campaign, his reputation banked on his road program, miles of weaving Jackson County pavement. "He pulled Jackson County out of the mud," one of Harry's old teachers from grade school said. Now Truman's roads were going to lead him out of the county, all the way to Washington, DC.

"What's a senator?" little Margie Truman asked her father, when she learned the family would be moving to the nation's capital. Both Bess and ten-year-old Margaret were devastated, having to leave their friends, family, and home in Independence. Margaret would remember "wailing dramatically."

Truman drove the family a thousand miles straight east to Washington. "I was nearly 51 years old at the time, [and] I was as timid as a country boy arriving on the campus of a great university for the first year," he later wrote. Bess picked out a furnished apartment in a red brick building at 3016 Tilden Street, about five miles from where Truman's office would be. The four-room apartment was not much bigger than their garage in Independence. The $150 rent made Truman's eyes bulge; he borrowed money from a local bank and filled the little home with furniture. The new job would raise his salary to $10,000, but that would still make Harry "undoubtedly the poorest Senator financially in Washington," as he said. As a consolation to Margie, he rented a piano from a local shop.

On January 3, 1935, Truman entered the Senate gallery for the first time, prepared to take the oath. Before the ceremony, he was called into the vice president's office down a corridor, where Vice President John Nance "Cactus Jack" Garner of Texas awaited him. Other freshman senators gathered, all strangers to Truman. "Men," Garner said, "before we enter into these ceremonies I'd like to have you all join me in striking a blow for liberty." Garner pulled out a bottle "that looked like corn liquor," according to one man present, and poured shots. Minutes later, well fortified, Harry was back in the Senate gallery. Seated in the audience were his wife and his daughter, and Jim Pendergast. Cactus Jack Garner banged an ivory gavel and "the teeming galleries were hushed, as though a curtain were being raised on a great drama," a reporter described the scene. Along with the other freshmen, Truman took the oath.

The Seventy-Fourth Congress was a boost for Roosevelt, now midway through his first term. The midterm 1934 election had been one of history's great landslides, the nation voting overwhelmingly Democratic, a clear mandate that the populace had embraced FDR's New Deal policies. Truman was assigned suite 248 in the Senate Office Building, the words MR. TRUMAN, MISSOURI painted on the door. In the Senate gallery he took seat 94, in the back row, with Sherman Minton of Indiana on his right and Rush Holt of West Virginia on his left. The Senate was known as "the Most Exclusive Club in the World." There was but one woman: Hattie Caraway, Democrat from Arkansas. Truman was instantly a curiosity in Washington, because he had arrived under dubious circumstances. He was called "the Senator from Pendergast," and many of his colleagues refused to speak to him.

"If you had seen Harry Truman . . . in the freshman row in the Senate, you would hardly have picked him as a future leader," an early Truman biographer wrote. "He seemed to be one of those inconspicuous political accidents – a nice fellow cast up by the workings of machine politics." According to a short *Washington Post* profile (commonplace for freshman senators), Truman was "not considered brilliant, either as an orator or as a scholar." Ignored by many, he got one good piece of advice from J. Hamilton Lewis, Democrat of Illinois.

"Don't start out with an inferiority complex," Lewis said. "For the first six months you'll wonder how you got here, and after that you'll wonder how the rest of us got here."

On the morning of February 14, 1935, Harry Truman crossed the White House threshold for the first time. He walked through the front door and down a hallway past bored newspapermen fingering cigarettes. Franklin Roosevelt's appointments secretary had written Truman's name in the president's calendar as "Sen. Thomas Truman" with the *Thomas* crossed out. Harry's appointment with the president was at 11:15.

"No one who hasn't had the experience can realize what it was like to enter the Oval Room and see Franklin Roosevelt behind that fabulous desk," Washington insider Donald Nelson once wrote. "There is no experience in the world quite like it." Inside the Oval Office, the walls were crammed frame to frame with pictures of ships, celebrating Roosevelt's love of sailing and his days as assistant secretary of the navy. His desk teemed with objects of curiosity, given to him by foreign leaders and baseball stars alike. The president smiled while receiving guests, but the cigarette in his black cigarette holder was the giveaway. If it was pointed up, he was in a good mood. Down – bad mood. On this day Truman would remember nothing of FDR's mood. He would only recall feeling terribly nervous.

"I was practically tongue-tied," he later said. It wasn't the president who made him so timorous, but rather the *presidency*. "I was before the greatest office in the world."

The meeting was short and inconsequential, a formality for a freshman senator.

Truman was now fully in the throes of his political education. He routinely was up at five and arrived at his office at seven in the morning. "That man was there earlier than everybody," recalled one of his secretaries, Edgar Faris. "I don't care if he went to bed at 2 a.m., he was up at five and he was down at that office. This man really worked." He learned the ins and outs of Congress. It was essentially a bill-generating machine. Members drummed up new laws or ways to alter existing ones. These ideas were put on paper, considered, argued, revised, passed on to the president, sometimes vetoed, sometimes not, and often hurled into history's dustbin along with the ambitions of the men whose name was on them. Committees tackled essential issues from commerce to foreign affairs. The Senate Chamber where the ninety-six gathered was a boxing ring where intellects sparred, hurling ideas, audacity, and at times inscrutable ideology at one another through a haze of tobacco smoke.

Truman had read bios of all the players, and now here they were in flesh and blood: Arthur Vandenberg, the Republican stalwart from Michigan, opinionated and irritable. Guy Gillette of Iowa, white-haired and dignified, the prototypical glamorous statesman. Huey Long of Louisiana, bombastic and radical, who would soon be felled by an assassin's bullet. Of the bunch, Truman remained one of the most reticent, content to study the mechanics of government and to vote when bills were called up for action.

He established himself as a firm New Deal Democrat, supporting the president at almost every turn. He supported the farmer, labor, and what he called "the average man for a happier and more abundant life" – people, that is, like himself, and most Missourians. A widely respected senator from Montana named Burton Wheeler took Truman under his wing and appointed him to the Interstate Commerce Committee, where he would do his most important work in this term, formulating new regulations to aid railroad companies that had crumbled due to the Depression (nearly a million railroad men were out of work, and some ten thousand miles of track had been abandoned).

Truman wasn't surprised when the press and fellow senators accused him of voting according to Tom Pendergast's wishes. The boss in Kansas City did ask Harry to vote certain ways. Truman followed orders on inconsequential matters, but his voting record on legislation sided with FDR almost every time — even when Roosevelt sparked controversy by trying to "pack" the Supreme Court by adding justices who would vote for his New Deal policies in 1937, a move that historians consider one of FDR's most embarrassing mistakes.

Meanwhile, Truman settled into the "Washington Merry-Go-Round." He learned that while much of the business of the Senate occurred on the Senate Chamber floor, more of it was accomplished over cocktails in offices and at Washington watering holes. "Kind of hard . . . to attend a dry lunch in this town," Harry told Bess. Margaret enrolled at a local girls' school, and she was now old enough to ride a streetcar alone to the Senate offices in the afternoons. "She would drop paper clips down my neck," recalled Truman's secretary, Reathel Odum. "Our desk chairs were on wheels and she'd roll me around." In summer, the Trumans headed back to Independence for the recess.

Gradually, Truman worked his way off the bottom of "the club" hierarchy. He earned a reputation as a hard worker and a deeply ethical thinker. As he told Bess, "There's a driving force inside me that makes me get into things." Still, he could not get the president's secretaries to return his phone calls.

Truman introduced the most important work of his first term, the Truman-Wheeler bill, in 1939. By the time it came up for argument on the Senate floor, however, his reputation had suffered a stiff blow. He was sitting in his office one day early in 1939 when he got a phone call. He was told that his mentor, some would even say his "boss," had been indicted on federal charges. Pendergast was going to prison. Truman — facing an election year in 1940 — knew that this was not going to go well for him.

Pendergast, now sixty-seven, pleaded guilty to evading income tax on more than $300,000, money collected illegally while "arranging a compromise" in a fraudulent insurance deal. Other Pendergast operatives had already been jailed for fixing elections in Kansas City. Whether any fraud ever occurred in an election won by Harry Truman has never been proven.

On May 29, Pendergast arrived at Leavenworth Federal Penitentiary, driven by his nephew Jim Pendergast, Harry Truman's close friend and war buddy. By lunchtime the man who had run the Kansas City Democratic machine for twenty years had heard the soul-shattering sound of iron prison doors slamming shut. Reporters and photographers appeared at Truman's office door in April 1939 for comment. Truman said, "Pendergast has been a good friend to me when I needed it. I am not one to desert a sinking ship when it starts down." To Bess, Harry was more honest: "The terrible things done by the high ups in K.C. will be a lead weight to me from now on."

///

Nearing the end of his Senate term, Truman was in trouble. "Never before or since," his daughter later wrote, "can I recall my father being so gloomy as he was in those latter months in 1939, after Tom Pendergast went to prison." The Truman-Wheeler bill – the most important work of his life so far – was being blocked on the Senate floor. "I feel as if my four years and a half hard work has been practically wasted," he wrote a friend. Truman had little money, and few prospects of a job if he was not able to win reelection in 1940, and given the Pendergast stain, few gave him any shot at all. As one Washington insider said of the nation's capital: "There is nothing more pitiful in this town than an 'ex.' A general without an army or a post, [or] a Senator who has been defeated."

One day the governor of Missouri, Lloyd Stark, paid Truman a visit in Washington. Like Truman, Stark faced the end of his term. Two years younger than Harry, the governor was a graduate of Annapolis who had also commanded an artillery outfit in World War I. He had made a fortune in his family business – Stark Nurseries – filling Missouri's grocery stores with Stark apples. The governor had been instrumental in bringing down the Pendergast machine, and had taken much credit for it, which infuriated Truman, who knew what other political insiders in Missouri knew: that Stark had made use of Pendergast's services earlier in his own career when he needed them.

Relaxing in Truman's office, Stark said, "Everybody keeps telling me that I ought to run for the Senate." He chuckled. "But don't worry about it, Harry. I wouldn't dream of running against you."

Stark made an exit, leaving Truman to think. He turned to one of his secretaries, Victor Messall, and said, "That S.O.B. is going to run against me."

10

WHILE AMERICA GEARED UP for the 1940 elections, the nation was falling into the grip of war paranoia. Stories of domestic contests were pushed off the front page for more pressing news from across the Atlantic. On May 10, 1940, the Nazis invaded Belgium, Holland, Luxembourg, and parts of France. One by one, Hitler's highly mechanized armies devastated their enemies. The French had the finest army of the European Allies; their forces surrendered within six weeks. The British knew they were next. When William Knudsen, president of General Motors (the world's largest corporation), visited London to check on his company's interests there, he found the population "scared stiff."

"Airplanes! Airplanes! Airplanes!" Knudsen reported back to his colleagues in the United States. "That is all they think about, and bombs go with them." In the United Kingdom, children were being evacuated from cities. Gas masks were being handed out by the thousands. "It was really bad," Knudsen said. "They were just hysterical."

Hitler's blitzkrieg — "lightning war" — was something the world had never seen. Hermann Göring, the Nazis' number two in command, defined *blitzkrieg* in an interview: "aerial attacks, stupendous in their mass effect, surprise, terror, sabotage, assassination from within, the murder of leading men, overwhelming attacks on all weak points in the enemy's defense, sudden attacks, all in the same second, without regard for reserves or losses."

In the United States, "war preparedness" became the nation's catchphrase, and the debate between interventionism and isolationism divided the political landscape. The questions on every citizen's lips: What role, if any, should the United States play in this conflagration abroad?

On a Saturday in St. Louis, in 1940, Truman gathered his closest friends in the Statler Hotel's lobby to discuss his political future, for he had a more immediate and personal confrontation ahead of him. Truman's friends leveled with the junior senator: He was washed up. Governor Stark had announced his candidacy for Truman's seat, and once again the battle would be for the Democratic primary, as whichever candidate won would skate past the Republicans in left-leaning Missouri. Already the papers had pointed out that Truman had "little chance of renomination." Truman had told the *Washington Post* what he thought about Stark: "I'll beat the hell out of him." Now he had gathered his friends to see who could help. The Pendergast team was gone. Truman had this bunch of Missourians in his corner — mostly poker buddies. Not one had any real national political experience.

"Harry, I don't think you can win," said Roger Sermon, an Independence grocer who also served as the town's mayor. "And that's not merely my personal opinion but after inquiry around."

"He had very little backing or encouragement at that meeting," noted John Snyder, a St. Louis banker. "As I recall it, there were only two or three that even suggested that he should run for a second term."

Truman said, "I'm going to file. I wouldn't have the guts to go home and face my people if I ran out." At the Statler that afternoon he outlined a platform for a campaign. According to the minutes of that meeting:

- *The Senator will not engage in personalities and asks his friends to do the same. Avoid mentioning the Senator's opponents in any way.*
- *Avoid getting into controversial issues [ie, Pendergast]. Stick to Truman — his record as a judge, as a Senator, as a military man.*
- *While others discuss issues not involved in the primary, each worker will carefully avoid getting into those traps.*
- *The press is a function of our free institutions. If they are wrong in their attitude, try to make them see the true light, but under no circumstances attack them.*
- *Political parties are essential to our republic, our nation, and we must not attack them. What we're doing is to show by our actions what we think our Party is destined to do: Provide basic laws for a more abundant life and the happiness and security of our people.*

Truman's friends did not respond positively. "We didn't give him a chance," recalled A. J. Granoff, a Kansas City lawyer. "We expected him to be beaten badly."

///

At 7:30 p.m. on June 15, Truman appeared in front of the Pettis County Courthouse in Sedalia, Missouri, to kick off his campaign. He had promoted a secretary in his Senate office named Victor Messall to be his campaign manager. The treasurer was Harry Vaughan, a former tie salesman who would be no help financially. ("I had a bank balance of three dollars and a quarter," Vaughan said.) Before the opening party in Sedalia, Messall had sent out campaign "Bulletin #1" advising all friends of Truman's to show up.

"An effort should be made to get as many cars as possible to come out to Sedalia on that night. All cars should be properly decorated with American flags, red and white streamers and carrying signs bearing catchy phrases such as 'Make Government Human with Men like Truman.'"

The morning of the campaign kickoff, eighty-seven-year-old Mamma Truman sat in the front row to cheer on her son. Bess and Margaret sat on the speaking platform. Remembered Margaret: "At 16, I was able to feel for the first time the essential excitement of American politics." The speech was another Truman special, embracing FDR's New Deal. "I believe in the brotherhood of man," he said. "Not merely the brotherhood of white men but the brotherhood of all men before the law." Soon after, Truman and Fred Canfil took to the road again. Truman's focus: the New Deal, the importance of the farmer in America, the emergency in Europe, and military preparedness.

He had a habit of clapping his hands when he wanted to make a point onstage, which created a horrible bark from the electric speaker system. A campaign aide had to instruct him: "You could refrain from slapping your hands together in front of the microphone." Compared with his opponent, Lloyd Stark, who was fabulously wealthy, Truman struggled with his campaign budget as usual. "I think that was the all-time low for a senatorial campaign," recalled treasurer Vaughan. Truman pulled $3,000 out of a life insurance policy to pay expenses. At one point he hadn't enough funds for a hotel room, so he slept in his car.

Newspapers called the candidate "a dead cock in the pit." "Without fraudulent votes from Jackson County," Truman's hometown paper, the *Kansas City Star*, claimed, "he could not have been elected" as a judge in the first place. The *St. Louis Post-Dispatch*: "Truman is through in Missouri. He may as well fold up and accept a nice lucrative Federal post if he can get it — and if he does get it, it's a travesty of democracy."

Truman sought Roosevelt's endorsement, but his campaign office received a polite telegram in reply on July 30, 1940, one week before the primary, from FDR's press secretary, Steve Early: "The President asks me to explain to you personally that while Senator Truman is an old and trusted friend the president's invariable practice has been not to take part in primary contests." Stark, meanwhile, was talking up his close relationship with the president to the press. He visited Roosevelt in April 1940 and bragged about his personal role in putting Tom Pendergast behind bars. Stark was so confident of his victory, he declared his candidacy for vice president at the 1940 Democratic National Convention in Chicago, handing out Stark Delicious apples to the crowds.

With time running out, Truman called on his only power base: his friends in the Senate. Burton Wheeler of Montana endorsed Truman on June 28, 1940. Two days later Tom Connally of Texas did the same. Alben Barkley of Kentucky flew to St. Louis to stump for Truman. Only three hundred people showed up in a space with a three thousand capacity, and Barkley was criticized afterward for throwing his weight behind a candidate who "owes his place to the notorious Pendergast machine."

On August 6, 1940, Harry and Bess cast their votes in the primary, in Independence. By this time, the whole Truman team was suffering exhaustion. Campaign manager Messall had ulcers so bad, he could not stomach a whiskey to settle his nerves. Truman had been traveling back and forth to Washington throughout the campaign, due to the war crisis, but on primary election night, he stayed at home in Independence. Friends and neighbors dropped by to pay respects, and as the sun set, the Trumans huddled by their radio. During the early returns, the contest appeared lost, and Harry told his wife: "I'm going to bed." She was astonished, and remained in front of the radio. At midnight Bess and Margaret retired feeling "very weepy and depressed," as Margaret recalled.

At 3:30 a.m., Bess was awoken by a phone call. She picked up to find a stranger on the line. "This is Dave Berenstein in St. Louis," the man said. "I'd like to congratulate the wife of the senator from Missouri."

"I don't think that's funny," Bess barked, and slammed the phone down. She was going back to bed when she remembered who Dave Berenstein was – one of Harry's campaign workers in St. Louis.

The state of Missouri had more faith in Truman than all the election experts expected, but still, the contest was so tight, he was not declared the winner until 11 a.m. the next day. By that time he was already rushing to catch a flight back to Washington. He slipped through the back door of the Senate Chamber the following day while Hiram Johnson of California was making a speech. At the sight of Truman, the chamber fell silent. One senator stood up and began to applaud, then another, and soon the entire Senate floor exploded in acclamation for Harry Truman. He felt hands slapping his back and saw toothy smiles on the faces of men who so rarely showed any emotion. "I thought Wheeler and Jim Byrnes were going to kiss me," he wrote Bess.

Once again, a political campaign had left Truman further in debt, and days after the primary, a bank foreclosed on the family farm in Grandview. Mamma Truman and Truman's sister, Mary Jane, were forced to move out of the home they had lived in almost all their days. Friends of Truman's said they had never seen him so furious, for Truman believed the foreclosure was a political stab in the back. Nevertheless, in Democratic-leaning Missouri, he won the general election in November, defeating his Republican opponent easily.

Harry Truman was the senator from Pendergast no more.

///

In the winter months of 1941, Truman took a road trip. He was suffering from exhaustion, and the highway called for him. Long drives were his preferred method of decompressing. Aiming to inspect new army camps, he motored thousands of miles in his old Dodge to Florida, up to Michigan, and through the flatlands of Missouri, living out of his suitcase. What he saw disturbed him, and so on February 10, 1941, he made a speech on the Senate floor. His daughter later referred to this speech as "fateful," for it was "to change the course of all our lives."

"I am introducing a Resolution," Truman began that Monday morning on the Senate floor, "asking for an investigation of the National Defense Program and the handling of contracts. I feel that it is my duty at this time to place before the Senate certain information which I have, and which I am sure is of vital importance to the success of the National Defense Program."

Less than five weeks earlier, Roosevelt had delivered his "Arsenal of Democracy" fireside chat, which drew the largest radio audience of all time. Roosevelt was calling for an unprecedented spending campaign. "Guns, planes, ships and many other things have to be built in the factories and arsenals of America," Roosevelt told his audience. Refer-ring to Hitler's conquering armies, the president said: "Never before since Jamestown and Plymouth Rock has our American civilization been in such danger as now." Due to the Depression and the neutral-ity acts signed by the president during the 1930s, the American military had grown anemic. The army ranked eighteenth in the world in size at the beginning of 1940 (smaller than Belgium's, Portugal's, even Swit-zerland's), with fewer than 200,000 men, compared with nearly 7 mil-lion trained Nazi soldiers. Roosevelt was demanding a modern military equipped with cutting-edge machinery. The president had recently re-ceived $10.5 billion in appropriations for emergency defense programs.

The spending, Truman told his fellow senators, "probably signifies the entry of our nation on a totally different path of destiny than it has ever trod before."

Construction of new factories was under way — "aircraft factories in San Diego, Columbus, St. Louis, Buffalo, Dallas," Truman said, "ship-yards in Oakland and Houghton (Washington); munitions plants in Chi-cago and Omaha; and engine works in Cincinnati and Paterson." In every one of those federally funded projects, Truman explained, there was ample chance of inefficiency and graft. "I have had considerable ex-perience in letting public contracts," Truman said, referring to his days as a Jackson County judge. "And I have never yet found a contractor who, if not watched, would not leave the Government holding the bag."

Truman's idea was to set up a Senate committee to police this gov-ernment spending. On March 1, 1941, the Senate passed Resolution 71, to create the Special Committee to Investigate the National Defense Pro-gram, with a budget of $15,000. It was barely enough to pay for secre-taries and stenographers. Truman's first move was to set up a bipartisan team of senators — five Democrats and two Republicans — so no barbs of party politics could be hurled at him. For staff, he wanted investigators who had no allegiances to the military or anyone else. For his first hire, he set his sights on Matthew J. Connelly, a well-dressed thirty-three-year-old Irish American who had experience as a congressional staffer with the Appropriations Committee. Connelly knew how things worked on the inside. The day he showed up at suite 248 in the Senate office building for his interview, he got his first taste of Truman's way of doing things.

"Come in," Truman said. "We have a very peculiar situation here." He gave Connelly his committee's pitch. "I don't know what I can pay you," he said, "but I will say this to you: If you go along with me you will never have any reason to regret it."

Connelly answered, "Senator, I came in here to say no, but the way you talk is refreshing in Washington and you've got yourself a deal."

Truman hired lawyers – notably Hugh Fulton, a bulldog prosecutor whom Truman described as "a big fat fellow with a squeaky voice." There was an FBI investigator named H. G. Robinson – "a man who could look at a person that he wasn't fond of with the fishiest coldest stare," according to one committee staffer. Truman added old friends such as Fred Canfil and, a little later, Harry Vaughan as errand runners, stretching the budget by putting certain committee members on the payrolls of other departments that had surpluses (Connelly's idea). The staff spread out around available desks in the Senate building, with headquarters in suite 449, where hearings would be held. The committee's most important space became known as "the Doghouse" – a small office attached to Truman's own, where he conducted confidential meetings and always kept the bar stocked. The senator's motto was "There is no substitute for a fact. When the facts are known, reasonable men do not disagree with respect to them."

The committee set out on its first series of investigations at army construction sites and quickly uncovered shocking inefficiencies. Some construction sites were costing the federal government as much as ten times the original estimates. One camp in Texas was supposed to have cost the army less than $500,000; the bill would eventually hit $2.54 million. "If our plans for military campaigns are no more extensive and no better than those for construction," Truman concluded, "we are indeed in a deplorable situation."

On April 15, 1941, less than two months after the committee was born, Truman conducted a hearing in Washington with the secretary of war, Henry Stimson, and army chief of staff General George C. Marshall, two of the nation's most high-profile defense figures. The committee grilled Stimson and Marshall in front of reporters, with chief counsel Hugh Fulton doing most of the talking. ("Hugh was a brilliant attorney," committee staffer Robert Irvin later said. "He had a tremendous, tremendous capacity to see the big picture and to see how all the pieces fit together.")

The following day the *New York Times* ran large pieces of testimony verbatim, with a big photo of Truman and the secretary of war together. "It was very widely seized upon by the press," Connelly recorded. "They realized that this was going somewhere . . . This would be news."

///

The afternoon of December 7, 1941, found Truman resting alone in a room at the Sinclair Pennant Hotel in Columbia, Missouri. He had stayed in bed for twelve hours the night before, had breakfasted at 8 a.m., and had retired back to bed because it was Sunday and he was suffering work exhaustion. His phone rang and he picked up to find a deputy U.S. marshal on the line.

"This is Roy Webb," the marshal said breathlessly. "Have you heard the radio?"

"No," Truman said.

"The Japs are bombing Pearl Harbor."

"Are you sure you know what you're talking about, Roy?"

"It's on the radio."

"My goodness, man," Truman said. "I've got to get to Washington."

Truman hung up the phone and dialed the St. Louis office of the airline TWA. He explained it was imperative that he be in the nation's capital the following morning. Shortly after hanging up, the phone rang again; Bess was calling from their Washington apartment to let him know that the secretary of the Senate had called to say there would be a joint session of Congress the following afternoon — Monday, December 8. In short time Truman was at the airport. He ended up in Pittsburgh at 3:30 a.m., then landed in Washington at 5:30 a.m., where his friend and secretary Harry Vaughan was waiting with a car. Truman got to his apartment in Washington at 6 a.m., where Bess made him breakfast, then he made it to the House Chamber, in time to hear Roosevelt deliver one of the most memorable pieces of rhetoric in American history.

The air in the vast room where presidents had given State of the Union speeches for years had never felt more electric with anticipation. The international situation had seemed foggy for months, but now, in retrospect, things seemed more clear. In May, six months earlier, Roosevelt had called for "an unlimited national emergency," in response to Nazi threats of world domination. In July, in response to Japan's occupation of Indochina, the president had frozen Japan's assets in America and had slapped Japan with an oil embargo. Japan was getting 88 percent of its oil from the United States. After the embargo took effect, many in Washington, including Truman, believed Japan would be left with no course of action except attack. And now it had come, a sucker punch at Pearl Harbor. Close to twenty-five hundred Americans had been killed, with nearly twenty naval vessels and more than three hundred airplanes damaged or destroyed – a devastating percentage of the Pacific Fleet.

A few minutes past noon Roosevelt's motorcade pulled up to the Capitol. With his legs locked by steel braces so he could stand at the podium, he faced a crowd jammed shoulder to shoulder. Behind Roosevelt at the podium sat the vice president, Henry Wallace, and Speaker of the House Sam Rayburn. The president began.

"Vice President . . . Mr. Speaker . . . members of the Senate . . . and the House of Representatives . . . Yesterday, December 7, 1941, a date which will live in infamy . . . the United States of America was suddenly and deliberately attacked . . ."

After Roosevelt left the Capitol, senators, in a roll call, voted unanimously for war. The House voted 388–1. The only negative came from Jeannette Rankin of Montana, a pacifist and the first female American congresswoman. Her vote sparked such fury, she had to take refuge from a mob by locking herself in a phone booth until police could escort her to her office. Due to the Tripartite Pact – which tied the Axis powers together – Germany and Italy declared war on the United States on December 11. The United States declared war on the Axis on the same day, at which point most of Europe's nations chose sides. Britain declared war on Bulgaria. Holland declared war on Italy. Belgium declared war on Japan.

Truman found himself in an extraordinary position. He knew how unprepared the nation was to face war against the Nazis and the Japanese simultaneously. His committee had investigations in progress all over the country, rooting out profiteers and inefficiencies in the national defense effort – an effort that would now take on incalculable importance.

Soon after Pearl Harbor, the committee released its first wartime report – ten months' worth of investigations into defense contracting inefficiencies. The report landed with a sonorous thud on desks all over the capital. "To thousands," the *Washington Post* noted, "the first question after the shock of the Truman report must have been: 'Who in the world is Truman?'"

The Senate Special Committee to Investigate the National Defense Program was now being called the Truman Committee, and the senator's work hours knew no end. "My committee has had so much publicity in the last sixty days that its work is not nearly as efficient as it was before that time," Truman wrote his daughter while on the road, two months after Pearl Harbor. "We are in a situation where the slightest mistake will cause us serious difficulty." By the end of 1942 the Truman Committee had held some seventy hearings, resulting in more than three thousand pages of testimony, covering shortages of aluminum, copper, lead, zinc, and steel; bottlenecks in aviation production and shipbuilding; labor, transportation, and housing problems; and more. Every report reflected the unanimous opinions of all seven of the committee's senators, Democrats and Republicans. The committee reports at times were highly critical of the Roosevelt administration. At one point the president refused to see Truman about a committee matter.

"He's so damn afraid that he won't have all the power and glory that he won't let his friends help as it should be done," Truman wrote Bess. If the president wouldn't see him, Truman told Bess, Roosevelt "could go to hell."

For the first time in his life, Truman was getting national publicity for something other than his Pendergast relationship. Among his staff he was deeply revered, though there were no illusions about him. "He had tremendous personal charm, and no airs," recalled committee investigator Robert Irvin. "I don't think anybody regarded him as a genius or a brilliant man . . . But they thought of him as a very, very able guy and a very honest guy, and a very dedicated guy. He was as patriotic as they come."

On March 8, 1943, Truman appeared on the cover of *Time*. The committee, according to the story, "had served as watchdog, conscience and spark plug to the economic war-behind-the-lines." It was "one of the most useful Government agencies of World War II." Truman himself was the "Billion Dollar Watchdog," and it was all kind of bizarre, *Time* stated, because Truman's seat in the Senate was itself the result of strange circumstances, involving a patron now at Leavenworth Federal Penitentiary. "Truman's presence in the Senate," *Time* noted, "is a queer accident of democracy." Still, in the context of the war, Truman was only one of a myriad of politicians making news. He was still considered by many in the Senate a low-profile figure.

The overwork and travel were taking its toll on Truman. In April 1943, the committee held a series of grueling hearings: on aircraft shortage (April 1–3), food waste (April 5), again on aviation (April 8), rubber tire shortage (April 9), aviation again (April 13–14), shipbuilding (April 16), and delays in barge and other oil shipments (April 17). Two days after that last hearing Truman checked himself into the U.S. Army and Navy General Hospital in Hot Springs, Arkansas, on the verge of nervous collapse.

LYING IN A HOSPITAL BED, Truman feared for his life. Bess rushed to Arkansas to be by his side. His heart was "beating too fast," he told his doctors, and he suffered bouts of vomiting. The doctors ran tests on his heart and lungs. They fed him a foul-tasting barium solution, then x-rayed his stomach. His blood pressure was not bad for a man his age: 126/86.

"He works under a great deal of pressure most of the time," a physician wrote in Truman's file, "and it seems likely his symptoms are largely associated with nervous tension and strain."

Truman was nearing his fifty-ninth birthday, and here in the hospital he had time to think. The pace of history had left him in a world he struggled to recognize. No generation had ever lived through such leaps of innovation so ruthlessly squeezed into a lifetime. The ubiquity of telephones, movies with sound, paved streets roaring with motorcar traffic, the rise of the supermarket with branded products such as Post Toasties cereal and Hellmann's Blue Ribbon mayonnaise – none of this had existed thirty years earlier. The war had accelerated the speed of modernization. Truman could recall as a young man of nineteen reading about the Wright Brothers' first controlled flights. Now the U.S. Army Air Forces were flying thousands of 56,000-pound B-24 bombers, equipped with radar and gyrocompasses that enabled the dropping of bombs on precision targets. Racial integration, women on assembly lines – it all felt like an H. G. Wells novel.

In the previous eighteen months the nation had been reborn, not just economically but psychologically. It was often said during this war that "America has come of age." Americans – especially in Washington – felt the pull of destiny, that their country had become the world's moral arbiter.

Despite the radical shifts in daily life, one thing for Truman had not changed. He was still smitten by his wife, whom he proudly called "the Boss." ("I just always had the impression that Mrs. Truman came first and her happiness was very important to him," one Truman Committee staffer said. "That wasn't true of all of the senators on the Hill.")

Truman left the hospital with a clean bill of health. Bess wrote Margaret, "Dad has been through the gov't clinic & they found nothing wrong but advised an *honest-to-goodness rest.*" But Truman had no time for rest. He jumped back into his committee work.

In the summer of 1943 he received a mysterious communiqué from his old friend Fred Canfil. There had been rumors about huge expenditures going toward a secret factory outside Pasco, Washington. Canfil had called the Truman Committee office from Pasco: "Something's going on up here," he said. "I'm going to find out what it is." Soon afterward, Truman got a call from the secretary of war, Henry Stimson. A transcript of this phone call exists.

SECRETARY OF WAR: Hello, is this Senator Truman?

TRUMAN: Yes, this is Senator Truman.

SECRETARY: Senator, I have been trying to get at you for two purposes.

[The two discuss a matter regarding the Moral Rearmament Group.]

SECRETARY: The other matter is a very different matter. It's connected with the plant at Pasco, Washington.

TRUMAN: That's right.

SECRETARY: Now that's a matter which I know all about personally, and I am one of the group of two or three men in the whole world who know about it.

TRUMAN: I see.

SECRETARY: It's part of a very important secret development.

TRUMAN: Well, all right then.

SECRETARY: And I —

TRUMAN: I herewith see the situation, Mr. Secretary, and you won't have to say another word to me. Whenever you say that to me, that's all I want to hear . . . You assure that this is for a specific purpose and you think it's all right. That's all I need to know.

SECRETARY: Not only for a specific purpose, but a unique purpose.

TRUMAN: All right, then.

Canfil was told to leave the matter alone. Two more years would pass before Truman would find out the truth about this secret project outside Pasco, and by that time he would be president of the United States. It was the world's first ever full-scale plutonium production reactor.

///

One morning in mid-July 1944, Truman was at home in Independence when his phone rang. It was about eight o'clock Missouri time, and he was preparing to leave for Chicago for the 1944 Democratic National Convention. He picked up the phone.

"Harry," he heard, quickly recognizing the southern drawl of James F. Byrnes, a former senator from South Carolina now serving as director of the Office of War Mobilization, the most powerful of Roosevelt's domestic war policy offices. Byrnes said, "The President has given me the go sign for the Vice Presidency and I am calling up to ask if you will nominate me."

This was big news but not unexpected, as Byrnes was a towering figure in Washington. He was often called "the Assistant President." Truman accepted the offer to give Byrnes a nomination speech in Chicago. On that same morning, however, Senate majority leader Alben Barkley called Truman in Independence. Barkley was asking if Truman would make *his* nomination speech for VP in Chicago. Apparently, Barkley had reason to believe *he* was the president's choice for number two. Truman explained that he had already given Byrnes his word, so he could not.

In the sultry July heat, Truman went out behind his house and pulled his 1941 Chrysler Royal club coupe out of the garage. Bess and Margie were in Denver, visiting Bess's brother, so they would meet Truman at the convention. With his suitcase packed, he pulled out of his driveway, bound for the Windy City.

The vice presidency had become the focus of the hottest gossip in Washington. The current VP, Henry Wallace, was rumored to be out of Roosevelt's favor. Wallace had proven himself so far to the left, Democratic Party officials referred to his supporters as "the lunatic fringe." The question was: Who could take Wallace's place? Truman had no intentions of gunning for the job, and neither did America have such intentions for him. According to a Gallup poll in July 1944, only one in fifty Democratic voters thought Truman should be the vice presidential candidate on the

1944 ticket. The great majority was focused on two others: Henry Wallace (65 percent) and Alben Barkley of Kentucky (17 percent). Byrnes, Virginia senator Harry Byrd, and Speaker of the House Sam Rayburn each had 3 percent.

Roosevelt had informed party officials that he would run for an unprecedented fourth term due to the wartime emergency, but that he would leave it up to the delegates at the Democratic National Convention to choose a vice presidential candidate. His specific reasoning would soon become apparent. The president himself would not attend the convention; he was too busy with war business, he said, though it was rumored that the real reason was because he was a severely ill man. An oft-spoken pre-convention slogan was "You are not nominating a Vice President of the United States, but a President." The convention would take place at the Chicago Stadium, an indoor arena where the city's hockey team played. Stadium officials had stocked up with 30,000 hot dogs, 125,000 soft drinks, 96,000 bottles of beer, and rivers of bourbon and rye. The Republicans had held their convention in the same hall three weeks earlier — having nominated Thomas Dewey of New York as their candidate.

James Byrnes checked into the Royal Skyway suite at Chicago's Stevens Hotel, an especially large room, believing he would need the space to hold meetings, as he was expecting to get the VP nomination. Roosevelt had told Byrnes to his face that he, Byrnes, was the smartest choice. Upon arrival in Chicago, Byrnes told Senator Tom Connally of Texas, "Truman will nominate me."

The current VP Henry Wallace was staying at the Sherman Hotel. Wallace believed *he* was FDR's choice for number two. He had it in writing from the president, and was planning to release this document at the opportune moment.

Alben Barkley, senator from Kentucky, appeared in Chicago with a twinkle in his eye. Days earlier, a rumor had swept through Washington that "the 'White House' has decided on Barkley," according to the diary of Senate reporter Allen Drury. Barkley believed he had a strong shot at making the 1944 ticket.

Truman stepped through the busy lobby of the Stevens Hotel on Michigan Avenue on Saturday, July 15. His room was on the seventeenth floor, offering a sprawling view of sapphire Lake Michigan. He was working on his speech to nominate Byrnes, unaware that forces were already at work to thrust the junior senator from Missouri into the VP slot.

///

On July 11, eight days before the Chicago convention kicked off, Roosevelt had held a meeting in the White House with party officials, to discuss the 1944 ticket. The night began at 7:30 p.m. with presidential martinis. The sun had beaten down on Washington on this day, and FDR appeared tired and listless, his focus wandering. After dinner, the group moved to the president's second-floor study for coffee and drinks, and conversation turned to the vice presidency. Present were Edwin Pauley, a California oilman and treasurer of the Democratic National Committee, and Robert Hannegan, the committee's chairman, among others.

Names bounced around the room, but each potential VP candidate posed a problem. The current vice president, Henry Wallace, was out, all agreed. Sam Rayburn, the Speaker of the House, was not popular anymore in his home state of Texas. Any potential candidate had to guarantee victory in his home state, if nothing else. Senator Barkley of Kentucky would be a popular choice, but the president had recently clashed with him on a political matter, and there was bad blood there. Jimmy Byrnes — though probably best qualified — was from the South and would alienate black voters. And he had abandoned the Catholic Church when he married a Protestant, so Catholics would not vote for him. The president favored William O. Douglas, a Supreme Court justice, but Judge Douglas had no political experience, and he was rumored to have a weakness for alcohol, which could make him a liability.

Robert Hannegan, who happened to be from Missouri, brought up Truman's name. Hannegan's opinions held a lot of weight in this room. Not only was he chairman of the Democratic National Committee, he was known for his incisive political mind. (He would later become president of the St. Louis Cardinals baseball team.)

Roosevelt admitted: he was not overly familiar with the senator from Missouri. The president knew of Truman as the man "in charge of that war investigating committee." "I hardly know Truman," Roosevelt had said on another occasion. "He has been over here a few times, but he made no particular impression on me."

The more the conversation focused on Truman, the more clear it became: Truman was not a strong candidate – in fact, he was quite obscure in comparison with men such as Byrnes and Barkley. Also, there was concern about Truman's age, that he was too old. But Truman had no enemies. He would not alienate any section of the electorate. Even with his Pendergast past, he seemed the least problematic choice. Roosevelt leaned forward in his wheelchair and placed his hand on Robert Hannegan's leg.

"Now, Bob," the president said, "you want Truman."

"Yes," came the answer. "I do."

Roosevelt turned to the committee treasurer, Edwin Pauley. "Ed, do you?"

"Yes."

"Do all the rest of you?" asked Roosevelt.

All said yes.

Exactly what Roosevelt said at this point has been debated, but sources present at this meeting have him saying something very similar: "Boys, I guess it's Truman."

"Truman just dropped into the slot," recalled Ed Flynn, a powerful Democratic figure from the Bronx, who was there that night. "It was agreed that Truman was the man who would hurt [the ticket] least," said Flynn.

Still, Roosevelt refused to make any commitment. Party officials realized that he could not choose any candidate without offending other party members. Instead, he would mollify the ambitious contenders by leading them all on, then he would make no final choice at all, leaving it up to the convention in Chicago. As Pauley later recalled: "Roosevelt was ducking the whole thing."

///

Two days before the convention was to open, Truman was resting in his room at the Stevens Hotel when a knock came on the door. It was Robert Hannegan. The two men knew each other well; Hannegan was from St. Louis, and Truman had helped get him his job as Democratic National Committee chairman. Hannegan gave the senator the hard sell: he should campaign to become vice president.

"Harry," said Hannegan, "the president wants you to be his running mate."

"Tell him to go to hell," Truman said. "I'm for Jimmy Byrnes." Then: "Bob, I don't want to be Vice President. I bet I can go down the street and stop the first ten men I see and that they can't tell me the names of the last ten vice presidents of the United States. I bet you can't tell me who was McKinley's vice president."

Hannegan could not.

As the day wore on, however, Truman realized that there was more to this situation than it appeared. Elements were conspiring. He met with Sidney Hillman, a powerful labor leader and Roosevelt advisor, the next morning in Hillman's suite at the Ambassador East. Truman asked Hillman to endorse Byrnes for VP. Hillman said he was for Henry Wallace, but if not Wallace, the labor faction of the Democratic Party could get behind another candidate. Truman asked whom.

"I'm looking at the other one," Hillman said.

The next conspirator was Roy Roberts, managing editor of the *Kansas City Star*, a man of 350 pounds who was reputed to drink one to two fifths of scotch a day and was known to order a steak dinner in restaurants immediately after already eating one. Roberts was in Truman's hotel room doing his best to convince the senator to gun for the VP job, with no success. Another knock came on the door. Truman opened the door to find an old friend from Missouri — Tom Evans, a businessman who owned a Kansas City radio station — standing in the hallway.

"What are you doing here, Roy?" Evans asked Roberts.

"Well, I'm Harry's campaign manager for Vice President," Roberts joked.

"You're fired," said Evans.

Roberts asked if he had heard Evans correctly.

"Yeah, fired, get out."

Roberts left the hotel room. Alone with his intimate friend Evans, Truman made his real argument. Campaigns were expensive, he began. "I just don't have any money."

"Your friends will take care of it," Evans responded.

"Well, I don't want to drag out a lot of skeletons out of the closet," Truman said.

Then he began to explain — and the more he talked, the more his real fears poured out. For starters, Truman admitted, he had put his wife on the Senate office payroll. Bess was earning a $4,500 salary, and not working terribly hard. Truman's entire reputation stood on honesty and integrity.

That idealism was the driving force of the Truman Committee, and thus everything he represented in the eyes of his colleagues and constituents. If he ran for office, no doubt Republicans would attack him for misspending tax dollars on his wife's paychecks. "The worst thing is that I've had the Boss [Mrs. Truman] on the payroll in my Senate office," Truman said to his friend Tom Evans, "and I'm not going to have her name drug over the front pages of the papers and over the radio," Truman said.

"Well, Lord," said Evans, "that isn't anything too great. I can think of a dozen senators and fifty congressmen that have their wives on the payroll."

"Yes, but I don't want them bringing her name up. I'm just not going through that." Besides, Truman said, he was sixty, retirement age. "I'm satisfied being a senator and I think I'm doing a good job. I think I have done the country a great favor [with the Truman Committee] and I just want to stay there and be let alone."

Most important, Truman did not want to be *president* of the United States. The rumors about FDR's health were rampant.

"I'm satisfied where I am," Truman said. "Just a heartbeat, this little," he said, gesturing with his fingers, "separates the vice president and the president."

It was clear to Evans: Truman was terrified.

///

On July 15 — the day Truman arrived in Chicago, and four days before the convention was to begin — a train pulled into the city's Fifty-first Street rail yard shortly after noon, to be serviced. One of the cars was the *Ferdinand Magellan*. From the outside, it looked like any old train car, but a close look revealed it was not ordinary at all. The train car weighed about 285,000 pounds, far more than a regular Pullman, due to its bulletproof window glass and ⅝-inch nickel-steel armor plate on the track. It had been purposely built with so much heft that a dynamite charge would not derail it. Aboard in his special train car was the president of the United States.

Roosevelt was bound for San Diego and a cruiser for Hawaii, where he would hold secret meetings with General Douglas MacArthur and Admiral Chester Nimitz regarding the Pacific war. In Chicago, Robert Hannegan, along with the city's mayor, Edward Kelly, climbed aboard the

Ferdinand Magellan to find the president huddled with Eleanor Roosevelt and Judge Sam Rosenman, speech writer and special White House counsel. Secret service men appeared especially nervous, as there was no security stationed at the rail yard. No one was supposed to know that the president was in Chicago.

The meeting aboard the train lasted fifty-two minutes. When Hannegan got off the train, he had with him a letter – a document that was about to set off a firestorm. It was dated July 19 (the first day of the convention, four days *after* this meeting). It read:

> Dear Bob [Hannegan]:
>
> You have written me about Harry Truman and [Supreme Court Justice] Bill Douglas. I should, of course, be very glad to run with either of them and believe that either of them would bring real strength to the ticket.
>
> Always sincerely,
> Franklin Roosevelt

According to Roosevelt's secretary, Grace Tully, Hannegan came out of the president's study on the train car with a handwritten note, and he asked her to type it up for him. He also asked, according to Tully, that she reverse the names of Truman and Douglas as they originally appeared in Roosevelt's note, so that Truman's would come first, and thus appear as if he was the preferred candidate. Hannegan later insisted this part of the story was apocryphal. Nevertheless, the train pulling the *Ferdinand Magellan* left Chicago with the president aboard. Hannegan kept the letter a secret.

///

Two nights before the convention opened, Senator Samuel Jackson of Indiana, the convention's chairman, released to the press a different document – also, apparently, a letter from Franklin Roosevelt addressing the mystery around 1944 ticket. This was the so-called "Wallace letter." It read: "I have been associated with Henry Wallace during his past four years as Vice President . . . I like him and I respect him, and he is my personal friend. For these reasons, I personally would vote for his renomination if I were a delegate to the convention. At the same time, I do not wish to appear in any way as dictating to the convention. Obviously the convention must do the deciding."

The letter caused chaos. Wallace now seemed the front-runner. And yet, powerful party officials were insisting Roosevelt was for Byrnes; they had even ordered Roosevelt and Byrnes signs from a print shop.

Truman was campaigning hard for Byrnes.

The *Washington Post* was saying the job was Wallace's.

The *Los Angeles Times* was saying Wallace was "out."

According to the *Post,* two others were still "prominently in the advance speculation": Alben Barkley and Senator Sherman Minton of Indiana.

In a last-ditch effort to get the president to make his own decision, a party leader in Chicago named Frank Walker called Roosevelt, managing to make the connection while the president was aboard his private train car. Roosevelt reportedly barked into the telephone: "Frank, go all out for Truman."

12

ON WEDNESDAY, JULY 19, 1944, at 12:04 p.m., with the words "Call to Convention" by a Democratic committee secretary, a hush fell over a crowded Chicago Stadium. Flags festooned the railings. Cigar smoke flavored the arena's stale air. Each state's delegation sat in a group with a stick rising up, bearing a sign with that state's name on it. Truman sat with the Missouri delegation; Bess and Margaret had arrived in Chicago, and they were with him. For hours the convention moved through a litany of speeches as the temperature rose steadily.

At one point on this day, likely in the afternoon after the convention had opened, Truman was summoned to a meeting at Robert Hannegan's suite at the Blackstone Hotel. He arrived with his friend Tom Evans of Kansas City. "In the room was a number of people," Evans later recalled. "It seems to me like a dozen or fifteen." Hannegan was clearly under strain; his eyes appeared reddened and he was sweating through his open-collar shirt. He called the president, who was in San Diego by this point. "Whenever Roosevelt used the telephone," Truman later recalled, "he always talked in such a strong voice that it was necessary for the listener to hold the receiver away from his ear to avoid being deafened, so I found it possible to hear both ends of the conversation."

"Bob," Roosevelt said to Hannegan, "have you got that fellow lined up yet?"

"No," said Hannegan. "He is the contrariest goddamn mule from Missouri I ever dealt with."

"Well, you tell the Senator that if he wants to break up the Democratic party in the middle of the war, that's his responsibility."

According to Tom Evans, Truman took the phone and spoke to Roosevelt. Evans remembered Truman saying these words: "Well, I just think, Mr. President, that I've done a good job where I am and I'm happy, and I want to stay there. Yes, sir, I know you're Commander-in-Chief. Yes, sir.

Yes, sir. Well, if that's what you want, that's what I'll do. I have always taken orders from the Commander-in-Chief."

Finally, Truman said into the phone: "I'll do it."

When he hung up, he turned to those dozen or fifteen people in the room. "I've just told the president that I would be a candidate and I don't want to lose," Truman said. "Now go out and work your heads off."

Soon after this conversation, Robert Hannegan shocked the convention by releasing the letter he claimed Roosevelt had given him aboard the *Ferdinand Magellan* days earlier. ("You have written me about Harry Truman and Bill Douglas . . .") The letter sparked a feeding frenzy among the press. Justice Douglas was not at the convention; he was hiking in the Wallowa Mountains of Oregon and had no idea what was happening in Chicago. More important, the authenticity of the letter was instantly attacked by Wallace supporters, who questioned among other things the date (the letter was dated the nineteenth, the first day of the convention, though Hannegan had admitted that he had obtained the letter from the president on the fifteenth). By this time, Jimmy Byrnes and Alben Barkley had been told that the president was backing Truman. Both were dumbstruck and furious; they had been betrayed by Roosevelt, and their shot at the White House had just vanished.

The contest was now between Truman and current vice president Henry Wallace. And Wallace was not planning on losing.

Delegates were scheduled to vote on the VP nominee on the convention's second day. Truman took his seat next to Bess in the sweaty hall. His friends had now been working furiously to obtain the confidence of the forty-eight delegations, to vote for Truman. He had the backing of the Democratic National Committee, which he believed would be enough to topple Wallace.

In the late afternoon hours, Alben Barkley stood at the podium in a crisp white suit and delivered a nomination speech for America's first three-term president to run for a fourth, calling Roosevelt "one who is endowed with the intellectual boldness of Thomas Jefferson, the indomitable courage of Andrew Jackson, the faith and patience of Abraham Lincoln." When the roll call began, the delegations threw their power behind Roosevelt in a foregone conclusion: 1,086 delegates went to FDR, against 90 for others. From a secret location, Roosevelt delivered a short speech broadcast via radio and over the convention's loudspeaker system. As soon as it was over, the highly anticipated roll call for VP began to electrify the crowd. Truman was all smiles.

"You seem to be in good humor," a *New York Times* reporter said to him.

"Yes, I am going to be nominated for Vice President," he answered.

"You seem to be pretty certain of it."

"You don't think I'd make a statement of that kind unless I knew what I was talking about."

The crowd, however, was suddenly booming with Wallace support. Chants could be heard in the arena's farthest corners, growing louder by the minute.

"We want Wallace!"

"The people want Wallace!"

Henry Wallace himself stood among the Iowa delegation shaking hands, his tall body capped by his trademark swoosh of gray hair. Looking around, Truman saw the arena had suddenly grown remarkably overcrowded. "To say the place became overcrowded is a mild statement," remembered the Democratic National Committee's Ed Pauley. "It was one of the world's catastrophes." Pauley remembers canvassing his assistants trying to find out what was going on. Where were all these people coming from? It turned out that Wallace supporters had flooded the arena bearing counterfeit entrance tickets. "No delegate can sit in his own seat," Pauley was told. "The Wallace people have taken the whole thing over."

By the time the roll call began, the arena had grown unbearably hot. From the stage, organizers called one state after the next, and with each, the arena roared in support of Wallace. When the Iowa delegation voted for their homegrown son, "bedlam broke out in the entire Chicago Stadium," recalled Neale Roach, the convention's assistant director. "[Wallace supporters] had planned their demonstration very well even to the point of seeing to it that the organist and the band played the Iowa corn song as long and as loud as they possibly could."

Realizing that Wallace was running away with the vote, Democratic National Committee members panicked. And yet, the organist kept playing the "Iowa Corn Song," in support of Wallace. Pauley turned to Neale Roach and said, "Stop that organ!" He pointed to a fire ax. "Neale," he said, "do you see that ax up there above the organ? Go up there, get that ax and chop every goddamn cable there is, every one. That's the only thing that will stop [the organist]. We're going to call off the convention tonight."

Minutes later the organ music suddenly stopped. Democratic Party leaders scrambled to end the proceedings, which they managed to do, claiming that overcrowding had caused a fire hazard. Mayor Kelly took the stage and declared, "By the authority of the Mayor of the City of Chicago, we herewith declare the hall be vacated, immediately."

///

By noon the next day – July 21, decision day for VP – the arena was once again jammed. Even before the convention chairman could call for order (which he did at 12:12 p.m.), the place was in a "high pitch of excitement," according to one *New York Times* reporter, "aroused by the imminence of nomination of a Vice President."

Truman was no longer on the floor with the Missouri delegation. He had moved with Bess and Margaret behind the stage, as he was now a candidate and was likely to be on the stage at some point. All over the arena, feet trampled over balled-up newspapers, and much talk that afternoon was dedicated to a stunning development in Germany. A plot to kill Hitler with a bomb had badly bruised the Nazi leader, and he had reacted with vengeance. HITLER EXECUTES PLOTTERS! read the top headline in the *Chicago Tribune*.

From his seat, Truman could see a sea of people, and innumerable Wallace and Truman banners. He had stayed up all night trying to sway delegates from Wallace to Truman. At 6:30 a.m. he was to be found in a room in the Drake Hotel trying to get the senior senator from Missouri, Champ Clark, to agree to give the nomination speech for him. Clark was drunk. Truman forces served him coffee and set him to work. Clark delivered his speech for Truman "extemporaneously," according to one reporter, around 1 p.m.; Truman had "all the qualities and all the qualifications" for the job "in this year of destiny."

The roll call began at 4:52 p.m. It took hours, and at the end, Truman had 319½ votes to Wallace's 429½. Fifteen other candidates had gotten votes, and no one man had a majority. Two things became clear: There would have to be a second ballot, and those who had voted for anyone other than Wallace or Truman would have to choose from one of those two, in order for one to achieve a majority – 589 votes. Democratic committee members scrambled to sway the vote in Truman's favor. The final ballot kicked off around 7 p.m. Halfway through, no clear winner had emerged – until, that is, the roll call reached Maryland. Governor Herbert O'Conor, who had himself received his state's 18 votes in the first ballot, switched all his delegation's votes to Truman. Maryland's choice started a chain reaction, and one by one, other delegations followed: Oklahoma, Texas, Virginia. The stampede for Senator Truman was on.

In their seats, Harry and his daughter were awed by the scene. "I reveled in the pandemonium," recalled Margaret. Bess had never wanted any of this to happen. "Mother was barely able to muster a smile," Margaret recalled. At 7:37 the Iowa delegation – Wallace's home state – moved that the nomination of Harry Truman be made unanimous, and at 8:13 the convention's chairman, Samuel Jackson, cut through the crowd to the stage. At this moment Truman was at a concession counter ordering a hot dog and a Coca-Cola. Jackson formally made the announcement.

"There being 1,176 qualified votes of which Senator Harry Truman has received more than the majority, I do now declare him to be the nominee of the Democratic Party for vice president and the next vice president of the United States."

The roar of the crowd was so loud, Truman heard none of this. He was standing behind the stage with a hot dog and a Coke in his hands as Jackson yelled into the microphone: "Will the next Vice President of the United States come to the rostrum? . . . Will the next Vice President come to the rostrum?" Finally, Truman heard the call.

"By golly," he said aloud. "That's me!"

With the help of a police escort on each arm, he moved through the crowd. He stood before a phalanx of microphones and made the shortest acceptance speech any politician in the hall had ever heard. It lasted roughly one minute. Through history's looking glass, however, his words were uncannily prescient. He would dedicate his work to "help shorten the war and win the peace," he said.

"I don't know what else I can say," Truman finished, "except that I accept this great honor with all humility. Thank you."

Immediately following Truman's acceptance, the convention chairman hurried through perfunctory resolutions, and the crowds made for the doors. Thousands poured out into the Chicago streets on the hot July night. The Trumans were bombarded with well-wishers and hand shakers. "We were blinded by the flashbulbs of a hundred photographers," recalled Margaret. "Women wept and flung their arms around us, all but fracturing our spines."

Truman could see his wife was not enjoying the attention. He asked some police officers to help get them out of there as quickly as possible. As they climbed into the back of a limousine, Bess leaned to Harry's ear and said, "Are we going to have to go through this all the rest of our lives?"

///

News from the Chicago convention sent shock waves through Washington, DC. Democrats were divided and upset. As the Senate reporter Allen Drury wrote in his diary post-convention, "Few people can hate one another with more cordial enthusiasm than a bunch of Democrats." Republicans, meanwhile, were set to attack. With his Pendergast stain, Truman offered them endless ammunition.

The night after the convention ended in Chicago, the Trumans received friends in Bess's suite at the Morrison Hotel. Fred Canfil manned the door, and only those close to the family were allowed inside. The following morning Harry spoke to reporters briefly.

"How does it feel to be Vice President?" he was asked.

He laughed. There was still an election ahead, he said. "I'll tell you when I'm elected."

Bess reluctantly held the first press conference of her life. She was introduced to the female political press corps, who fired questions and watched as she squirmed in discomfort. When asked her age, Bess said that no woman older than twenty should have to answer that question. When asked if she planned to become a public figure, Bess answered, "I never have and I never intend to make any speeches."

When the Trumans piled into Harry's Chrysler and made for Independence, the mood in the car was ice cold. Harry knew what Bess was thinking: he should have said no.

13

TRUMAN CALLED HIS NATIONAL DEFENSE COMMITTEE together on the morning of August 8, 1944, in room 160 of the Senate building, where most of the staffers had their desks. He was resigning as chairman of the Truman Committee, he explained. The 1944 election would be all-consuming, and as VP nominee, he could not have his actions in committee work be construed as political, so he was stepping down. He was proud of the committee's work. Their efforts had saved taxpayers $15 billion, he estimated.

"It was obvious sincerity," recalled committee investigator Walter Hehmeyer. "And when he got all through there was a sort of silence and everybody in the room stood at their desks." Truman walked around and shook every hand, thanking every committee worker personally. "This is the kind of man that Truman was," said Hehmeyer. "He clearly wasn't looking for votes. I mean, there was no crowd, no reporters."

Truman's name on the 1944 ticket predictably caused concern among party members. The press called him "the Missouri Compromise." "He is no great campaigner, no sparkling public figure," wrote one *Christian Science Monitor* political reporter. "Poor Harry Truman. And poor people of the United States," wrote the political columnist Richard Strout in the *New Republic*, noting the rumors about Roosevelt's health. "[Truman] will make a passable Vice President. But Truman as President of the United States in times like these?"

Even Mamma Truman had something to say. "I would rather have had him stay in the Senate," said the ninety-one-year-old. "He did not want it. They shoved him into it."

Ten days after resigning from his committee, Truman went to the White House as the vice presidential nominee for the first time. He arrived in a slightly off mood, because the night before, Bess, in Independence, had informed him over the phone that the sons of two of his friends had died in action overseas. The White House had a way of intimidating visitors, anyway. The president gave Truman a hero's welcome.

"You'd have thought I was the long lost brother," he wrote Bess.

Outside on the South Lawn the two men sat underneath a magnolia tree planted years earlier by Andrew Jackson. Servants brought tea and sardines on toast. It was hot, and they sat in shirtsleeves, Truman in a hanging tie, Roosevelt in a bow tie. When Roosevelt lifted the teapot, Truman's eyes bulged. The president's hands shook so much, he could barely pour a cup of tea. The conversation moved to the war, difficulties in China, and the upcoming campaign. Roosevelt was so busy with war business, he said, he would rely on Truman to carry the load. Truman suggested he use an airplane for easier travel, but Roosevelt did not like the idea.

"One of us has to stay alive," he said.

The pair smiled for photographers — "the flash light newspaper picture boys," as Truman called them. Then the VP nominee headed back to his office in the Senate building, where his friend Harry Vaughan was hanging around.

"You know," Truman said soberly, "I am concerned about the president's health. I had no idea he was in such feeble condition. In pouring cream in his tea, he got more cream in the saucer than he did in the cup. His hands are shaking and he talks with considerable difficulty. It doesn't seem to be any mental lapse of any kind, but physically, he's just going to pieces."

Nevertheless, Harry had an election to plan for. It would be America's first wartime presidential election since Lincoln beat George McClellan in 1864.

///

In early October 1944, Truman kissed his wife and daughter good-bye and set off on a 7,500-mile nationwide campaign tour. Aboard his train car were Matthew Connelly, who would work on speeches ("What do I know about politics?" Connelly asked before their departure, to which Truman responded, "Nevermind that, you've got a pretty good teacher"), and Eddie McKim, who would serve as security. McKim would stand next to Truman during speeches and rallies, pretending to have a gun. "Nobody knew whether or not I was a Secret Service man," McKim noted. The candidate had worked through hard-fought Missouri elections before, but this was a national campaign. The Democratic National

Committee called the shots and covered the bills. The committee's secretary, George Allen, was the "advance man," going from town to town to drum up a crowd so when Truman arrived on his train, he could step out onto a platform on the back, where a loudspeaker system was set up. He would give a speech — sometimes to hundreds, other times to a dozen people — then head to the next town.

At Madison Square Garden a young crooner named Frank Sinatra introduced Truman. In Pittsburgh, the Truman entourage enjoyed a twenty-six-motorcycle police escort to a speaking hall, where the film star Orson Welles turned up to campaign for the ticket. Truman's speeches were still awkward and devoid of charisma. "His voice is good but his delivery . . . gallops," one reporter wrote that summer. "It sounds like 'Oh-God-when-will-I-be-finished' while he's talking and 'Thank-God-I-*am*-finished' when he hits the last sentence."

The candidate's appeal was his everyman persona. He was your neighbor, or the guy standing on line at the pharmacy, who just happened to be running for VP. Truman was "one of the most amazing stories in American democracy," wrote one *Boston Globe* reporter. "It is the story of an average man, swept to dizzy heights against his will, a little bewildered by it all and doubting whether it is really true." His message was a simple one: Now, in the climactic moments of the world war, was not the time to change chief executives.

"There will be no time [for a new president] to learn," Truman told a group of three thousand in Lamar, Missouri — unable at the time to pick up on the extraordinary irony of this statement. "And mistakes once made cannot be unmade . . . At no time in history has a President possessed such knowledge of foreign leaders and their problems."

He knew he would be attacked for his Pendergast connection, and he weathered the storm. As he had anticipated, the story of his wife on the payroll played big. The prominent writer and congresswoman Clare Boothe Luce taunted Mrs. Truman, calling her "Payroll Bess." The *Chicago Tribune* published the most vitriolic anti-Truman columns, with titles such as "Meet Truman, Pendergast's Oiler of Roads," and "Truman Reign in County an Epic of Waste."

One night Truman was asleep aboard his train in Peoria, Illinois, when reporters suddenly mobbed his car. The Hearst press, he learned, was about to print a story saying Truman had once been a member of the Ku Klux Klan, back in his early days in Jackson County. In the middle of the night the White House's press secretary, Jonathan Daniels, called Democratic National Committee secretary George Allen, who was in a hotel room in Peoria.

"Jonathan was worried," Allen recalled. "And so was I."

Early the next morning Allen boarded the Truman train. He pushed Truman into a bathroom – the only place they could talk alone. If the story was true, Allen said, it would be a disaster to Roosevelt's candidacy. If it was not, they would sue Hearst. Truman insisted it was a lie, but he did not want any lawsuit. He would deny the story and let it go. His associates would never forget Truman's composure. "It shook the whole universe except one man," recalled Tom Evans, the candidate's hometown friend, who was aboard the Truman train at the time. "Mr. Truman wasn't a bit worried."

The KKK story splashed across newspapers all over the country. Truman issued calm denials, and a crafty researcher was able to find a *Kansas City Star* article showing that the Klan had opposed Truman in a 1926 Jackson County election. ("We are unalterably opposed to Harry Truman," the story quoted Klan officials saying.) The scandal blew over, as Truman said it would.

In early November the train pulled into Kansas City. In front of his hometown crowd, Truman delivered the most ironic sentence of his life: "Ask yourself if you want a man with no experience to sit at the peace table with Churchill, Stalin, and Chiang Kai-shek." The irony was apparent to no one at the time.

///

On election night – Tuesday, November 7, 1944 – the extended Truman family rallied around Mamma Truman in Grandview, while Harry, Bess, and Margaret stayed at the Muehlebach in Kansas City, in the hotel's penthouse suite, not far from where the Truman & Jacobson haberdashery once stood. Truman paced through the crowd of guests, saying, "Everybody around here is nervous but me." He loved bourbon, but he was an expert at nursing a drink; others were not so skilled. Bess and Margaret were appalled by the evening's drunkenness. At one point a radio announcer reported that Truman's home state of Missouri might tilt Republican.

"Wow," Truman said, "I think this calls for a concert." News photographers snapped away as he sat at a piano and regaled guests with Paderewski's Minuet in G.

All night the race rocked back and forth, and the clock read 3:45 a.m. in Washington when Dewey conceded. Franklin Roosevelt would be the first fourth-term president, and Harry Truman his number two. That night, after the guests had gone, Truman eased himself onto a bed in his suite at the Muehlebach Hotel. No longer in the public eye, he felt the impact of what was about to happen. A friend named Harry Easley was with him. "[Truman] told me that the last time that he saw Mr. Roosevelt he had the pallor of death on his face and he knew that he would be President before the term was out," Easley recalled. "He said he was going to have to depend on his friends."

It seemed only yesterday that Truman was plowing fields in Grandview, daydreaming about the adventures of Andrew Jackson. At so many points over the previous twenty years, it appeared his career in politics would not survive. Now he had been elected Missouri's first vice president. Roosevelt cabled Truman directly the next morning.

Hon. Harry S. Truman
Hotel Muehlbach [*sic*]
Kansas City, Missouri

I am very happy that things have gone so well. My thanks and congratulations for your splendid campaign. I will see you very soon in Washington.

Roosevelt

///

Thousands shuffled through a thin layer of snow onto the White House lawn on the morning of January 20, 1945, to see the president's fourth inauguration. The ceremony was held on the White House's South Portico rather than at the Capitol. It would be the smallest and soberest inauguration on record, out of deference to soldiers fighting overseas. The Marine Band played "Hail to the Chief"; the Episcopal bishop of Washington, Reverend Angus Dun, offered a prayer; then Chief Justice Harlan Stone approached the speaker's platform. In the crowd were Eddie Jacobson, Truman's old haberdashery partner, and Ted Marks, the best man at Truman's wedding. So too was Jim Pendergast, the nephew of Tom Pendergast.

The incoming VP was the first to take the oath, and Bess and Margaret watched from nearby. Flanked by American flags, he spoke the historic words; it was so cold, his frozen breath could be seen from a distance. In seconds it was done, and he retreated to his chair.

Roosevelt was next. With legs locked straight by steel braces, Roosevelt stood coatless and hatless in a bitter wind; his speech was brief — barely longer than Lincoln's Gettysburg Address. The world had changed so much in recent times, he told his audience. "We have learned to be citizens of the world," he said. "We have learned the simple truth, as Emerson said, that 'the only way to have a friend is to be one.'" Roosevelt looked so weak at this moment, his jaw dangled open, as if he was too weary to pull it closed. Many would recount their shock at his appearance. Recalled Margaret: "I suddenly found myself feeling depressed at the climax of a day that I had thought was going to be one of the high points of my life."

As Truman greeted well-wishers outside, a dramatic scene unfolded in private inside the White House. The president went to the Green Room to rest, where he was seized suddenly by stabbing chest pains. He grabbed his son James's arm and said, "Jimmy, I can't take this unless you get me a stiff drink. You'd better make it straight." A minute later, Roosevelt was pouring whiskey into his mouth, fortifying himself for the reception.

Truman left the proceedings forty minutes before it was over, catching a ride with a friend back to the Senate building. When he got to his office (he chose to keep the same one, suite 240, which he had recently moved into), a custodian was painting a new sign on the door: THE VICE PRESIDENT. He took the opportunity to call his mother.

"Now you behave yourself," Mamma Truman told him.

With correspondence piled on his desk, Truman began his new job — what little of it there was.

///

Two days after the inauguration, Truman presided over the Senate for the first time. He received an ovation, and when the moment was right, he smacked a gavel to begin the proceedings. The gavel was said to be carved from a tree planted on the Capitol grounds by George Washington. One day later, January 23, Roosevelt left for Yalta with his entourage, where the group would meet with the Soviets and the British in what would turn out to be the most controversial of the secret Grand Alliance conferences. All of Roosevelt's trusted advisors would attend, from Jimmy Byrnes to Harry Hopkins, Admiral Leahy to George C. Marshall. Truman remained behind in Washington.

The same week that Roosevelt left for Yalta, Truman arrived in his office one morning, and Matthew Connelly — who was now his confidential secretary — approached him with a strained look on his face. The conversation, as Connelly recalled it:

"I've got some bad news for you," Connelly said.

"What's that?"

"Tom Pendergast died."

Truman understood: this would be a major issue. If he went to the funeral, he would be bitterly criticized. If he did not, he would disappoint himself. Crook or not, Pendergast had given Truman more political opportunities than any other figure by far.

"Tom died?" Truman said. "What do you think I should do?"

"I know what you're going to do," said Connelly. "You're going to his funeral."

"That's right."

With Connelly's help, Truman commandeered a military plane and took off. His presence at Pendergast's funeral was the talk of the town in Washington; even Truman's political opponents had to admit, it was a gutsy move. "That was one of the greatest things he ever did in the minds of the political public," Connelly said. "It was awfully popular."

Roosevelt was still aboard the ship *Quincy* steaming home when news of the secret, historic Yalta conference was published around the globe. Plans for a joint occupation of a defeated Germany, for the future of former Nazi-occupied nations such as Poland, for the foundation of the United Nations, were now all in place. The war was reaching its climax. In Europe, Allied forces had stormed the beaches at Normandy and had defeated the Nazis in the Battle of the Bulge. Russia's Red Army was preparing a major offensive from the east toward Berlin. In the Pacific, U.S. forces under General MacArthur and Admiral Nimitz had pushed from one atoll to the next, turning sparsely populated, jungle-thick islands into roaring airports where bombers could strike at mainland Japan. The Japanese had proved fanatical in their resistance. Upon losing the struggle for Saipan, Japanese citizens had committed mass suicide — mothers with their children, hurling themselves from cliffs. *Time* magazine put a prescient question to readers: "Do the suicides mean that the whole Japanese race will choose death before surrender?"

Over the next weeks, secluded from the public, Roosevelt engaged with Stalin in secret via transatlantic cable, as the diplomatic relations between the Soviet Union and the United States took a frightening turn. Ambassador Averell Harriman's communiqués from Moscow sounded the alarm; the mood in Moscow had suddenly turned paranoiac and sinister. "We now have ample proof that the Soviet government views all matters from the standpoint of their own selfish interests," Harriman cabled the State Department in early April, just days before Roosevelt's death. "We must clearly realize that the Soviet program is the establishment of totalitarianism, ending personal liberty and democracy as we know and respect it."

Truman had almost no more knowledge of the international situation than the average American who studied the newspapers. Privately, the president disparaged Truman. "He never regarded the new Vice President as part of his operational relationships," said Thomas Blaisdell, who worked in Washington's Office of War Mobilization and Reconversion. "I was custodian of the President's secret war files," recalled White House assistant naval aide William Rigdon. "But not once had I been instructed to show any document to the vice president. He simply had not been worked into the Roosevelt administration."

Then came April 12, the day of Roosevelt's death, and the day when Truman's presidential odyssey began. When Truman drifted off to sleep on the night of April 12 after taking the presidential oath, he knew that the following day was likely to be the hardest day of his life. And it would only be day one of his administration, with nearly four years left to go.

As Thomas Jefferson — America's second VP and its third president — once said: "The second office of this government is honorable and easy. The first is but a splendid misery."

Part III

April–May 1945

He came in like a man on a rocket.

— Jonathan Daniels, White
House press secretary

*I am alarmed and concerned over the
Russian situation. It is deteriorating so
rapidly that it is frightening.*

— State Department official Joseph Davies

ON THE MORNING OF APRIL 13, Truman awoke early as usual. His first
day as president fell on the birthday of Thomas Jefferson — a good omen,
he could only hope, for if he identified with any political philosophy at
this point in his career, he was a Jeffersonian Democrat. As a man of
routine, he walked out his apartment door to go on his morning walk.
Outside, however, the world appeared a wholly different place. Police
patrolled his apartment building's hallways and the grounds outside. Increased secret service detail followed his every stride. Even the scatter-
ing pigeons seemed to see him in a new light. Truman was wearing a gray
double-breasted suit, a dark tie, and black shoes, with a crisply folded
pocket square poking out of his chest pocket. After a quick breakfast, he
headed for the motorcade parked behind his building when he saw Tony
Vaccaro, a political reporter for the Associated Press, standing nearby.
Vaccaro was aiming for a scoop, and Truman obliged him.

"Come on in, Tony," Truman said, climbing into the back of a bulletproof limousine. "Let's get started."

A bit stunned, Vaccaro got in. As a driver throttled for 1600 Pennsylvania Avenue, Truman asked Vaccaro for a favor. He wanted people to know
that he was the same old Harry. He was worried he would not be able to
see his friends anymore, particularly the boys from the 129th Regiment.

"You know, if I could have my way, I'd have them all come in without
knocking," Truman said. The days when his war buddies could drop by
to "strike a blow for liberty" were gone. "I'm going to miss all of that."

The president's car cut through the morning traffic and pulled to
a stop in front of the White House's executive wing just before 9 a.m.
As Truman stepped out, some two dozen photographers dove forward,
camera flashes popping.

"My," Truman said, smiling, "I seem to be popular this morning."

A newsman asked if Truman had any statement.

"No, nothing beyond what I said yesterday."

The White House was unusually crowded, especially at this early hour. Roosevelt had rarely left his bedroom before 9:30 a.m. "Men stood mob-thick in the big lobby of the Executive Offices," recorded press secretary Jonathan Daniels. All eyes were on Truman as he walked at army pace through the corridors to his new office. "It was an amazing day," Daniels recalled, "to see the transition from the aristocrat of Hyde Park to what those of us who had been with Roosevelt at that time thought was this little guy from Kansas City."

When Truman sat down in the president's chair for the first time, he could see FDR's presence everywhere his eye turned – Roosevelt's maritime paintings crowding the walls, his stained ashtrays and canine statuettes all over the desk. Truman swung around in the chair "as if he were testing it," Daniels recalled. "I felt a little sorry for him . . . It seemed still Roosevelt's desk and Roosevelt's room. It seemed to me, indeed, almost Roosevelt's sun which came in the wide south windows and touched Truman's thick glasses."

Truman was ready to begin the business of the day. He asked an assistant to clear FDR's possessions from the desk and preserve them for Mrs. Roosevelt. Matthew Connelly was on hand to become the president's confidential secretary. Outside the Oval Office, the staff moved about the maze of warrens tensely; many of them had worked for Roosevelt for twelve years. "They were confused, shocked, stunned," recalled Connelly. "Because none of them knew [Truman] and he didn't know any of them." Assistant press secretary Eben Ayers spoke for all the White House staff that morning when he wrote in his diary, "I had no idea, and nobody else around of the old staff, had any idea of what was going to happen next."

Characteristic of Truman, he thought of his family, Bess in particular. She was succeeding the most influential First Lady the country had ever known. Now Bess would have to somehow fill Eleanor Roosevelt's shoes. Truman phoned his secretary, Reathel Odum, in his Senate office, and asked that she report to the White House. When she arrived ("I was frightened to death," she recalled), Truman asked her to go to the Connecticut Avenue apartment to help "the Boss." Odum's new job would be secretary to the First Lady.

At 9:30 a.m. gangly Bill Simmons – who manned the Oval Office door – showed guests in to see the president: radio executive Leonard Reinsch, who had helped Truman with his public speaking during the vice presidential campaign, and Eddie McKim, the Omaha insurance man. McKim had been waiting for Truman in the Statler Hotel the night before, ready for a poker game, when he heard on the radio of FDR's death. Truman got up from his desk and approached McKim, apologizing because, as one of his best friends, McKim should have been invited to witness the on-the-spot inauguration in the White House. For decades McKim had called his friend Harry, or sometimes Captain. But not today.

"Well, Mr. President," McKim said, "it doesn't count what's gone before. What counts is what happens now."

Truman returned to his seat. McKim stood in front of him, not knowing what to say.

"Do you have to stand there?" Truman asked.

"Well, Mr. President, I suddenly find myself in the presence of the president of the United States and I don't know how to act."

It was a telling moment. This was how it was going to be from now on.

Across the country, journalists in every city were chronicling the end of an epoch and, with the incoming administration, the beginning of a new age of anxiety. "No man ever came to the Presidency of the United States under more difficult circumstances than does Harry S. Truman," a *Los Angeles Times* columnist wrote. The *Wall Street Journal* on this morning called Truman's job an "almost superhuman task." "Riding to work this morning," Senator Vandenberg of Michigan wrote in his diary, "I got to wonder whether the country wasn't just as anxious and perplexed about the future as I was."

Less than a month before his sixty-first birthday, Truman was the oldest man to become president since James Buchanan (1857–1861), and only the second president from west of the Mississippi River (Herbert Hoover, born in Iowa, being the first). He was the seventh vice president to ascend to the top office following the chief executive's death, the first being John Tyler in 1841, who took on the moniker "His Accidency." Only this time the new president was inheriting more power than any had ever possessed upon entering office, in the midst of the biggest war ever known. As the Supreme Court justice Robert H. Jackson uttered in a eulogy for Roosevelt on this day, April 13, 1945: "No Alexander, or Caesar, or Hannibal, or Napoleon, or Hitler, ever commanded such an aggregation of physical force."

The United States was a nation of some 140 million people. The military numbered 12,096,651 according to the latest War Department figures (army, army air forces, navy, marines, coast guard) — 5,403,931 of whom were currently deployed overseas. As of March 31, the current world crisis had cost the U.S. Army 802,685 casualties (killed, wounded, and prisoners of war) and the navy 93,392.

If Truman had one strength coming into the White House, it was his intimate knowledge of the home front, how the United States had become a boiling industrial machine. At the beginning of the war, Roosevelt had imagined an "Arsenal of Democracy" that would provide the tools of war for all the Allied armies, built on assembly lines according to mass-production principles that were themselves uniquely American. "Every single man, woman, and child is a partner in the most tremendous undertaking of our American history," Roosevelt had said two days after Pearl Harbor. Now, on April 13, 1945, that dream had been realized. War production had reached its absolute peak. In every corner of the country, industrial miracles were at work.

In one factory, situated in what had been open fields and orchards just five years earlier, Ford Motor Company was churning out B-24s at a rate of one per hour, turning what had been the nation's largest and most destructive bomber aircraft at the beginning of the war into the most mass-produced American military aircraft of all time (and still to this day). The Kleenex company was building machine gun mounts; a casket factory was making airplanes; an orange juice squeezer company was now at work on millions of bullet molds. In New Orleans one man, Andrew Higgins, was designing and building so many naval vessels, Hitler would call him "the new Noah." The United States was producing 45 percent of the world's armaments and nearly 50 percent of the goods. Factories had produced so many airplanes, jeeps, tanks, ships, submarines, and amphibious vehicles, Joseph Stalin had declared the United States "the country of machines."

Truman was now chief executive of all this industrial and military might. The power was tangible in the Oval Office, radiating from the national symbolism that now surrounded him: the American flag standing tall, and the bald eagles, the nation's official emblem, woven into cascading blue window shades behind his desk. He had only a few classes of formal education beyond high school, but as Washington officials were soon to find out, he was remarkably educated. His lifetime's reading had familiarized him with the triumphs and tragedies of innumerable world leaders. Now he had become one of them.

///

At 10:15 a.m. Secretary of State Stettinius arrived with the Joint Chiefs of Staff and the war cabinet. Truman knew these men — towering figures, the brain trust of American military power — but only superficially.

General George C. Marshall, sixty-five, was not only the army's chief of staff, he was a man whose military judgment was rarely challenged, even by the likes of Winston Churchill and Joseph Stalin. As Secretary of War Henry Stimson was to say of Marshall that summer: "I have seen a great many soldiers in my lifetime and you, sir, are the finest soldier I have ever known." Marshall had been busy this morning, hurling all the resources of the Pentagon into a state funeral for Roosevelt, which was to begin in roughly twenty-four hours. (Already, Roosevelt's body was traveling by train from Warm Springs to Washington, the route guarded by two thousand soldiers dispatched from Fort Benning.)

Also sitting before Truman: Secretary of the Navy James Forrestal, fifty-three, a man of extraordinary intensity and nervous energy. A former amateur boxer, Forrestal had a flattened nose and was known for his complete lack of sense of humor. (In four years' time, he would suffer a nervous breakdown and hurl himself to his death from a hospital window.) The group also included seventy-seven-year-old Secretary of War Henry Stimson, bleary-eyed insomniac and the deeply respected elder statesman of the bunch, and Fleet Admiral William Leahy, the president's chief of staff and the nation's highest-ranking military officer. The military men came in uniform, while the civilians (the secretaries of navy, war, and state) wore suits.

Every one of these men except Truman was a product of wealth and the best schools, from Yale and Princeton to the United States Naval Academy, and all could sense the tension in the room. As Leahy recorded, "One cannot yet see how the complicated critical business of the war and the peace can be carried forward by a new president who is completely inexperienced in international affairs."

The secretary of state asked to be heard. "Take as long as you want," Truman said. Stettinius brought up the United Nations Conference in San Francisco. It was less than two weeks away.

"I have decided that I shall not go to San Francisco," Truman said.

Roosevelt had appointed a delegation, to be led by the secretary of state himself. "You will go to San Francisco and conduct the meeting with great success," Truman said to Stettinius. "If you wish me to deliver a message, I shall be glad to do so." Stettinius agreed that this would be appropriate. The secretary also suggested that Truman should meet personally with Prime Minister Churchill, as soon as possible.

"Do you wish me to take steps to push that along?" Stettinius asked.

"Any steps you take to encourage an early visit by Winston Churchill to this country will be a great service," Truman said, tacitly stating that it would be the British leader's duty to come to America, not the other way around.

Marshall and Leahy then spoke, outlining the current military situation. "They were brief and to the point," Truman recalled. They believed it would take at least six more months to defeat Germany, while operations in the Pacific would take longer. It would take another eighteen months to bring Japan to her knees, the Joint Chiefs believed. There was a lot of war left to fight. All of the top military officials agreed that Japan would have to be taken by an invasion of ground forces. The success of Operation Overlord, the D-day invasion of Europe, buttressed this argument. The invasion of Japan – code name Operation Downfall – was now in the planning phase inside the offices of the Pentagon.

Truman said he thought he should make a statement before Congress, to assure the peoples of the world that he would carry on the policies of Roosevelt, and that the campaign to force unconditional surrender on the Germans and Japanese would continue with all the resources the Allies could bring. All agreed it was a good idea. And so Truman's first message to Congress was scheduled for Monday, in three days' time. All in this room knew, the announcement of Truman's speech would ignite intense anticipation, for it would be the new president's debut on the national stage.

With that, the secretaries and Joint Chiefs of Staff took their leave. As General Marshall and Secretary of War Stimson exited the White House together, Stimson used the word "favorable" to describe his impression of Truman.

"We shall not know what he is really like," General Marshall responded, "until the pressure begins to be felt."

In Truman's office, Admiral Leahy remained behind to talk one-on-one. As the top military advisor to Roosevelt, Leahy was suffering through this grim day. He had enjoyed a special connection with Roosevelt for many years, the common language being the love of sailing and the sea. Notoriously stiff and cranky, Leahy was defined to the core by his navy uniform. He had lived, it seemed, for lifetimes on the cutting edge of this war, serving as ambassador to Vichy France during the Nazi occupation and then chief of staff to the president. At sixty-nine he was considerably older than Truman, and he possessed more up-to-date military information than any other American, on any given day. As a military man, he understood the chain of command, but privately he could not help expressing his dismay at reporting to a chief executive he believed to be a "bush leaguer." Since shortly after Pearl Harbor, Leahy said, he was the man who met with Roosevelt each morning to report on military affairs.

"I want you to do the same for me," Truman said. "I should like very much for you to remain in the office for so long as it is necessary for me to pick up the strands of the business of the war with which you are familiar, and with which I am not."

Leahy only knew how to do his job one way, he told Truman. "If I am to remain as your Chief of Staff," he said, "it will be impossible for me to change. If I think you are in error I shall say so."

"That," Truman said, "is exactly what I want you to do. I want you to tell me if you think I am making a mistake. Of course, I will make the decisions, and after a decision is made, I will expect you to be loyal."

///

At exactly 12:15 p.m. secret service logged Truman out of the White House. It would take a long time before the president would get used to the amount of activity that hinged on his decision to go anywhere, at any time. He headed to Capitol Hill and found himself walking through the Capitol's hallways surrounded by armed guards, through corridors where he had walked alone for a decade.

Surprised faces turned to him, and he smiled uncomfortably, entering the familiar office of Les Biffle – "Biffle's Tavern." Inside, senators and congressmen greeted him – Senate majority leader Alben Barkley of Kentucky, House majority leader John W. McCormack of Massachusetts, Senate minority leader Wallace H. White of Maine, House minority leader Joseph Martin of Massachusetts, Speaker of the House Sam Rayburn, and about a dozen other senators. Truman shook their hands two at a time. These men had not expected him, and were told only at the last moment that he would be arriving. "It shattered all tradition," Senator Vandenberg wrote in his diary. "But it was wise and smart."

For years Roosevelt had employed wartime powers to exclude Congress from much decision making, causing friction between the executive and legislative branches. These congressmen now believed that Truman — their great friend from the Senate — would reverse this trend and put power back into their hands. "It means that the days of executive contempt for Congress are ended," Vandenberg wrote in his diary, "that we are returning to a government in which Congress will take its rightful place."

Truman, meanwhile, saw the situation from the other side. He knew that as president he would have interests that were bound to clash with those of his friends on Capitol Hill. As he would later say: "[A] president who didn't have a fight with Congress wasn't any good anyhow." Now was the time to lay a foundation of goodwill. (Later this day Truman sent a messenger with the last box of cigars he had in his Senate office to Vandenberg — one of the most powerful of the ninety-six — with a note: "Our swan song.")

Lunch was served — salmon, corn bread, peas. Truman held a drink in his hand and admitted he was overwhelmed. He said he would make a statement before a joint session of Congress, in three days' time. Some in the room thought it a bad idea — too soon after Roosevelt's death. Truman had made up his mind. "I am coming and prepare for it," he said. He then pleaded with these men for their help. They all knew him to be an honest, nose-to-the-grindstone worker. They also knew how unprepared he was to be the president of the United States, and that he had never coveted this "terrible job." He was going to need their support, regardless of political party.

"I'm not big enough," Truman told Senator George Aiken of Vermont on this day. "I'm not big enough for this job."

When he walked out of Les Biffle's office, a group of reporters had gathered. Truman knew these men well. They had been told: no interviews. But they came anyway to pay their respects.

"Well, isn't this nice," Truman said, again shaking hands two at a time. "This is really nice."

"Good luck, Mr. President," shouted one reporter.

When he heard these words, Truman's eyes filled with tears. "I wish you didn't have to call me that," he said.

Jack Bell of the Associated Press remembered this moment poignantly: "We had called him Harry all the time. But we couldn't do that. We couldn't say 'Harry' and we couldn't swallow enough to say 'Mr. President,' so we just addressed him as 'You.'"

Truman made a statement that stunned those reporters, for even these seasoned Washington journalists had never heard a politician speak with such frankness. "I don't know if any of you fellows ever had a load of hay or a bull fall on you. Last night the whole weight of the moon and stars fell on me." He paused. "If newspapermen ever pray, pray for me."

///

At 2:30 p.m. on Truman's first day in office, James F. Byrnes arrived at the White House. Blue-eyed Jimmy Byrnes, sixty-two, was a Washington legend, a South Carolina–bred New Deal Democrat who had never finished high school and had climbed the ranks as a lawyer before becoming an elected official on Capitol Hill. Career was Byrnes's life; he was childless and had little time for distractions from his ambitions. Not nine months earlier, Byrnes had traveled to the Democratic National Convention in Chicago, expecting the VP nomination, only to be scorned by Roosevelt. Byrnes had suffered the betrayal intensely, quitting his job as director of the Office of War Mobilization and leaving Washington for his home in South Carolina, where he had designs on a governorship.

Now FDR was dead. At ten minutes past midnight on the morning of April 13, Byrnes had cabled Truman: "If I can be of service call on me." He had flown immediately to Washington, and now here he was in Truman's office. As Truman would later learn, Byrnes was feeling no doubt that he could handle the presidency far better than Harry could. The presidency, Byrnes thought, should have been his.

They discussed "everything under the sun," Truman recalled. He had heard that Byrnes had made shorthand notes of the meetings at Yalta between Churchill, Stalin, and Roosevelt. Byrnes agreed he could hand his notes over to Truman. Then Truman said he was considering Byrnes for secretary of state. The head of the State Department was next in line for the presidency, and the current secretary, Stettinius, had come from the private sector. If Truman were to die or become incapacitated, he wanted a successor who had held public office, who had been elected by the American people to serve. And he trusted Byrnes, who had nearly twenty-five years' experience in Congress. Besides, Byrnes, like Truman, had come from humble beginnings.

Byrnes "practically jumped down my throat to accept" the job, Truman recalled. The current secretary of state was about to leave for the San Francisco United Nations Conference. The Byrnes appointment was as good as done but would have to remain a secret for the time being. It would soon become the worst-kept secret in Washington.

Before leaving Truman's office, Byrnes brought up a taboo subject. "With great solemnity," Truman recalled, "he said that we [the United States] were perfecting an explosive great enough to destroy the whole world." Truman was aware of this extraordinary project's existence, he told Byrnes, but he knew few details. Byrnes believed the new invention had potential not just as a military weapon but as a political one as well — that "the bomb might well put us in a position to dictate our terms at the end of the war," as Truman recalled Byrnes saying.

Time was short, and again the president was left with little information about the Manhattan Project. He was also left with assurance that James F. Byrnes was about to become one of his most trusted advisors.

///

Soon after Byrnes's departure, Secretary of State Stettinius returned to Truman's office for a final meeting of the day. This time Stettinius dove into the Moscow conundrum. He explained to Truman that relations with the USSR since the Yalta Conference had "deteriorated." Truman understood this, and asked why. This was not an easy question to answer. The secretary of state asked if Charles Bohlen might be given an opportunity to speak; he was Roosevelt's Russian interpreter and a respected State Department point of view on American-Soviet relations. Bohlen was shown in. "I had not met Truman at the time he became president," Bohlen recalled. "He was an obscure vice-president, who got to see Roosevelt much less than I did and who knew less than I did about United States foreign relations."

Bohlen gave an account of the ping-pong of cables between Stalin and Roosevelt, right up to the moment when Roosevelt lost consciousness the day before. Stalin appeared to be turning his back on many critical promises he had made at Yalta, and Poland had become the crux of the problem. Bohlen had been among the first wave of State Department officials to staff the Moscow embassy when it opened in 1934, and he had a keen understanding of the situation. The Soviets wanted control of Poland, and in spite of the perceived agreements at Yalta, they intended to have it. "For the Soviets," Bohlen later wrote in his memoirs, "Poland was a question of life and death, as well as honor, because in thirty years it had twice served as an invasion corridor [for Germany to attack Russia]."

It would now be up to Truman to decide how to proceed with Stalin, and the new president made it clear that he intended to be firm with the Russians. "He gave me the impression," the secretary of state wrote in his diary after this meeting, "that he thought we had been too easy with them."

Stettinius had with him an extraordinary communiqué from Moscow, from Averell Harriman, the ambassador to the Soviet Union. Harriman explained in his cable to Truman how he had "a most earnest and intimate talk with Marshal Stalin." The Soviet leader was shocked by the death of Roosevelt, and the event had evidently moved him to act. "In speaking of President Roosevelt and yourself," Harriman wrote Truman, "Stalin said . . . President Roosevelt has died but his cause must live on and we shall support President Truman with all our forces and with all our will."

According to Harriman's report, Stalin had now agreed to send his number two, Vyacheslav Molotov, to the San Francisco United Nations Conference set to start in twelve days, as a gesture to Truman. The Russians had previously informed Roosevelt that Molotov would not attend, due to the faltering relations between the two countries. If the Russians did not attend the San Francisco conference, the United Nations was sure to fail. Now the Russians had agreed to send representation. The entire existence of the UN lived and died on this decision; already, it seemed, history had been made before Truman's first day in office was over.

If Molotov was going to travel to the United States, Truman thought, he should come to Washington. A cable shot off to Moscow ordering Ambassador Harriman to set up the meeting, setting the stage for Truman's first face-to-face with the Soviets.

Before Truman's first day in office was over, chief of staff Leahy helped the president construct his first correspondence with Winston Churchill regarding the global emergency and the standoff on Poland.

"There are . . . urgent problems requiring our immediate and joint consideration," Truman wrote Churchill. "I have in mind the pressing and dangerous problem of Poland and the Soviet attitude . . . Our next step [is] of the greatest importance."

15

AT DUSK, police and secret service locked down the building at 4701 Connecticut Avenue, so that Truman could enter his second-floor home. Never had this apartment felt so small. Margaret wrote in her diary that she had not left the place all day. "We have an army of secret service men around us at the apt. and everywhere we go," she wrote. "Stayed in all day today." As Truman wrote, "There was no escaping the fact that my privacy and personal freedom were to be greatly restricted from now on."

No record of the family's conversation at the dinner table exists, but surely Harry, Bess, Margaret, and Mrs. Wallace knew they had to pack their bags and fast. They would leave their furniture behind for the time being. Mrs. Roosevelt was still living in the White House. Truman decided to move the family to the Blair House, an official residence normally used to house visiting dignitaries, until Eleanor Roosevelt could move her possessions out of the home where she and her husband had lived for more than twelve years.

Truman had read more words on this day than he ever dreamed possible, but that evening he settled down to a new routine: wading through documents long into the night, his exhausted eyes straining to soak up page after page of information. Earlier in the day the secretary of state had placed a thick memorandum on the desk of Matthew Connelly, a memo that aimed to "bring [Truman] up-to-date on the vital developments." It provided a snapshot of the global playing field and a crash course in international relations. Truman read the memo that night, when he could do so without interruption.

Great Britain — the United States' most important ally — was first on the memo's list. Britain was a nation suffering a grave identity crisis. "The British long for security but are deeply conscious of their decline from a leading position to that of the junior partner of the Big Three," the State Department document noted. Churchill had exhibited a deep animosity and growing paranoia toward the Russians. "The British government has been showing increasing apprehension of Russia and her intentions," the document read. Churchill was a trustworthy friend, but it must never be forgotten that he held Britain's interests paramount, at whatever cost to his allies.

France was next on the list. Paris required construction of a new government following liberation from the Nazis. General Charles de Gaulle had taken power, but he was an erratic figure obsessed with national and personal prestige. France, therefore, had "from time to time put forward requests which are out of all proportion to their present strength and have in certain cases . . . showed unreasonable suspicions of American aims and motives."

National policy toward Germany prioritized the following goals: destruction of the Nazi regime, punishment of war criminals, banishment of Hitler's military government, and the prevention of any military manufacturing whatsoever. The American, Russian, and British governments had agreed that Germany would be divided into sectors after the Nazi surrender. Each of the three nations would govern its own sector, with France subsequently given a fourth sector. Thus the mechanics of post-Nazi occupation were roughly in place. That aside, the future of this nation was still a subject of debate in Washington and abroad. What would become of Germany, post-Hitler?

The State Department document pointed out serious problems in Italy, notably Yugoslavia's occupation of an important piece of the nation's northeast around Trieste. Further issues plagued Austria and Argentina. "A problem of urgent importance to the United States is that of supplies for areas liberated from enemy occupation," the document pointed out. "The chaos and collapse which may result in these countries from starvation, unemployment and inflation can be averted principally by making available essential civilian supplies." If the peoples of bombed-out Europe could not obtain food and coal for heating, they would become easy prey for "extremist groups" — for communist revolution.

The most pressing problem, the State Department document pointed out, was clearly Russia and its control of Poland. As Truman later explained the situation: "The plain story is this. We and the British wanted to see the establishment in Poland of a government truly representative of all the people. The tragic fact was that, though we were allies of Russia, we had not been permitted to send our observers into Poland. Russia was in full military occupation of the country . . . and had given her full support to the so-called Lublin government — a puppet regime of Russia's own making."

Stalin had placed his signature next to Roosevelt's and Churchill's on the Declaration on Liberated Europe, at Yalta in February. He had agreed in contract that nations liberated from the Nazis would have the opportunity to "create democratic institutions of their own choice." Now the Russians were boldly flouting democracy in Poland. Truman knew from his time in the Senate how sensitive Congress was to the Polish matter. The freedom of people to choose their own government was the kernel of the ideology for which United States and British soldiers had fought and died in this war. As Senator John Danaher of Connecticut had said on the Senate floor not long before, "There are literally thousands upon thousands of boys of Polish extraction who . . . are fighting all over the world in the firm belief that they are going to help restore the pre-war borders of the homeland of their parents." Representative John Dingell of Michigan: "We Americans are not sacrificing, fighting, and dying to make permanent and more powerful the Communistic Government of Russia and to make Joseph Stalin a dictator over the liberated countries of Europe."

If Stalin was to succeed in installing a puppet government in Poland, what was to stop him from doing so again, in all the other eastern European nations liberated from Hitler's grasp?

///

Roosevelt's casket was scheduled to arrive in Washington on the morning of April 14, Truman's second full day in office. Truman was to meet the train at Union Station. Beforehand, he squeezed in early morning appointments, in a continued attempt to gather the reins of government. He had outlined the broad strokes of the speech he would give before a joint session of Congress in two days' time, and set a speech-writing team to work in a White House conference room, poking his head in to monitor the progress.

Everywhere in the White House, chaos reigned. "I doubt that there have been few more dramatic, confused moments in American history than the ingress of the people who saw power in their hands under

Harry Truman," wrote press secretary Jonathan Daniels. "There were weird people [in the White House] like a fellow named McKim. I, at this time . . . had the feeling that the aristocracy of Democracy had passed away and the Pendergasts of politics were pouring in." That feeling was palpable all over the West Wing. "There is a feeling of an attempt by the 'gang' to move in," assistant press secretary Eben Ayers wrote in his diary. "Missourians are most in evidence . . . I have no desire to remain here if we are to have a Democratic 'Harding administration,' as some are hinting." (President Warren G. Harding is remembered for Pendergast-style scandals, notably the Teapot Dome scandal of the early 1920s.)

First to see the president officially on April 14 was John Snyder, a St. Louis banker and one of Truman's closest personal friends and poker buddies. Truman needed to appoint a new federal loan administrator, and he told Snyder he was the man for the job.

"I don't think you ought to appoint me to that job," Snyder said, sitting uncomfortably in the president's office. "I'm not sure I'm the right man."

"I think you are the right man," Truman said. "I'm sending your name to the Senate."

Jimmy Byrnes was in the room, and said, "Harry, you forget who you are. You're the president of the United States. Order him to do it."

Later Truman called Jesse Jones, a powerful New Dealer who had until recently served as secretary of commerce. Truman said "the President" was appointing Snyder as federal loan administrator.

"Did he make that appointment before he died?" Jones said, thinking of Roosevelt.

"No," Truman answered, incredulously. "He made it just now."

A quick meeting with Secretary of the Treasury Henry Morgenthau followed. For years Morgenthau had served as one of Roosevelt's most trusted advisors and in fact had been Roosevelt's neighbor in Hyde Park, New York. Like Roosevelt, Morgenthau was East Coast establishment, raised by a wealthy diplomat father and educated at the finest academic institutions (the Dwight School in Manhattan, then Cornell). Of late, Morgenthau had come under fire for his theories on how Nazi Germany should be handled after surrender — the so-called Morgenthau Plan, which would strip Germany of all its industrial assets, leaving an agrarian nation in the wake with no ability to form a military or any other sort of industrial enterprise. The plan was a subject of heated debate in Washington. The Treasury secretary was the only Jewish cabinet member, and thus many suspected his Morgenthau Plan to be more about vengeance than cogent policy. Nevertheless, he greeted Truman soberly on the morning of April 14.

Truman said, "I think I admired Mr. Roosevelt as much as you did."

"I don't think that's possible," Morgenthau awkwardly returned. He said, "I feel this war very strongly. I have one son with General Patton and another in the Pacific, and his ship has just been torpedoed for the second time. My first idea is to win the war and then I want to win the peace."

"That's what I want to do," Truman said.

Conversation steered toward the matter at hand. Morgenthau was a man of extraordinary power who knew more about the world's financial ebb and flow probably than any other individual alive. Truman asked for a full report on the finances of the war and the nation. As Morgenthau moved for the door, Truman said, "Now I want you to stay with me."

"I will stay just as long as I think I can serve you," Morgenthau answered.

"When the time comes that you can't, you will hear from me first direct," Truman said.

("Truman has a mind of his own," Morgenthau wrote of this meeting in his diary. "The man has a lot of nervous energy, and seems to be inclined to make very quick decisions.")

The president cut out to Union Station at 9:45 a.m., where navy men in crisply pressed uniforms moved Roosevelt's casket onto a caisson pulled by seven white horses, the casket covered in an American flag. The funeral procession crawled through the streets, turning west onto Constitution Avenue and past the Capitol, the casket surrounded by dozens of police officers on Harley-Davidson motorcycles. Crowds mobbed the sides of the streets, behind rows of soldiers holding rifles topped with bayonets. The president's motorcade followed behind the casket, Truman sitting between Jimmy Byrnes and the former vice president and current secretary of commerce Henry Wallace. Mrs. Roosevelt rode in another car, and the crowds craned their necks to glimpse her. An estimated 300,000 people stood along the route to witness the procession. Truman would never forget the sight of the grief-stricken faces, many weeping without restraint. Above, two dozen B-24 Liberator bombers roared, striping a blue sky with trails of white exhaust.

Nearing 4 p.m. the funeral services were set to begin in the White

House's East Room, a space that had seen its share of historic moments. The East Room had hosted numerous presidential family weddings over the decades. The funeral services for William Henry Harrison, Zachary Taylor, and Abraham Lincoln had taken place here. Theodore Roosevelt had hosted boxing matches in this room. Now it would be remembered as the site of Franklin Roosevelt's White House funeral service.

 Mourners had already filled the room when Truman entered, with Bess and Margaret by his side. According to custom, people stood when the president of the United States walked into a room. This time no one did. "I'm sure this modest man did not even notice this discourtesy," recalled Robert Sherwood, FDR speech writer, who was present. When Mrs. Roosevelt arrived, however, everyone stood. Flowers filled the corners of the room from floor to ceiling, and heat drew beads of sweat from the formally dressed mourners. The service began with "Faith of Our Fathers," Roosevelt's favorite hymn, and ended with the dead president's most famed pronouncement, delivered in his first inaugural address: "The only thing we have to fear is fear itself."

Later, at 10 p.m., a funeral train left Union Station on an all-night journey bound for Roosevelt's home in Hyde Park, where he would be interred. The train was seventeen cars long, packed with high-powered government officials, the Trumans staying in Roosevelt's train car, the *Ferdinand Magellan.* It was 9:30 a.m. when the train pulled into Hyde Park. Harry, Bess, and Margaret stood in the crowd as West Point cadets in scarlet capes moved the casket to Roosevelt's final resting place. Few could forget the sight of Eleanor Roosevelt with her head bowed in the rose garden of the Roosevelt mansion on the Hudson River, as soldiers shoveled dirt into the grave.

By noon, the Trumans were once again aboard the *Ferdinand Magellan,* headed back to Washington. Truman could see out the window thousands of Americans who had gathered along the railroad tracks to glimpse the train rushing by. "Old and young were crying on the streets," he wrote in a diary. "Old Negro woman sitting down on curb with apron up was crying like she had lost her son. Most of the women and half the men in tears."

Truman spent most of the ride attempting to work on his speech, but he was interrupted constantly. "Now, the real politicking began," recalled Margaret. "Every congressman and senator on the train was trying to get to see the president." Truman had never enjoyed the gift of oration. In twenty-four hours' time, he would make his presidential debut before Congress with a speech he hoped would spark confidence in the new administration. In all his life, he had never shouldered such pressure. That night, as he lay in his bed, he prayed that he would be up to the task.

///

When Truman entered the House Chamber in the Capitol on April 16, the day after FDR's burial, the eyes of Washington were on him. He was greeted by a standing ovation. The applause for Truman was so loud it reverberated in the chamber's nearly hundred-year-old bones. The time was 1:02 p.m. when Truman climbed the stairs to the podium, and when he looked out at the crowd, he spotted Bess and Margaret in the gallery, glancing at them so quickly, he could not see that tears were rolling from Bess's eyes. "Dad was terribly nervous up there on the rostrum," Margaret recalled. "He was always nervous before a speech, but this one, so enormously important, doubled his normal tension." He put his lips before the podium's microphones and started in, but Speaker of the House Sam Rayburn stopped him.

"Just a minute, Harry," Rayburn whispered, forgetting to address Truman as Mr. President. "Let me introduce you." Rayburn turned and said at great volume, "The president of the United States!" Again, the room roared – senators, congressmen, military leaders, the justices of the Supreme Court.

Had there ever been more of an underdog standing on this rostrum? The ovation was as much for Roosevelt as it was for Truman, but one got the sense that the American people wanted Harry Truman to succeed.

He began. "Mr. Speaker . . . Members of the Congress . . . It is with a heavy heart that I stand before you, my friends and colleagues in the Congress of the United States. Only yesterday we laid to rest the mortal remains of our beloved president Franklin Delano Roosevelt. At a time like this words are inadequate. The most eloquent tribute would be a reverent silence. Yet, in this decisive hour, when world events are moving so rapidly, our silence might be misunderstood and might give comfort to our enemies." Truman spoke of Roosevelt ("no man could possibly fill the tremendous void left by the passing of that noble soul"), the war ("we dare not permit even a momentary pause in the hard fight for victory"), and the role of the United States in a world engulfed in violence, death, and outrageous acts of evil.

"Today, the entire world is looking to America for enlightened leadership to peace and progress," Truman said. "All of us are praying for a speedy victory," he told his audience. "Every day peace is delayed costs a terrible toll . . . Our demand has been, and it remains . . . unconditional surrender."

The speech ended with a prayer, a quote from King Solomon: "Give therefore thy servant an understanding heart to judge thy people, that I may discern between good and bad; for who is able to judge this thy so great a people?" Truman had but a fraction of FDR's gift for oratory, but his voice was steady and firm. For twelve years the president who addressed the world from this pulpit spoke in the intonations of the moneyed East Coast establishment. This voice was different. It was the voice of a common man, asking God for guidance, and the response was the loudest affirmation Truman's ears had ever encountered.

Secret service logged the president back into the White House at 2:37 p.m., which already made him late for his afternoon meetings. He had been gone from his office only a little over two hours. Much of the afternoon would be spent worrying over the Russians.

On this day Truman met with British officials for the first time, notably Churchill's foreign minister, Anthony Eden, and together they finalized wording for a communiqué to Joseph Stalin — Truman's first direct communication with "the Man of Steel" regarding the situation in Poland. The cable was titled "Personal and Secret from the President and the Prime Minister for Marshal Stalin," and it pleaded with the Soviet leader to back down on his position. "The British and United States Governments have tried most earnestly to be constructive and fair in their approach and will continue to do so," the communiqué read. The cable was signed in all capital letters: TRUMAN.

But the friction with the Soviet Union had grown only more heated. The day that Truman addressed Congress, he received reports of a meeting between ambassador to Moscow Harriman and Stalin, in the Kremlin, a meeting that grew so acrimonious, one American official present noted that Harriman and Stalin had nearly come to physical blows. Stalin accused the Americans of using army aircraft in Poland to aid the anticommunist Polish underground, now organizing an uprising against the Soviets. Harriman thundered back that Stalin's information was false, that he was accusing the Americans of treachery, and thus he had insulted the integrity of the commander of the United States Army, General Marshall. "You're impugning the loyalty of the American high command and I won't allow it," Harriman yelled at the Soviet dictator. "You are actually impugning the loyalty of General Marshall."

Meanwhile, Harriman had gotten a firm commitment that Vyacheslav Molotov would meet with Truman. The Soviet number two would leave Moscow the following day (April 17), traveling the longer route over Russia rather than over Europe, out of fear for his safety. En route to the San Francisco conference, Molotov would make an appearance in Washington on the twenty-first, in five days' time.

///

That night Truman left the White House to the now familiar chant from the usher in the lobby: "The President has left his office." During the day, Bess, Margaret, and Mrs. Wallace had moved out of the Connecticut Avenue apartment and into the elaborately furnished Blair House, diagonally across the street from the White House on Pennsylvania Avenue, so Truman decided to walk to his new home. This threw his secret service detail into a fury of last-second preparations. The yellow four-story stucco Blair House dated back to 1813 and had played host to numerous visiting dignitaries during the war, from King Peter II of Yugoslavia to General Charles de Gaulle. But never had a president of the United States lived in it, even temporarily.

In his new study that night, Truman got a chance to catch up on correspondence. Letters had begun to pour into the White House mailroom from friends in Missouri; these missives would arrive by the bushel for days to come. "Little did you think when you were first elected Judge of the Eastern Division of the Jackson County Court, or did your fellow townsmen ever think, that you would become President of the United States," wrote Rufus Burrus, a Jackson County lawyer. "You are a good man, Harry," wrote C. D. Hicks, a St. Louis railway equipment manufacturer, "and God will direct you." Of all the missives Truman received from his Missouri friends, none were likely to move him the way Eddie Jacobson's did. "You know that I am not the praying type," his old haberdashery partner wrote, "but if ever we did pray, we did on the night of April 12. The task you inherited is unequalled in world's history."

Truman wrote his mother and sister from the Blair House on the night of April 16. "I have had the most momentous, and the most trying time anyone could possibly have, since Thursday, April 12th. My greatest trial was today when I addressed the Congress. It seemed to go over all right . . . Things have gone so well that I'm almost as scared as I was Thursday when Mrs. R told me what had happened. Maybe it will come out all right." He signed the letter, "Your very much worried son + bro, Harry."

16

THE DAILY SCHEDULE of the president could be described in a word: relentless. As Truman wrote in his memoirs, "Being President is like riding a tiger. A man has to keep on riding or be swallowed." "It takes about 17 hours a day," he said on another occasion. "And then you get as much sleep as you can, start over again and do the next 17 hours as best you can. No man can do it as it should be done."

On the morning of April 17 Truman began a new routine. After breakfast, he left the Blair House, making the two-hundred-yard commute to the White House on foot. He had to cross an intersection with a traffic light at Pennsylvania Avenue and Jackson Place, and when he reached this corner, secret service magically turned all the lights at the intersection red so the president could cross. Newspapermen and secret service clung to Truman's heels, perspiring as they attempted to match his pace, forming a farcical retinue. The White House correspondent Merriman Smith: "This limousine-infested Capital saw something today it hadn't ever seen – the president of the United States walking to work." Truman shook the hands of wide-eyed women who happened to be walking by. Cabdrivers motoring past honked their horns and yelled, "Good luck, Harry!"

Mornings in the White House began with a military briefing from Admiral Leahy, who delivered the critical news from all corners of the globe. These meetings took place either in Truman's office or in the White House Map Room, an extraordinary space filled with the most technologically advanced cryptographic and communications equipment ever invented. All top-secret cables to and from foreign leaders and embassies came through this room. National Geographic maps hung on the walls, pinned with codified colored markings noting the location of Allied and Axis troops and ships, so that the president could grasp at a glance the broad strokes of the military situation and, with Leahy's help, how it had changed from the day before. Roosevelt had set up this secret space in a former women's cloakroom in the White House basement soon after Pearl Harbor. It was so secret, not even the First Lady was allowed inside. Few people who worked in the White House knew of its existence.

After the president's military briefing came a 9 a.m. staff meeting, which Truman would hold six days a week (including Saturdays). He called this "the morning meeting." About a half dozen staffers sat around his desk, including correspondence secretary Bill Hassett (who responded to the majority of Truman's mail), appointments secretary Connelly, the press secretary and assistant press secretary, and Truman's portly poker pal Harry Vaughan, whom he had made an official military aide and was fast becoming the unofficial White House jester. These informal meetings lasted from twenty to forty minutes, often veering into storytelling, such as the time when a full-blown discussion dove into Winston Churchill's startling "capacity for drink," or the time when the group addressed French leader Charles de Gaulle's astonishing pomposity. "I don't like the son-of-a-bitch," Truman said.

Then came the day's appointments, which stacked up in small blocks of time. On Tuesday, April 17 – Truman's fourth full day in office, and the day after he addressed Congress – he was handed an official meetings schedule for the first time, prepared by Matthew Connelly. His morning on the seventeenth was devoted mostly to the press. A *New York Times* artist was given thirty minutes to sketch him for the Sunday magazine. (During this meeting, Truman pulled from his wallet a folded piece of paper with a section of the poem "Locksley Hall" printed on it. He read the poem "slowly and with feeling," the *New York Times* man recalled. Then the president said, "Tennyson wrote that in 1842." Truman had carried this poem with him everywhere he went since he was a little boy.)

At 10:30 a.m., dozens filed into the Oval Office for Truman's first press conference. Standing behind his desk, he greeted reporters as they pushed into the room, which quickly grew uncomfortably crowded. Regular presidential press conferences were a tradition going back to Woodrow Wilson, who on March 15, 1913, set a precedent of welcoming newspaper reporters into his office to answer questions. Roosevelt had held two a week and had elevated these meetings to high art. Wielding his cigarette holder as if conducting an orchestra, he would deliver soliloquies that would entrance his guests, while almost always failing on purpose to answer any question posed.

On April 17 the largest crowd ever assembled for a presidential press conference pushed into the Oval Office – 348 men and women reporters – all aiming to size up the new chief executive. Some were forced to stand on the terrace outside the president's office – lucky ones, because the room got exceedingly hot.

"Good morning," Truman said, "good morning."

"Good morning, Mr. President," someone in the crowd said. "Will you take it sort of slow for us today, please, sir?"

"Surely, surely," Truman said. "Anything I can do to accommodate you."

No one in the room could help making comparisons to Roosevelt. For one thing, this president was standing up. "We all knew that Roosevelt had gone to Groton and then Harvard," recalled White House correspondent Robert Nixon, who was getting his first crack at Truman that morning. "That [Roosevelt] came from a quite old, well-to-do family; that he moved in what is known as the best circles all of his life . . . Truman was a small town, Midwestern Missourian of farm origin . . . The contrast was in appearance, voice mannerisms, and even their attire. President Roosevelt, while a casual dresser, was very well tailored . . . Truman dressed like he had just come off of Main Street in Independence."

The new president called for attention. "The first thing I want to do to you is to read the rules," he said. After telling the reporters what they already knew – everything he said was background material, no direct quotes were allowed unless there was specific permission – he began by announcing that most of the Roosevelt staff would stay on, and that Matthew Connelly had been appointed his confidential secretary. Truman read a letter aloud from Mrs. Roosevelt, thanking everyone for their wishes, "which have brought great comfort and consolation to all of us." Due to the wartime paper shortage, Mrs. Roosevelt would not be responding to all correspondence. Instead, she had asked Truman to read her thank-you letter to the press.

Truman then opened the floor. He answered questions about reciprocal trade, race relations, the wartime ban on horseracing, and the historic United Nations Conference set to open in eight days.

"Mr. President," said one reporter in the crowd. "Will Mrs. Truman have a press conference?"

"I would rather not answer that question at this time."

At numerous moments Truman delivered witticisms that sparked laughter in the room. The Missourian had a simple way of speaking that amused his counterparts in the press. He whittled his ideas down to the fewest words and handed them over. Unlike Roosevelt, Truman actually answered questions, and if he chose not to, he said just that.

"His first press conferences were wonderful," noted press secretary Daniels. At the end of this first one, something happened that had never occurred in any of Roosevelt's meetings with the press: the room erupted in spontaneous applause.

///

Nearing the end of his first week in office, Truman had inadvertently become the world's most fascinating man. Reporters had overturned every stone to explore the man's curious character.

How big was he? (Five feet nine inches, 165 pounds.) His gustatory pleasures? (Meat and potatoes, pie a la mode.) What did the middle initial S. stand for? (Nothing specifically.) Though Truman was associated with Kansas City, a hotbed of swinging jazz, he was no fan of what he called "modern noise," preferring Beethoven and Bach. His favorite pastime was poker. Madame Tussauds of London asked for the president's exact measurements and physical attributes, so the museum could build a lifelike wax statue of him. The White House delivered them: gray eyes, size 9B shoes, 35½-inch waistline.

No one was more surprised by the hoopla than Truman himself. "Six days President of the United States," he wrote in a letter to his mother and sister on Wednesday, April 18. "It is hardly believable."

Comparisons were made to Andrew Jackson, the first common man to become president – much to Truman's pleasure, because Jackson was of course his hero. The famed quote "If Andrew Jackson can be President, anyone can!" was refashioned as "If Harry Truman can be President, so could my next door neighbor!" Others compared Truman to Abraham Lincoln; both Truman and Lincoln had come from humble beginnings in the Midwest, both had served as small-town postmasters at one time (Truman for a *very* short time), and both were failed store owners (Berry & Lincoln; Truman & Jacobson).

In reality Truman was like no other man who had ever served as president, and the family's obscurity only brightened the spotlight. It seemed as if they had come out of nowhere. "Mr. and Mrs. Truman lived so inconspicuously in their senatorial days that few people knew them," wrote *Washington Times-Herald* columnist Helen Essary. "He brings to the

White House a background and personality which has had no counterpart among any recent or remote Chief Executive," wrote Luther Huston in the *New York Times*.

The powerful men who reported to Truman crystallized their first impressions. Undersecretary of State Joseph Grew wrote in a letter to a friend that he had "seen a good deal of [Truman] lately" and could report "nothing but the most favorable reaction . . . I think he is going to measure up splendidly to the tremendous job which faces him." "When I saw him today," Grew wrote of Truman in another missive, shortly after FDR's death, "I had fourteen problems to take up with him and got through them in less than fifteen minutes with a clear directive on every one of them. You can imagine what a joy it is to deal with a man like that." Even the notoriously cranky Admiral Leahy was disarmed by the president's affability. "Personally," Leahy wrote, "he proved to be easy to work with and, to use a trite phrase accurately, one of the nicest people I have ever known."

As the man who worked most closely with Truman on an hourly basis, handsome Matthew Connelly became a subject of intrigue. Connelly met with the press the same day that Truman did.

"How do you spell your name?"

"C-O-N-N-E-L-L-Y. That is Matthew J."

"Are you going to function as the appointment secretary?"

"That's right."

Connelly was from Clinton, Massachusetts. He was thirty-seven, married with one daughter. A graduate of Fordham University, he had worked on Wall Street, then as an investigator with congressional committees. The press wanted to know if he had any political experience.

"Not in actual politics, no."

"Do you drink, or chase women, or anything like that?"

"You should know." (Laughter.)

The president's family members came under the spotlight. When Margaret returned to class at George Washington University after the shock of FDR's death, the press followed her around campus. "Back to school and photographers all over the place!" she wrote in her diary. Bess Truman had become the subject of public fascination, a fact that pleased her none at all. Eleanor Roosevelt had radically altered the role of the First Lady by holding weekly press conferences for women reporters and writing her own newspaper column. Now the pressure was on Bess to do the same; Mrs. Roosevelt had sent her a note saying that this would be good for women across America.

Unlike Mrs. Roosevelt, who enjoyed the public eye, Bess remained a mystery. "Few citizens of the capital have even had a glimpse of her," a Washington bureau AP reporter wrote. Those who did know Bess found it hard to imagine this small-town sixty-year-old housewife as the First Lady of the United States, or a speech giver, or a newspaper columnist. Bess announced she would hold a press conference on April 17, but then she called it off, agonizing over the decision.

The first in-depth interviews with Truman's extended family members surfaced. "My first thought was that Harry was president and we didn't want him to be," said Bess's brother George Wallace. "I really can't be glad he's President because I am sorry that President Roosevelt is dead," said Mamma Truman. "If he'd have been voted in, I'd be out waving a flag, but it doesn't seem right to be very happy or wave any flags now." She had listened to her son's speech to Congress over the radio. "Every one who heard him talk . . . will know he's sincere and will do what's best," she said.

(Truman's press advisors told him that Mamma Truman's comments could not have been more perfect; it was as if they had been written by a seasoned press agent. Truman wrote his mother on the matter on April 18: "I told them that my family all told the truth all the time and that they did not need a press agent.")

Mamma Truman was correct: Her son's speech *had* given the nation a boost of morale, at a time when it was desperately needed. The stock market soared the afternoon after Truman's first speech. "Everywhere one hears the remark, 'He's doing all right,'" noted one political columnist. Senate reporter Allen Drury wrote in his diary the day after Truman's speech, "Few Presidents in history have started off on such a wave of universal good will and good hope as has come to Harry Truman."

Meanwhile, the most fevered gossip in the nation's capital centered on power in the new administration. Rumors were, Secretary of State Ed Stettinius was out and Jimmy Byrnes would take his place. Treasury secretary Morgenthau was likely to go. Who would fill his role? Republicans were sure that FDR's New Deal was dead, that the midwestern values of the new president would move the political metronome further right from Roosevelt's far left, if not smack in the center. But the true nature of the president's politics had yet to be seen.

By all accounts, Truman was off to a brilliant start. Privately, however, his presidential odyssey was unfolding differently. He was a poker player, and he knew that the deck was unlikely to spit out aces. The future was sure to thrust upon him contention and perhaps even public embarrassment. All he had to do was open a *Time* magazine, and there it was, talk of his incompetence: "Harry Truman is a man of distinct limitations, especially in experience in high level politics." Even in his private conversations with his wife, the doubt was crushing.

"He shared so many moments of doubt and discouragement with her," recalled Margaret of the early days of the Truman presidency. "This frankness combined with her natural pessimism to produce a lack of confidence." Bess feared what everyone else in America feared. According to Margaret: "She was not sure he could do the job."

THE RELENTLESS PACE OF HISTORY seemed to quicken during the first week of the Truman administration. From around the globe came stark reports of anarchy and murder.

In the battle for Okinawa, Japanese forces were employing a campaign of mass suicide missions to repel American forces: kamikaze planes, kamikaze boats, even suicide swimmers immolating themselves with explosives anywhere they could to affect damage and death. Military leaders in Tokyo were determined to make a statement, and the timing happened to coincide with Truman's inauguration day and his first days in office. Suicide planes rained from the sky — 256 of them, according to navy sources, starting the day before Roosevelt's death. Admiral Chester Nimitz, commanding the U.S. Navy in the Pacific, reported that "large numbers of enemy aircraft made desperate attacks on our forces in the Okinawa area." Antiaircraft gunners downed dozens of Japanese planes, but the enemy sank one destroyer in the process, and caused wreckage to numerous other American ships. The blows were not only physical; they were psychologically brutalizing. The Japanese had employed suicide tactics before, "but never so extensively and so earnestly" as they now were in Okinawa, according to a *New Yorker* reporter embedded with the marines. The suicide missioners had become "a branch of hysteria . . . developed highly in this war."

Meanwhile the American forces hammered Japanese strongholds on the island with combat troops supported by ships and planes hurling thousands of tons of shells. Some 140,000 island citizens were caught in the crossfire. On the island, Japanese soldiers hid in a maze of caves and seemed intent on fighting to the last man. The casualty reports reaching the Pentagon stunned War Department officials — nearly 2,700 American soldiers and sailors in the first nine days of the Okinawa campaign.

But Okinawa was only a part of the story in the Pacific war. In Tokyo, miles of neighborhoods were still smoldering from firebombings unleashed by Major General Curtis LeMay and his Twenty-First Bomber Command. LeMay had ordered an incendiary mission the night of April 13–14, which was April 12–13 in Washington, which meant that Tokyo had begun to boil with explosions and flames just a handful of hours after Truman had recited the presidential oath. Crews returning from those missions told of devastating results. "We saw great clouds of black smoke, higher than our plane," reported Corporal David Menor of Kansas City, Missouri. "We could still hear explosions when we were better than 100 miles away on our trip home." This one firebombing mission would destroy over 170,000 buildings, leaving roughly 2,500 dead (mostly civilians), about the same number of Americans who died at Pearl Harbor.

Soon after this mission – on Truman's third full day in office – Curtis LeMay declared from his headquarters on the island of Guam that the defeat of Japan could be achieved, he believed, by striking the mainland with incendiaries, by burning Japanese neighborhoods until the nation could no longer summon the will to fight.

As Truman was beginning his presidency, LeMay's reputation was soaring in the Pentagon. A month earlier the Ohioan had single-handedly changed the strategy of the attacking forces in the Pacific theater, with no permission from anyone. LeMay had been sent from the European theater to the Mariana Islands in the Pacific to take command of a new fleet of the army air forces' B-29s. These new aircraft were the biggest, most destructive weapons systems ever devised. Four 2,200-horsepower Wright engines could power the airplane to 357 miles per hour. The Superfortress had a wingspan nearly as long as half a football field, and could carry ten tons of bombs. Boeing had designed the aircraft to attack at high altitudes to avoid flak, and thus it was the first American military aircraft with a pressurized cabin. It was also the first with remote-control machine guns.

General H. H. "Hap" Arnold, head of the army air forces, had gambled $3 billion – and his entire career – on the development of the B-29 Superfortress. (The B-29 program cost taxpayers considerably more than the Manhattan Project did.) The stress of the B-29's development had caused Arnold to suffer numerous heart attacks. By autumn 1944, the airplanes were finally arriving in the Pacific. At only thirty-nine years of age, LeMay had been given the command. His direct superior, General Larry Norstad, had told him (according to LeMay's account): "You go ahead and get results with the B-29. If you don't get results, you'll be fired . . . If you don't get results it will mean eventually a mass amphibious invasion of Japan, to cost probably half a million more American lives."

In the winter of 1944–1945, LeMay's B-29 crews flew 2,037 sorties, attempting to knock out precise targets in darkness from high altitudes, a strategy considerably safer for the men aboard these ships. LeMay was not satisfied with the results.

"Our attempts to bomb precision targets at night have failed," he wrote the army air forces' chief, General Arnold. Weather and the ability of the bombers to hit targets from such high altitudes proved the major problems. So LeMay came up with a new plan of attack. "It was against this background," according to a Twenty-First Bomber Command report, "that the decision was reached early in March 1945 to launch a series of low level incendiary night attacks against Japanese urban areas." LeMay's idea was to strip out all possible excess weight from the B-29s — including the armament, the guns, and the gunners — and load them with firebombs. The aircraft would then fly at low altitude to be sure to hit their targets, which were urban neighborhoods tightly woven with wooden-framed buildings that would explode in towering columns of flames.

The plan was entirely in conflict with American policy, which was to use airplanes for "precision bombing" — to strike precise targets of military importance with conventional TNT, to weaken the enemy's ability to wage war while causing as little damage to civilian populations as possible. The United States had condemned urban bombing. Earlier in the war, Roosevelt had appealed to the world to keep armies from perpetrating "the ruthless bombing from the air of civilians in unfortified centers of population," calling this form of warfare "inhuman barbarism." While American air power did take part in the ruthless bombing of Dresden, no American officials publicly embraced this form of warfare, the way the British did.

LeMay knew that if he asked permission to utilize firebombs in low-altitude attacks against urban areas, he would be turned down. So he asked no permission. His aim had never been to kill women and children but to put an end to Japan's ability to wage war, and much of Japan's war making counted on "home industries carried on in cities or settlements close to major factory areas," according to a secret Twenty-First Bomber Command report. In other words, urban areas where civilians lived.

The first incendiary mission was flown March 9–10, using bombs loaded with white phosphorus and napalm; the latter substance was a new highly flammable fuel gel developed in a Harvard laboratory. The B-29 crews had been instructed on the best way to drop their payloads, to create the maximum amount of fire: "The bombs from a single ship must be spaced so as to assure a merging of the fires started by each bomb into a general conflagration before fire fighters have had time to put them out . . . With a full bomb load . . . of M-69 incendiaries, the area burned out by a single ship should be around 16 acres."

The night that first raid flew, LeMay paced in his headquarters until sunrise. "I'm sweating this one out myself," he told a subordinate. "A lot could go wrong . . . If the raid works the way I think it will, we can shorten this war."

That first firebombing of Tokyo resulted in the largest death toll of any air raid, in any war ever, up to that point – an estimated 100,000 Japanese, likely more. Civilians hiding in dug-out holes that served as crude bomb shelters were baked alive by the towering flames, the heat reaching 1,800 degrees F. Others took refuge in canals only to be boiled to death in the searing heat. LeMay awaited response from Washington. The White House (still under Roosevelt) remained strangely silent. LeMay himself had this to say on the matter: "We don't pause to shed any tears for uncounted hordes of Japanese who lie charred in that acrid-smelling rubble. The smell of Pearl Harbor fires is too persistent in our own nostrils."

The major general was becoming a curiosity not just for the deeds of the Twenty-First Bomber Command but for the unapologetic resolve with which he faced the killing of civilians, and the boldness for which he claimed personal responsibility. He had become known by his nickname, "Iron Ass." "I was a machine," the Ohioan said of himself. "When I went to the bathroom, it wasn't in the ordinary human process. If I defecated, I defecated nuts and bolts. I was made of metal throughout. Iron Ass LeMay."

LeMay had ended these missions on March 19 for one reason: he ran out of firebombs. But his stock had once again filled, coincidentally, right at the time Truman became president. Reports of the April 13–14 firebombings claimed that fifteen square miles of the city were still in flames forty-eight hours after the raid. Even at the time of FDR's funeral, the city of Tokyo was still burning. When General Arnold received aerial photographs of the devastation, he wrote LeMay directly: "A quick glance at the map certainly gives the impression that something over half of Tokyo is now gone. [The] Tokyo incendiary operations have certainly been among the most effective in the entire history of bombing. Keep up the good work."

///

In Europe the advancing Allied armies liberated more concentration camps during Truman's first week in office. On April 15, three days after FDR's death, the British Second Army reached Bergen-Belsen. What they found there defied description, according to the Second Army's commander, General Miles Dempsey. "Anything you have seen doesn't even begin the story," he told reporters. Prisoners from camps closer to the front had been moved to Bergen-Belsen over the past year, swelling the population to about sixty thousand living people. Due to sanitary conditions, the camp was rife with typhoid, tuberculosis, and other diseases. Heaps of corpses lay scattered around, with one major pit filled with blackened bodies. The victims were Jews, political prisoners, "asocials," Jehovah's Witnesses, and homosexuals, among others.

"There were children – 500 of them – in the midst of this," reported the *Chicago Tribune*. "Babies were born here daily." Estimates put the death toll at thirty thousand, just in the previous few months, and more investigation would push that number considerably higher.

During this same week, the Allies liberated Nazi death camps at Dora-Mittelbau, Buchenwald, and Westerbork. Within a few days, the U.S. Ninetieth Infantry Division would reach the camp at Flossenbürg, where more horror was discovered.

Reports in newspapers and over the radio during the first days of the Truman administration revealed the details of Hitler's most horrifying secret. "And now, let me tell you this in the first person," Edward R. Murrow said over CBS Radio on Truman's third day as president. Murrow had visited Buchenwald, where the Nazis had murdered at least 56,000 male prisoners, roughly 11,000 of them Jews. Murrow told of bodies "stacked up like cordwood," innumerable victims of starvation and torture, and hundreds of dying children. "God alone knows how many men and boys have died there during the last twelve years . . . At Buchenwald they spoke of the president just before he died. If there be a better epitaph, history does not record it."

Hitler and his band of gangsters would soon be held accountable,

Truman was sure. Top Nazi officials were hiding somewhere in Berlin. They could only hope the Americans would get to them first, before the Russians, who unlike American soldiers bore the scars of a Nazi invasion of their country. Nor did the Soviet army hold itself to what the Americans considered a code of moral conduct in the European war.

Concentration camp prisoners were not the only innocents dying in Europe. The liberation of Nazi-occupied nations brought on problems that American officials found potentially unsolvable, notably starvation and pestilence. The War Department had sent one of its officials, John J. McCloy, on a fact-finding mission in Europe, and McCloy had now returned. His report was delivered to Truman during the early days of the new administration.

"There is complete economic, social and political collapse going on in Central Europe," McCloy wrote, "the extent of which is unparalleled in history unless one goes back to the collapse of the Roman Empire, and even that may not have been as great an economic upheaval . . . One of the chief elements of disorder is the immense number of previously enslaved people who will be running around loose, as well as Germans who have been made homeless by the devastation of [the Allies'] victory."

According to the State Department, seven million displaced people were now in Germany or in formerly Nazi-conquered territory, with nowhere to go and no infrastructure to help them. There was little food, and little coal production for heating. Railroads, canals, and roads had been destroyed, making transportation – the arterial system of all economies – almost nonexistent. The most basic human comforts were unavailable to vast populations throughout the continent. An April 16 memo to the president pointed out that "without drastic action," hunger and pestilence in liberated areas would lead to more political unrest, and could derail the formation of the United Nations: "The success of any plans agreed upon at San Francisco can be seriously jeopardized, if not defeated, by internal chaos in the liberated countries."

Still another complication arose during Truman's first week. On the day of Roosevelt's death, Eisenhower's troops had established a bridgehead on the Elbe River near Magdeburg, some sixty miles west of Berlin. It was here that Eisenhower was to make the most controversial decision of his military career. The commanding general ordered his armies to stop at the Elbe, rather than push on toward the German capital. In the days before FDR's death Eisenhower and Churchill had engaged in a contentious debate over the general's plans to halt the Anglo-American armies at the Elbe. The Russians were pushing toward Berlin from the east. Churchill urged, almost desperately, that Eisenhower push past the Elbe to capture Berlin, before Stalin's armies got there.

"Why should we not cross the Elbe and advance as far eastward as possible?" Churchill cabled Eisenhower. The prime minister feared that if the Russians captured all of Austria and Berlin, this would "raise grave and formidable difficulties in the future." The Soviets were allies, but from the prime minister's point of view, the Anglo-Americans and the Red Army were in a race to fill the power vacuum left by the conquered Nazis.

Eisenhower chose to halt at the Elbe. His reasoning would be debated by historians for generations, but the following are logical conclusions: First, zones of post-surrender occupation had already been drawn, and Eisenhower's armies had already pushed past the border of where the American occupation zone was to be, and into the Russian zone. So why conquer more territory at the cost of American lives knowing that, once the Germans surrendered, Eisenhower would have to give that territory back to the Soviets? Second, Eisenhower feared what would happen when the American and Russian armies finally met, joining the eastern and western fronts. This meeting was likely to happen in a matter of a few days. The Elbe River would serve as a convenient buffer when it did. The third reason was that Berlin was a political objective. Eisenhower was a general, and had to make decisions in the field based on military objectives – not political ones.

From the White House, Truman supported Eisenhower's decision. What would happen next was anyone's guess. As Secretary of War Henry Stimson described the situation: "The armies had outrun the policy makers." Only one thing seemed for sure. As McCloy had concluded in the report on his fact-finding mission in Europe: "In this atmosphere of disturbance and collapse, atrocities and disarrangement, we are going to have to work out a practical relationship with the Russians. It will require the highest talents, tolerance and wisdom in order to accomplish our aims."

///

At 9:45 a.m. on April 20 – Truman's eighth full day as president – Henry Morgenthau arrived in the Oval Office.

"Mr. Secretary," Truman said.

"Before you were President," Morgenthau came back, "you called me Henry. I wish you would continue to do that." Then: "Mr. President, if you don't misunderstand me, as a citizen, I would like to say that I think you have done extremely well in the first week."

"I have had all the breaks," Truman said.

Morgenthau had only fifteen minutes scheduled with Truman. He handed over a memo – pages full of facts that Truman had requested from him. This memorandum was the first of many aimed at developing a snapshot for the president of the nation's economy, and how it fit into the current global emergency. For a man who had been a financial failure all his life, Truman was skilled with handling budgets and spotting leaks in the flow of capital, a skill he had first picked up as a judge in Jackson County during the Depression. Only now the numbers were astronomical, for the United States currently formed the largest, most powerful economy in the history of the world. The federal government had become the purchaser of nearly half the products of the nation's industries. This was a situation that had no precedent. Truman had only six weeks before he would have to deliver his first military budget to Congress. He was facing very difficult decision making.

According to Morgenthau's memorandum, fiscal year spending for 1945 equated to some $99 billion, $88 billion of which was for war activities. Receipts, exclusive of borrowing, were estimated at $46 billion, or about 46 percent of the total. The federal government's income flowed through taxes and war bonds, the latter of which 85 million Americans had invested in. For fiscal year 1946, Morgenthau estimated the budget at $82.5 billion, with $69.5 billion marked for war activities, though there was no way to know what war expenditures would be, as they would depend on the results of military action as yet to play out.

The gap in spending and income had resulted in unprecedented national debt, already well over $250 billion and growing fast. Roosevelt had promised when he entered the White House in 1933 that he would balance the budget, something the previous president, Hoover, had failed to do. However, FDR had subsequently been influenced by the British economist John Maynard Keynes, who argued that in times of emergency (such as the Great Depression and the war), "public authority must be called in aid to create additional current incomes through the expenditure of borrowed or printed money." In other words, Keynes urged deficit spending. This radical theory, along with the spectacular rise in economic activity spurred by the war, was greatly responsible for pulling the United States out of the Depression.

The war had electrocuted the economy. The gross national product had more than doubled during the war years, and consumer income had risen sharply. Average weekly earnings in America were $24.20 in 1940; now, in 1945, that number hit $44.39. However, supplies of goods from toaster ovens to automobiles had declined or disappeared altogether. This equation — tremendous demand, very little supply — resulted in the frightening specter of runaway inflation. The federal government's army of economists had strategized an elaborate price-control system to stem inflation. But the price controls could not remain in place forever. Some critics claimed FDR and Keynes had steered the American economy head on for a cliff ledge. Economists had learned a lot from the last war, but still, this was uncharted territory.

Above all of this financial turmoil hung the dark cloud of reconversion. Someday — and that someday would come soon, Truman could only hope — thousands of government-owned factories, building war materiel, would have to stop producing. As soon as the war ended, the federal government was set to cancel billions of dollars' worth of war contracts almost instantly, and in fact, this process had already begun. Unemployment was predicted to skyrocket. Millions of soldiers would return from overseas with money earned fighting, money they would want to spend, which would only fuel further inflation. Massive budget deficit, price controls, with reconversion soon to arrive — never before had any economy faced what the American economy did at the time Truman took over.

From his discussions with Morgenthau, Truman also concluded that he did not have faith in the Treasury secretary's loyalty. Morgenthau came off as petulant and hungry for power. Already, the new president was considering who could take the secretary's place.

///

The White House Cabinet Room adjoined the Oval Office in the West Wing, separated only by the president's secretary's office. For years the Cabinet Room had served as a theater where Roosevelt extemporized performances with rambling stories and often incisive polemics, for fidgety cabinet officials crowded around a mahogany conference table.

For Roosevelt, cabinet meetings were long-winded solo performances. Truman's first cabinet sessions were a study in contrast.

"The quickest Cabinet meeting that I remember since I came into the War Department in 1940," Stimson commented in his diary after Truman's first, on April 20, his eighth day in office. "The President took command and galloped . . . through the meeting in an hour." Truman wanted a different culture from the one fostered by Roosevelt. He went around the table and directed each department secretary to speak. FDR liked to foster rivalries among his cabinet officers, which sometimes turned turbulent and often played out in the newspapers. The new president wanted no backbiting, no feuds. Truman wanted a team. "He was very vigorous, decisive, and hardboiled in presenting [this] viewpoint," Secretary of Commerce Henry Wallace wrote in his diary after Truman's second cabinet session.

The founding fathers had created the cabinet in article 2 of the Constitution – department heads whose job it was to advise the president on matters pertaining to their offices. George Washington had appointed the first cabinet: Secretary of State Thomas Jefferson, Secretary of the Treasury Alexander Hamilton, Secretary of War Henry Knox, and Attorney General Edmund Randolph. By Truman's time there were ten officers, all Democrats but one (Secretary of War Stimson). Cabinet secretaries were appointed by the president and confirmed by the Senate by simple majority. And that meant they were the easiest positions of power for a president to replace, as they were not elected officials. It was here, within the cabinet, where Truman was going to make his first changes, in an effort to build his own team.

He had already formed his initial opinions of the cabinet figures he had inherited. Secretary of State Edward Stettinius was "a fine man, good looking, amiable, cooperative, but never an idea new or old." Secretary of the Treasury Henry Morgenthau was a "block head," a "nut." Secretary of War Stimson was "a real man – honest, straight forward and a statesman." Secretary of Labor Frances Perkins, the only female cabinet member, was "a grand lady – but no politician," while navy secretary James Forrestal was painfully indecisive: "Poor Forrestal . . . He never could make a decision." Only four of these ten figures would remain in their job through the end of 1945. Truman was preparing numerous cabinet changes within the next month. In fact, he would shape a new cabinet faster than any succeeding VP ever had.

His first major appointment was not a cabinet official but nonetheless, a high-profile job — press secretary. On the evening of April 19, Charlie Ross arrived to meet with the president. Ross was part of the legendary class of 1901 at Independence High — along with Harry and Bess Truman. Ross had been valedictorian. He had since worked his way up to chief political reporter for the *St. Louis Post-Dispatch,* winning a Pulitzer Prize along the way for his reporting on the Depression. Ross had not always been kind to Truman in print. In fact, Ross had eviscerated him years earlier for his Pendergast connections. But the president knew that he, Harry Truman, was fair game, that any other good reporter would have done the same thing in Ross's shoes. Now he thought Ross was the right man for press secretary — wise, hardworking, well connected. He could count on Ross to be 100 percent loyal. When Ross appeared at the White House, the two greeted each other as old friends.

Lanky and intense, with piercing green eyes and greased brown hair, Charlie Ross had a cigarette habit to rival any. When he spoke, the words sounded like they were pumping out of a smokestack. He would have to take a massive pay cut to join Truman's team, he informed the president, from $35,000 to $10,000, and he feared he would lose his pension if he quit the *Post-Dispatch,* a paper owned by Joseph Pulitzer Jr.

"Matt," Truman barked to Matthew Connelly, "get that no-good Pulitzer on the phone. I want to talk to him." Connelly managed to get Pulitzer, who must have been surprised to hear from the president of the United States that evening. With Ross sitting by, and Truman doing the negotiating, Joseph Pulitzer agreed to allow Ross a two-year leave from the newspaper, and he could keep his retirement.

It was agreed. Truman sent for cocktails to celebrate. Then he ordered Connelly to make another phone call. He wanted to talk to Miss Tillie Brown of Independence, Missouri.

"Who's Miss Tillie Brown?" Connelly asked.

"Charlie and I know. She was our school teacher."

Connelly made the phone call through the White House operator, and Miss Tillie Brown picked up in Independence. Truman grabbed the phone and said, "Miss Tillie, who do you think this is?"

"Well, I don't know," answered the elderly woman.

"This is Harry Truman."

"The President?"

"Miss Tillie, who do you think I have with me?"

"Who do you have with you?"

"Charlie Ross. He's going to be my press secretary."

Connelly would recall tearing up while listening to this phone call. So too did Stephen Early, Roosevelt's longtime press secretary, who happened to be at the White House that night. At the end of the night Early said to Connelly (according to Connelly's recollection): "Boy, what a man. I'll never forget it. I loved Roosevelt, but we have a President."

Truman made the announcement the next day at his regular press conference – Charlie Ross would begin May 15. "Charlie and I graduated in the same high school class," Truman told the packed room.

"What was that year, sir?" one reporter asked.

"1901. Do your own figuring. [Laughter.] That covers everything, doesn't it?"

Over the next few days Truman announced more appointments: Edwin W. Pauley as U.S. representative on the Allied Reparations Commission, with the rank of ambassador. It would be Pauley's job to figure out a method of forcing Germany to pay the Allies back for war damages after the Nazi surrender. Robert Hannegan of St. Louis would take over as postmaster general, which was a cabinet position. Justice Robert H. Jackson of the Supreme Court would take on the most daunting position. As Truman described Jackson's appointment officially, the justice would be "Chief Counsel for the United States in preparing and prosecuting charges of atrocities and war crimes . . . to bring to trial before an international military tribunal." Justice Jackson was going to begin to build cases and the foundation for an international court to try them, to bring Nazi war criminals to justice. The only member of the current United States Supreme Court who had never completed law school, Jackson – widely considered brilliant – would become chief prosecutor at the Nuremberg trials.

///

"Dear Mamma + Mary," Truman wrote on April 21, "I've been the president for nine days. And such nine days no one ever went through before, I don't believe." Even before Truman was sworn in, "it was necessary for me to begin making decisions," he wrote. "And I've been making them ever since."

Each morning Truman arrived in his office to find his daily calendar stacked up with meetings of high national and international consequence. Senators and congressmen came and went in the time it might take a man to chat with an acquaintance on the street, often groups of visitors scheduled for five-minute blocks. The issues at hand were innumerable and often so complex, it required hours of reading to have a rudimentary grasp on them before Truman was forced into dialogue. At 3 p.m. each day, Roberta Barrows – the assistant appointments secretary – delivered to the president what she called "legal sheets," bios of all the people who would be meeting with the president the following day. These required Barrows to perform careful detective work. "I had to know their background and what they were going to talk to the president about," she recalled.

"There are no minor problems that come to his desk," recalled Truman's friend and now administrative assistant Eddie McKim. "They are all major . . . Everybody was there on appointment; they had to be there on a major problem, or they wouldn't get in . . . There was no two of them alike. That's the Presidency."

On April 19, President Osmeña of the Philippines arrived at the White House for Truman's first visit with a foreign leader. The Philippines had been a U.S. colony since 1898 and would be granted independence at the war's end, but Truman needed reassurance that the United States could maintain military bases there.

A day later Truman met with Rabbi Stephen Wise, president of the Zionist Organization of America, to discuss the critical issue of displaced Jews in Europe, who should be granted land in Palestine to form a Jewish state, the rabbi argued. The secretary of state had prepared the president with a confidential memo for the Wise meeting: "We have interests in [Palestine] which are vital to the United States, [and] we feel that this whole subject is one that should be handled with the greatest care." Truman made Dr. Wise no commitments.

The president met with J. Edgar Hoover, chief of the Federal Bureau of Investigation. Hoover's powers in an era of wartime paranoia had expanded alarmingly, Truman believed. "We want no Gestapo or Secret Police," he wrote in a diary. "FBI is tending in that direction. They are dabbling in sex-life scandals and plain blackmail . . . *This must stop.*"

Truman was also grilled by black leaders seeking to know how the new president would stand on racial issues. The war had forced integration as nothing ever had. However, about half of the employers in the United States still refused to hire black workers, and blacks were forbidden from serving alongside white soldiers in the military. Black leaders could see progress made on the labor front; the war economy had put more African Americans to work than ever before. As one female black American famously said: "Hitler was the one that got us out of the white folks' kitchen." As of 1944, 7.5 percent of war production jobs were held by African Americans, while their overall percentage of the nation's population at the time was 9.8 percent. A black reporter from the *Chicago Defender* put it to Truman: "Would you comment on these matters and any others that may give reassurance to 13 million of your fellow Americans who today look hopefully to you?" The reporter walked away satisfied that the new president would support black issues as much as Roosevelt had.

As busy as a president could be, Truman was still a man who each night went home to his family, who had to keep track of bills, and who had doctor and dentist appointments. (The White House dentist made house calls; Truman's teeth were in fine shape, but Margaret had nine cavities, having not seen a dentist in five years.) On April 19, between appointments with army chief of staff George Marshall and the Chinese foreign minister, T. V. Soong, Truman took a few minutes to entertain some special guests. His brother, Vivian, and Fred Canfil showed up at the White House. They took turns sitting in the president's chair and swam in the White House pool before Truman had enjoyed a chance to test the waters.

Truman had made Canfil a U.S. marshal in Kansas City, and it was Canfil who drove to the nation's capital, from Missouri. "We all wanted to see Harry and that's why we drove to Washington," Canfil told Duke Shoop of the *Kansas City Star*, which promptly published a photo of the strange-looking Canfil smiling crookedly in front of the White House. (The trip got Canfil in trouble, as the long drive violated rationing rules on the use of gasoline.)

The Trumans also had the added stress of moving again. On April 20, a procession of twenty army trucks could be seen parked at the White House, as movers hauled Eleanor Roosevelt's possessions out of the executive mansion. ("I was saying goodbye to an unforgettable era," she told her newspaper column readers.) Mrs. Roosevelt stopped by the Blair House on her way out of town, as a courtesy to Bess and Margaret.

She apologized for the state of the White House, and admitted that she had recently seen a rat scamper across a porch railing while she was having lunch with friends on the South Portico. Due to the war emergency, the Roosevelts had no time to keep up the home. When Bess and Margaret went to look at the place, they were not happy.

"The expression on Mother's face when she saw the dingy, worn furniture and the shabby white walls, unpainted in twelve years, was more expressive than any paragraph of exclamation points," Margaret recorded. Bess insisted that the walls be painted and new furniture be purchased before the new First Family could move in.

ON APRIL 19, the day Truman's brother and Fred Canfil visited the White House, and also the day Charlie Ross arrived, Admiral Leahy led the president to a safe in the executive mansion. Inside were some extraordinary documents — secret agreements that Roosevelt had made with Stalin, at Yalta. Around this same time Jimmy Byrnes produced his notes from Yalta. Together the documentation disclosed startling information that would have immeasurable impact on the future of the world.

According to these secret protocols, Stalin had agreed at Yalta to join the war against Japan two to three months after Germany's surrender, whenever that would be. He would need that much time to amass his troops and equipment on the other side of the globe from Europe. The Red Army's addition to the attacking forces would surely shorten the war against Japan and save countless American lives. And so this policy was unanimously embraced by top State and War Department officials and the Joint Chiefs of Staff, Truman now learned.

Stalin had demands in return, however: (1) the restoration of certain former rights of Russia, lost in the Russo-Japanese War of 1904–1905, including the Kurile Islands and lower Sakhalin, and control of Port Arthur and Dairen in Manchuria; (2) recognition of the independence from China of pro-Soviet Outer Mongolia; and (3) Soviet control of China's South Manchurian and Chinese-Eastern railroads. Roosevelt had agreed to all of this.

Truman could see why these demands benefited Stalin, giving him strategic territories for military bases and open access to seaports and trade routes. The secret Yalta agreements caused one major problem, however. Roosevelt's commitments would require large concessions on the part of the Chinese. Nobody had informed the Chinese. If the Chinese refused to abide by these secret agreements, of which they were never consulted, the entire picture of the war in the Far East would alter, as the Russians could then refuse to join the fight against Japan. Thousands of American lives would hang in the balance of these negotiations, and it would now be Truman's job to solve this vexing problem.

The president needed to know all the secrets before he sat down with Vyacheslav Molotov; Stalin's number two was set to arrive in the United States just three days after Truman learned of the secret Yalta agreements. The more the president studied the situation, the more he realized that he had but a glimpse of this complex picture.

At noon on April 20, Averell Harriman, the fifty-three-year-old ambassador to Moscow, arrived in Truman's office for their first meeting. Weary from the long journey (Harriman had traveled from Moscow to Washington by aircraft in record time – forty-nine hours and twenty minutes), he appeared haggard and nervous. To say his reputation preceded him would be a laughable understatement. The son of a railroad tycoon, educated at Groton (where he first met members of the Roosevelt family) and then Yale, Harriman was chairman of the board of the great Union Pacific Railroad. He had inherited a fabulous fortune at a young age and had traveled to the Soviet Union before the war as a principal of Brown Brothers Harriman, a Wall Street investment firm. He was a renowned polo player, an accomplished billiards and badminton competitor, and he had founded the American West's first ski resort, at Sun Valley, Idaho, in the 1930s. Roosevelt had recruited Harriman months before Pearl Harbor – at the height of the Battle of Britain – to serve as a special envoy of the United States, telling Harriman, "I want you to go over to London, and recommend everything that we can do, short of war, to keep the British Isles afloat." Harriman agreed to do the job, at his own expense.

So began his diplomatic career. He had taken over the Moscow embassy in 1943, running it with his daughter Kathleen as his hostess – a striking beauty who spoke Russian and rode Stalin's horses with abandon. Harriman's second in command at the Moscow embassy, George Kennan, described him during the war: "[Harriman] recognized no interests outside his work. Personal life did not exist for him . . . Accustomed to doing things in a big way and endowed with a keen appreciation for great personal power . . . he dealt only with people at the top . . . I once asked a Russian friend what the Russians thought of him. 'They look at him,' she replied, 'and they say to themselves: There goes a man!'"

As of April 1945, Harriman had spent more hours in Stalin's company than any other American. However, the stress of running the embassy – in the Spaso House, one mile from the Kremlin – had begun to wear him down. Life in the Spaso House had become overbearing – boarded up windows shattered during the Nazi invasion, lack of coal for heating. As the point man for American-Soviet relations, he carried the stress in bags under his eyes, and had become increasingly pessimistic about the future.

In the Oval Office, Secretary of State Stettinius presented Harriman to the president. Also in the room: Chip Bohlen, the Russian expert and interpreter, and Joseph Grew, the State Department's second in command. Truman asked for a report on the Soviet situation, and what Harriman had to say was chilling.

"The Soviet Union had two policies," Harriman said, according to this meeting's minutes, "which they thought they could successfully pursue at the same time – one, the policy of cooperation with the United States and Great Britain, and the other, the extension of Soviet control over neighboring states . . . Soviet control over any foreign country did not mean merely influence on their foreign relations but the extension of the Soviet system with secret police, extinction of freedom of speech, etc."

The Russians were fixed on domination, and it started with Poland. What the world was facing, said Harriman, was "a barbarian invasion of Europe."

Truman said he was not afraid of the Soviets. "And anyway," he said, "the Russians need us more than we need them." The president was speaking specifically of money and resources; the Americans were shipping the USSR hundreds of tons of food and military equipment weekly, and the Soviets (like the British, for that matter) were hoping to reap billions in loans from the United States for postwar reconstruction.

The president was adamant: the Soviets' puppet government in Poland had to go. According to the meeting's minutes, "[Truman] added that he intended to tell Molotov just this in words of one syllable." Truman admitted he was "not up on all details of foreign affairs," that he would rely on his secretary of state and Ambassador Harriman. But he planned "to be firm in his dealings with the Soviet government."

Through the discussion, Harriman realized how closely Truman had studied the Yalta negotiations. "I gained great respect for Truman at once," he recorded, after their first meeting. "Although I also was disturbed, during this first conversation and others that followed, because he kept saying – too often, I thought – that he was not equipped for the job, that he lacked experience and did not fully understand the issues."

Nevertheless, the stage was set for the Truman-Molotov meeting. No one had yet to discover a way to solve the impasse with the Russians over Poland. The State Department's Archibald MacLeish, who happened to be a Pulitzer Prize–winning poet, put the situation in these words: "It would be a blessing to the world if we could walk straight up to this question." Truman intended to do exactly that.

///

On Saturday night, April 21, a motorcade pulled up in front of the Blair House. As one secret service man recalled, seven "GPU guys" (Russian secret police) jumped out of a handful of cars, under the cloak of night. Without a word to anyone, they charged into the Blair House. "I followed them around and they tried the windows, tried this, pulled the drawers out, dashed up and down stairs, cased the joint [for] ten minutes," recalled the secret service man. Then Vyacheslav Molotov entered the residence. He would be staying in a different section of the Blair House from the Trumans, putting the president and Molotov in awkwardly close proximity.

By this time Truman and his advisors had held numerous meetings on how to handle Molotov. The president received memo after memo regarding every detail of the visit, which would require no military honors, at the Russians' request. Truman received a State Department bio of Molotov. "Real name is Skriabin, a Slav," it read. "Born in 1890 of a worker's family; entered the [Communist] Party in 1906; engaged in revolutionary work prior to the [Communist Revolution] and imprisoned and exiled many times." Once Stalin took the reins of the Soviet government in 1929, Molotov rode on his coattails to the very center of power in the Kremlin. "He has always carried out Stalin's policies and instructions in a painstaking and effective manner," the State Department's bio read. Molotov had a reputation for bluntness. He could be exceedingly rude.

At 8:30 p.m. on Sunday, April 22, Truman's tenth day in office, he received Molotov at the Blair House. The Russian stood taller than Truman, with a bulging forehead, wispy salt-and-pepper hair, and a shaggy mustache. The two men exchanged formalities, with Chip Bohlen standing by as interpreter. Molotov's trip by air had been long but bearable, he said. Truman said he had "the greatest admiration for Marshal Stalin and the Soviet Republic" and that he "hoped that the relations which President Roosevelt had established between our two countries would be maintained." Truman hoped they could navigate "difficulties" that "lay in the path." Molotov assured Truman this could be done, and they agreed that Truman and Stalin must meet in person as soon as possible.

Not until the following day did the two men get down to business. Molotov spent the morning of April 23 in a meeting with State Department and British foreign service officials, in hopes that the Polish situation could be cleared up without any confrontation with Truman. At 2 p.m. Truman met again with his top officials: Ambassador Harriman, Secretary of State Stettinius, Secretary of War Stimson, Admirals Leahy and Ernest King, General Marshall, and Secretary of the Navy Forrestal. Stettinius reported that meetings with Molotov over Poland that morning had gotten nowhere.

"It was now clear that the Soviet Government intended to try to enforce upon the United States and British Governments this puppet government," Stettinius recorded.

If anything, the situation had worsened. Truman received a State Department communiqué on this day detailing the scene inside Poland. A French official who had been allowed into Warsaw described the political situation as "appalling." "He states that the 'so-called' Warsaw government has practically no support and that its authority would be nonexistent if it were not maintained by the Red Army [and that] unless something is done, Poland as a nation will cease to exist within a year," the report read.

Surrounded by foreign-relations and military advisors, Truman went around the room asking for each's opinion on how to handle Molotov. But he had his own ideas, too. The conversation, as recounted in Averell Harriman's memoirs: "It was now or never, [Truman] said. The Yalta agreements so far had been a one-way street and that could not continue." If the Russians would not stand by their agreements, Truman said, they could "go to hell."

At 5:30 p.m. Molotov was shown in. Others in the room included Harriman and Stettinius. Molotov brought with him a translator, Vladimir Pavlov, and Moscow's minister of foreign affairs, Andrei Gromyko. After a warm greeting, Truman spoke with the kind of frankness he had learned in hard-nosed Kansas City politics. "The United States government could not agree to be a party to the formation of a Polish government which was not representative of all Polish democratic elements," Truman said. The U.S. government was "deeply disappointed" by the failure of the Russians to stand by their agreements, Truman said, and this disappointment "cast serious doubt upon our unity of purpose in regard to postwar collaboration."

The one-sided conversation continued for thirty minutes. "How I enjoyed translating Truman's sentences!" recalled Bohlen. "They were probably the first sharp words uttered during the war by an American President to a high Soviet official." At the end, Truman said, "That will be all, Mr. Molotov. I would appreciate it if you would transmit my views to Marshal Stalin."

According to Truman's account of this conversation, Molotov then said: "I have never been talked to like that in my life."

"Carry out your agreements," Truman fired back, "and you won't get talked to like that."

As Molotov stood up to leave, Truman handed him a memorandum that he wished the Russian to pass on to Stalin. The document reiterated the points the president had just voiced, in equally strong language. Molotov took his leave.

All over Washington the next day, news of the Truman-Molotov meeting spread, leaving government officials astonished. Chief of staff Admiral Leahy was thrilled. Secretary of War Stimson was deeply concerned, fearing that the Polish issue would result in "a head-on collision" between the United States and the Soviets. Ambassador Harriman was equally troubled: "I did regret that Truman went at it so hard because his behavior gave Molotov an excuse to tell Stalin that the Roosevelt policy was being abandoned."

Not long after the Molotov meeting, Truman met with Joseph Davies, a State Department official who had served as a Moscow ambassador before Harriman. Davies had written a best-selling memoir about his years in the Moscow embassy called *Mission to Moscow;* it had been turned into a popular movie in 1943, with Walter Huston playing the part of Davies and Ann Harding playing Mrs. Davies, who was none other than Marjorie Merriweather Post, heir to the Post cereal fortune and one of the richest women in the world.

"I gave it to him straight," Truman told Davies of his meeting with Molotov. "I let him have it. It was the straight one-two to the jaw. I wanted him to know that our cooperation had to be two sided." Then Truman asked Davies, "I want to know what you think. Did I do right?"

Davies was alarmed. He explained that he too had talked with Molotov, as they knew each other well. The Russians were very nervous about having to deal with an American leader other than Roosevelt, whom they knew and respected. With Roosevelt, the Russians believed they would arrive at peace, a fruitful friendship, after the war. With Truman, Davies explained, that assurance was gone. To understand the Russians, Davies believed, one had to see things as they did. The Soviets saw themselves as "an island surrounded by a sea of enemies," Davies believed. In all decisions, they would move to protect their security.

"It would be too bad," Davies told Truman, "if the seeds of a new world war were sown even before the fighting in this war had ended."

APRIL 25 would prove a momentous day for Truman. At the office that morning he held his usual staff meeting minutes after nine. "There was little on the appointment list of much importance," recalled assistant press secretary Eben Ayers. How wrong he would prove to be.

Between 9:15 a.m. and noon, the president met with eleven congressmen in eight different meetings, fifteen minutes apiece, plus the outgoing postmaster general, Frank Walker. Then, at noon, the secretary of war Henry Stimson, entered the Oval Office. He had written a note to the president the day before asking for a discussion "as soon as possible on a highly secret matter." Stimson arrived bearing a file. Through a second door in the Oval Office, another man entered, whom Truman quickly recognized. Major General Leslie Groves had been ushered into the White House through a back door and had walked through underground corridors, so as not to arouse the press who stalked the area around the West Wing's main entrance. Groves was a robust man — nearly six feet and about 250 pounds — whose mustache curled around a mouth eternally fixed into a scowl. He had risen in the army through the Office of the Chief Engineers and had supervised the building of the Pentagon. He had since taken over a new project, as Truman was about to learn.

Stimson handed Truman a memo, and the president read it carefully while Stimson and Groves sat quietly. The memo began with the following sentence: "Within four months we shall in all probability have completed the most terrible weapon ever known in human history, one bomb of which could destroy a whole city."

The secretary of war's memorandum detailed a new invention in the making called the atomic bomb. Some basic science needed explaining. Groves had also penned his own long memorandum containing rudimentary information, which he handed to Truman. "An atom is made up of neutrons, electrons and protons," it read. "When a free neutron, from outside the atom, strikes an atom of U-235 [uranium], the collision causes the atom to break into two parts freeing more neutrons and releasing a relatively large amount of energy."

An atom bomb might explode with the equivalent of anywhere from 5,000 to 20,000 tons of TNT, Groves's memorandum explained, which could make it the most powerful weapon ever imagined, if it in fact worked. The project was being called the Manhattan District Project. Groves's memo also made the following statement: "The successful development of the Atomic Fission Bomb will provide the United States with a weapon of tremendous power which should be a decisive factor in winning the present war more quickly with a saving in American lives . . . If the United States continues to lead in the development of atomic energy weapons, its future will be much safer and the chances of preserving world peace greatly increased."

Groves and Stimson proceeded to pull the curtain off the most ambitious industrial and scientific undertaking in human history.

///

The U.S. government's atomic bomb experiment had begun with a letter to Franklin Roosevelt almost six years earlier, dated August 2, 1939. It was a curious missive that would become as famed a document as any produced during the Roosevelt presidency. Signed by the theoretical physicist Albert Einstein, it told of how "the element uranium may be turned into a new and important source of energy in the immediate future . . . This new phenomenon would also lead to the construction of bombs, and it is conceivable – though much less certain – that extremely powerful bombs of a new type may thus be constructed."

Roosevelt knew that theoretical scientists had a tendency to dream wildly. But Einstein's dreams had a way of becoming reality. As the eminent physicist Arthur Compton noted, "Probably no other scientist since Charles Darwin had won as high a place in the history of human thought." The president discussed Einstein's letter with an economic advisor named Alexander Sachs (it was Sachs who had hand-delivered the Einstein letter to FDR). If such a bomb could be devised, Sachs was wondering, could the Nazis build it first? "Alex," Roosevelt said, "what you are after is to see that the Nazis don't blow us up." The president called in an assistant and pronounced three words that set the atomic bomb project in motion: "This needs action."

In the fall of 1939 the federal government transferred the first funds for a special military project — $6,000 to purchase materials, including a quantity of uranium. On June 27, 1940, Roosevelt created the National Defense Research Committee, a think tank headed up by Dr. Vannevar Bush, president of the Carnegie Institution; Dr. James Conant, president of Harvard; Dr. Richard Tolman of the California Institute of Technology; and Dr. Karl Compton, president of the Massachusetts Institute of Technology, among others. This group set to work gathering the brightest minds in physics, employing them in top-secret work devising methods of splitting atoms, to find out if in fact such highly theoretical ideas could be weaponized. The secretary of war first learned of this work on November 6, 1941 (just a month before Pearl Harbor). "Vannevar Bush came in to convey to me an extremely secret statement," Stimson wrote in his diary, "a most terrible thing." (Stimson was the only high-level government figure involved from this point up until the meeting with Truman on April 25, 1945.)

The bomb project fell under the command of the United States Army. Through the early years of research, while war was raging in Europe and the Far East, army chief of staff George Marshall followed the work carefully, often confused by its extraordinary complexity. "I would spend so much time with the *Encyclopedia Britannica* and the dictionary trying to interpret . . . that I finally just gave it up, deciding that I never would quite understand," he later said.

General Marshall and the secretary of war agreed to hand the day-to-day supervision of the project to Major General Leslie Groves on September 17, 1942. Groves was tasked with directing the expansion of work from the theoretical to the industrial phase. In June 1942, he appointed J. Robert Oppenheimer to be scientific director of a new secret laboratory, where the bomb would be built. Oppenheimer's appointment letter read, in part:

> The laboratory will be concerned with the development and final manufacture of an instrument of war, which we may designate as Projectile S-1-T. To this end, the laboratory will be concerned with:
>
> a. Certain experimental studies in science, engineering and ordnance, and
>
> b. At a later date large-scale experiments involving diffi-

cult ordnance procedures and the handling of highly dangerous material.

It was Oppenheimer who chose the location for his laboratory, barren land outside the village of Los Alamos, New Mexico, where he had spent part of his youth camping and riding horses in the high desert plains. There was an air of fate about this rugged land; as a young man, Oppenheimer had once said, "My two great loves are physics and New Mexico. It's a pity they can't be combined." Now, at Los Alamos, that dream had been realized.

The federal government secretly funneled millions of dollars into Oppenheimer's work, without the knowledge of Congress. An entire town had to be built at Los Alamos, with infrastructure to supply a population of scientists and military figures and their families, who would need clean water, shelter, schools, medical care, supplies of food, and all manner of technical equipment.

Groves, meanwhile, supervised the construction of two facilities even more ambitious than the Pentagon, all in secret. The first was at Oak Ridge, Tennessee, where uranium would be enriched for bomb making. The main building where this work took place spread out across forty-four acres, making it the largest building in the world. Housing had to be constructed for tens of thousands of workers, who had no idea what it was they were laboring to produce, because the project was so secretive. The site was not far from the city of Knoxville. "While I felt that the possibility of serious danger was small," Groves later recalled, "we could not be absolutely sure; no one knew what might happen, if anything, when a chain reaction was attempted in a large reactor."

The second site was at Hanford, Washington – the world's first full-scale plutonium production reactor, a facility that required a perimeter of 12 by 16 miles, 25,000 gallons per minute of water for cooling, and an immeasurable amount of electricity for power. Groves planned the site to be at least 20 miles from any town of one thousand inhabitants (the nearest real town was Pasco) and at least 10 miles from any highway. At Hanford, scientists were attempting to turn uranium into plutonium – another fissile material they hoped could be weaponized.

Everything Groves set in motion was potentially dangerous and extraordinarily expensive, and the end results of this work were unknown. "Never in history has anyone embarking on an important undertaking

had so little certainty about how to proceed as we had then," he recorded.

Keeping this work secret from the American public required the
strictest of security measures, and a bit of luck. Roosevelt had agreed
with Churchill at a conference in Quebec in August 1943 to share all
atomic technology with the British, that the two nations would work
together on the project, which Churchill code-named "tube alloys" in
his top-secret correspondence with the president. And yet the work at
Los Alamos, Oak Ridge, and Hanford remained mostly an American
phenomenon. The early army budget appropriations were not nearly
enough to pay for the project, so Stimson approached a select group of
congressional leaders. He informed them of the secret work, and they
were able to pilot funds through the Senate and the House without dis-
closing the money's purpose.

Even two years after Pearl Harbor, among the highest echelons of
government, few knew anything of this work's existence. Jimmy Byrnes,
the "Assistant President," did not find out about the project until the
summer of 1943, during a conversation with Roosevelt in the Oval Office. At this time, according to Byrnes, Roosevelt believed the Nazis were
ahead of the Americans in the race to produce a bomb. Byrnes was as-
tounded "with the scientists' prediction of what atomic energy would
do," he recorded.

By the end of September 1944, Secretary of War Stimson had been
informed of the following information regarding the atomic bomb, in
a memorandum written by Arthur Compton of the National Defense
Research Committee: "(1) By next summer this will become a matter of
great military importance. (2) The art will expand rapidly after the war,
and the military aspects may become overwhelming. (3) This country has
a temporary advantage which may disappear, or even reverse, if there is
a secret arms race on this subject." Stimson struggled with this information; the Manhattan Project had become not just a military matter but
an existential one.

"We were up against some very big decisions," Stimson wrote in his
diary. "The time is approaching when we can no longer avoid them and
when events may force us into the public on the subject. Our thoughts
went right down to the bottom facts of human nature, morals and government."

All the while, Roosevelt feared what the Nazis were doing. If Hitler produced a bomb first, the face of humanity would never be the same. On December 4, 1943, the *New York Times* published an article quoting an official from German High Command saying that the Nazis "intended by one fell, drastic stroke" to strike back against the Allies, that "the retaliation will be so powerful . . . [it] will find quite a different and surprising expression spiritually as well as politically." The German official concluded: "Mankind is not far from the point where it can at will blow up half the globe."

Were the Nazis building an atomic bomb? If so, could they complete and deliver the weapon before the Allies had crushed them for good?

The secretary of war's last meeting with Roosevelt on the subject had been less than a month before Roosevelt's death. They discussed fears that the whole bomb project would fail, that the scientists had "sold the president a lemon." Roosevelt had also received a memo from Jimmy Byrnes on this subject. "I understand that the expenditures from the Manhattan Project are approaching $2 billion with no definite assurance yet of production," Byrnes wrote. He was worried. "If the project proves a failure," he warned, "it will then be subjected to relentless investigation and criticism."

Admiral Leahy, the nation's highest-ranking military officer, was vocal with his opinion to President Roosevelt. The weapon, Leahy believed, was not going to work.

///

Such was the state of the atomic bomb on April 25, when Truman learned of its details for the first time. When he asked for a timeline for a bomb to be ready, the only thing Stimson could offer was "within four months."

Truman fired questions at Stimson and Groves. The president was amazed that an operation of this size, requiring $2 billion, massive forces of labor and materials on three built-from-scratch sites spread out across the country (Los Alamos, Oak Ridge, Hanford), could have remained so secret. Stimson suggested a few members of Congress be sent on a secret mission to see the plant at Oak Ridge, Tennessee; this would aid in clearing secret appropriations for the project in the future. Truman agreed to the idea.

The president understood how this weapon could force Japan to surrender unconditionally. But there were political matters to consider, and a terrifying future potentially, after the war. As Groves recalled Truman's questioning during this meeting: "A great deal of emphasis was placed on foreign relations, and particularly on the Russian situation." Stimson was sure that the USSR was spying on the work at Los Alamos, and – at this point, with Nazi Germany's imminent collapse – he believed that the Soviets were the only nation capable of putting such a bomb into production within the next five years. Stimson concluded that the world could "be eventually at the mercy of such a weapon. In other words, modern civilization might be completely destroyed."

///

Soon after Truman's meeting with Stimson and Groves on the atomic bomb, his day took an unexpected turn. The first sign of the Nazi surrender reached the White House on this afternoon, April 25. Truman received word that Heinrich Himmler, head of the Gestapo and one of the chief architects of the Nazi Final Solution, had submitted a surrender proposal to a high-ranking member of the Swedish Red Cross. Whether or not this surrender proposal had any validity was unclear. At 1:40 p.m. Truman left the White House in a motorcade bound for the Pentagon, where he was ushered into the secretary of war's office, and from there to a secret communications room.

Surrounded by some of his highest-ranking advisors (Leahy, Marshall, Admiral King), Truman picked up a telephone and was patched through to Britain. He heard for the first time the unmistakable voice of Prime Minister Winston Churchill, crackly over a secure transatlantic phone line. A transcript of this conversation exists.

"Is that you, Mr. President?"

Truman said, "This is the president, Mr. Prime Minister."

"How glad I am to hear your voice."

"Thank you very much, and I am glad to hear yours."

Churchill told Truman that Himmler had approached Count Folke Bernadotte of Sweden, claiming that Hitler had suffered a cerebral hemorrhage and was not expected to survive long. Thus Himmler was offering the surrender of the German forces to the United States and Britain. However, nothing was said of the Russian forces, who had on this very day surrounded Berlin completely.

Truman said, "I think he [Himmler] should be forced to surrender to all three governments – Russia, you, and the United States. I don't think we ought to even consider a piecemeal surrender." If the American and British governments were to accept any terms without the approval of the Soviet Union, Truman would infuriate his military ally, Joseph Stalin. It looked like the Germans were trying to "sow discord between the Western Allies and Russia," Truman said into the phone. Churchill agreed. The United States and Britain would not entertain any such surrender offer from the Nazis.

"We are walking hand in hand together," Churchill said.

"Well, I want to continue just that."

"In fact," concluded Churchill, "I am following your lead, backing up whatever you do on the matter."

"Thank you," Truman said. "Good night."

Immediately after this conversation, Truman received confirmation from the United States ambassador to Sweden that Himmler had in fact made contact. Truman cabled Stalin later that day informing him of this extraordinary development. He promised that no surrender terms would be considered outside of unconditional surrender to all three Allied governments. But it appeared that the death knell of the Third Reich was at hand.

///

At the very moment that Truman was speaking via secure Pentagon telephone with Churchill, at hotels throughout San Francisco, the delegations of nearly fifty nations were hurrying through final preparations to launch the United Nations peace conference. The opening ceremony started at 4:30 p.m. Pacific time at San Francisco's Opera House – a monument to Beaux-Arts architecture where for the past few years operas had been staged under the strict supervision of air-raid wardens.

The Americans, headed by Secretary of State Stettinius, had set up headquarters at the Fairmont Hotel's penthouse, while the British checked into the Mark Hopkins Hotel. The Soviets, led by Molotov, had taken up on a ship docked in San Francisco Bay, for security purposes. (Reportedly the ship was loaded with secret communications technology, and endless caviar and vodka.) The conference had been years in the making and was set to begin amid disillusion due to the declining American-Soviet relations, most specifically regarding the government in Poland.

"The conference began in the midst of deep disturbances and tensions," wrote a *New Yorker* correspondent covering the event. "You could feel them in the roots of your hair. Over the city the Polish question hovered like a foul bird." It was up to Stettinius more than any other figure to iron out the problems with the Russians and see the United Nations to the finish line. "I'm counting on you," Truman had told him. "I have complete confidence in you."

Just before 7:30 p.m. eastern time, Truman walked into the Diplomatic Reception Room in the White House, where Roosevelt had delivered his fireside chats over radio to the nation. Radio equipment was all set up, microphones with cords snaking along the floor. Truman sat at a desk with a speech spread out before him. His address would be broadcast directly into the Opera House in San Francisco, where already the delegations had hushed to silence in anticipation, and over radio at home and abroad. His comments were brief and to the point. Invoking the "great humanitarian" Roosevelt, Truman told the gathering in the Opera House: "You members of this Conference are to be the architects of the better world. In your hands rests our future . . .

"The world has experienced a revival of an old faith in the everlasting moral force of justice," Truman said. "At no time in history has there been a more important Conference, nor a more necessary meeting, than this one in San Francisco, which you are opening today."

San Francisco had become a litmus test for American-Soviet tension. Senator Arthur Vandenberg, who would do much of the negotiating by Stettinius's side as a key figure in the American delegation, wrote bluntly of his disillusion in his diary: "It would be a relatively simple matter to dynamite the new Peace League . . . What would *that* do for Poland? It would simply leave Russia in complete possession of everything she wants . . . There would be no hope for justice except through World War Number Three immediately."

This was not the first time the international community had attempted to create a global peace league. Truman could recall as a young man reading avidly of Woodrow Wilson's attempts to convince Congress to embrace the treaty of the League of Nations, after World War I. The League of Nations would save the world from future wars, Wilson argued. But Wilson failed in his mission to get Congress on board, and the League of Nations failed, as a result. The league's collapse crushed Wilson physically (he suffered a stroke) and — many believed — had a great deal to do with the war now being fought all over the world.

Truman could only hope that this time the new peace league would survive, and that it would fulfill its role: to prevent war. After his meeting about the atomic bomb earlier in the day, he knew that the stakes in global affairs were rising fast, beyond anything that Woodrow Wilson had ever confronted.

One can only surmise as to his conversation with Bess when he returned to the Blair House that night. It had been a long day. He had been fully briefed on the war's greatest secret for the first time. He had spoken to Winston Churchill for the first time, regarding the imminent collapse of the Third Reich. He had addressed the United Nations Conference and the world via radio. He could only imagine what kind of surprises tomorrow would bring.

ON THE SAME DAY Truman first learned the detailed story of the bomb, outside Torgau, a war-ravaged village twenty-eight miles northeast of Leipzig in Germany, an American officer named William Robertson of Los Angeles stepped over a fallen girder from a destroyed bridge at the Elbe River and introduced himself to a Russian soldier, patting the Russian on the back. The local time was 4:45 p.m. Second Lieutenant Robertson, from General Courtney Hodges's U.S. First Army, reached out his hand to shake the Russian's.

"Put it there," the American said.

It was the handshake heard around the world.

Minutes later a Russian voice came over the radio in the Americans' encampment: "This is the Red Army. This is the Red Army calling the American Army. We are calling to establish radio contact."

Eisenhower's armies and the Soviet forces had met. They had cut Nazi Germany in two, joining the eastern and western fronts.

Also on this same day, some sixty miles eastward, Russian troops began to storm neighborhoods of Berlin, which had been reduced to piles of rubble by the Allied bombing campaigns. The city "looked more like a giant junk heap today than the heart of the Capitol of the Third Reich," wrote one embedded American war correspondent. The Germans continued to return fire, but it was now clear in short time that the Russians would capture Berlin. Somewhere within the city, Hitler was hiding.

Truman, Stalin, and Churchill had already agreed on a statement each government would issue upon news that the Russian and Anglo-American armies had joined at the Elbe River. From Washington, Truman released the statement on April 27. Stalin did the same in Moscow, where residents' ears were soon assaulted by twenty-four salvos of ceremonial gunfire, the shots punctuating the jingle of thousands of bells ringing all over the city. In London, Churchill made the announcement simultaneously, and Londoners poured from their homes to gather in the streets.

"The last faint, desperate hope of Hitler and his gangster Government has been extinguished," Truman's statement read. Then: "This is not the hour of final victory in Europe, but the hour draws near, the hour for which all the American people, all the British people and all the Soviet people have toiled and prayed so long."

Over the next few days events moved swiftly. On April 28, the day after Truman released his Elbe Day statement, German officials appeared at Allied headquarters in Italy, where they were handed paperwork documenting the surrender terms for the Nazis in that country. Representatives of the American, British, and Russian armies were present. On this same day, at Giulino di Mezzegra near Lake Como, Italian partisans shot to death former Fascist dictator Benito Mussolini along with his young mistress, Clara Petacci, and seventeen other Fascist followers. Mussolini – who had aligned himself with Hitler and the Axis powers and had hurled Italy into the war with all the resources he could muster – had been caught trying to flee into Switzerland. His last words before execution were, reportedly, "No! No!" The *partisani* took his corpse to Milan, and there he was left on display in a city square. Locals lined up to spit on Mussolini's bullet-pierced head. One reporter described the scene: "The brains which took Fascist Italy into the war oozed onto the filth of a dirt plot in the center of Milan."

On April 29, one day after the Mussolini execution, German military officials – wearing civilian clothes – signed the surrender orders at Allied headquarters in Caserta, and the war in Italy ended. Truman gave a statement that Japan as well as Germany should "understand the meaning of these events."

On this same day United States forces liberated the Nazi death camp at Dachau. Among their findings there were more than thirty railroad cars containing decomposing corpses. More than thirty thousand prisoners were living at Dachau at the time of liberation.

The following day, April 30, an unconfirmed report came over BBC Radio in Britain, claiming that "Hitler died at noon today in his underground headquarters in the Tiergarten in Berlin with [propaganda minister Joseph] Goebbels at his bedside." One day later, radio stations within Germany also reported that Hitler was dead. While no officials were confirming any reports, Truman received word from army intelligence that the story was true. At the time he was informed, he was lying on a table in his bathing suit getting a massage in the White House, surrounded by chatting aides, when a messenger delivered the news in a memorandum on a yellow piece of paper. Truman read the memo, and the group discussed the news, their language surely peppered with epithets. "The words were the comments of men in a bathhouse," recalled one man present.

During Truman's regular press conference on May 2, a reporter put forward the question: "Mr. President, would you care to comment on the death of Adolf Hitler reported, or Mussolini?"

"Well, of course, the two principal war criminals will not have to come to trial," Truman said, the room jammed as usual. "And I am very happy they are out of the way."

"Well, does that mean, sir, that we know officially that Hitler is dead?"

"Yes . . . We have the best — on the best authority possible to obtain at this time that Hitler is dead. But how he died we are not — we are not familiar with the details as yet."

(The facts were as follows: Hitler's wife, Eva Braun, whom he had married on April 29 in a private ceremony in his secret Berlin bunker, committed suicide by swallowing prussic acid, on April 30. With her slumped body to his left, Hitler shot himself in his right temple with his 7.65-millimeter Walther. He was ten days past his fifty-sixth birthday. Nazi propaganda minister Joseph Goebbels followed the next day, shooting his wife and then himself. The Goebbels's six children were poisoned. While the bodies of Hitler, Goebbels, and their spouses were burned, the Goebbels children were found laid next to one another unblemished, as if asleep in a bed. All were wearing white.)

On the same day that Truman acknowledged Hitler's death, Stalin announced officially that Berlin had fallen. The Red Army had taken the German capital. Also on May 2, Eisenhower cabled the combined chiefs of staff (the top military leaders in both Washington and London) from Allied headquarters in Reims, France, advising that General Blumentritt, a German group commander, had made contact, promising to surrender his group the following day. Eisenhower noted that he would make sure Russian general Susloparov would be informed and invited to the proceeding.

Over the next days Truman received reports, sometimes hourly, on the collapse of the Third Reich. The Americans feared what the Nazis would do to U.S. war prisoners still being held. Truman gave a statement on the matter, and this statement was later dropped in massive numbers of leaflets from airplanes over Germany: "Any person guilty of maltreating or allowing any Allied prisoners of war, internees or deported citizens to be maltreated, whether in battle zone, on lines of communication, in a camp, hospital, prison or elsewhere, will be ruthlessly pursued and brought to punishment." Eisenhower reported that German soldiers and commanders had begun surrendering en masse to the Americans and British to be taken prisoner, because they feared torture and execution if they were taken prisoner by the Russians. "All resistance collapsed," Eisenhower recorded. "Swarms of Germans . . . began giving themselves up to the Anglo-American armies. American troops standing on the Elbe daily received these prisoners by the thousands."

All that remained before the war in Europe would end was the formalities of the final unconditional surrender – still a week away.

In the wake of the Third Reich's collapse, Europe was left annihilated, and American officials were just beginning to understand the depths of the despair. In France, according to the nation's Ministry of Public Health, more than 50 percent of children in industrial areas had rickets, while 70 to 80 percent suffered diminished growth due to malnutrition. A third of children in Belgium were tubercular. Truman called on Herbert Hoover – the only living former American president – to report on Europe's food problem. Hoover had made similar studies during World War I, and so he set to work again. Among his reports, he made the following conclusion: "It is now 11:59 on the clock of starvation." White House special counsel Judge Sam Rosenman had gone on a fact-finding mission in Europe, and his report landed with a thud on half the desks in Washington.

"The needs of the liberated countries of Northwest Europe are grave," Rosenman wrote. It would fall to the United States to feed the world's hungry, and quickly. "It is the established policy of this Government to accept this responsibility as far as it is possible to do so."

Soon the four powers – the United States, Britain, Russia, France – would move into their respective zones within Germany. Only now this occupation plan seemed fraught with danger. When it was made, the Russians appeared a trusted ally, with expectations of friendship and postwar collaboration. Now a different image of Stalin and his Red Army had come into focus. The Soviets had pushed Axis forces over a thousand miles across the continent in a campaign of savage fighting; rumors of these Red Army soldiers' behavior had reached the West, stories of pillage and rape reminiscent of conquering armies from medieval times.

"I fear terrible things have happened during the Russian advance through Germany to the Elbe," Churchill cabled Truman. "The proposed withdrawal of the United States Army to the occupational lines which were arranged with the Russians and Americans . . . would mean the tide of Russian domination sweeping forward 120 miles on a front of 300 or 400 miles." Poland, Austria, Czechoslovakia, the frontier from the North Cape in Norway across the Baltic – all this territory could easily fall into the Soviets' grasp. The Russian frontier "would include all the great capitals of Middle Europe, including Berlin, Vienna, Budapest, Belgrade, Bucharest, and Sofia." Churchill concluded: "This constitutes an event in the history of Europe to which there has been no parallel."

///

Throughout the final days of April, as Truman received updates from Eisenhower's headquarters in Europe, he was also receiving regular reports from the other side of the globe, in San Francisco. If the United Nations Conference was a litmus test of American-Soviet relations, the initial readings were frightening.

The Russians and the Americans could not agree on the first matter: who would chair the conference. As host, the American delegation should chair the meetings, Stettinius insisted. That was tradition for the hosting nation at international conferences. Molotov would not stand for it, arguing for four equal conference presidents, from the United States, Britain, Russia, and China. If the two countries could not agree on this simple matter, how were they going to come to agreement on a charter for a new world peace organization?

From the Fairmont Hotel, an exasperated Edward Stettinius called the president. He asked if he should "stick to my guns" and demand that, as host, he remain the conference's presiding officer. "It is precedent," Stettinius told Truman. "There never has been an international conference where the host is not presiding officer."

"Stick to your guns," said Truman.

The delegations faced so many disagreements in the opening days at San Francisco, it seemed the UN Conference was destined not to bring the world together but to push the major forces farther apart. The two powers quarreled over which countries should be recognized and invited to the conference, which should get votes in the UN Security Council, and whether or not a world peace organization should take precedence over already-established regional treaties. Still, Poland remained the crux of the problem. During the first days of May, a shocking news story further complicated the Polish situation. Sixteen members of the Polish underground had been invited to Moscow for negotiations; once they arrived, they were arrested and had since vanished. Their lives were presumed to be in grave danger. The American delegation in San Francisco was meeting in the penthouse suite at the Fairmont Hotel when the news arrived, via telephone call. "A serious shadow fell across the meeting," Senator Vandenberg wrote in his diary. "This is bad business."

And still, Molotov was demanding that the Soviet puppet regime in Poland be recognized and invited to the conference. Stettinius flatly refused. The only thing the delegations in San Francisco could agree on was how beautiful the city was.

One night early in the conference, Chip Bohlen of the State Department walked into the bar at the Fairmont and found Jan Masaryk, the Czech foreign minister, sipping a whiskey and soda. "Bohlen," Masaryk said, "what can one do with these Russians?" Without waiting for a response, Masaryk said, "Out of the clear blue sky I got a note from Molotov saying Czechoslovakia must vote for the Soviet proposition in regard to Poland, or else forfeit the friendship of the Soviet government. What kind of way is that to behave to a country that is trying to be friendly?" He paused. "You can be on your knees and this is not enough for the Russians."

ON THE MORNING OF MAY 7 the Trumans moved into the White House — Harry, Bess, Margaret, and Bess's mother, Mrs. Wallace. It had required twenty trucks to haul Eleanor Roosevelt's possessions out of the executive mansion. The Trumans required one to move in, for they owned very little, and most of what they did own was in Missouri. Truman had never had the money to buy his own house. Now he was living in the most famous house in America.

The home smelled of fresh paint — Nile-green hallways, off-white rooms, with a cream color for the president's second-floor bedroom and lavender-gray for the First Lady's suite. (Harry and Bess would sleep in separate bedrooms, as was custom in the White House.) Getting the pianos (one for Harry, one for Margaret) into the house was a challenge; movers had to take off the legs and swing them through a second-story window. Bess had supervised the purchase of new furniture and other necessities with the help of a Kansas City decorator. A bill for $419.45 from the Washington department store Woodward & Lothrop — covering everything from eight shower curtains to a new mattress and box spring — was paid by the National Park Service, which was responsible for the White House. The National Gallery provided paintings on loan for the mansion's walls.

There was much to learn. Edith Helm, the White House social secretary, was on hand to help. As was Mrs. Nesbitt, who ran the kitchen, and who, the Trumans would soon learn, had a habit of serving overcooked brussels sprouts with unfailing regularity. Tall and kind-faced, Alonzo Fields was the first African American to serve as head White House butler, having gotten the job under Herbert Hoover thirteen years earlier, just before the Roosevelts moved in. In the basement, the White House's nervous chief of mails, Ira Smith, carefully inspected all incoming packages with a staff of twenty-two. "Cranks are just as likely to use the postal service as any other method of trying to get explosives into the president's office," Smith admitted.

The White House staff — housekeepers, servants, gardeners, carpenters, a total of thirty-two, with head usher Howell Crim ranking highest — was paid out of a $150,000 annual appropriation. The president was responsible for food, however, for his family and for the staff. For the first time in his life, Truman was making a lot of money; the president's salary was $75,000, up from $15,000 as VP. But food for the staff and for personal guests could get expensive. Mr. Crim advised Truman to set aside $1,000 a month for food. That was half as much as the Roosevelts allowed, but as Crim told the president, surely the Trumans would not live on the grand scale that the Roosevelts did. Mrs. Roosevelt had left the kitchen well stocked, so Bess wrote her a check and a thank-you note.

The home had an unmistakable aura. "Visiting the White House in person is a little like meeting a celebrity face to face," Margaret later wrote. "You get impressions and feelings that a newspaper . . . can't communicate." Every president except George Washington had resided here. One could walk through the winding warrens from room to room and dream of what the place looked like when Thomas Jefferson lived here, with his abundant collections of fossils, musical instruments, books, and wine. Or during Andrew Jackson's administration, when the wildest party ever thrown in the White House went off, a post-inaugural bacchanal in 1829 where the promise of free liquor lured an unexpected mob.

"Everything seems larger than life," Margaret wrote, "a kind of waking dream, outside time, yet paradoxically immersed in time . . . The White House continues to envelop you the way history surrounds nations, a huge silent presence that is inescapable."

The mansion's main entrance came through the North Portico into a large lobby. Andrew Jackson had once kept a fourteen-hundred-pound wheel of cheddar cheese in this room — a gift from one of his supporters. Some claimed that on a hot day, you could still sense its odor. The Green Room contained the George P. A. Healy presidential portraits of John Quincy Adams, Martin Van Buren, and James K. Polk. The China Room held nearly three hundred pieces of chinaware, silverware, and glassware, displayed in fragile glass cases. Margaret Truman had asked that the "dark, clunky furniture" in her sitting room be moved. This furniture, it turned out, had been purchased during Abraham Lincoln's administration, and the Trumans had it moved to a room on the opposite end of the house, into a space renamed the Lincoln Bedroom — an ironic name, since Lincoln never slept in it. (He had used this space as his office, and it was in this room where, on January 1, 1863, he signed the documents that emancipated slaves in the eleven seceded Southern states.)

The current version of the West Wing was built in 1902, under Theodore Roosevelt. It housed the president's office, the Cabinet Room, an appointments lobby, and offices for assistants. Truman had grown to like walking to work from the Blair House, but his morning commute would be a lot shorter now.

The Trumans moved into the White House just in time for Harry to celebrate his sixty-first birthday the following day. As history would record, there would be quite a festive party.

///

"At 0241 hours this morning," General Eisenhower cabled the War Department on May 7, the day the Trumans moved into the White House, "the German representative, General Jodl, signed the instrument of military surrender." Hostilities were scheduled to end one minute after midnight on the night of May 8/9, Eisenhower reported.

The three Allied governments had made arrangements to announce the unconditional surrender of Nazi Germany simultaneously. However, Stalin refused to make the announcement. He was getting reports that the Nazis were still fighting the Russians, and as it would turn out, these reports were true. So deep was the hatred between these armies, the Germans and Russians would not let go of the shooting war. And yet, German radio stations were already announcing the unconditional surrender. Already, on May 7, a half million Americans had crowded Manhattan's Times Square to celebrate. Churchill demanded to make a statement immediately, but Truman would not allow it — not without Stalin's agreement. Admiral Leahy spoke at length with Churchill by secure phone from the Pentagon. Churchill was furious.

"What is the use of me and the president looking to be the only two people in the world who don't know what is going on?" Churchill barked at Leahy over the phone. "I feel it absolutely necessary to go off at 6 p.m., and I will telegraph to Stalin the very message that I am sending to you, in view of the fact that the Germans have blasted it all over the world."

In the White House the press corps had grown nearly hysterical, and

Truman was forced to issue a statement: "I have agreed with the London and Moscow governments that I will make NO announcement with reference to surrender of the enemy forces in Europe or elsewhere until a simultaneous statement can be made by the three governments. Until then, there is nothing I can or will say to you."

Churchill was forced to wait as well.

That night Truman slept in the White House for the first time, in the bed where Roosevelt had slept for the previous twelve-plus years. Mamma Truman and the president's sister, Mary Jane, would be arriving in four days to visit, so they could see the new home. Truman awoke early on May 8, as usual, and soon after sunrise he stole a moment to write a letter.

> The White House
> Washington
>
> Dear Mamma & Mary: —
>
> I am sixty-one this morning, and I slept in the president's room in the White House last night. They have finished the painting and have some of the furniture in place. I'm hoping it will all be ready for you by Friday . . . This will be a historic day. At 9:00 o'clock this morning I must make a broadcast to the country: announcing the German surrender. The papers were signed yesterday morning and hostilities will cease on all fronts at midnight tonight. Isn't that some birthday present?
>
> Lots & lots of love to you both,
> Harry

By 8:35 a.m. Truman was at his desk, and already his office was crowded with members of his cabinet, Senate and congressional leaders, military representatives including General Marshall and Admiral Leahy in crisp uniforms, and Bess and Margaret, all of whom sat in chairs behind and to the side of the president. Senator Kenneth McKellar of Tennessee offered Truman a special greeting that morning.

"You're forty years old!"

"Yes, forty years old — plus!" Truman responded, and giddy laughter filled the room.

Truman gave the signal, and a White House usher opened the office door. Newspaper reporters charged through. "Good morning," Truman said, rising from his seat. "I sure made you all get up this morning, didn't I? [More laughter.] Yes, indeed . . . Still at it, I see . . . Still coming, I see . . ."

The room was jammed tight. A voice shouted, "All in," and Truman began his remarks.

"I want to start off by reading you a little statement," he said. "This is a solemn but glorious hour. General Eisenhower informs me that the forces of Germany have surrendered to the United Nations. The flags of freedom fly all over Europe. It's celebrating my birthday, too — today, too."

Voices shouted, "Happy birthday, Mr. President!"

Truman hushed the crowd. "Our rejoicing is sobered and subdued," he continued, "by a supreme consciousness of the terrible price we have paid to rid the world of Hitler and his evil band. Let us not forget, my fellow Americans, the sorrow and the heartache which today abide in the homes of so many of our neighbors."

The president gave a clear message to the enemy: "We are going to be in a position where we can turn the greatest war machine in the history of the world loose on the Japanese." He demanded unconditional surrender of the enemy in the Far East.

When he finished, the news reporters made a mad scramble for the door. "Did you ever see such a rush!?" Senator McKellar said to the president. Merriman Smith of the United Press — one of the nation's most revered Washington correspondents — tripped and fell to the floor, fracturing his arm. But still the stampede continued. Truman headed to the Diplomatic Reception Room, where he was going to read his statement again over the radio.

"Our victory is but half-won," he said. "The West is free, but the East is still in bondage to the treacherous tyranny of the Japanese." Millions heard these words, huddled around their radios. Among them, in her home in Hyde Park, New York, Eleanor Roosevelt listened in. "I can almost hear my husband's voice make that announcement, for I heard him repeat it so often," she wrote of this moment in her newspaper column. She could not celebrate, for Americans were still fighting and dying for the cause. "Some of my own sons," she wrote, "with millions of others, are still in danger."

For the rest of the day, Truman received visitors, including the ambassador from Argentina and Governor Jimmie Davis of Louisiana, in short meetings, mostly fifteen minutes long. In the afternoon he was able to squeeze in a birthday party — a toast of bourbon with friends.

Across the country, celebrations were subdued. Bars and churches filled wall to wall. In Washington the War Department ordered all posts to maintain normal schedules. Traders on the New York Stock Exchange and Chicago's Board of Trade paused for two minutes of silence, then dove back into the heat of battle. Detroit's war factories remained open, as did the steel mills in Pittsburgh. All business in Cleveland closed down, while in Chicago, industry proceeded "at half-pace," the *Wall Street Journal* reported.

In Britain, where buildings still lay in rubble from Nazi bombers, the scene was far wilder. "There are no words," the American radioman Edward R. Murrow reported from London. "Just a sort of rumbling roar. London is celebrating today in a city which became a symbol. The scars of war are all about. There is no lack of serious, solemn faces. Their thoughts are their own." As Murrow concluded, on this day much of Britain was focused on America, for the United States would carry the weight of creating the peace for the future world and, to a large extent, aiding the victims suffering from years of explosive violence — the hungry, sick, and displaced. "Our nation," Murrow said, "which was created by men who wanted to leave Europe, is the center of the hopes and some of the fears of millions who are in Europe today."

There was no celebration in Moscow, for even now after the surrender documents had been signed, Nazi soldiers were still firing upon the Red Army.

Truman finished his work on VE-day beset with worry. The news from San Francisco was bad. The Russian and American delegations clashed at every turn. On his desk in the Oval Office at that very moment, statistics spelled out a horrific bloodletting on the isles of the Pacific. To capture Iwo Jima, eight square miles of volcanic rock, the marines had suffered 25,489 casualties, roughly a third of the landing force. At Okinawa — still now ablaze with military action — the statistics were even worse.

"Things have moved at a terrific rate since April 12," he wrote his mother and his sister on this day. "So far luck has been with me. I hope it keeps up. It can't stay with me forever however and I hope when the mistake comes it won't be too great to remedy."

///

The day after VE-day, at 9:30 a.m., a group of men led by Dr. Vannevar Bush and Dr. Karl T. Compton of the National Defense Research Committee arrived at the secretary of war's office in the Pentagon, along with General Groves, for the first meeting of the Interim Committee. Secretary of War Stimson had created the committee, with Truman's approval, as a think tank to gauge the pace of the Manhattan Project and to advise the president on all issues regarding the atomic bomb, military and political. The bomb had become a Promethean undertaking; scientists were unlocking the secrets of the universe. What would be the challenges of completing the weapon and delivering it over a target? What were the consequences of using this science in ways that generations hence could judge as singularly evil, rather than good?

Once this project was no longer secret – after the bomb had been born and employed – Congress would likely build a new committee to "supervise, regulate, and control the entire field," according to Stimson. Until that time, this committee would serve as the government's primary policy advisor on the subject. Thus its name – Interim. Truman had asked that he have a personal representative present, and Stimson had suggested Jimmy Byrnes, who was in the secretary of war's office this morning, May 9.

Stimson began the meeting with the following words: "Gentlemen, it is our responsibility to recommend action that may turn the course of civilization."

The discussion that followed got everyone up to speed on the progress of this project. Already, Groves had a Target Committee working on the selection of cities in Japan. This committee had come to some conclusions. The B-29 Superfortress would have a fifteen-hundred-mile range while carrying the estimated weight of the bomb. That would be enough distance to place the weapon on a primary target inside mainland Japan, from an air base in the Mariana Islands. Visual bombing was essential, so that firsthand accounts of the detonation could be made. The middle of the afternoon would be the best time to deliver the bomb, and weather would be a major factor. Groves was not prepared to allow hazardous weather to jeopardize this $2 billion enterprise, or to eclipse the explosion from the camera equipment. Groves thought there would be a bomb ready in July, August, or September, but those were the worst weather months in Japan.

He had a list of thirty-three primary targets. First on the list as of early May: Hiroshima. "Hiroshima is the largest untouched target not on the 21st Bomber command priority list," the Target Committee had reported. Thus, it was a virgin target, so the damage of the bomb could be gauged with accuracy.

As for delivery, the army's 509th Composite Group had been training at the newly constructed Wendover Army Air Base in Utah, for a top-secret mission, with specially outfitted Superfortresses stripped of all their gun turrets, except one in the tail, so the aircraft could accommodate the weight of the bomb. These B-29s had especially rugged fuel-injected engines, electrically controlled reversible propellers, and a host of other modifications to make them the finest, most technologically advanced four-engine bombers in the army air forces. Pilots had been practicing sharp diving turns and bombing runs with hyper-fast getaways. Recently the 509th had moved to the South Pacific, continuing training at an air base on the island of Tinian. Not one man in the 509th had any knowledge yet of what he was training for, with the exception of one — a crack pilot who had been specifically chosen to fly the B-29 that would drop the first bomb, Colonel Paul Tibbets of Quincy, Illinois.

Soon the bomb would be ready, members of the Interim Committee believed, and so would the delivery system. Sitting in the first Interim Committee meeting as Truman's personal representative, Jimmy Byrnes found himself "thoroughly frightened" as he listened to Groves and Stimson deliver details on the progress. "I had sufficient imagination to visualize the danger to our country when some other country possessed such a weapon," Byrnes recorded. "Thinking of the country most likely to become unfriendly to us." Byrnes was thinking of the Soviet Union.

The committee's first meeting ended after ninety minutes, with more meetings scheduled throughout the month of May. Never during this first meeting was the subject of whether or not to use the weapon raised. For all present, it seemed self-evident that it would be used — if in fact the scientists at Los Alamos could complete it.

Immediately after the committee left the secretary of war's office, another group of men was entering. Twelve congressmen walked into Stimson's office, along with General George Marshall and six personnel from the War Department. The congressmen had just returned from Europe, where they had toured liberated Nazi death camps, at General Eisenhower's request, and they now planned to report their findings to the secretary of war. For Stimson, who was presiding, the juxtaposition of this meeting with the Interim Committee meeting just before it made his day unlike any the seventy-seven-year-old could recall, in his decades of public service. The senators and congressmen began their testimony.

"We saw, of course, what everybody has seen there," Senator Alben Barkley reported, "the instruments of torture, the starvations, barbarisms, unsanitary conditions, dead, cremations, strangulations, everything that has been represented as being there . . . We found in that camp [Buchenwald] where they had a crematory that had six ovens, six compartments, and the capacity of that crematory was to burn 200 a day." Barkley told of a room with forty-eight hooks, where prisoners were strangled with rope, and if they did not die fast enough, they were beaten with mallets to quicken the process. "They told us that one day they had executed 126 of these people on these hooks."

"By strangulation?" asked Stimson.

"Yes, and by the use of this mallet."

The senators and congressmen continued with details "so gruesome that it is difficult to realize that such a thing could happen," as Barkley put it. Congressman James Richards of South Carolina ended the meeting on a sickening note. "Many of the inmates of the camps we inspected," he said, "testified to us that other camps were much worse to be in than the camps we saw."

Thus far, a majority of the Nazi archcriminals were still on the loose.

///

The same week as the first Interim Committee meeting was held, Truman received a cable from Churchill regarding "U.J." — Uncle Joe, the nickname that Churchill and Roosevelt had given to Stalin, an attempt at comic relief. "It seems to me that matters can hardly be carried farther by correspondence," Churchill wrote Truman, "and that, as soon as possible, there should be a meeting of the three heads of governments." The war had seen two famed Big Three conferences, where Roosevelt, Stalin, and

Churchill conferred in person under strict secrecy – Tehran (1943) and Yalta (earlier in 1945). Churchill's cable was the impetus for what would become Potsdam, the third and final Big Three World War II meeting.

The Russian situation was continuing to decline. The Red Army had liberated Austria from the Nazis, and Stalin had now installed a new government in Vienna, without consulting the other Allies. The Red Army had closed off Austria's borders and grounded American airplanes. Would Austria become another Poland? Truman cabled Stalin directly: "I am unable to understand why the Soviet authorities are now refusing to permit American and Allied representatives to proceed to Vienna."

In Bulgaria, according to a State Department memorandum to the president, the Soviets, "using one excuse or another, have imposed severe restrictions on the actions and movements of the members of the U.S. Representation . . . They will allow no planes or personnel to enter or leave Bulgaria without previous clearance from them . . . It appears that a concerted effort is being made by the Russians to keep the influence and prestige of the United States at an absolute minimum with the goal of increasing the prestige of the completely Communist-dominated Bulgarian Government and the USSR."

Regarding Poland, Churchill had transmitted another stern cable to Stalin calling for a new Democratic regime in Warsaw. Stalin had written back, and this communiqué was forwarded to Truman. Stalin indicated that Churchill's attitude "excludes the possibility of an agreed solution of the Polish question." Stalin admitted that the Soviets had arrested the sixteen members of the Polish underground. They were "undergoing investigation" for "planning and carrying out diversionary acts" and "maintaining illegal wireless transmitting stations." Their safety could not be assured.

The dark shadow of Stalinist communism was cast across eastern Europe. It appeared that Ambassador Harriman's fear – that the Russians were planning "a barbarian invasion of Europe" – was becoming fact.

Truman agreed with the prime minister: correspondence could only go so far. It was imperative that the three leaders meet in person. "There should now be no valid excuse for Stalin's refusing to come west toward us," Truman wrote Churchill. With regard to timing, the president noted that he would not be able to leave the country "before the end of the fiscal year (June 30)."

Churchill urged Truman to plan this tripartite meeting sooner. "Mr. President," he cabled on May 11, "in these next two months the gravest matters in the world will be decided." The next day Churchill cabled again:

> I am profoundly concerned about the European situation. I learn that half the American Air Force in Europe has already begun to move to the Pacific theatre. The newspapers are full of the great movements of the American armies out of Europe . . . Anyone can see that in a very short space of time our armed power on the Continent will have vanished, except for moderate forces to hold down Germany. Meanwhile, what is to happen about Russia? . . . I feel deep anxiety because of their misinterpretation of the Yalta decisions, their attitude towards Poland, their overwhelming influence in the Balkans, excepting Greece, the difficulties they make about Vienna, the combination of Russian power and the territories under their control or occupied, coupled with the Communist technique in so many other countries and above all, their power to maintain very large armies in the field for a long time.

"An iron curtain is drawn down upon their front," Churchill wrote, using the term *iron curtain* for the first time. "We do not know what is going on behind."

22

ON SATURDAY, MAY 11, Truman stood at an army airstrip outside Washington as the *Sacred Cow* — Roosevelt's specially outfitted airplane — descended from a clear blue sky and touched down, with Truman's mother and sister aboard. The first aircraft built to fly a president, the *Sacred Cow* was a Douglas VC-54C Skymaster with a quartet of 1,450-horsepower engines and a long, gleaming silver fuselage. It had an elevator built in to lift FDR's wheelchair into the cabin, and a top speed of roughly 300 miles per hour. Roosevelt's circle had christened this airplane the *Flying White House,* but the press had renamed it the *Sacred Cow,* and that name had stuck. It was an idiom meaning *above criticism,* and while the name referred to the high security surrounding this aircraft, reporters joked that the moniker referred more to FDR than to the vehicle itself.

After the *Sacred Cow* taxied, its hatch opened and Truman went aboard to fetch his mother and sister, who had flown in from Missouri. When frontier-bred Mamma Truman emerged from the president's plane with her son's arm in one hand and a cane in the other, she scowled at the crowd of photographers and newsmen awaiting.

"Oh, fiddlesticks!" said Mamma Truman. "If I'd known that, I wouldn't have come."

"And how are all at home?" Truman asked his mother.

"Oh, fine, just fine."

Next Truman fetched his sister, Mary Jane, and the three stood for photographers, Harry waving his gray hat in the air, his face "wreathed in smiles," as one reporter chronicled. Mamma Truman stole the show. She looked like what she was: a ninety-two-year-old farm woman walking right out of the nineteenth century, in her best Sunday clothes — a long and simple dark-blue dress and a blue straw hat with a gardenia on it nearly as big as her head. "She's certainly a grand old lady," the *Sacred Cow*'s pilot, Lieutenant Colonel Harry T. Myers, said. It was Mamma Truman's first airplane ride, her first visit to Washington, and her first time seeing her son since he had become president of the United States.

When the Trumans arrived at the White House, Bess, Margaret, and Mrs. Wallace were there to meet them. For the first time since April 12, Truman had no official appointments on his calendar. His Saturday was free, and his mother's visit coincided with Mother's Day weekend. He played a joke on his mother, escorting her into the Lincoln Bedroom, with the family in tow.

"Mamma," Truman said, "if you've a mind to, you may use this bed while you're here."

"What?" she cried. "Sleep in the bed THAT MAN used?"

She still had not gotten over the South's losing the Civil War, and she certainly would not be sleeping in any bed of Abraham Lincoln's. She chose a less heralded spot down the hall, much to the amusement of the whole Truman family.

White House staffers were surprised to see Mamma Truman wandering the mansion's hallways during her visit, engaging surprised strangers in conversation. She liked to tell anyone who would listen: "When he was a boy, Harry could plow the straightest furrow in Jackson County." Truman introduced his mother to the State Department's Joseph Davies at a dinner in the White House. "She is a dear little old lady . . . bright as a squirrel, and 'All American,'" Davies wrote in his diary. She told Davies she had come "to see that Harry was started right." During the conversation, the name of a certain politician from a northern state was mentioned.

"Isn't he a Yankee?" Mamma Truman asked.

"Yes, Mamma," Harry said, "but you know there are good Yankees as well as bad and good Rebels."

"Well," she said, "if there are any good Yankees, I haven't seen one yet."

Truman knew his family had suffered through his unlikely rise, and their discomfort grated on him. He liked to think that it no longer mattered what the press said about him. "Nothing they can say about me that hasn't been said," he wrote in the summer of 1945. "They can't do me any harm now. As Ed McKim says, there is no promotion to this job." But his family was not used to the spotlight. "It is a terrible, and I mean terrible nuisance to be kin to the president of the United States," he wrote in one letter. "Reporters have been haunting every relative and purported relative I ever heard of and they've probably made life miserable for my mother, brother and sister. I am sorry for it, but it can't be helped."

Now Mamma and Mary Jane were in the White House, and Truman was hoping they would find some fun in it.

On Sunday morning the Trumans went to services in the chapel of the National Naval Medical Center in Bethesda, Maryland. Truman had, by presidential proclamation, made this a national day of prayer in lieu of VE-day, and because it was Mother's Day. After the service, the Trumans headed to the Washington Navy Yard to board the USS *Potomac* — which Roosevelt had christened the presidential yacht. A cruise aboard "the Floating White House" offered views of the banks of the Potomac River, which had played such an important role in the war that Mamma Truman could never let go of, the war lost by the Confederacy in the days of Lincoln.

All over the country on this weekend, newspapers chronicled the story of the end of the president's first month in office. It was also the end of the official mourning period for Roosevelt, so flags could be raised to the top of their masts on the following Monday morning, all over the United States and at embassies from Moscow to Mexico City. The month had flown by in a montage of historic events. The Axis surrender in Italy, the execution of Mussolini, the suicide of Hitler, the Russian capture of Berlin, Nazi Germany's unconditional surrender, the liberation of death camps, the firebombings of Japan. The United Nations Conference was under way in San Francisco, and the president had been briefed on the most startling secret in human history.

Truman was a man who knew how to savor the finer moments, and his family's visit surely must have felt like one of them. He was surrounded by the four most important people in his life — his mother, his sister, his wife, and his daughter — on the first Sunday after the end of the European war. They could remember not long ago when his political career seemed sure to end, after the Pendergast imprisonment just before Truman's 1940 Senate reelection campaign. By all odds, he should have celebrated his sixty-first birthday quietly in Independence, awaiting his Senate pension check in the mail. All of this would be a dream to awaken from. But it was real.

///

Now in Truman's second month in office, the White House had taken on his personality. At some point during those early days, a sign appeared on his desk displaying a motto borrowed from Missouri's own

Mark Twain: ALWAYS DO RIGHT. THIS WILL GRATIFY SOME PEOPLE AND ASTONISH THE REST.

He liked the business of government to run efficiently — as crisp as the folds in his pocket square. When he learned that the average White House lunch for employees cost the government $2.50, he wanted to know why, since the army fed its men at 50 cents. He agreed with many of his cabinet officers who had criticized Roosevelt for his disorganized administrative style. Roosevelt, as summed up succinctly by historian Arthur Schlesinger Jr., "deliberately organized — or disorganized — his system of command to insure that important decisions were passed on to the top. His favorite technique was to keep grants of authority incomplete, jurisdictions uncertain, charters overlapping." The new president wanted teamwork and loyalty as unifying principles, an organized chain of command, and trustworthy heads of departments who could make wise decisions on their own.

Truman also stressed the kind of work ethic he had learned from his father — a farmer's work ethic. "You have no idea how hard he worked," recalled Roberta Barrows, Matthew Connelly's assistant.

The president's egalitarianism caught the White House staff off guard. Unlike the Roosevelts, who were accustomed to ignoring hovering servants, Truman insisted on addressing the kitchen staff by first name. His driver, secret service man Floyd Boring, recalled his first conversations with Truman while at the wheel. "By the way," Truman said to him, "I see you are driving most of the time. How are you connected with me?"

"Well, Mr. President," said Boring, "I've been assigned to drive you."

"Well, could you tell me your name?" It was Floyd Boring. "You don't mind if I call you Floyd, do you?"

Recalled Boring: "So that's the kind of guy he was."*

Fueled by restless energy, Truman darted from office to office between his appointments, rather than remaining behind his closed door, as Roosevelt did. Roberta Barrows, whose desk was near the Oval Office door, jumped to her feet each time the president stepped out, and she

---

* Boring led a fascinating career in the secret service. He had become the president's driver under FDR, on a day when Roosevelt's usual driver was discovered to be intoxicated. Boring was with Roosevelt in Warm Springs the day Roosevelt died, and he later took part in a gunfight during a 1950 assassination attempt on President Truman, which left one shooter and a secret service man dead.

curtsied. The curtsying struck Truman as odd; why would anyone curtsy for him, Harry Truman? One day he emerged from his office, saw Barrows curtsy, and said, "Now look, I know you respect the office of the president of the United States, but I cannot sit in that office by myself, between appointments, all day long. I want to know what is going on. I'm used to the Capitol. And you'll see me every day, in and out of other people's offices, so I want you from here on in not to rise."

"I appreciate that," she said. "Thank you, sir." The curtsying stopped.

The president could inspire laughter, sometimes in spite of himself. People enjoyed poking fun at his attire. He wore "matching combinations of socks, tie, and handkerchief for his breast pocket," assistant press secretary Eben Ayers wrote in his diary. "Perhaps it's a hangover from the days when he was in the clothing business." The British fashion writers in particular picked apart Truman's wardrobe. (He responded that it was none of their business.) His sense of humor many found startling in its impropriety. At one dinner in the White House, Truman told a group of cabinet officers that he should never have been president but rather a piano player in a whorehouse.

"That would have been too bad," responded Lewis Schwellenbach (whom Truman appointed secretary of labor in 1945), "because then we never would have known you!"

"Why be so high and mighty," Truman came back, "as though you had never been in a whorehouse!?" (Commerce secretary Wallace wrote in his diary that Schwellenbach "seemed to be genuinely shocked.")

The men in the pressroom roared with laughter over another Truman story. "Just a few days after Truman became President," recalled correspondent Robert Nixon, "without any notice to anybody, [he] suddenly walked to the front door of the White House (he was a very rapid walker), went bouncing down the stairs, down the driveway and out through the gate. The astonished Secret Service did a double take . . . He took them *completely* by surprise. Finally they went running after him." Truman needed some pocket change, so he was headed to his bank. "People were turning around, staring at this man walking briskly down the street. They remarked, 'You know, that looks like President Truman.' Which it was, but they wouldn't believe their eyes."

Truman's favorite leisure activity was poker. He liked an eight-card hand and he dealt left-handed, and by May 1945, some notable players had sniffed out his Friday-night games in the White House, which were a regular release from the relentless pressure of politics. "You know, I'm almost like a kid," he once said of his poker outings. "I can hardly wait to start." These were never big money games, for Truman did not have big money. When reporters asked what the beverage of choice was, he answered: "Kentucky bourbon." Old friends Harry Vaughan and federal loan administrator John Snyder had played with Truman for years. But new faces appeared, such as ambassador to the Soviet Union Harriman, who, although rich beyond most people's ability to fathom, "guarded his chips as though he were on relief," as White House legal counsel Clark Clifford recalled. A young congressman from Texas named Lyndon Baines Johnson also found his way to Truman's poker table, where he was particularly cunning and aggressive.

Insiders had thus far one major criticism of Truman: his friends. Harry Vaughan – the White House jester and military aide to the president (Truman would make him a general in the army before the end of the summer) – walked around in an ill-fitting uniform. As Truman Committee investigator Walter Hehmeyer put it: "Harry Vaughan was as out of place in the White House as a hippopotamus in a bird bath." Truman's crony Eddie McKim, now a White House administrative assistant, had a tendency to embarrass the president with an ill-founded sense of power, a strange condition the Truman family had begun to call "Potomac fever." McKim enjoyed telling people in the executive mansion what to do, though he had no authority to do so. At one point, McKim ordered staffers to stop responding to Eleanor Roosevelt's condolence letters, noting that "Mrs. Roosevelt is no longer riding the gravy train." Then McKim took twenty-one-year-old Margaret out on the town, not bringing her home until past midnight, without informing either the president or secret service. Truman was forced to fire McKim. "I just can't have him around anymore," he told a Missouri friend, Harry Easley. "That's all there is to it. So he's gone."

"Truman brought in a bunch of incompetents down to the White House," noted Nixon, the White House correspondent. "They didn't know first base from breakfast." When asked about this matter, the president responded: "How can I bring big people into government when I don't even know who they are, and they don't know me?"

America was getting to know the new First Family too. When Truman's sister, Mary Jane, took a trip to see a cousin in Texas in May 1945, she was surprised by a welcoming ceremony with photographers and the mayor of Dallas bearing a dozen roses. Reporters followed her all over town. One concluded, "The more we see and hear of these Trumans, the better we like them."

Margaret enjoyed the perks of being the president's daughter. She had her own car and driver, and she had a library of films to choose from in the White House movie theater. But the job of First Daughter came with difficulties. "I had to learn to say as little as possible when reporters were around," she recalled. "And most annoying of all, I had to accept the fact that I was a public property. Not only did everyone in the world feel entitled to know all the details of my life, but there were any number of people, both in and out of the media, who felt free to comment on my appearance. My nose was 'crooked' and ought to be 'fixed.' I had 'heavy' legs . . . I was 'immature.' I was too 'mature.'" Margaret's new companion lightened the emotional load – Mike, an Irish setter puppy given to her in May 1945 by Robert Hannegan, whom Truman had just appointed postmaster general.

Bess, meanwhile, was counting the days until June, when she could leave Washington for Independence, where she planned to spend the summer months. The North Delaware Street house offered a respite from the caginess of Washington, which she despised. She had released a statement saying that she never would hold any press conferences, and had managed to keep her name out of the news. She did, however, host her first White House tea, at 5 p.m. on May 24. Bess Truman had never imagined any party quite like this one. Dozens of women – the wives of diplomats – converged, representing thirty-nine nations, including Bolivia, Cuba, Iran, Latvia, Paraguay, Thailand, and Russia.

When Bess went to her bridge club to play cards with her friends for the first time since she had become First Lady, all the women rose and applauded when she entered the room. She felt humiliated.

"Now stop it," she said, "stop it this instant. Sit down, every darn one of you."

Her mother, Mrs. Wallace, now eighty-eight, was as unfriendly to Harry as she had always been – even now that he had become president. As historian Michael Beschloss wrote of Mrs. Wallace, "The imperious dowager, proud of her place atop the social hierarchy of Independence, Missouri, still believed that this dirt farmer and failed haberdasher was unworthy of her daughter Bess."

Despite the stress of their sudden thrust into celebrity and world affairs, the Truman family was making the White House their home. Truman had replaced Roosevelt's ship paintings in the Oval Office with pictures of early airplanes. A portrait of Roosevelt was mounted nearby on Truman's right, while a statue of Andrew Jackson stood atop a stand to the president's left, both crowded close as if they were whispering into Truman's ears. In the kitchen, old Mrs. Nesbitt — famed for turning out "meals so gray, so drooping, and so spectacularly inept that they became a Washington legend," as put by one *New Yorker* writer — had suddenly decided to retire, after an uncomfortable run-in with Bess, probably over the ubiquity of brussels sprouts on the dinner table. The Trumans asked Vietta Garr, an African American housekeeper and cook from Independence, to join them in the White House as cook and companion, and she agreed. (Garr had worked for Madge Wallace for years at the North Delaware Street home and had a close relationship with Margaret.)

The Trumans could now enjoy more exciting aromas from the White House stoves, Vietta Garr's Missouri home cooking — fried chicken, baked ham, sweet potatoes, and Harry's favorite angel food cake. Meanwhile, Alonzo Fields, the head butler and an accomplished mixologist, had perfected old-fashioneds according to the Trumans' tastes — bourbon over rocks with water and nothing else. "Now that's the way we like our old-fashioneds," Bess said approvingly.

On the job, Truman was proving tougher than people thought he would be. He had announced that he was cutting $7.5 billion from shipbuilding programs and from eight government agencies. That was a lot of jobs sliced — a wise decision for the economy, most believed, but not for a man who ever intended to get elected again. Truman had vetoed the Agricultural Deferment Bill, which would allow farmers to avoid military service. Roosevelt had supported the bill, but Truman won over Congress. He "challenged the [farm] bloc on a matter of broad national policy and won," noted the *New York Times*.

Truman knew America's warm glow was destined to fade. He had feared the inevitable moment when he would make a grave error — a mistake that would embarrass him on the public stage — and that day came in early May. As Clark Clifford, a young lawyer working in the Truman administration at the time, wrote of government: "At the savage intersection of policy, ambition, and history, it is impossible to be right all the time."

Harry Truman (left) in the Truman & Jacobson haberdashery in Kansas City, circa 1920. The store failed (as did most of Truman's early business ventures). "I'm still paying on those debts," he wrote, some twelve years after this picture was taken. HISTORICAL CORBIS/GETTY IMAGES

Pandemonium at the 1944 Democratic National Convention in Chicago, where Truman shocked the political world. Although only 2 percent of Democratic voters favored him for vice president, the Missourian was named to the '44 ticket with Franklin Roosevelt. BETTMANN/GETTY IMAGES

A stunned Truman accepts the VP nomination in Chicago. Up to this moment, he was adamant that he did not want the job. "He did not want it," his mother, Martha Ellen Truman, said. "They pushed him into it." GORDON COSTER/GETTY IMAGES

Truman and Roosevelt meet at the White House to discuss the 1944 election. "His hands are shaking and he talks with considerable difficulty," Truman said of the president after this meeting. "It doesn't seem to be any mental lapse of any kind, but physically, he's just going to pieces." UNIVERSAL HISTORY ARCHIVE/ GETTY IMAGES

Truman recites the presidential oath of office, at 7:09 p.m. on April 12, 1945. To his left: his wife, Bess, and only child, Margaret. He described this moment in these four words: "The lightning has struck!" Said one reporter at the time: "No man ever came to the presidency of the United States under more difficult circumstances than does Harry S. Truman." ABBIE ROWE, NATIONAL PARK SERVICE/HARRY S. TRUMAN LIBRARY & MUSEUM

FDR's funeral procession winds through Washington, DC. In the White House, chaos reigned. "I doubt that there have been few more dramatic, confused moments in American history than the ingress of the people who saw power in their hands under Harry Truman," recalled press secretary Jonathan Daniels.

KEYSTONE FEATURES/GETTY IMAGES

During Truman's first week in office, Allied armies liberated Nazi death camps in Europe. This photo inside Buchenwald was taken April 16, 1945, the day the new president addressed Congress for the first time.

UNITED STATES ARMY SIGNAL CORPS/ HARRY S. TRUMAN LIBRARY & MUSEUM

The battle for Okinawa raged during Truman's early days in office. In this death struggle, the Japanese employed suicide bombers, suicide boats, even suicide swimmers. Pictured: a Japanese kamikaze attack on the USS *Bunker Hill* on May 11, 1945.

UNIVERSAL HISTORY ARCHIVE/ GETTY IMAGES

Major General Curtis LeMay at Twenty-First Bomber Command headquarters on the island of Guam. LeMay architected fire-bombings of Japan that killed thousands during Truman's first four months in office.

HISTORICAL CORBIS/GETTY IMAGES

The Boeing B-29 Superfortress — the most technologically advanced weapons system of its time — was the main aircraft used in the firebombings of Japan. The development of this aircraft cost the American government more than the Manhattan Project did.

BERNARD HOFFMAN/ GETTY IMAGES

Two of the most power-ful figures in the early Truman administration: General George C. Marshall (left), the army chief of staff, and Henry Stimson, sec-retary of war. Stimson headed up the atomic bomb project from a governmental level.

BETTMANN/GETTY IMAGES

Truman at the United Nations Conference in San Francisco, where the peace organization was formed, on June 26, 1945. On the right: Secretary of State Edward Stettinius. On the left: Alger Hiss of the U.S. delegation. (Hiss was later outed as a Soviet spy.) Behind Truman: close friend and unofficial White House jester Harry Vaughan.
BETTMANN/GETTY IMAGES

June 27, 1945: The biggest crowds in Jackson County history turned out for Truman's homecoming as president for the first time. Here he exits his airplane, the *Sacred Cow*, with his daughter, Margaret.
HARRY S. TRUMAN LIBRARY & MUSEUM

From left: General Dwight Eisenhower, General George Patton, and the president, watching an American flag rise over former-Nazi Berlin. The flag was the same one that flew over the White House at the time of Pearl Harbor and was also raised over Paris when the city was liberated from the Nazis. Truman wrote in his diary on this day, July 28, 1945, "Flag was [flying] on the White House when Pearl Harbor happened. Will be raised over Tokyo." BETTMANN/GETTY IMAGES

Less than four months into his accidental presidency, Truman meets British prime minister Winston Churchill for the first time, in front of the Little White House in Soviet-occupied Germany. Churchill had earlier cabled Truman: "You and I will have to bear the great responsibility for the future." IMPERIAL WAR MUSEUM/GETTY IMAGES

As Truman and Churchill confer for the first time, the world's first atomic explosion — the Trinity shot — goes off in the New Mexico desert. When Churchill learned of Trinity, he exclaimed, "The atomic bomb is the second coming of wrath." JACK AEBY/HARRY S. TRUMAN LIBRARY & MUSEUM

Truman's first meeting with Soviet dictator Joseph Stalin (July 17, 1945), one day after the Trinity atomic bomb test. From left: Vyacheslav Molotov (Stalin's number two), Truman's secretary of state James F. Byrnes, Truman's Russian translator Chip Bohlen, the president, Truman's chief of staff Admiral Leahy, and Stalin, the Man of Steel. The historic Potsdam Conference would begin later that night. UNITED STATES ARMY SIGNAL CORPS/HARRY S. TRUMAN LIBRARY & MUSEUM

On August 2, four days before the Hiroshima bombing, Truman and Jimmy Byrnes meet with Britain's King George VI. At lunch, Truman's chief of staff Admiral Leahy said of the bomb, "I do not think it will be as effective as expected." The king said, "Admiral, would you like to lay a little bet on that?"

The Nagasaki bomb (August 9, 1945) — the second atomic strike. Was Truman justified in using atomic weapons against Japan?

The dramatic scene inside the Oval Office as Truman announces the unconditional surrender of Japan on August 14, 1945 — four months and two days after the death of FDR. ABBIE ROWE, NATIONAL PARK SERVICE/HARRY S. TRUMAN LIBRARY & MUSEUM

Following the announcement of Japan's surrender, Harry and Bess Truman wave at tens of thousands who have gathered at the White House gates, chanting, "We want Harry!" It was, in the words of one reporter present, "the wildest celebration this capital ever saw." ABBIE ROWE, NATIONAL PARK SERVICE/HARRY S. TRUMAN LIBRARY & MUSEUM

OF ALL WASHINGTON'S WARTIME LEGISLATION, none was arguably more controversial than Lend-Lease. The brainchild of FDR, the Lend-Lease bill was conceived in the winter of 1940–1941, before the United States entered the war, and Roosevelt signed it into law on March 11, 1941. It enabled Roosevelt, and now Truman, to send munitions and supplies to "the government of any country whose defense the president deems vital to the defense of the U.S." All over the world, because of Lend-Lease, Soviet, Chinese, British, French, and other soldiers had fought with and, in some cases, were still fighting with tools of war built in American factories, and gaining sustenance from food grown on American farms, at the expense of the American taxpayer. (Over the course of the war, more than thirty countries would benefit from Lend-Lease, totaling some $50 billion in American assistance.) As Churchill famously said, "Give us the tools and we will finish the job." He called Lend-Lease "the most unsordid act in history."

Without Lend-Lease, Hitler could never have been defeated. That did not mean that the American taxpayer had to like this law. Foreign countries were supposed to pay for this food and these tools of war years down the line (albeit, at a huge discount), but the war was bankrupting the Allied governments, the United States aside. The American taxpayer was not likely to see all this debt paid back.[*] As Senator Arthur Vandenberg had said of Lend-Lease: It must not extend "one minute or $1 into the post-war period."

On May 11, Truman received a memo signed by Undersecretary of State Joseph Grew and Foreign Economic administrator Leo Crowley stating: "Deliveries of supplies under the current lend-lease programs for the

---

[*] Britain finally paid off its World War II debt to the United States in 2006. The Soviets settled their debt as part of a 1972 trade package.

U.S.S.R. should be adjusted immediately to take account of the end of organized resistance in Europe." Some Lend-Lease military equipment should continue to flow to the Soviets considering their secret plan to join the war against Japan, the document pointed out. "Other lend-lease supplies now programmed for the U.S.S.R. should be cut off immediately as far as physically practicable."

According to the latest figures on Truman's desk, the United States had sent 593,259 long tons of Lend-Lease goods to the Soviets in the month of April 1945. That number was up from 484,829 long tons the month before. Shipments included aircraft and trucks built on the assembly lines of Detroit, and ship hulls full of bullets, but also (during the month of April) 16,866 short tons of wheat, flour, and cereals; 23,459 short tons of butter; and 26,213 short tons of animal fats and cured meats.

Truman knew from his days in the Senate how touchy Congress was on the issue of Lend-Lease. As Representative Karl Mundt of South Dakota – a member of the House Foreign Affairs Committee – said on the floor of the House, "There can be no post-war economic activities by Lend-Lease except through the most flagrant violation of the intent of Congress." Now the war in Europe was over.

The president approved the plan to cut off many supplies to the Soviets, and also to the British, immediately. Had he thought this matter through completely? The fact was, he was exhausted and he signed the document without reading it, trusting his advisors on the matter. A number of high-level officials had singled out a curious trait about Truman. "He . . . seemed eager to make decisions of every kind with the greatest promptness," Commerce secretary Henry Wallace wrote of Truman in his diary, following a cabinet meeting. "Everything he said was decisive. It almost seemed as though he was eager to decide in advance of thinking." According to ambassador to the Soviet Union Averell Harriman, "You could go into [Truman's] office with a question and come out with a decision more swiftly than any man I have ever known."

Over the next few days, the chain of command reached ships at sea, brimming with supplies headed for the Soviet Union and Britain. Those ships were ordered to turn around. They contained cargo loads of food desperately needed by the British and Soviets, whose territories had seen infrastructure devastation that the United States had not. Stalin

and Churchill were sure to be furious over Truman's Lend-Lease decision, as soon as they learned of it.

///

One night in May, Truman was aboard the presidential yacht playing
a game of poker with friends. He was holding cards when a naval aide
handed him an alarming memorandum regarding the Yugoslavian dictator Tito. According to intelligence sources, Tito was attempting to lay
claim to territory in northern Italy – a piece of Venezia Giulia, notable
for the port city of Trieste. Truman said, "Tell the son of a bitch he'll have
to shoot his way in."

"Aye aye, sir," the naval aide said. And Truman went back to his game.

Over the next few days, however, the standoff in Italy grew hot, and
the threat of mass violence became imminent. According to State Department reports, Yugoslavian forces had hung their own flags all over
Trieste and had even changed the street signs from Italian to their own
language. The Yugoslavian military had complete control. Tito seemed
willing to gamble the lives of his soldiers, and it was hard to gauge a bluff
from across the Atlantic Ocean.

Venezia Giulia bordered the Balkan States and had been subject to
territorial dispute before. The current situation alarmed Truman for two
reasons: (1) Tito had a large army of 300,000 to 400,000 soldiers, and his
regime was "no less dictatorial than Stalin's," bearing "little resemblance
to democracy and [affording] few opportunities for freedom," according
to a report to the president from William "Wild Bill" Donovan, head of
the Office of Strategic Services (the OSS spy agency, precursor to the
CIA); and (2) Tito was another puppet of the Soviet government. "In foreign affairs, as in internal affairs, Russia is the lodestone governing Tito's
policies," the spy agency stated. "In every international issue, whether it
is the direct concern of Yugoslavia or not, Tito and his press assiduously
follow Moscow's lead . . .

"The issue, therefore, is hardly an Italian-Yugoslavian dispute, but a
basic and clear-cut U.S.-Soviet conflict," concluded the OSS. "In this
conflict the United States holds very good cards . . . there is an overwhelming superiority of [American and British] troops in the area."

On May 11, Truman spelled out the situation in a cable to Churchill. "You
are no doubt receiving the same reports," he wrote. Tito's threatening

and expansionist tactics felt "all too reminiscent of those of Hitler and Japan."

Through State Department channels, the United States sent a firm message to Tito, who refused to move his troops. He had won this frontier from the Nazis in late April, and thus Yugoslavia "has all the rights to hold this territory," Tito argued in a cable to the U.S. State Department. "It would be unjust to deny [the] Yugoslav Army the rights of military occupation of 'Venezia Giulia.'"

General Eisenhower and Britain's Field Marshal Harold Alexander, the Allied commander in Italy, were given orders to reinforce troops in the disputed area and to prepare for the worst. These forces were not to fire, unless fired upon first. Appeals were sent to Stalin to defuse the situation, but Stalin had everything to gain by allowing the dispute to continue. Daily the situation worsened. Refugees by the tens of thousands were lingering in the area, and there was little food to feed either them or the local populations. On May 15 Undersecretary of State Joseph Grew reported that "many Italians of all classes are being arrested and local industrialists have been told that their property is now Yugoslav." Grew also reported that Tito was making incendiary moves in Austria. "The Yugoslavs are making excessive and ridiculous demands and charges." The American and British military leaders began moving refugees and POWs out of the area around Trieste, "so as to leave our troops mobile for whatever happens," Grew informed Truman.

On May 16, Truman wrote Churchill again. "I am unable and unwilling to involve this country in a war with the Yugoslavs unless they should attack us, in which case we would be justified in using our Allied troops to throw them back." Four days later he cabled again, "I must not have any avoidable interference with the redeployment of American forces to the Pacific."

"We had another explosive situation on our hands," Truman recorded.

At every turn, it seemed, Truman saws signs of more war coming. And each new arising conflict seemed to place the Americans and the Soviets on a crash course. On May 12, as the Tito drama was unfolding, Truman received a startling telephone call from Secretary of State Stettinius in San Francisco, where negotiations between the American and Russian delegations were continuing to unravel. Vyacheslav Molotov was insisting that members of the UN Security Council — a group formed of delegations from the world's most powerful nations — should have a veto privilege. What that meant, according to the Russian definition, was the ability of a Security Council nation to veto any action of which the rest of the Security Council nations approved. According to the Russian definition, the veto would allow one nation to block a matter from even being discussed by the Security Council. The Americans found this position indefensible.

At one point, during a discussion over regional treaties at the San Francisco conference, a Latin American official made the following statement, and his reasoning exemplifies the perceived assurance of impending war between the United States and the USSR: "Any country seeking to attack the United States in the future would attack through the weakest point, which is in South America. The next war will be between Russia and the United States, not between any two countries in Europe. [An] attempt will be made to [out]flank the United States through South America."

In Germany, meanwhile, Allied forces were scheduled to meet in Berlin on June 5 to move the occupation into the next phase. The United States, the United Kingdom, the Soviet Union, and France would take over their respective occupation zones, each with its own military government ruling over a desperate population totaling some 70 million. The Americans would govern the southeastern section of Germany and would have to withdraw some two hundred miles from their current military position at the Elbe River. The Soviets would take the northeastern zone (which, in four years' time, would become the communist nation of East Germany). The British would take over the northwestern part of Germany, which was closest to Britain itself, while France would take a smaller section to the southwest.

Already State Department officials had grave reservations that these occupation mechanisms – dreamed up during a time when American-Soviet relations were far rosier – would work. George Kennan, Ambassador Harriman's top aide in the Moscow embassy, wrote around this time, "The idea of a Germany run jointly with the Russians is a chimera. The idea of both the Russians and ourselves withdrawing politely at a given date and a healthy, peaceful, stable, and friendly Germany arising out of the resulting vacuum is also a chimera. We have no choice but to lead our section of Germany . . . to a form of independence so prosperous, so secure, so superior, that the East cannot threaten it." (Thus the future foundation of West Germany, which formed its official government four years later, in 1949.)

A new image of Europe was coming into focus. The continent would be increasingly influenced by democratic regimes from the West and Soviet-backed regimes from the East. The Soviets had Poland, Austria, Yugoslavia, Bulgaria, Romania, Hungary – all of it in their sights. A report to the president from the OSS on May 18 revealed that Czechoslovakia too was falling to communist influence: "Sources declare that the Communist Party appears to be the only organized political group and the only one with a program . . . Source also reports that the Czech Communist Party has demanded that workers be armed."

Even in the Far East, the Soviets were spreading communist influence, in surprising ways. On Monday, May 14, at 2 p.m., Truman met with the Chinese foreign minister, Dr. T. V. Soong. Joseph Grew attended, to take the meeting's minutes. Dr. Soong spoke beautiful English, as he had studied economics at Harvard and Columbia Universities, and had worked in banking in New York for a short time. At age fifty, he had already spent twenty years at the highest levels of Chinese government. He outlined for Truman an extraordinarily complex situation in China, as the two sat together in the White House over a map of the Far East. The prime objective of Soong's government was to drive out Japanese forces occupying Chinese territory, he explained, and he would need continued Lend-Lease military supplies from the United States. Truman assured that these supplies would continue until the Japanese surrendered. But the Chinese situation, Dr. Soong said, had also gotten tangled with the Soviet problem.

China had been divided by two forces from within – the old republic under Chiang Kai-shek, friendly with the United States, and Communist forces in the north, under Mao Tse-tung. "[Dr. Soong] discussed at some length the attitude of Soviet Russia," according to Grew's account of this May 14 meeting with Truman. The Soviets had allied with Chiang Kai-shek's government during the war, but lately "there had been a change and the Soviet Government seemed to be supporting the Chinese Communists rather than the National Government," Soong said.

What was to keep the Soviets from supplying arms and soldiers to Mao and the Communists in China, to foment a communist revolution in one of the most powerful nations in the East?

Three months earlier, at the end of the Yalta Conference, American-Soviet relations had reached a peak of goodwill. Now the State Department's number two, Joseph Grew, had come to this conclusion: "A future war with Soviet Russia is as certain as anything in this world."

///

The week after VE-day Truman went in search of advice, canvassing the brightest political minds in Washington on how to stem the decline in American-Soviet relations. There had to be a way to avoid more war, for any war with the USSR would slaughter inconceivable numbers of people. After all, as different as these nations were, they had common ground. Both the United States and the Soviet Union had been born of violent revolution, and both were now in this war due to surprise attacks – the United States at Pearl Harbor and the Soviets at the hands of the Nazis. As the two countries that would emerge from the war as superpowers, they would play the two biggest roles in creating whatever new world lay in the future.

Truman started with a former ambassador to Moscow. On Sunday, May 13, the State Department's Joseph Davies arrived at the White House for an informal tête-à-tête with Truman in his second-floor study. Truman was "much disturbed" over the Russian situation, as Davies recalled. The newspapers – "these damn sheets," Truman called them – were fueling the fire. Davies was a trusted sounding board, and he was hearing the same alarm bells. He told Truman that he had just written him a letter, and had yet to mail it. He had brought it with him, and Truman asked him to read it aloud.

"The rapid and serious deterioration within the last few weeks in the relations between the Soviets, Britain, and ourselves, and particularly with ourselves, has alarmed me," Davies said. "The potentialities are beyond words . . . In my opinion, you are in the best position to avert [conflict] for our country and for the world." Davies urged Truman to avoid contention – to avoid "the 'tough' approach" – and to handle Soviet relations "with generosity and friendliness." In such cases, "the Soviets respond with even greater generosity . . . It is . . . wrong to assume that 'tough' language is the only language that they can understand. That is commonly urged. My experience has been to the contrary . . .

"The situation today is, in my opinion, grave," Davies concluded. "But it is not without hope."

Two days later, after his regular press conference, Truman held another

meeting on the Soviet situation with Averell Harriman and other officials. These men were recommending the opposite approach from the
one Joseph Davies had urged. According to the meeting's minutes, "Ambassador Harriman said that the problem with our relations with Russia
is the number one problem affecting the future of the world and . . . at
present moment we were getting farther and farther apart."

Harriman believed a hard line was now the last-ditch approach, the
only one that the Soviets would understand. Navy secretary Forrestal
described Harriman's position in his diary: "He said that their [the Russians'] conduct would be based upon the principle of power politics in
its crudest and most primitive form. He said we must face our diplomatic
decisions from here on with the consciousness that half and maybe all of
Europe might be communistic by the end of next winter."

What was the best approach: the hard line that Harriman (the current
Moscow ambassador) urged, or the soft line that Davies (a previous Moscow ambassador) advocated?

At noon the following day – Wednesday, May 16 – the secretary of war
came to the Oval Office to suggest yet another path. Stimson was deeply
concerned about the power vacuum forming in Europe following the
Third Reich's collapse.

"All agree," he informed the president in a memo he delivered during
this meeting, "as to the probability of pestilence and famine in central
Europe next winter. This is likely to be followed by political revolution
and Communist infiltration."

Stimson believed a primary focus in gaining global political stabilization, particularly regarding the Soviets, should be the reconstruction of
Germany. Only a strong Germany would be able to resist the spread of
communism, and the German nation anchored the very center of Europe. Stimson argued intensely against the Morgenthau Plan – Treasury
secretary Henry Morgenthau's idea to reduce Germany to an agrarian
nation, without the industrial capacity to build a military. It was in the
United States' best interest to help rebuild Germany, Stimson argued.
If Germany did not have a sound economy, with citizens whose basic
needs of life were met, the country would become easy prey to Soviet infiltration. "A solution must be found for [Germany's] future peaceful existence and it is to the interest of the whole world that they should not
be driven by stress of hardship into a non-democratic and necessarily
predatory habit of life," Stimson argued.

"All of this is a tough problem requiring coordination between the Anglo-American allies and Russia," Stimson concluded.

During Truman's meeting with Harriman, the ambassador to the Soviet Union had warned the president of frightening consequences if he did not move up the timeline of the proposed Big Three meeting: "The longer the meeting [is] delayed, the worse the situation would get." Stimson believed otherwise. In two months' time, the United States was likely to have more power to bargain with. In a direct reference to the atomic bomb, Stimson informed Truman, "We shall probably hold more cards in our hands later than now." Truman concurred: it was best to wait.

Stimson believed the bomb could be the key to solving some of these conundrums. "It may be necessary to have it out with Russia . . ." he had written in his diary a day before his meeting with Truman, "Over any such tangled wave of problems, the S-1 secret [the atomic bomb] would be dominant." Regarding the upcoming tripartite meeting, "it seems a terrible thing to gamble with such big stakes in diplomacy without having your master card in your hand."

///

"It seems to me that the need for our triple meeting at the earliest moment is very great," Churchill cabled Truman on May 21, expressing deep anxiety over "the grave discussions on which the immediate future of the world depends." The longer it took to work out acceptable agreements with Stalin, Churchill argued, the more difficult it would be.

Truman did not want this meeting to occur until after the first atomic bomb test, but the secret nature of the bomb made this delay impossible to explain, even to Churchill.* Something had to be done in the meantime. An idea came from Harriman and Chip Bohlen in the State Department.

On May 19, at 11 a.m., Truman summoned Harry Hopkins to the White

---

* Historians have never agreed on whether Truman's delay for setting up the tripartite meeting was in fact because of the bomb, and this gray area has proven controversial. Certainly Truman wanted to delay so that he could become educated enough in international relations to negotiate with the likes of Churchill and Stalin. Still, this author sides with those who believe Truman's delay was directly linked to the bomb, as evidenced in these pages.

House. Hopkins, Truman said, was going to embark on a mission of unparalleled importance.

Few more enigmatic figures could be found on the Washington scene
in 1945 than Harry Hopkins. Nearing his fifty-fifth birthday, the Iowa-
born former social worker had been, arguably, Roosevelt's best friend.
During the war years, Hopkins had actually lived in the White House
with the Roosevelts, and FDR bestowed upon him extraordinary power.
Hopkins had no real job in the State Department, no particularly impres-
sive education, nor any distinctive background that would suggest a career in diplomacy. But Roosevelt trusted him as he did no other. "When
he's talking to some foreign dignitary," Roosevelt said of Hopkins, "he
knows how to slump back in his chair and put his feet up on the conference table and say, 'Oh, *yeah?*'" One observer described Hopkins as having "the purity of St. Francis of Assisi combined with the shrewdness of
a race track tout." He dressed in poorly fitting suits, the shoulders frequently flaked with dandruff, and his face often showed frustration, as if
his eyes were searching for something they would never find.

By the time Hopkins arrived in Truman's office, one glance was
enough to know that Hopkins was dying. He had been hospitalized for
cancer seven years earlier, and doctors had removed more than half of
his stomach. Ever since, he had struggled with his health, with hospital stays, a bout of jaundice, difficulty walking, one ailment after another.
Hopkins had lost his youngest son in the war, eighteen-year-old Stephen, a marine killed in action in the Marshall Islands. The horror of losing Stephen had done his health no good. At Roosevelt's funeral service,
five weeks before his meeting with Truman, Hopkins "looked like death,"
according to Robert Sherwood, one of Roosevelt's chief speech writers.
"The skin of his face [was] a dreadful cold white with apparently no flesh
left under it. I believed that he now [at the time of the funeral] had nothing left to live for, that his life had ended with Roosevelt's."

The new president had one final mission for Hopkins. It would not
be an easy one.

"I asked him to go to Stalin," Truman wrote in notes of this meeting,
"provided his health permitted, and tell [Stalin] just exactly what we intended to have in the way of carrying out the agreements purported to
have been made at Yalta – that I was anxious to have a fair understanding
with the Russian Government." Truman told Hopkins to "make it clear to
Uncle Joe Stalin that I knew what I wanted – and that I intended to get –

peace for the world for at least 90 years." Truman told Hopkins he could use "diplomatic language or a baseball bat."

Truman must have known that a Moscow mission could kill Hopkins. But the president had reason to believe that Hopkins could get results, for Hopkins knew Stalin personally. Roosevelt had sent Hopkins to meet Stalin shortly after the Nazis invaded Russia, in 1941. As put by Ambassador Harriman: "Hopkins was the first Western visitor to Moscow after the German attack, when things were going pretty badly. Stalin evidently saw in Hopkins a man who, in spite of ill health, had made that long, exhausting and hazardous journey to bring help. It was an example of courage and determination that impressed Stalin deeply. He had not forgotten."

Wisely, Truman concluded that he would upset Churchill by sending Hopkins to meet with Stalin, that the prime minister would seize on the absence of Britain's presence in these meetings. So Truman sent for Joseph Davies, who arrived at the White House at 9 p.m. on May 21. "He wanted me to go to London," Davies recorded. "He wanted me to explore matters of possible differences with Churchill and get his ideas." Truman also wanted Davies to stall for time. He revealed to Davies why he could not move up a tripartite meeting, that it could not take place before July. "He told me then of the atomic bomb experiment," Davies wrote in his diary. "The test was set for June, but had been postponed until July." Truman wanted to know whether or not he had an ace in the hole before he sat down at the table with Churchill and Stalin.

On May 23, Harry Hopkins flew to Paris with his wife, Ambassador Harriman, and interpreter Chip Bohlen, en route to Moscow. That same day, Davies took off for London. "Hopkins and Davies left simultaneously and will arrive in London and Moscow about the same time," Truman wrote in his notes. "[They] will be back in less than ten days and we will see what the result is."

IN THE EARLY MORNING HOURS OF MAY 24, under the cover of darkness in Tokyo, air-raid sirens signaled oncoming waves of American B-29 Superfortresses. From the ground, the bombers could be heard before they could be seen, thousands of 2,200-horsepower engines roaring. Then the ships appeared against the moonlit sky, gliding through moving columns of searchlights casting from the ground. One person in Tokyo described the vision of these bomber aircraft: "unreal, light as fantastic glass dragonflies . . . their long, glinting wings, sharp as blades." Major General Curtis LeMay had dispatched 550 Superfortresses from bases in the Marianas. The attack wave swept low, under 10,000 feet, the planes slicing through Tokyo's sky before sunrise and releasing canisters that ignited the city.

"The sheer number of the bombs was incredible," recalled a French journalist who was living in Tokyo, Robert Guillain. "The carpet [of bombs] unrolled with pitiless regularity, spreading its mat of fire over the flat districts between the port and the hills . . . As soon as they touched the ground, the cylinders spewed fire that leaped, the newspapers said, 'like bounding tigers.'"

All the next day, Tokyo's fire crews worked to put out the flames. The following night LeMay's bombers roared again, and they faced little opposition. This time the Superfortresses struck the grounds of the emperor's palace. Emperor Hirohito was safe, hiding in a concrete-enforced underground shelter. Firefighters abandoned whole neighborhoods to the flames to save the palace, leaving vast sections of Tokyo to burn. Search crews would collect the bodies from the ashes many hours later. Wrote Guillain: "The last of old Tokyo's architectural treasures — the ones that had survived the 1923 Earthquake — were burned to the ground: the Shiba pagoda; the Yoyogi temple where 'the ashes of the true Buddha,' given to Great Japan in 1942, were kept; the black-and-gold-lacquered tombs of the Tokugawa shoguns; all these perished in the tragic forty-eight hours from May 24 to 26."

At operational headquarters on Guam, LeMay paced all night during these attacks while chewing on his ever-present cigar. He was all-consumed by the war, and by the idea that his command could end it. Nothing else seemed to exist for him. Of this new attack wave, LeMay later wrote in his memoirs: "We plastered the as-yet-unburned areas of Tokyo with nearly nine thousand tons of incendiaries on the 23rd and 25th." (The planes took off on those dates and reached their targets after midnight, on the 24th and 26th.) LeMay had recently written to his superiors in the Pentagon: "I feel that the destruction of Japan's ability to wage war lies within the capability of this command, provided its maximum capacity is exerted unstintingly during the next six months, which is considered to be the critical period."

American newspapers reported the May 24 firebombing on their front pages. No outrage came from the American public. All the critics who had hurled calumny at the British for their willingness to bomb civilian population centers in Nazi Germany now remained silent. In fact, popular American opinion now seemed to embrace this form of warfare. Newspaper articles ran long columns with pictures of the factories where the firebombs were built. FILLING "GOOP BOMBS" THAT ARE FRYING JAPAN LIKE MIXING CAKE DOUGH, stated a *Boston Daily Globe* headline. "The M-69s [firebombs] become miniature flamethrowers," reported *Time* magazine, "that hurl cheesecloth socks full of furiously flaming goo [napalm] for 100 yards. Anything these socks hit is enveloped by clinging, fiery pancakes."

Only Secretary of War Stimson urged an end to the indiscriminate killing. Stimson went to see the president. "I told him I was anxious about this feature of the war for two reasons," Stimson wrote in his diary. "First, because I did not want to have the United States get the reputation of outdoing Hitler in atrocities; and second, I was a little fearful that before we could get ready the Air Force might have Japan so thoroughly bombed out that the new weapon would not have a fair background to show its strength."

Why had the rules changed – from precision bombing to the firebombing of civilian neighborhoods? What about the Japanese was different, in the eyes of America, from the Third Reich?

Historians have made much of the inherent racism in America against the Japanese during the war, and the fact that the War Relocation Authority had gathered up approximately 120,000 "individuals of Japanese ancestry" and interned them in camps located around the West Coast, under the jurisdiction of the Department of the Interior. The mainstream press printed cartoons of "Japs" as apes swinging from vines with machine guns in their paws. They were "yellow bastards," "yellow monkeys," and vermin-infested "louseous Japanicas." But American feelings toward the Japanese went beyond racism. A hatred had sunk deep into the American consciousness following Pearl Harbor, a hatred that did not come into play in the European war, even toward the Nazis.

Even before the United States entered World War II, it became apparent that the war in the Far East was different from the one in Europe. Americans read about frenzies of killing by the Japanese, notably the Rape of Nanking in 1937. ("Japanese atrocities marked fall of Nanking," the *New York Times* reported. "Nanking invaders executed 20,000.") A cult of death among Japanese soldiers terrified the Allies and set these soldiers apart from the German forces fighting in Europe. Mass suicides among both civilians and warriors, the idea that death was a better choice for the Japanese soldier than to be captured as a POW — this form of warfare labeled the Eastern enemy as zealots willing to die for their emperor, whom they revered as a deity. Thus the popular press in the United States characterized the enemy in the East as a "racial menace" fighting a holy war.

Atrocities committed by the Japanese could not be characterized as anything more evil than the Nazi Final Solution. But the Nazis had not attacked Americans on American soil. And among high-level military ranks, there was more to the story. It was the Japanese treatment of prisoners of war that sparked hatred toward the Eastern foe among Pentagon operatives, who would have had access to information regarding treatment of American and British POWs. Allied intelligence had plenty of evidence of beheadings, torture, and executions.

American military officials felt it their duty to finish the Japanese off at the cost of as few of their own soldiers as possible. That meant crushing the enemy, using any and all tools at the military's disposal, firebombs included. As Admiral Leahy wrote, "The best psychological warfare to use on those barbarians was bombs, and we used bombs vigorously." General Hap Arnold, head of the army air forces, summed up what many military figures in America were thinking, in his diary during the days of the Tokyo firebombings:

"Apparently, the atrocities by the Japs have never been told in the US; babies thrown up in the air and caught on bayonets, autopsies on living people, burning prisoners to death by sprinkling them with gasoline and throwing in a hand grenade to start a fire . . . More and more of the stories, which can apparently be substantiated. Stories of men and boys being killed while all girls and women from ten years of age upward were raped by 1 Jap division retreating from this section of Manila. They are not pretty stories but they explain why the Japs can expect anything . . . There is no feeling of sparing any Japs here, men, women, or children; gas, fire, anything to exterminate the entire race exemplifies the feeling."

Arnold admitted in his diary that these specific instances could not be entirely verified, but the torture and executions of POWs could be, and they explain much about the attitude of American military decision makers in 1945. The firebombing raids of Major General Curtis LeMay were the most clear example.

Still young in his presidency, Truman followed in the footsteps of his predecessor Roosevelt. He responded with no action following LeMay's widely reported firebombings, leaving the conduct of the war to his trusted military commanders. Soon fate would thrust this decision making into his own hands.

///

On May 25, in the Pentagon, the Joint Chiefs met to formulate their final plans for the future of the war with Japan. They disagreed with Curtis LeMay, who believed firebombing alone could bring Japan to its knees. As they had earlier, the Joint Chiefs came to the conclusion that a ground invasion of the Japanese islands was imperative in forcing unconditional surrender. They laid out the strategy for victory in the East as follows, according to the meeting's minutes:

A. Apply full and unremitting pressure against Japan by strategic bombing and carrier raids in order to reduce war-making capacity and to demoralize the country, in preparation for invasion.

B. Tighten blockade by means of air and sea patrols, and of air striking force and light naval forces to include blocking passages between Korea and Kyushu [the southernmost island of Japan's mainland] and routes through the Yellow Sea.

C. Conduct only such contributory operations as are essential to establish the conditions prerequisite to invasion.

D. Invade Japan at the earliest practicable date.

E. Occupy such areas in the industrial complex of Japan as are necessary to bring about unconditional surrender and to establish absolute military control.

Three days after this Joint Chiefs of Staff meeting, Undersecretary of State Joseph Grew came to see Truman with a novel idea. Grew arrived at Truman's office at 12:35 p.m. on May 28 with special counsel to the president Sam Rosenman, a man of gifted intelligence and thoroughly trusted by Truman. With Rosenman listening, Grew laid out a scenario. Even before Truman took over on April 12, Pentagon officials had decided that the invasion of Japan was a necessity. The aim in Japan was to defeat the enemy with the least possible loss of American lives. "The Japanese are a fanatical people," Grew noted, "and are capable of fighting to the last ditch and the last man. If they do this, the cost in American lives will be unpredictable." The Japanese worshipped their emperor like a god, Grew said, and Grew would know. He had served as ambassador to Japan for much of the 1930s, and at the time of Pearl Harbor. If the emperor's fate was in the balance, Grew believed, the Japanese would never surrender.

"If some indication can now be given the Japanese that they themselves ... will be permitted to determine their own future political structure," Grew argued, "they will be afforded a method of saving face, without which surrender will be highly unlikely."

Grew was suggesting that the Japanese might surrender if they knew that their emperor could remain in power. The idea was incisive, yet problematic. Roosevelt and subsequently Truman had demanded unconditional surrender of the Japanese, as they had demanded and achieved with the Nazis. Allowing the emperor to remain in power would be considered a major condition.

Would FDR have approved of such an idea? Would Congress stand for it? And the American people? As *Time* magazine put it at the time:

"The Emperor Hirohito was Japan ... The war against Japan was inevitably a war against the Emperor."

Truman understood the challenging nature of this proposition. He could not know, however, that this question would become a pivotal one in world history and would weigh heavily on his legacy.

In the Pentagon, the secretaries of war and navy, General Marshall, and other State Department and military officials argued these matters through the end of May and beyond. The only thing they could agree on was the incertitude of it all. "The Japanese campaign involves therefore two great uncertainties," Stimson wrote in May 1945. "First, whether Russia will come in [to the war against Japan] though we think that will be all right; and second, when and how S-1 [the atomic bomb] will resolve itself."

ON MAY 28, Truman experienced for the first time the awestriking pageantry of a White House State Dinner. The regent of Iraq – Prince Abd al-Ilah – arrived in Washington with his entourage. The prince was his nation's most powerful figure; he had "all the prerogatives of the King of Iraq," according to a State Department memorandum to the president. White House chief of protocol George Thomas Summerlin sprang into action. Every detail down to the most minute had been planned out, as the prince's visit was a performance in which everyone involved had a careful role to play. As host, Truman found himself confronting the affair with great anxiety.

A motorcade of officials left the White House to collect the regent and his party, who arrived by train at Union Station at 4:30 p.m. Strict instructions were given for the order of introductions. The Americans addressed the regent as "Your Royal Highness" and the prime minister of Iraq as "Mr. Minister."

As instructed, Truman walked onto a White House portico at the exact moment the motorcade pulled up in front of it via the Northwest Gate. The president greeted the prince and his men, then both parties assumed a formation according to a diagram the protocol chief had produced. Photographers clicked away. Truman, in a black double-breasted suit, and the regent, in a light-tan officer's uniform, stood three paces in front of their entourages, as the White House Marine Band performed military honors. Truman then led the prince into the White House to present Mrs. Truman. The prince – a thin, affable man with a delicate mustache and boyish features – spoke clear English. He presented the president with a gift: a silver coffee set. Truman found the gift rather odd but kept this notion to himself for the moment, thanking the prince profusely.

On the day of his death, Roosevelt had signed a letter inviting the prince to Washington. The Mideast was a knot of political and trade interests, the various strings leading back to capital cities all over the globe, notably London, Paris, Moscow, and Washington. Iraq was a nation that had grown out of the Fertile Crescent, the land of Baghdad and the Tigris and Euphrates Rivers. The country was smaller than the state of Texas, and yet the United States had much to gain through Iraqi friendship. The State Department had instructed Truman to prevail upon the prince to allow U.S. airlines to make use of airfields in Iraq. "If such rights are given to us," the State Department advised, "Iraq will become one of the crossroads of our post-war aviation system." Confidential sources had revealed that the British were secretly trying to block the United States' landing rights in Iraq, because of their own interests in the Mideast.

More important was the region's black gold. "Iraq is extremely rich in oil," the State Department advised. "Some geologists believe that the oil resources of Iraq are greater than those left in the whole United States." American investment was extracting considerable profit from oil fields in the Mideast, and the British were doing well too.

"Our real interest in the Middle East and Iraq, however, is believed to be much greater than any profits which might be derived from trade," the State Department advised Truman. "Our primary interest in this part of the world is one of world security."

Two major challenges faced the Mideast. The first was Zionism, which was now becoming one of the world's major issues, following the liberation of Jews from Nazi concentration camps. According to the State Department, "The Arabs, not only in Palestine but throughout the whole [Mideast], have made no secret of their hostility to Zionism and their Governments say that it would be impossible to restrain them from rallying with arms." On the day of his death, FDR had communicated in his letter to the Iraqi prince that "no decision affecting the basic situation in Palestine should be reached without full consultation with both Arabs and Jews." Surely the prince had come to Washington for one reason above all others: to implore the United States not to support Zionism. Truman assured his advisors that he would respect FDR's promise, and make no commitments either way as of yet.

The second problem facing the Mideast was the economic ambitions of predatory nations, who saw resources in these weak countries that could be used to fortify their own security. France was refusing to remove troops from Syria and Lebanon; violent clashes between troops and local populations had embittered these citizens. The British, the Soviets, and the United States had troops in Iran, another nation rich with oil. If the United States could forge ties with Iraq, this strategic relationship could only help in creating peace and security in a part of the world where everyone stood to gain.

At 8 p.m., Truman and the regent descended the White House grand staircase, with all the dinner guests gathered below. The crowd included cabinet members, Admiral Leahy and General Marshall, Chief Justice Harlan Stone, senators, congressmen, and various friends of Truman's. "It was truly a magnificent sight," Margaret Truman recalled. "The paneled walls and Corinthian pilasters, the marble mantel, the gilded wall sconces, the dining table set with gold flatware and gleaming crystal and china." The State Dining Room was like an American history museum. There was George P. A. Healy's portrait of Abraham Lincoln — Honest Abe peering out while holding his chin in his hand. The prayer that John Adams gave at formal dinners — a blessing on the White House — was inscribed on a mantel near the president's seat at the table.

At one point during the evening Truman asked Admiral Leahy to sit between himself and the prince. Truman had no experience socializing with royalty, while Leahy had been an ambassador to France and a governor of Puerto Rico and was seasoned in such environments. After dinner and toasts, Truman rose to make his remarks. "I want to say to the Regent of Iraq that we are most happy to have him as the guest of the people and the Government of the United States," he began.

It was the first time in Truman's life he had presided over an affair with such pomp and circumstance. Roosevelt had excelled at such moments. His prestige was the defining character of events such as these, and Truman knew he could only pale in comparison.

The next day, however, he told his staffers in the morning meeting that hosting his first state dinner was not as uncomfortable as he thought it would be. "He told us in the morning that, in spite of himself, he had a good time," recalled Eben Ayers. Truman was confused by one thing, however. The Iraqi prince had given him a silver coffee set as a gift, and the cups had no handles. The practical Missourian wondered: How can one pick up a hot cup of coffee in a metal cup with no handle? It was a conundrum.

///

Now six weeks into his presidency, Truman still struggled to confront his reality. At his morning meeting on one of the last days of May, he confided in his staff that he still could not believe it was all true. "I'm one American who didn't expect to be President," he said.

Ever since April 12, momentum had been building behind Truman. He had become a symbol for ordinary Americans, who saw in him the hopes and dreams of their own lives and those of their children. By the end of May, America was in a full-blown love affair with the new president. Daily, bags full of letters were dumped onto the floor of the White House mailroom from citizens who saw a piece of themselves in the unlikely story of the "Man from Missouri." "There are letters addressed to the president by every Tom, Dick, and Harry in the country," Eben Ayers wrote in his diary on May 28. One citizen, identifying himself as "A Convalescent Taxpayer," wrote to the president, "I cannot speak for the country but I can speak for myself and one hundred percent of the people I know. We are delighted with what you are doing. We feel the country has its feet on the ground again."

The outlook of the whole nation had changed, according to a story in the *Washington Post* entitled "Whole Nation Reflects Era of Good Feeling Inspired by President": "The mood of the United States is one of extraordinary friendliness. Americans appear to be more at ease with each other. They are more inclined to talk about national affairs, less inclined to argue. In short there is a cordiality in the air that this country hasn't known in years." *The New Yorker* summed up America's passion for Truman: "There is one thing about President Truman – he is made in the image of the people. You go into a men's shop to buy a pair of pajamas, President Truman waits on you. You go to have a tooth X-rayed, Truman takes the picture. You board a downtown bus, Truman is at the wheel. Probably it's those glasses he wears, but whatever it is, we rather like having a President who always seems to be around. President Roosevelt was for the people, but Harry Truman *is* the people."

Not yet two months into the Truman administration, the *Washington Post* published early polls on the 1948 presidential race, in a story by George Gallup. An overwhelming majority of Americans (63 percent) favored Truman as the Democratic nominee, even though less than a year earlier a majority of Americans had no idea who Truman was. In second was Henry Wallace, forty-three points behind. "Although President Truman stepped into the presidency at one of the most critical periods in world history and followed a man of overshadowing universal fame, he has so far received both the favor and support of an overwhelming majority of his fellow citizens," Gallup wrote.

Universities had contacted the White House staff offering honorary degrees to the president, who of course had no college degree, and he turned these offers down politely because he did not believe he deserved them. Perhaps the people most surprised by Truman were those who reported directly to him. "He is capable and an extremely fine gentleman for whom everyone has the highest regard," one White House staffer wrote in his diary at the end of May.

Meanwhile, the new administration was coming together – the new faces of power in Washington. At his final press conference in May, Truman announced more cabinet appointments. Secretary of state was the biggest of them all, but Truman still could not announce the Byrnes appointment until after the San Francisco conference. Others would come first.

"I have some Cabinet changes I want to tell you about," he told a packed room. "Mr. [Francis] Biddle's resignation has been accepted, and Tom Clark of Texas will be appointed in his place as Attorney General." Truman also named Clinton P. Anderson of New Mexico as secretary of agriculture, in place of Claude Wickard. Roosevelt had generally relied on the East Coast establishment for his appointments – the Harvard and Yale crowd. Truman's appointees thus far came mostly from west of the Mississippi.

"Mr. President, were any of the resignations requested by you?" one reporter asked.

"They were not. I have the resignation of every member of the Government who can resign since I have been President! [Laughter in the room.] I can accept them or not as I choose." (Attorney General Francis Biddle was said to be "sore" as a result of his sacking, to which Truman responded, "I don't give a damn what he says.")

From the point of view of everyday citizens, Truman's presidency was unfolding far better than any could have predicted. Certainly Truman himself felt the same. Two things occurred at the end of May, however, that darkened the mood in the Oval Office considerably. The first involved Lend-Lease. From Moscow, Harry Hopkins was keeping Truman up to date on his discussions with Joseph Stalin. During Hopkins's second meeting with Stalin in the Kremlin, on May 27, the Soviet generalissimo confronted Hopkins over Truman's new Lend-Lease policy. Truman had cut off supplies to the Soviets, and Stalin was furious. According to the minutes of this Stalin-Hopkins meeting, "[Stalin] said that if the United States was unable to supply the Soviet Union further under Lend Lease that was one thing but that the manner in which it had been done had been unfortunate and even brutal."

Stalin believed Truman was using Lend-Lease as leverage to extract concessions from the Soviets, and that such behavior was not the attitude of a friend. "If the refusal to continue Lend-Lease was designed as pressure on the Russians in order to soften them up then it was a fundamental mistake," Stalin said, adding that "if the Russians were approached frankly on a friendly basis much could be done but that reprisals in any form would bring about the exact opposite effect."

By this time, Truman was hearing from Churchill too. "I am distressed to have to bother you . . . ," Churchill cabled, "but the machine has come to a standstill on the subject [of Lend-Lease]." Churchill had made agreements with Roosevelt, the prime minister told Truman, to the effect that Lend-Lease would continue. The British were broke. "I now hear that your War Department has told our people in Washington that they are expecting so large a cut . . . [and] that supplies to us must be drastically curtailed."

The Lend-Lease cuts damaged Truman's standing gravely in the eyes of Churchill and Stalin, at a critical moment in international relations. Millions of Soviet citizens were starving, while the British too were suffering shortages of every resource. As White House correspondent Robert Nixon explained, "This cut the pipeline. This was taking the bread and butter out of the mouths of starving people . . . It shocked Churchill and Stalin to the bottoms of their feet." The Truman administration would be able to kickstart Lend-Lease again, but the damage had been done.

Just as the Lend-Lease debacle began to play out, Congress and colleges broke for recess, and Bess left the White House for Independence, taking Margaret and Mrs. Wallace with her. They were off to spend the summer at home in Missouri, leaving Truman alone in the White House. Truman accompanied his family on the train as far as Silver Spring, Maryland, in a private car. He hated to be alone, and in saying good-bye, he struggled to hold back tears. "Daughter was in a very unsatisfactory humor," he recorded of this moment. "I hope – sincerely hope, that this situation (my being President) is not going to affect her adversely."

As for Bess, Truman knew that his job had forced her into a life she had never wanted, and perhaps in all their twenty-six-year marriage, he had never felt her so distant.

He learned a hard lesson in these first few days with his wife and daughter gone: how lonesome and isolated the presidency could be. As Woodrow Wilson had once said, "It is the extraordinary isolation imposed upon the president by our system that makes the character and the opportunity of his office so extraordinary." So many unsolvable problems gnawed at Truman's nerves. The United Nations Conference was dragging on. He had to confirm plans to fly to San Francisco to address the closing session — if in fact the delegations could agree on anything and get the conference completed. The Tito standoff in Venezia Giulia could result in a breakout of violence at any second, at the cost of more American lives. The president's military budget had to be completed in time for the scheduled budget message to Congress, on June 11. He was working to reorganize the cabinet, and the largest federal agencies too. He wanted chains of command in the agencies, with the top figures trustworthy and loyal, and he knew he would have to step on a lot of toes to get this done. Over all this hung the dark cloud of impending economic chaos, sure to follow the war's end, and an upcoming tripartite meeting that would place Truman at the negotiating table opposite Winston Churchill and Joseph Stalin.

"The White House becomes especially lonely at night," Margaret Truman wrote of her father. "The pressures of the impossible job do not go away . . . Throw in a few personal problems and between midnight and dawn you have a very lonely man . . . When you go down the long, high-ceilinged second-floor hall and hear the wind sighing in the trees, you can easily imagine you are the last person left on earth, and any moment you, too, may disappear into the shadows."

///

On May 29 the Big Three leaders decided on a time and a place for their upcoming tripartite conference, which now promised to be a political brawl of historic proportions.

"I shall be very glad to meet you and President Truman in what is left of Berlin in the very near future," Stalin cabled Churchill, who forwarded the note to the president. "I hope this might take place about the middle of June." Truman responded that he would not be able to leave the

United States until July, and Stalin replied directly to Truman: "I have no objections against the proposed by you date — July 15th."

And so the date was set for the meeting, in bombed-out Berlin. Truman was considering a one-on-one with Stalin first, before Churchill joined in, as the future of the world clearly depended on the negotiations between the United States and the Soviet Union. Britain's role was no longer primary. The prime minister certainly would not like the idea of a Truman-Stalin meeting without the United Kingdom represented, but Churchill might not have a choice, Truman figured.

Churchill continued to plead for a sooner date. "I will gladly come to Berlin with a British delegation," he cabled Truman. He added some biting British sarcasm: "But I consider that July 15, repeat July the month after June, is much too late for the urgent questions that demand attention between us, and that we shall do an injury to world hopes and unity if we allow personal or national requirements to stand in the way of an earlier meeting."

The prime minister could not understand what felt to him like procrastination. Truman could only hope the bomb was going to work.

"Nothing really important has been settled yet," Churchill cabled Truman, "and you and I will have to bear the great responsibility for the future."

Part IV

June–July 1945

We see no acceptable alternative to direct military use.

— J. Robert Oppenheimer on the
atomic bomb, June 16, 1945

HISTORY DOES NOT DEFINITIVELY RECORD THE DAY when Truman realized that he would soon face the most controversial decision that any
president had ever faced, and perhaps would ever face, in all of time. But
evidence suggests that the first of June was that day.

It began on a high note. Staffers arrived in the Oval Office at nine
fifteen for the morning meeting to find the president in a great mood.
He was wearing new spectacles, his eyesight fading from all the reading. He told his staff that Harry Hopkins had achieved something marvelous in Moscow. Hopkins had brokered an agreement between Stalin
and the Poles, allowing exiled Polish leaders in London to return to
Warsaw to help create a more democratic regime. Truman had received
a cable to this effect first thing in the morning from Hopkins: "It looks
as though Stalin is prepared to return to and implement the [Yalta] decision and permit a representative group of Poles to come to Moscow,"
the cable read. This communiqué was immediately followed by one from
Churchill: "Harry Hopkins has just sent me a most encouraging message
about the Polish situation."

The staffers were surprised — a nice way to begin a Friday morning.
"If this is true," Eben Ayers wrote in his diary, "it will be a major accom-
plishment in removing one of the most serious issues threatening Rus-
sian-Allied relations."

The president faced another relentless day of meetings, and his
morning calendar on this day exemplifies how grueling his daily life
could be. A fifteen-minute ceremony with the regent of Iraq, a half
hour with the secretary of the Treasury, twenty minutes with Senator Styles Bridges of New Hampshire, and the weekly press conference; then Truman hosted the Civil Service Commission's Arthur S.
Flemming (thirty minutes); civilians Paul D. Hoffmann, Howard Myers,
and William Benton (fifteen minutes); Dr. L. S. Rowe (fifteen minutes);
George Messersmith (fifteen minutes); Dr. Gilbert Grosvenor, Dr. John

Oliver La Gorce, and Robert V. Fleming (fifteen minutes); Senator Frank P. Briggs, Dr. C. Robert Starks, Dr. Chester D. Swope, Dr. George J. Conley, and Dr. Phil R. Russell (fifteen minutes); Miss Gertrude Ely (fifteen minutes); and a group of labor representatives — thirty-two of them (five minutes). This schedule only got him to lunch, at 1 p.m.

The White House released a Message to Congress from the president on this morning, informing the American people of the Allies' "plans for bringing about unconditional surrender of Japan."

> We are now engaged in a process of deploying millions of our armed forces against Japan in a mass movement of troops and supplies and weapons over 14,000 miles — a military and naval feat unequalled in history. The Japanese have more than four million troops under arms — a force larger than the Germans were ever able to put against us on the Western Front . . . We have not yet come up against the main strength of the Japanese military force . . . Substantial portions of Japan's key industrial centers have been leveled to the ground in a series of record incendiary raids. What has happened to Tokyo will happen to every Japanese city whose industries feed the Japanese war machine. I urge Japanese civilians to leave these cities if they wish to save their lives.

In Truman's first meeting after a short lunch, he welcomed Justice Robert Jackson, who had just returned from the rubble of Europe, where he was laboring to set up military tribunals to try Nazi war criminals. Jackson's progress fascinated the president. Already, a number of the most loathed German officials had been stripped of their freedom. ("I always get those dirty Nazis mixed up," Truman wrote of these figures. "But it makes no difference.") Heinrich Himmler — the Nazi minister of the interior, and a chief architect of the Final Solution — had been captured by the Soviets and had already committed suicide. Hitler's most senior ranking military official, Wilhelm Keitel, and the evil Ernst Kaltenbrunner, boss of the feared Gestapo, were both in custody. Joachim von Ribbentrop, Hitler's foreign minister, was still at large. (He would be captured thirteen days later.)

Thus far, Hermann Göring was the most intriguing Nazi in custody. With Hitler dead, there was no more high-profile Nazi alive than

Göring. A former World War I pilot who had spent time in a sanitarium in a straitjacket before rising to be Hitler's number two for much of the Third Reich's life-span, Göring had surrendered on his own volition to American forces, fearing what the Russians would do with him if he were captured by the Red Army. Truman had received Göring's jewel-covered baton as a gift from some generals. "Can you imagine a fat pig like that strutting around with a forty thousand dollar bauble – at the poor taxpayer's expense and making 'em like it?" Truman said of Göring and his baton. "It goes in a military museum."

Justice Jackson had, by this time, fixed Nuremberg as the place for the trials to take place. He had come across one unexpected obstacle. The British did not favor military tribunals, when it came to the handful of top war criminals who were easy to positively identify. As Jackson informed the president, "Their [the British] unanimous view was that these criminals be not given a trial, but that they should be . . . shot forthwith." Jackson was insisting even the most heinous Nazis receive the rights of habeas corpus. These proceedings would be studied for generations. The moral obligations were imperative.

///

As Truman met with Justice Jackson in the Oval Office, Secretary of War Henry Stimson was presiding over the last of a series of climactic meetings in the Pentagon regarding the atomic bomb. The purpose: to cement final recommendations for the president on the Manhattan Project. These meetings spread out over four days and called on all the major players: Jimmy Byrnes, Generals Marshall and Groves, even Robert Oppenheimer and four of his top scientists, who had traveled to Washington from Los Alamos.

Stimson was now focused exclusively on the atomic bomb. He had become transfixed by its potential historical impact. He had prepared handwritten notes for these meetings, which curiously read like modernist poetry. The verse was a window into the secretary of war's state of mind.

> Its *size* and *character*
> We don't think it *mere* new *weapon*
> *Revolutionary Discovery* of Relation of man to universe
> Great History Landmark like

Gravitation
Copernican Theory
But,
Bids fair *infinitely greater*, in *respect* to its *Effect*
— on the ordinary affairs of man's life.
May *destroy* or *perfect* International *Civilization*
May [be] *Frankenstein* or means for World Peace

In terms of military judgment, no one in Stimson's meetings overshadowed General Marshall, who came to the secretary of war armed with some convincing ideas. What if the United States government was to give the Japanese an evacuation warning, so that the bomb could be used against Japan without killing innumerable civilians? "He thought these weapons might first be used against straight military objectives such as a large naval installation," according to meeting minutes, "and then if no complete result was derived from the effect of that, he thought we ought to designate a number of large manufacturing areas from which the people would be warned to leave — telling the Japanese that we intended to destroy such centers."

"Every effort should be made," Marshall argued, "to keep our record of warning clear. We must offset by such warning methods the opprobrium which might follow from an ill-considered employment of such force."

Marshall also brought up chemical weapons, which might be used in the savage battle currently being fought on the island of Okinawa. "[Marshall] spoke of the type of gas that might be employed. It did not need to be our newest and most potent — just drench them and sicken them so that the fight would be taken out of them — saturate an area, possibly with mustard [gas], and just stand off." It was no less humane than the flamethrowers currently in use to flush Japanese soldiers out of caves, General Marshall argued.

When the Los Alamos scientists were given the floor, they captivated their audience. Oppenheimer was appearing before the Interim Committee for the first time. While managing the stress and deadlines of Los Alamos, Oppenheimer's five-foot-ten-inch body had withered to less than 130 pounds. He appeared as long and thin as the cigarette he was incessantly lighting, and he had striking facial features — bright blue eyes framed between pronounced cheekbones and heavy black eyebrows. As biographers Kai Bird and Martin Sherwin wrote of Oppenheimer, "Every feature of his body was of an extreme." Here also was Italian-born Enrico Fermi, who had created the first controlled nuclear chain reaction, in 1942; Arthur Compton, who with Fermi and others had designed the first plutonium-producing reactor, at Hanford, Washington, during the war years; and Ernest Lawrence, inventor of Berkeley's cyclotron, a machine later called "the granddaddy of today's most powerful accelerators." Each one of these scientists, with the exception of Oppenheimer, was a Nobel laureate. In introducing them, Stimson expressed that "this project should not be considered simply in terms of military weapons, but as a new relationship of man to the universe."

"This discovery might be compared to the discoveries of the Copernican theory and the laws of gravity," Stimson said, "but far more important than these in its effects on the lives of men."

The scientists updated the committee on their progress. Dr. Compton noted that production of enriched uranium and plutonium at the Oak Ridge and Hanford facilities was now at a rate of pounds or hundreds of pounds but that soon scientists would be capable of producing many tons. Though no bomb had yet been detonated, Compton felt the explosive capability of the work at Los Alamos was "a scientific certainty."

Oppenheimer reviewed expectations for the test shot, now scheduled for July 4 — a day of obvious symbolism. One bomb might produce anywhere from 2,000 to 20,000 tons of TNT equivalent; it was impossible to know for sure at this stage, he explained. But he assured the group that the visual effect would be "tremendous." He described what sounded like the creation of a new sun, a "brilliant luminescence, which would rise to a height of 10,000 to 20,000 feet." Future bombs, he believed, could detonate with the force of 50,000 to 100,000 tons of TNT, and later, as much as 100 million tons. Oppenheimer added that, while the "immediate concern had been to shorten the war," he envisioned a future where this new revolutionary means of exploiting power could be used for peacetime purposes. "The basic endeavors in the field should be the enlargement of human welfare," he said.

He also had strong opinions about how to handle the USSR. He argued that the United States should approach the Soviets now, in hopes of a postwar cooperation in this field. If the Americans sprang the bomb on the world as a surprise, the Soviets were certain to react with exponentially greater distrust and aggression.

The others in the room were surprised to hear the theoretical physicist speak so bluntly of politics, and on this matter Byrnes objected. If the Russians were given knowledge of the project, even in general terms, Byrnes believed, "Stalin would ask to be brought into partnership."

The Interim Committee came to some conclusions. There should be no warning given to the Japanese. What if a warning were offered, and the bomb failed to explode? Or, if the weapon did explode and failed to bring about a surrender — would the critical element of surprise have been wasted? Also, the strategists believed that the Japanese could move American POWs into the target area, if they were told ahead of time where it would be. The committee agreed that the bombing should not occur in a civilian area. However, they also agreed that they "should seek to make a profound psychological impression on as many of the inhabitants as possible."

The secretary of war asked Oppenheimer to create his own committee at Los Alamos, so that the scientists themselves could make recommendations on what should be done with their work. Did the scientists believe that this weapon should in fact be used? Oppenheimer was to form this advisory committee quickly, as time was of the essence. However, it appeared to the scientists that the decision to use the bomb had already been made. As Compton noted, it seemed from these committee discussions like "a foregone conclusion that the bomb would be used."

///

After the Interim Committee's final session, Byrnes crossed the Potomac River in his car, motoring from the Pentagon to the White House for an unscheduled meeting with Truman. Byrnes gave a blow-by-blow of the decisions made — the recommendations to the president from the highest military, political, and scientific thinkers. Byrnes himself had been among the strongest voices in these proceedings. He had made the following recommendations at the end of the final session, all of which the Interim Committee had approved. These were the decisions that Byrnes voiced to Truman on this day, June 1: *"While recognizing that the final selection of the target was essentially a military decision, the present view of the Committee was that the bomb should be used against Japan as soon as possible; that it be used on a war plant surrounded by workers' homes; and that it be used without prior warning."*

The implications of this were frighteningly clear to Truman. In the end, no matter what recommendations were made, the final decisions regarding the bomb would be his, and his alone.

Never before in American history had the president been personally responsible for a major military tactical decision during the course of a war. But then, everything about the bomb was unprecedented. As a child, Truman had begun his political education through his reading. He had learned that history moves in cycles, that political circumstances in the present so often have occurred before, in different places and different times, from Philadelphia in 1776 to ancient Greece. But nothing in history could prepare humanity for the bomb, and for the potentially apocalyptic global picture now in Harry Truman's focus.

Around this time, Leonard Reinsch – the radio executive who was serving in the White House as a publicity advisor – met with Truman, finding him deeply disturbed. Truman explained that he had just been briefed on something explosive; exactly what, he told Reinsch, he could not say.

"Leonard," Truman uttered, according to Reinsch's recollections, "I have just gotten some important information. I am going to have to make a decision which no man in history has ever had to make. I'll make the decision but it is terrifying to think about what I will have to decide." Truman said again and again, "I wish I could talk to you about it." But he could not.

///

"This is a lonesome place," Truman wrote his wife of the White House, on the morning of Sunday, June 3. Bess, Margaret, and Mrs. Wallace were in Independence, and the president had a rare day with no official appointments. He had his breakfast alone, then got dressed. "I'm always so lonesome when the family leaves," he wrote in a diary on this morning. "I have no one to raise a fuss over my neckties and my haircuts, my shoes and my clothes."

Without informing any security detail, Truman snuck out of the White House. He walked alone through Lafayette Square to Saint John's Church at Sixteenth and H Streets. A few soldiers and sailors stopped in their tracks when they saw the president walking alone through Washington, saluting him formally. But mostly, he went unnoticed. "Don't think over six people recognized me," he recorded. Parishioners were not surprised to see the president among the crowd that Sunday morning, as Saint John's was the closest chapel to the White House, and every president since James Madison had made an appearance here. Truman found the services "rather dull," he wrote in his diary, "but I had a chance to do some thinking and the time wasn't wasted."

That night he dined alone on the South Portico, looking out over the White House lawn. Staff was at his beck and call. Truman had everything he needed, with the exception of emotional support he had never in his life required more. He was accustomed to sharing his thoughts with Bess about a day's work. She was the only person to whom he could reveal himself completely. He longed for Margie, too. In his letters to her from this time, he revealed himself to be what so many fathers of daughters become: intensely vulnerable. He felt her pain. When Margaret left for Independence, Washington's most popular political gossip columnist — Drew Pearson, in his "Washington Merry-Go-Round" column — put an uncomfortable spin on her departure.

"It came as something of a shock to Washington dowagers and socially-minded young naval officers when attractive, dynamic Margaret Truman suddenly was whisked out of Washington at the very height of the gay June season," Pearson wrote. "A very wise presidential papa wasn't happy about the featured newspaper articles of his daughter shagging at this party, cocktailing at that, and bitting merrily through Washington society with the war still bitterly contested in the Pacific."

Truman felt personally wounded. Pearson's column was the most widely read syndicated newspaper column in the country, and it suggested whimsy and heartlessness on the part of Margaret Truman. He wrote Margie from the White House to apologize, on the day the story was published.

"You evidently are just finding out what a terrible situation the president's daughter is facing," he wrote. "That was the main reason for my not wanting to be Vice-President. I knew what it would mean to you and your mother — to your Aunts and Uncles and Grandmothers and cousins." He called Pearson's column "a tissue of lies" and pleaded with his daughter to "keep your balance and go along just as your dad is trying to do."

Alone at night, the president buried himself in budget figures and State Department papers. But he had to escape what he began to call "the Great White Jail." On his first bachelor weekend he attended the annual Jamboree of the Burning Tree Golf Club in Bethesda, Maryland, a popular watering hole for Washington's elite. Guests at the jamboree that night heard someone playing piano. When they looked up, they were stunned: there was the president of the United States, his fingers on the keys. Imposing secret service men stood cold-faced as a crowd gathered around the piano. "I'm just a prisoner," Truman joked, nodding toward his bodyguards. "Look at my keepers. But you don't know what fun I'm having tonight."

The following Saturday night, June 9, Truman invited guests aboard the presidential yacht for a game of poker. At the card table, Truman could forget his worries and lose himself in the game. Players would sometimes forget to call him Mr. President (such as the time the jurist and politician Fred Vinson addressed Truman as "you son of a bitch"). It was hot aboard the *Potomac* that night, the seasonal humidity thickening the air. The game went on, and surely some bourbon bottles were opened. One frequent Truman poker pal, the White House correspondent Robert Nixon (who was almost certainly aboard the *Potomac* that night, as six newsmen had been invited as guests), said of Truman: "He loved these wild games. Boy, there were some so wild they'd make your hair stand up."

But the poker table could only serve as a temporary escape. "Have been going through some very hectic days," he wrote in his diary in early June. "Eyes troubling somewhat. Too much reading 'fine print.' Nearly every memorandum has a catch in it and it has been necessary to read at least a thousand of 'em and as many reports. Most of it at night."

He confessed in his diary that he was nearly helpless when Bess was gone: "I'm a damn fool I guess because I could never get excited or worked up about gals or women. I only had one sweet-heart from the time I was six . . . I'm old fashioned I guess, but it's a happy state to labor under in this terrible job I fell heir to on Apr. 12, '45."

MUCH TO TRUMAN'S SURPRISE, international tension eased during the first week of June. The news regarding a new Polish government was a boost. Stalin also agreed in early June to help defuse the Tito standoff at the border of Italy and Yugoslavia. Negotiations were taking place for a peaceful solution; the United States, British, and Yugoslavian governments would in fact sign an agreement for the future disposition of Venezia Giulia on June 9. It would remain part of Italy.

From San Francisco, Secretary of State Stettinius had kept Truman up to date on the UN negotiations by phone. The gravest disagreement between the Americans and Soviets remained the veto in the Security Council. Could a member nation veto action by the others? The Soviets insisted on a veto, which could render the UN impotent to act, in the case of one nation's attack on another. The Americans were against the veto, as the Soviets defined it. Molotov refused to negotiate, so Stettinius decided on a bold move — to go over Molotov's head, reaching out directly to Stalin in Moscow through Harry Hopkins. On June 6, Hopkins had his last meetings with Stalin, after which he cabled Truman directly regarding the UN veto: "Stalin overruled Molotov and agreed that the American position was acceptable to him."

Once again, Harry Hopkins had come through. He had saved the UN peace organization. In San Francisco, Stettinius was ecstatic; this victory humiliated Molotov, in front of all the UN delegations. Stettinius informed the president that it now appeared the conference would come to a close successfully, around June 15, at which point Truman would travel west to address the delegations at the closing ceremony.

The Americans celebrated one other major triumph in the first week of June. This victory came over the French, and gave Truman particular satisfaction. French forces under Charles de Gaulle were occupying a piece of northern Italy and were refusing to leave. They had ignored orders from General Eisenhower to move out of Italy and were threatening to protect their claim to this section of Italy along the French border with military action. On June 6, Stimson met with the president to discuss the matter. Stimson spoke of "this clash with the French."

"I was fully in sympathy with the necessity of curbing DeGaulle," Stimson wrote in his diary, "whom I was coming to regard as a psychopathic. [Truman] interrupted me to say that was his opinion too."

This situation bordered on the absurd. The British and American forces had saved France from the Nazis. The United States government had delivered – and was still delivering – immense amounts of supplies to France through Lend-Lease. (France had a separate Lend-Lease agreement signed before Truman took over, which allowed for continued deliveries of supplies after VE-day.) Now de Gaulle was attempting to claim territory that did not belong to France – threatening to fight against American troops with tools of war supplied by America. "Those French ought to be taken out and castrated," Truman said in one of his morning meetings.

Truman wrote de Gaulle a letter, dated June 6, noting "the almost unbelievable threat that French soldiers bearing American arms will combat American and Allied soldiers whose efforts and sacrifices have so recently and successfully contributed to the liberation of France itself. Indeed, this action comes at the time of the very anniversary of our landings in Normandy which set in motion the forces that resulted in that liberation."

The president informed de Gaulle that Lend-Lease supplies headed for France would be stopped at once if France refused to relinquish this section of Italy. Very soon after Truman's letter was delivered, the president was informed by Allied headquarters in Caserta, Italy, that "General DeGaulle agrees to withdrawal of French troops west of 1939 Italo-France frontier."

The French affair sparked chuckles in many offices of the War Department and the Pentagon, and reinforced the stature of the president. Truman considered releasing the correspondence to the press; it would have embarrassed de Gaulle so severely, the French leader may have been forced to resign, but Truman decided against this move.

On June 8, a few minutes before 2 p.m., Truman took his seat in the Cabinet Room for his regular cabinet meeting. Undersecretary of State Joseph Grew opened the proceedings that day. "Mr. President," he said, "I don't believe as a rule in crowing before the sun is really up but I may say that the international scene is a great deal better today than it was two days ago."

///

Joseph Davies returned to the United States from his meetings with Churchill, arriving at the White House for dinner with Truman at 6:45 on the night of June 4. He found Truman in his second-floor study reading documents with his sleeves rolled up.

"Tell me," Truman asked, "how were you received?"

Davies began his account of his British sojourn, a story replete with intense conflict and moments of comic relief. One thing stood out for Davies: the prime minister was in a very nervous and agitated state. He was terrified of the Russians.

Soon after his arrival in the United Kingdom, Davies was whisked off to Chequers, a sixteenth-century mansion in Buckinghamshire that served as the official country retreat of the prime minister. A formal dinner for political luminaries followed, after which Churchill and Davies retired to a private study, the prime minister with scotch and soda, and Davies – in bad health with heart problems – having "chemical soup" (broth synthetically made, since real broth was not obtainable in Britain due to the war, even by the prime minister). According to Davies, this first private talk "was not a 'smooth' session."

Davies told Churchill that – regarding the upcoming Big Three conference – Truman was considering meeting with Stalin alone first, then Churchill would be invited. The prime minister was instantly enraged. He insulted the honor of the United States to Davies's face, and Davies – who had just arrived in England – threatened to leave immediately. Churchill then calmed down and agreed to cooperate with the United States (Truman interjected in the story here: "Great, you did a splendid job. You got exactly what I wanted on Churchill's own suggestion."). That first discussion with Churchill continued until 4:30 a.m., Davies explained. The two men then offered cloying good-night speeches, in the English tradition. As Davies recalled the conversation:

"To the great American Envoy," Churchill said.

"Goodnight to you, Sir," Davies came back, "the greatest Englishman of all time, who lived what Shakespeare dreamed, and who translated into deeds what England's greatest had taught."

The discussions began again the next morning in Churchill's private quarters. Apparently, the prime minister had no compunction about conducting high-level diplomacy while still in bed in his pajamas. From here on out, over the next few days, Davies and Churchill got to the bottom of the prime minister's fears, which Davies listed for the president.

Churchill was bitter toward the French. "He was completely fed up with de Gaulle and out of patience," Davies told Truman. The prime minister was "even more bitter towards Tito," who was "a communist, and completely under the domination of Moscow." Most important, Churchill was violent in his criticism of the USSR. Davies was shocked by his vitriol. Churchill believed the Soviets had sent "communist propagandists and leaders, 'like locusts,' to establish communist cells" all over Europe, Davies recounted. "What was more horrible to him than Communism," Davies reported, "was the imposition of the Secret Police and Gestapo methods."

"As I listened to his denunciation of the Soviets," Davies continued, "I was horrified in the realization of what it meant to Peace."

Churchill feared what was going to happen to Europe once the American military forces were gone from the continent. He understood the priorities in the Far East; the war against Japan had to be won. But with the withdrawal of American troops, Davies quoted Churchill, "Europe would be prostrate and at the mercy of the Red Army and of Communism." The prime minister was clear about how high the stakes had grown, and who would shoulder the responsibilities ahead. "Perhaps it would fall to a very few men to decide in the next few weeks the kind of life that would confront several generations to come," Churchill told Davies.

Davies left the United Kingdom with quite an impression of Churchill: "A great man, but first, last, and all the time, a great Englishman for Britain and the Empire, first, last, and all the time, with even Peace a second consideration."

///

Nine days later, on June 13, Harry Hopkins arrived at the White House, returning from Moscow. Servants had set a breakfast table on a portico that offered a rare view of the capital city: the Washington Monument poking at a humid sky, and – behind it, on the banks of the Potomac –

the Jefferson Memorial (completed two years earlier). Along with Truman, Joseph Davies and Admiral Leahy sat down at the breakfast table to hear Hopkins's account of his mission to Moscow.

Truman told Hopkins that he was looking spry. The president admitted that when he sent Hopkins off to Moscow, he feared Hopkins might not make it back alive. In truth, Hopkins was concealing a 102-degree fever on this morning. He had lost so much weight, his seersucker suit dangled from his shoulder bones. Hopkins had kept Truman up to date on his discussions with Stalin through long cables from the Moscow embassy, so Truman knew the basic story. The meetings had spread out over twelve days, in Stalin's office in the Kremlin. The Russians were most obsequious in their attempts to impress the visiting Americans, taking a particular liking to Mrs. Hopkins — a former editor for the fashion magazine *Harper's Bazaar* — who had accompanied her husband to supervise his health. ("[She] had an extraordinary effect on the Soviet marshals," translator Chip Bohlen recalled. The Soviet military men crowded around her, "practically rendering her invisible.")

From the start, Hopkins laid out the situation for Stalin. "Two months ago," Hopkins began, according to meeting minutes, "there had been overwhelming sympathy among the American people for the Soviet Union and complete support for President Roosevelt's politics which the Marshal [Stalin] knew so well." Since then, the American citizens "were seriously disturbed about their relations with Russia. In fact, in the last six weeks deterioration of public opinion had been so serious as to affect adversely the relations between the two nations."

Stalin countered. In the Soviet Union, influential circles "felt a certain alarm in regard to the attitude of the United States Government," he said. "It was their impression that the American attitude towards the Soviet Union had perceptibly cooled once it became obvious that Germany was defeated." The Soviets believed that, with Hitler out of the picture, the Americans no longer needed their friends in Moscow. Herein lay the reason why Truman's cancellation of Lend-Lease had such a stinging impact in the Kremlin.

When Hopkins steered the conversation to the Far East, the gimlet-eyed Soviet had some surprises for the Americans. For the first time, Stalin committed to a date on which the Soviets would join the war against Japan: August 8. On that day the Red Army would be "properly deployed" to attack Japanese forces occupying the Manchuria region of China. Stalin explained that the Russian people "must have a good reason for going to war." Truman wanted the Soviets to join the war against Japan because he knew this would save American lives. However, it would also mean the blood of Soviet soldiers, and Stalin was not about to give this away for free. In exchange for Soviet participation in the Far East, on top of the demands he was making of China, Stalin had other trophies in mind. According to excerpts of Hopkins's report, Stalin had come to the following conclusions regarding Japan:

1. Japan is doomed and the Japanese know it.
2. Peace feelers are being put out by certain elements in Japan . . .
   a. The Soviet Union prefers to go through with unconditional surrender and destroy once and for all the military might and forces of Japan . . . [If the Japanese were not forced into unconditional surrender] they will start at once to plan a war of revenge.
   b. However, he [Stalin] feels that if we stick to unconditional surrender the Japs will not give up and we will have to destroy them as we did Germany.

Then Stalin uttered what appeared to be his main prize. According to Hopkins's report: "The Marshal expects that Russia will share in the actual occupation of Japan and wants an agreement with the British and us as to occupation zones."

This was a red flag. Truman had no interest in having the Soviets occupy any part of Japan.

Stalin promised that, when his troops poured over the Chinese border into Manchuria to push out the Japanese occupying forces, he would have no designs on Chinese territory itself. "He stated categorically that he had no territorial claims against China and mentioned specifically Manchuria and Sinkiang and that in all areas his troops entered to fight the Japanese he would respect Chinese sovereignty," Hopkins informed Truman.

The question was, should the Americans trust that Stalin would keep his word? Or would Soviet influence move deep into China, on the coattails of the Red Army? And then into Japan itself? The American government would have to respond to Stalin's demands, which put the president in an extraordinary position. If he agreed to Soviet demands, Stalin's influence would push into the East. If Truman did not, the United States would fight Japan without Soviet assistance, and more American soldiers would die.

Truman informed Hopkins and Davies that their missions were important moments in the context of this war, and the American people deserved to know about them. In the United States the free press warranted information, and they would get it. The group moved down to the Oval Office, where doors were then flung open for the press. At that moment, "a battery of photographers greeted us," recalled Davies. Hopkins and Davies answered questions from newspaper reporters and smiled for newsreel cameras. As Harry Hopkins's biographer (and FDR speech writer) Robert Sherwood later wrote, "This was an extraordinary moment in Hopkins's life, for he now found himself in the thoroughly unfamiliar position of enjoying a very good press. He was even, for a few days, something of a national hero."

The mission to Moscow was the last for fifty-four-year-old Harry Hopkins. He was soon back in the hospital, and he died less than eight months later — January 29, 1946.

28

BY THE END OF TRUMAN'S SECOND WEEK alone in the White House, he began to feel like a haunted man.

"I sit here in this old house and work on foreign affairs, read reports, and work on speeches," he wrote Bess on June 12, "all the while listening to the ghosts walk up and down the hallway and even right in here in the study. The floors pop and the drapes move back and forth — I can just imagine old Andy [Andrew Jackson, presumably] and Teddy [Roosevelt] having an argument over Franklin [Roosevelt] . . . The din is almost unbearable." Truman was now two months into his presidency. "Just two months ago today, I was a reasonably happy and contented Vice President," he wrote Bess. "Maybe you can remember that far back too. But things have changed so much it hardly seems real." Three days later Truman wrote Bess again, following a phone call: "It was nice to talk with you last night. I was so tired and so lonesome I did not know what to do."

Eleanor Roosevelt attended a luncheon at the White House around this time, and she described Truman in these terms: "His family is gone, the house is bare & stiff & he's the loneliest man I ever saw. He's not accustomed to night work . . . and he doesn't like it. He's not at ease & no one else is. I am so sorry for him & he tries so hard."

In his first two months as president, Truman had devoted a majority of his time to foreign affairs, but domestic issues were becoming increasingly critical. He submitted his first military budget to Congress on Monday, June 11. (The total program for the new fiscal year would run $39,019,790,474 — a 25 percent cut in military spending from the year earlier, reflecting the end of hostilities in Europe.) There were labor strikes that required executive orders from the president, so the federal government could take over factories, coal mines, and railroads, all critical to the war effort. Truman called on farmers across the nation to increase food production in every possible way: "The supply lines to feed our troops and the millions fighting and working with them are the longest in the history of warfare."

He was still searching for advisors he could trust with respect to the home front. He confided in his press secretary, Charlie Ross, his federal loan administrator, John Snyder, and White House special counsel/ speech writer Sam Rosenman that they were his three most trusted confidants with respect to domestic policy. "Took Ross, Snyder and Rosenman to the 'House' for lunch," Truman wrote in a diary entry. "Gave them a libation before we went to the daily dining room for lunch. Told the three of them that they were most in my confidence and that I wanted frank and unadulterated statements of fact to me from them – and that when they couldn't treat me on that basis, they'd be of no use to me."

Regarding his politics, he "has answered by actions the question on every lip at the time of the death of Franklin D. Roosevelt," noted a *Chicago Tribune* columnist. "What kind of President will Truman make?" He had proven a Jeffersonian Democrat, as he defined the term. He was out for the little guy, the common man, workers and farmers, for all those who fell easy prey to the greed and manipulation of the powerful forces that capitalism sometimes fostered. His liberalism raised some eyebrows on Capitol Hill even among some right-leaning Democrats, but Truman was prepared to dig in and fight on domestic issues, as Americans would soon find out. As he once said, "The President has to look out for the interests of the 150 million people who can't afford lobbyists in Washington." He would fight for the kind of man he had once been but was no more – an ordinary American.

Still, as a wartime president, he had to focus primarily on the global emergency. June 18 would prove to be a critical day, for the Truman administration and the war.

///

At 3:30 p.m. on June 18, Truman called a meeting to order of his Joint Chiefs of Staff and his top civilian cabinet advisors from the War Department. The brain trust of the American military gathered. Here sat General George Marshall, Fleet Admiral Ernest King, Lieutenant General I. C. Eaker of the army air forces (representing General Arnold, recovering from a heart attack), and the chief of the president's staff, Fleet Admiral Leahy. Secretary of War Stimson was in the room, as were Assistant Secretary of War John J. McCloy and Secretary of the Navy Forrestal. The president wanted to know from each an opinion on the most efficient means of forcing Japan to surrender unconditionally, and to bring the war to an end.

General Marshall spoke first, reiterating arguments he had already posed but now with more detail. The situation in Japan was "practically identical" to the situation in Europe before the Normandy invasion, Marshall said. He believed that "the only course to pursue" with respect to Japan was the course that had brought the Nazis to their knees: a ground invasion. He had chosen the island of Kyushu at the southern end of Japan's mainland for the landing, and he set D-day at November 1 – four and a half months' time.

Marshall listed the reasons for the timing: "Our estimates are that our air action will have smashed practically every industrial target worth hitting in Japan as well as destroying huge areas in Jap cities," he said. "The Japanese Navy, if any still exists, will be completely powerless. Our sea action and air power will have cut Jap reinforcement capabilities from the mainland to negligible proportions." Any delay past November 1 could force a further delay of up to six months due to winter weather, he explained.

The general then discussed what could be expected in casualties. The United States had suffered roughly 20,000 casualties (killed, wounded, missing) in the invasion of Iwo Jima, against an estimated 25,000 Japanese (killed and taken prisoner, for there was no way to even guess how many were wounded). In Okinawa – the fiercest fought ground battle of the Far East war, and one in which the U.S. forces were on the brink of declaring victory – the Americans had suffered 34,000 army and 7,700 navy casualties, against 81,000 Japanese (the latter number being "not a complete count," according to the military statisticians). U.S. casualties in the first thirty days of the Normandy invasion had been 42,000. There was no way to estimate the number of casualties expected in the invasion of mainland Japan, but Marshall did say this: "It is a grim fact that there is not an easy, bloodless way to victory in war and it is the thankless task of the leaders to maintain their firm outward front which holds the resolution of their subordinates."

Marshall was convinced that "every individual moving to the Pacific should be indoctrinated with a firm determination to see [the invasion] through." He put the number of troops required for the operation at 766,700. The invasion plan was as follows: (1) to have the Russians attack the Japanese occupying Manchuria in China; (2) to "vitalize the Chinese" with air support and supplies so they could handle the Japanese occupying other parts of their country; and (3) all of which would allow the Americans – with British aid – to go after mainland Japan.

Truman went around the room and heard not a single dissent. Lieutenant General Eaker of the air forces noted that he had a fresh cable from his boss, General Arnold, saying he too agreed the invasion should move forward. Stimson went along with the plan, with reservations. He had visited Japan years earlier when he had served as governor-general of the Philippines, under President Coolidge, and he had followed the politics of Japan for longer than anyone else at the table. He felt he knew the Japanese more personally. He believed that there were a lot of Japanese citizens not interested in fighting this war, but if this "submerged class" was attacked on their homeland, they would fight savagely. It would be a terrifying, bloody ordeal. Truman also wondered aloud if the invasion by the white man would further impel the Japanese to combat with religious zeal.

Leahy brought up unconditional surrender. He feared that an insistence on unconditional surrender "would result only in making the Japanese desperate and thereby increase our casualties." Leahy believed unconditional surrender was unnecessary, that the United States could agree to softer terms in exchange for fewer lives lost. For example, the United States could allow the Japanese emperor to remain in power. Might not the enemy surrender, if the enemy was told it could retain its monarchy?

Truman was increasingly wary of this argument. The shock of Pearl Harbor was still fresh in the American consciousness. Would a conditional surrender be construed as a failure on the part of the Truman administration? Even a stab in the back of the deceased former president, FDR? This whole war was a result, many believed, of the failure of the United States to force complete unconditional surrender on the enemy in the last war. If the Americans had truly accomplished that after World War I, the argument went, there was no way Pearl Harbor or the rise of Hitler could have occurred. As Eleanor Roosevelt had written in June 1944: "We gave up unconditional surrender the last time . . . and now we have sacrificed thousands of lives because we did not do a thorough job."

The pressure was on Truman to not make that mistake again.

The Soviets had promised to join the war on August 8. Truman asked if the decision on the invasion should be delayed, as the declaration of war by the USSR could be enough to push the Japanese to surrender unconditionally. All agreed, this matter was of major importance.

When the president asked one final time if there was unanimous opinion in the room regarding plans for a ground invasion, all agreed, it should be a go. Leahy remembered watching Truman at this meeting. "Truman was always a good listener," Leahy recalled, "and I could not gauge exactly what his own feeling was. He did indicate in our discussion that he was completely favorable toward defeating our Far Eastern enemy with the smallest possible loss of American lives."

At the end of this meeting, Truman turned to Assistant Secretary of War John J. McCloy, who had not yet spoken.

"McCloy, you didn't express yourself," Truman said (according to McCloy's recollections), "and nobody gets out of this room without standing up and being counted. Do you think I have any reasonable alternative to the decision [on the invasion] which has just been made?"

McCloy turned to his boss, Stimson, who said, "Say what you feel about it."

"Well, I do think you've got an alternative," McCloy said. "And I think it's an alternative that ought to be explored and that, really, we ought to have our heads examined if we don't explore some other method by which we can terminate this war than just by another conventional attack and landing."

McCloy began by saying that he agreed that the Japanese might surrender if they were given word that they could retain their monarch, Emperor Hirohito. Then McCloy brought up the bomb. "Well as soon as I mentioned the word 'bomb' — the atomic bomb — even in that select circle, it was sort of a shock," he recalled. "You didn't mention the bomb out loud; it was like mentioning Skull and Bones in polite society at Yale. It just wasn't done."

McCloy argued that the United States should tell the enemy of the bomb, and if Japan did not surrender, it would be used. He said, "I think our moral position would be better if we gave them a specific warning of the bomb."

The response, as McCloy remembered the conversation: "We don't know that it will go off; suppose it doesn't go off; our prestige will be greatly marred."

"All the scientists have told us that the thing will go," McCloy said.

"It's just a matter of testing it out now, but they're quite certain from re-ports I've seen that this bomb is a success . . ."

Truman said the group should "explore this," but decisions with re-gard to the bomb could not be made until it was tested successfully. Tru-man ordered the Joint Chiefs to move ahead with plans for a ground invasion of Japan, an order that would begin the process of putting more than three quarters of a million Americans in harm's way.

///

At the time of this June 18 conference, Manhattan Project scientists at Los Alamos in New Mexico were straining to meet the July 4 deadline for the first test of an atomic bomb. The scientists had instructions to prove that a bomb could work before Truman left the country to sit at the bargaining table with Stalin and Churchill at the upcoming tripartite meeting in the Potsdam suburb of Berlin. As Oppenheimer later told an interviewer, "We were told that it would be very important – I was told I guess by Mr. Stimson – that it would be very important to know the state of affairs before the meeting at Potsdam at which the future conduct of the war in the Far East would be decided."

By June 1945, Oppenheimer's secret laboratory in the New Mexico desert had become a full-blown town. The pace of the work was astound-ing, especially to the men performing it daily. In March 1943, "Oppie" (as most people at Los Alamos called him) had arrived with the first mem-bers of his research team. Now, barely more than two years later, about 4,000 people were living at Los Alamos in some 300 newly constructed apartment buildings, some 50 dormitories and 200 trailers. The residents had their own radio station and their own Los Alamos town council.

Throughout the existence of the Manhattan Project, these scientists and military men worked according to a simple ideology. As put by Op-penheimer: "Almost everyone knew that if [the bomb] were completed successfully and rapidly enough, it might determine the outcome of the war." Now that the first test was near, however, many of these figures had begun to confront an ambivalence over the morality of their work. Some scientists at Los Alamos had begun hosting meetings to discuss their fears about the effects this bomb would have on Japan and what it would mean for the future of humanity, but Oppenheimer did not ap-prove. That was the work of politicians, he said. Their work was to build a weapon that would end the war. It was only a matter of time, however, before the voice of dissenting scientists demanded to be heard.

On June 11, James Franck – a Nobel laureate – produced a petition signed by seven Manhattan Project scientists in Chicago. Franck attempted to place this document in the hands of the secretary of war. "We feel compelled to take a more active stand now because the success which we have achieved in the development of nuclear power is fraught with infinitely greater dangers than were all the inventions of the past," the petition read. The scientists determined that there was no hope of avoiding "a nuclear armament race" among nations in the future, particularly with the USSR. Just because the bomb was being born, these scientists believed, did not mandate that it should be used against human targets. The petition pointed out that the United States had "large accumulations of poison gas, but not use them."

Ultimately, the petition called for "a demonstration of the new weapon . . . before the eyes of representatives of all the United Nations, on [a] desert or a barren island."

This petition was signed seven days before Truman's June 18 meeting with his Chiefs of Staff and war cabinet, on the planning of the Japanese invasion. The president was never made aware of it at the time. He was, however, almost certainly made aware of another document, dated June 16: the findings of Robert Oppenheimer's Scientific Advisory Committee, formed to allow the Manhattan Project scientists to voice an opinion on what should be done with their work. Oppenheimer summed up the findings as follows:

> The opinions of our scientific colleagues on the initial use of these weapons are not unanimous; they range from the proposal of a purely technical demonstration to that of the military application best designed to induce surrender. Those who advocate a purely technical demonstration would wish to outlaw the use of atomic weapons, and have feared that if we use the weapons now our position in future negotiations will be prejudiced. Others emphasize the opportunity of saving American lives by immediate military use . . . We [Oppenheimer's Scientific Advisory Committee] find ourselves closer to these latter views; we can propose no technical demonstration

likely to bring an end to the war; we see no acceptable alternative to direct military use.

///

On the same afternoon as Truman's meeting with his military advisors on Japan (June 18), General Eisenhower made his triumphant return to Washington. Roughly a million people lined the streets to praise Eisenhower – "definitely the biggest crowd in the capital's history," according to the city's police department. Here was "Iron Ike," who had led Operation Torch, the invasion of North Africa in the fall of 1942; who had commanded the 1944 D-day invasion of Normandy; who had served as supreme commander of the Allied Expeditionary Force in Europe. When he marched down the aisle in the House Chamber to the speaking platform, a who's who of political and military power was there to see him: the Joint Chiefs of Staff, Supreme Court justices, senators, congressmen, diplomats, Mrs. Mamie Eisenhower, everyone but Harry Truman, who chose not to appear, to give Eisenhower all the spotlight. The *Washington News* called Eisenhower's roaring reception Congress's "greatest ovation in 25 years."

At the speaker's podium, the general "looked nervous and embarrassed and rather like the high school valedictorian just prior to his speech," recorded one reporter in the crowd. When Eisenhower began his remarks, many in the crowd believed that they were listening to a speech from the next president of the United States.

That night Truman hosted Eisenhower at the White House for a "stag party." More than a hundred guests attended. Eisenhower was "a real man," in Truman's words, and the president enjoyed himself immensely. The Marine Band Orchestra delivered all the White House favorites. Truman escorted Eisenhower into the State Dining Room, where the formality of place cards was omitted. Eisenhower brought his son John with him, who had graduated from West Point on June 6, 1944 – D-day – and had then joined his father on the beaches of Normandy. The day after Eisenhower's White House fete, Truman wrote Bess: "Eisenhower's party was a grand success . . . He is a nice fellow and a good man. He's done a whale of a job. They are running him for President, which is O.K. with me. I'd turn it over to him now if I could."

The timing of Eisenhower's return to Washington was fortuitous, for the day after his speech at the Capitol, word came from the Far East that Okinawa had fallen. Truman received a communiqué from a naval aide on June 19: "Okinawa: It is officially stated that the enemy resistance was broken today. A breakthrough was made in two places. The enemy is being pushed off the southern end of the island. Mopping up is under way." One of the most bitterly fought battles of all time was ending. Officially, the Allies would not declare the victory until June 22. Churchill sent Truman a heartfelt congratulatory cable that summed up this historic battle succinctly: "The strength of will-power, devotion, and technical resources applied by the United States to this task, joined with the death-struggle of the enemy, of whom 90,000 are reported to be killed, places this battle among the most intense and famous in military history."

Even before the final shot was fired, nearly 100,000 military engineers and construction workers began turning the island of Okinawa into a sprawling staging area with airfields and living quarters for hundreds of thousands of soldiers, in preparation for the November 1 invasion of Japan.

AT 8 A.M. ON JUNE 19, the morning after Eisenhower's party at the White House, the president's motorcade pulled onto the tarmac at an airfield outside Washington. The crew of the *Sacred Cow* was readying the aircraft in anticipation of a long flight due west, with Truman aboard. Eisenhower showed up to see Truman off ("I didn't know you could get up this early in the morning, Ike," Truman joked). It was Truman's first jaunt aboard this Douglas VC-54C. He had logged his share of flight miles over the years, but he had never flown like this.

The *Sacred Cow*'s unpressurized cabin had an executive conference room with a big desk located next to a bulletproof window. There was an electric refrigerator in the galley and a fold-down bed; the president had his own private lavatory too. The aircraft's four Pratt & Whitney engines produced close to 3,000 horsepower, and a sensational amount of noise and vibration.

Truman's flight to Tacoma, Washington, was set to land at 5:40 p.m. He planned to visit the state's capital, Olympia, for a few days' rest as the guest of an old friend, Governor Monrad Wallgren, who as a senator had served on the Truman Committee. Then the president was scheduled to continue on to San Francisco to address the delegations of fifty nations at the closing ceremonies of the United Nations Conference.

That morning the *Washington Post* made for good airplane reading. Drew Pearson's Washington gossip column — "Washington Merry-Go-Round" — was all about the president. "Harry Truman has now been President of the United States for a little over two months — two of the most historic months in the nation's history," the column began. There was a new atmosphere in the White House that could be summed up in a word: businesslike. "Truman gives the impression of having a firm grasp on all domestic problems," Pearson wrote. "He knows them thoroughly — undoubtedly better than Franklin Roosevelt during his latter years, when he was devoting all his time to the war . . . One thing that worries [Truman] most is our foreign affairs. The new President frankly realizes it is his main weakness."

The *Sacred Cow* touched down at McChord Field three minutes early (the Washington-to-Tacoma flight took twelve hours and sixteen minutes nonstop). By that time, two other planes had landed at this same airfield – one carrying the White House press corps, the other secret service. Truman stepped out onto the tarmac, where Governor Wallgren and his wife awaited.

"Hello, Harry," the governor said, offering his hand.

"It sure is swell for you and Mrs. Wallgren to meet me here," Truman said.

They climbed into an open car and a motorcade cruised through Washington's capital city, both sides of Olympia's streets lined with swelling crowds on tippy-toes, straining to catch sight of the new president. The crowds formed "a human lane up the main street," as one reporter put it. Never had Truman imagined a moment like this one, to be the focal point in such an ebullient celebration of presidential iconography and Americanism. And this western trip was just getting started.

His next few days would enable him to at least attempt to relax; he had but one official appointment, to present a congressional Medal of Honor to a soldier wounded while fighting with General Patton's Third Army. Truman and Wallgren went fishing. They hiked around Mount Rainier, where the thinness of the air from the high elevation took the president's breath away. Secret service allowed Truman to drive a car, something he truly enjoyed, and that felt like a grand luxury now. Each morning the press met with Charlie Ross at Governor Wallgren's mansion, hunting for a story, but there was little Ross could report. Instead, Ross waxed humorously between cigarette puffs about the delicious breakfasts the president and his party were having, knowing that the newsmen were forced to eat Spam, due to rationing.

Behind the scenes the business of running the nation continued. Truman signed bills and issued executive orders. He nominated twelve army officers for three-star general promotions, including Nathan Farragut Twining, a future chairman of the Joint Chiefs of Staff. The planning of the Big Three meeting was moving along, cables discussing the details dashing back and forth between continents at electronic speed.

At 9 a.m. on June 25, Truman took off in the *Sacred Cow*, landing at an airfield in Marin County just north of San Francisco, in the afternoon.

With Secretary of State Stettinius sitting beside him, the president rode through Marin. "The whole countryside seemed somehow influenced by the honor of the occasion in which the president of the United States passed by," Stettinius wrote in his diary. "Suddenly over the shoulder of a hill, there was a view of the mystic white city across the bay – San Francisco, with just a soft touch of sunlight upon it."

Crossing the Golden Gate, Truman saw a giant WELCOME sign fastened to the bridge's towering red spires. In the city there was pandemonium; half a million people were out in the streets. "The whole city was all keyed up with excitement," recalled Henry Reiff of the U.S. delegation to the UN. "Flags flying, crowds gathered about the Hotel Fairmont waiting to catch a glimpse of the president. My, what excitement all over the place!"

Truman must have thought of Woodrow Wilson's heralded arrival in Paris after World War I, for the League of Nations Conference. Congress had failed to approve the League of Nations treaty, but this time the story would be different. Certainly public opinion was all for the UN. According to the American Institute of Public Opinion, over 80 percent of Americans believed the United States should join this "world organization with police power to maintain world peace."

At the Fairmont, someone leaned over to Truman and said, "What a tribute this has been to you," referring to the city's wild excitement.

"It's what we stand for – the United States," Truman said. "They were cheering the office, not the man."

That afternoon, behind closed doors, Truman had a private talk with Edward Stettinius. Truman had sent ahead a messenger, George Allen of the Democratic National Committee, to inform Stettinius that he would be replaced by Jimmy Byrnes as secretary of state. Stettinius was out, and he could not hide his disappointment. At this triumphant moment for the United Nations – which Stettinius could claim as a great personal victory – he was a wounded man. Truman was appointing him the first U.S. representative to the UN.

"Well, you certainly have done a grand job out here," Truman said, steadying himself with an old-fashioned. "Are you satisfied with what I am planning?" he asked, referring to Stettinius's new job.

"We can have a leisurely talk tomorrow," Stettinius said in between sips of a martini.

"You have got to be satisfied," Truman said earnestly. "I want you to be." He promised Stettinius that, with the aid of Charlie Ross, they could spin the move to make it look like somewhat of a promotion for Stettinius. "Don't you have full confidence in Charlie Ross? Don't you trust him?"

Stettinius said, "First I want you to know that I respect you and I think you are a straight shooter." But then: "Mr. President, do you really believe that you can do this thing and put Byrnes in without its appearing publicly like a kick in the pants for me?"

"I sincerely believe it can be done that way," Truman said.

The following day, Truman, Stettinius, and the other members of the U.S. delegation entered the War Memorial Veterans Building for the signing of the United Nations Charter. The charter itself was laid on a circular table surrounded by the flags of fifty nations, which represented over 80 percent of the world's population. The charter was five hulking tomes, facsimiles in five languages – English, Russian, French, Chinese, and Spanish. The logistical challenges of creating this document were staggering; a staff of 135 translators had worked around the clock in seven-hour shifts for days, on twenty electric reproduction machines.

Stettinius signed the charter, then Senators Tom Connally and Arthur Vandenberg signed as the two other ranking members of the U.S. delegation. It took hours for all fifty nations to sign, and even then the United Nations had not yet been born, from the point of view of the Americans. The charter would be flown back to Washington, where the Senate would have to vote on it.

As it now stood, the UN consisted of a fifty-nation General Assembly, an eleven-nation Security Council (which would serve as the most powerful peace enforcement agency in the world), an eighteen-nation Economic and Social Council, plus smaller agencies such as a Trusteeship Council and an International Court of Justice. It was, in the words of one reporter covering the conference, "an omen of great hope." After the signing, the delegations settled in to hear the keynote speaker. Every seat was full when Harry Truman stepped up to the rostrum to address the crowd.

"The Charter of the United Nations," he said, "which you have just signed, is a solid structure upon which we can build a better world. History will honor you for it. Between the victory in Europe and the final victory in Japan, in this most destructive of all wars, you have won a victory against war itself."

There were some Battery D boys in the audience that night, personal guests of the president. Many noticed the strange absence of Bess Truman in the crowd. Truman's speech was well written by all regards, but he had never mastered the art of public speaking. When he delivered his climactic sentence, he shook his hands in the air awkwardly. The United Nations was being born, he said, for one major purpose: "to *find* a *way* to *end* war!"

At the close of ceremonies, Truman looked forward to laying his head on his pillow in a quiet room at the Fairmont. The English version of the United Nations Charter, with all its signatures, was couriered by a special messenger to an army plane for transport back to Washington. The special messenger's name was Alger Hiss, a member of the United States delegation to the UN Conference who would later, in 1948, be accused of spying for the Soviet Union, and would be convicted in 1950 of perjury due to this charge. At the time, however, Hiss was an official entrusted with the delivery of this charter. On the airplane, the UN Charter sat inside a locked safe with its own parachute in case of emergency. The safe bore a sign that read, FINDER! DO NOT OPEN. SEND TO THE DEPARTMENT OF STATE, WASHINGTON.

The day after the closing ceremony, Truman boarded the *Sacred Cow* again for a flight to Kansas City, where he was about to experience the homecoming of a lifetime.

///

The biggest crowds in the history of Jackson County turned out to meet the president when he arrived home in Missouri. His flight landed at 1:28 p.m. on June 27 at Fairfax Field outside Kansas City, Kansas. As soon as the gangway was in place, Margaret Truman ran inside the airplane to hug her father. Bess remained at home, far from the popping camera bulbs. When Truman stepped out of the *Sacred Cow,* his old friend Roger Sermon — the mayor of Independence — stepped forward.

"By jove, look who's here," Truman said. "Hi, Roger, how are you?"

Truman's motorcade swept through Kansas City, Kansas, and over the bridge into Kansas City, Missouri, led by a squadron of motorcycle police. He sat in the back seat of an open car, with Margaret and his brother, Vivian, sitting next to him. A parade of cars followed, many of them open automobiles overflowing with locals. A sign at Grand Avenue read, WELCOME HOME, HARRY! Mobs pushed from the sidewalks into the streets.

From the windows of a Woolworth's store, women waved mini-American flags mounted on little sticks. In front of Kansas City's Jackson County Court House, which Truman had led the charge to build eleven years earlier, a familiar face yelled, "Hello Harry!" Others screamed for "Mr. President" awkwardly – as if, one *Washington Post* reporter noted, "the things that had happened to put this man in the White House were still a bit incredible."

When Truman arrived in his Independence neighborhood, soldiers with white helmets and MP brassards on their arms lined the roads to keep the crowds back. He could see that the old family house at 219 North Delaware had received a fresh coat. It wouldn't do to have the "Summer White House" – as the press was now calling it – badly in need of paint. The house sat on roughly three quarters of an acre, and gardeners had spruced up the property. Along the driveway, red, pink, and white peonies – Bess's favorite flowers – were in bloom. On the northwest corner of the lawn, Truman saw a brand-new thirty-four-foot flagpole set in cement. It was a gift from the city of Independence, and the Stars and Stripes had been raised on this pole for the first time the day before his arrival. Behind the house, there was a new doghouse for Margie's Irish setter, topped by a sign with the dog's name, MIKE.

The family gathered in the house. There was one particular piece of news to celebrate. During Truman's 1940 Senate campaign, a bank had foreclosed on the family farm in Grandview, where Truman had toiled for years as a farmer and where his mother had lived for most of her life. Now, with the financial help of some friends, the family had repurchased the home, and the deed was fully paid off.

"That gives you a rent free home for the rest of your life," Truman informed his mother and his sister. "So now take good care of yourselves and live as long as you can."

In the afternoon Truman enjoyed a quiet moment with his daughter in his backyard, then he rushed off to hold his regular press conference, this time at Independence's Memorial Hall. Every seat in the place was full, but no one was sitting when the president walked onto the stage, where a simple desk and chair had been placed for him. Reporters sat in chairs in the front row, with seemingly the entire town of Independence behind them. Press secretary Charlie Ross called the meeting to order.

"Gentlemen, and ladies – ladies and gentlemen." (Cries of *shshshshhhh.*) Ross read the rules: No direct quotes, unless it's a formal announcement.

"Now, no one is to leave the conference until it is adjourned." Ross turned to Truman. "I believe that's all, Mr. President."

"All right," Truman said. "I guess we'll start."

He began by announcing that Edward Stettinius would be moving to a new job: representative of the United States to the United Nations. He refused at that moment to name the new secretary of state.

One reporter yelled, "Is it Mr. Byrnes, Mr. President?"

Laughter filled the room, for Byrnes's appointment had by this point become common knowledge.

"That question," Truman said, "I cannot answer."

Following the press conference, Truman was whisked off to a dinner with old army buddies at Independence mayor Roger Sermon's house, then to the auditorium at the town's Reorganized Latter Day Saints Auditorium, where again locals jammed the room to see the president, who stood on a stage and spoke extemporaneously. The flag-festooned church auditorium had thousands of seats, and Truman packed the house. Behind him on the stage sat Bess and Margaret, and one Miss Caroline Stoll, age eighty-four, who had been a grade school teacher of Harry's. "This is the most wonderful day of my life," she said. "To think that God should let me live to see this come to pass."

"Time and again, I have tried to fill this great auditorium," Truman said, referring to his adventures as a novice politician in Jackson County, "and this is the first time I have succeeded." He told the story of the night he had become president. "I arrived at the White House and went to Mrs. Roosevelt's study and she informed me that the president had passed away. You can understand how I felt at that moment. It was necessary for me to assume a greater burden, I think, than any man has assumed in the history of the world."

There were two things Truman needed to achieve as president, he explained. "The first one is to win the war with Japan, and we are winning it." The crowd erupted in thunderous applause. "The next one," Truman said, "is to win the peace." He spoke of the Big Three meeting in Berlin, fast approaching, where negotiations would lead, he hoped, to "peace of the world, for generations to come."

///

Truman's homecoming cast a spotlight on the state of Missouri the likes of which its residents had never known. The whole country wanted to know about the place that had given rise to this figure who had inadvertently become a subject of intense fascination. Missouri had never had its own president of the United States before. It had, however, cast its vote for every president since the turn of the twentieth century, and thus it was said that, as Missouri goes, so too goes America. The state had both northern and southern roots (southerners were more likely to pronounce Missouri with an *a* at the end), and while it was home to two vastly different cities – St. Louis and Kansas City – the majority of the land was carved into farming communities. Missouri did not practice segregation on buses, elevators, or streetcars, but it did in schools, toilet facilities, restaurants, and hotels.

Kansas City, the metropolis most associated with the president, still had the air of the Wild West. It was cut in half by the chocolate-colored Missouri River, with Kansas City, Kansas, on one side and Kansas City, Missouri (the larger, more well-known metropolis), on the other. More than three hundred passenger trains and five hundred freight trains passed through Union Station in Kansas City, Missouri, every day. Until recently, the city had boasted some of the most celebrated jazz clubs in the country, stages that had given rise to Bennie Moten, Count Basie, and hometown saxophone wunderkind Charlie "Yardbird" Parker. But many of those clubs had shuttered during the war, and many of those musicians were now serving in the military. While the sizzling Kansas City steak was the local gustatory claim to fame, this cut's smoky fragrance had all but disappeared, due to rationing.

The war had fueled the city's booming economy. Action in the slaughterhouses had pushed Kansas City past Chicago during the war as the world's largest cattle market. Aviation and ordnance plants employed tens of thousands, notably a freshly constructed B-25 bomber plant on the Kansas side of the Missouri River. One example of the wartime boom: the Vendo Company of Kansas City, Missouri – previously a soda vending machine company with 150 workers – had become a military electronics factory employing 1,500.

Independence, meanwhile, was a town that could be dropped into any other state and not look out of place. It had shops, auto garages, banks, corner drugstores, all surrounding Independence Square. There was one thing Independence had, however, that other towns did not: Harry Truman.

"It looks to us," one longtime resident told the *New York Times,* "like you writers and newspaper people are trying to paint a lot of glamour on a fellow who just won't glamorize. Harry Truman isn't any genius. He's just like the rest of us around here, only he's a little smarter. We've known that ever since he was a kid."

The day after Truman's appearance at the church auditorium, he went for a walk through Kansas City, with secret service in tow. At Thirty-Ninth and Main Streets he visited an old friend — Eddie Jacobson — in Jacobson's new shop, Westport Men's Wear.

"Hello there, Eddie," Truman said, shaking his old friend's hand.

"Hello, Harry."

Surely the memories flashed before Truman's eyes — running the canteen with Jacobson at Camp Doniphan in Oklahoma, two young soldiers on their way to war. Or the ill-fated Truman & Jacobson. That shop had now been closed for twenty-three years. Jacobson had opened his new store just months earlier.

"I want some shirts," Truman told Eddie. "Size 15½, 33 lengths."

Jacobson searched the store, but he did not have Truman's size. By this time, mobs had crowded the front door, and photographers snapped away at the old partners. It was a moment neither man would ever forget.

Once again, Bess managed to escape the attention, secluding herself behind the doors of 219 North Delaware during her husband's visit. Thus far, she had decided the role of First Lady did not suit her. (A year later, in 1946, Bess was asked, "If it had been left to your own free choice, would you have gone into the White House in the first place?" She answered, "Most definitely would *not* have." Would she want Margaret to become a First Lady? "No." Did she think there would ever be a female president? "No." Had living in the White House changed her view of politics and people? "No comment.")

Truman promised his family that he would have no official duties on his last full day at home — Saturday, June 30 — for he could not even guess when he would be able to come home again. But pleas from the press lured him out onto his front porch with Margaret for some pictures, in the late afternoon. The photographers asked for Bess to be in the photographs, and Truman went inside to fetch the First Lady. He came back alone. As Margaret remembered, "Mother had flatly refused to join us." Truman offered a halfhearted smile, telling the photographers, "Take a few more of us, why don't you, boys."

Early the next morning, July 1, the president's limousine left Independence for the airport. Truman arrived back in Washington at 2 p.m., alone without his family in the White House again. Later in the afternoon he was at his desk looking over documents in his second-floor study when a knock came at the door. White House staffers Bill Hassett, Eben Ayers, and Matt Connelly entered, along with Charlie Ross and Sam Rosenman. A few minutes later a naval aide ushered in Alger Hiss of the State Department, who held in his hands the UN Charter.

Truman suggested a drink to celebrate — with ice, as the summer heat was bearing down on the White House. He made a call, and minutes later servants brought in a tray of glasses, a bucket of ice, and bottles of bourbon and scotch. Truman raised a toast to the United Nations.

The following day, just after lunch, he stood at the podium in the Senate Chamber and formally presented the charter. As an international treaty, the document would have to be approved by the Senate by a two-thirds vote, or it would land in history's dustbin, right next to Woodrow Wilson's League of Nations charter. Truman delivered a short, heartfelt speech.

"No international document has been drawn in a greater glare of publicity than has this one," he said. "The choice before the Senate is now clear," he continued. "The choice is not between this Charter and something else. It is between this Charter and no Charter at all."

The Senate began its talks the moment Truman left the gallery. The deliberations would grow heated at times, the UN hanging in the balance.

At 11 a.m. the following day, James F. Byrnes was sworn in as secretary of state. Truman watched Justice Richard Whaley conduct the ceremony on the White House's East Portico, which was surrounded by rosebushes in bloom. The affair was quick, simple, and sultry hot, with Mrs. Byrnes and Henry Stimson standing by as witnesses with the president.

Byrnes now joined Truman as chief architect of American foreign policy. Ever since Thomas Jefferson served as the first secretary of state, the role had been defined by decisions as to how much the United States should get involved in other nations' conflicts, and how to exploit international relations for the purpose of national security and economic growth. The end of World War II would pose complexities that no secretary of state had faced before.

The new secretary of state was a polarizing figure – certainly more so than Truman realized at the time. Byrnes had a rare résumé; he had served in all three branches of government – executive (as secretary of state), judicial (as a Supreme Court justice), and legislative (as a former senator from South Carolina). He had angered some of his colleagues in the past, who considered him Machiavellian and, at times, remarkably self-interested. Before his swearing in, Sam Rosenman, White House special counsel, had warned Truman: "I don't think you know Jimmy Byrnes, Mr. President. You think you do. In the bonhomie of the Senate, he's one kind of a fellow; but I think you will regret this [appointment], and if I were you, I wouldn't do it." Others were furious over the sacking of "Brother Ed" Stettinius, who was responsible more than any other man for bringing the UN Charter to fruition. "It just shows how cruel and ruthless 'politics' can be," Senator Vandenberg wrote in his diary.

Truman felt sure that in Byrnes he had the right man. "My, but he has a keen mind," he wrote of Byrnes. The timing of the appointment was key. The president was set to leave for Berlin in two days' time, and blue-eyed Jimmy Byrnes would be by his side as his most trusted advisor.

30

"I SURE DREAD THIS TRIP worse than anything I've had to face," Truman wrote Bess of the upcoming Berlin conference. He was set to leave the White House on the night of July 6, and the race to prepare had set the city of Washington on edge. In the midnight hours, office lights could be seen flickering in the executive mansion, the old State and War Building, the Pentagon, and elsewhere, as officials tapped out thick position papers for Truman on every subject from Zionism to the evolving government in Poland to the future economy of Germany. At port in Newport News, Virginia, the crew of the USS *Augusta* was readying the ship for the president. Truman's party was now set at thirty-seven individuals, while the secretary of state's traveling staff would total twenty-six. The Joint Chiefs of Staff's party would total seventy-five, not including the chiefs themselves.

The Russians were set to host the meeting inside Soviet-occupied territory. The conference would be held in the Berlin suburb of Potsdam, since the city of Berlin had been destroyed, in a prince's palace that had not suffered bombing damage. Harriman carried the heavy load of making the arrangements for the conference with the hosting Soviets, while Eisenhower's office was in charge of arranging on-site accommodations. The latter in particular had become a headache, signifying how difficult it was going to be to negotiate with the Soviets on anything. American reconnaissance personnel headed by General Floyd Parks had been refused access to secure a safe location for the president and his staff in Potsdam.

"All attempts to secure permission for General Parks and party to proceed to Berlin immediately for reconnaissance and making necessary arrangements for conference have been unsuccessful," Eisenhower's office in Frankfurt cabled Washington. General Parks himself cabled: "No explanation can be given for such a delay except the lack of permission from the Soviet authorities to undertake necessary arrangements." Only after strong lobbying from Harriman was General Parks allowed to enter Potsdam, to insure safety, inspect quarters, and to set up high-frequency communications systems. Mess, laundry, medical, and pharmaceutical aid — all of it had to be arranged under the careful watch of Soviet intelligence.

Britain was holding an election for prime minister, and the results would not be known at the start of the conference, so Churchill informed Truman that he would bring his opposing candidate, Clement Attlee of the Labour Party, with him, "in order that full continuity of British policy may be assured," whether Churchill remained prime minister or not. Experts in the State Department had informed Truman that they expected Churchill to win the election, but who knew? Electioneering was full of surprises, as Truman knew as much as anybody.

The names of Truman's party represented great intrigue in Washington. "There isn't any doubt that James F. Byrnes, Secretary of State, has emerged as the man closest to President Truman," the *Boston Globe*'s chief Washington reporter noted. Secretary of War Stimson was not on the list to attend Potsdam. Neither was Secretary of the Treasury Henry Morgenthau, who was infuriated. The rumor mill buzzed that Morgenthau was going to get replaced by Fred Vinson, director of the Office of Economic Stabilization. Vinson had been invited to the Potsdam Conference. Morgenthau had not. Morgenthau insisted on talking over the matter with Truman, face-to-face.

The two met in the Oval Office at 10:15 a.m. on the day before Truman was scheduled to set sail. By this time, the Oval Office appeared entirely Truman's. All remnants of Franklin Roosevelt had vanished — a fact not lost on Morgenthau, who had considered himself one of FDR's closest confidants and had spent countless hours with Roosevelt in this room. Even the desk was different. Truman had given FDR's desk to Eleanor Roosevelt and had replaced it with a walnut desk that had belonged to Theodore Roosevelt. Upon this desk now sat a framed photograph of Bess—the same picture that Truman had kept in his pocket while fighting as a soldier in World War I.

"You are leaving," Morgenthau said, "and there's all this gossip which has been increasing more and more about my being through." Morgenthau wanted to know: Was he in or out?

"Let me think this thing over," Truman said, trying to find a polite way out of the conversation.

"Mr. President, from several remarks you have dropped you must have something in your mind. Either you want me or you don't, and you know it now."

Morgenthau offered his resignation. He said that if he was not invited to Potsdam, he should step down. The president had heard enough.

"All right," Truman answered, "if that is the way you feel, I'll accept your resignation right now."

Soon afterward Truman was hosting his regular press conference, prepared to announce Morgenthau's resignation. When reporters entered his office, they found him sipping a glass of water ("just taking a little something for my nerves!" he said) and wielding a sword that had come off a swordfish ("a good letter opener," he said). The press had come to rely on Truman's jocularity as an icebreaker, but Truman's voice turned sober as he announced the Treasury secretary's resignation. Morgenthau had run the Treasury for eleven years. When reporters asked Truman if he had decided on a successor, he said, "I have a successor in mind, but he will not be announced until I get back from Europe."

Fred Vinson would in fact be the new Treasury secretary, and had already begun to assume the role.

///

Not long before Truman's departure for Europe, the secretary of war came to see him. Stimson came to discuss Japan. He produced a document, and Truman read the memorandum – called "Proposed Program for Japan" – carefully, as Stimson sat by. The planning for the invasion of Japan was "now actually going on," Stimson wrote. "There is reason to believe that the operation for the occupation of Japan following the landing may be a very long, costly and arduous struggle on our part." Stimson was second-guessing the invasion plan. He believed that the Japanese would refuse to surrender, under any cost, if their homeland was invaded by foreigners. They would fight to the last man and the last square foot of territory. The United States would have no choice but to destroy Japan completely, at the cost of countless American casualties.

"A question then comes," Stimson's memo read. "Is there any alternative to such a forceful occupation of Japan which will secure for us the equivalent of an unconditional surrender of her forces and a permanent destruction of her power again to strike an aggressive blow at the 'peace of the Pacific'?" The memorandum read further: "Japan has no allies . . . She is terribly vulnerable to our concentrated air attack upon her crowded cities, industrial and food resources . . . We have inexhaustible and untouched industrial resources to bring to bear against her diminishing potential. We have great moral superiority through being the victim of her first sneak attack. The problem is to translate these advantages into prompt and economical achievement of our objectives."

The secretary of war did not mention the atomic bomb in this memorandum. (As Stimson noted, "On grounds of secrecy the bomb was never mentioned except when absolutely necessary.") Behind closed doors in the president's office, however, they spoke freely on the matter.

Stimson recommended a kind of warning to Japan, and he had written a draft of what such a warning would look like, with the help of his colleagues. It spoke of the "overwhelming character of the force we are about to bring to bear on the islands." It spoke of "the inevitability and completeness of the destruction on which the full application of this force will entail." Whether or not such a warning would use the words *atomic bomb* was a subject to be discussed. But either way, Stimson argued, by issuing a public and official warning, the United States could convince Japan to capitulate. And if Japan did not (more likely the case), history would record the moral position of an attacking nation that had done its best to warn its victim of what was to come — annihilation of a city, perhaps more than one.

Truman liked what he was hearing. Stimson's memorandum was the impetus for what would become the Potsdam Declaration — an ultimatum to Japan that the whole world would see, warning utter destruction.

The secretary also believed that no harm would come from allowing the emperor to remain in power in Japan. He believed such an offer would "substantially add to the chances" that Japan would surrender. Truman remained uncommitted on this matter.

Finally, Stimson thought it would be a good idea to inform Stalin at the upcoming meeting about the atomic bomb, before it was used. (The secretary was assuming at this point that Oppenheimer's test shot would be a success, which was not assured.) Stimson thought Truman should tell Stalin "that we were busy with this thing working like the dickens and . . . that we were pretty nearly ready and we intended to use it against the enemy, Japan." The time was now to inform Stalin of the bomb, Stimson urged, "with the purpose of having it make the world peaceful and safe rather than to destroy civilization." Here again, Truman was in agreement. The question remained: How to inform Stalin?

Before leaving the president's office, Stimson asked why he had not been invited to Potsdam. He was nearing his seventy-eighth birthday; he was an elder statesman who was clearly pained by the idea of missing out on what would be the climactic moment of a much heralded career. He wondered aloud to the president: Was it because of his age?

"Yes," Truman answered, trying to lighten the moment with a bit of laughter. "That was just it." He feared Stimson's overexertion.

Stimson was fit and ready. He could produce nothing less than the endorsement of the surgeon general of the United States, he said. He thought he could do some good if he came along in an unofficial capacity. Truman agreed, and Stimson left to go make last-minute arrangements for the most important trip of his life.

///

On the eve of Potsdam the global picture looked grim. The course of international relations depended on various plot lines of which Truman had no control, and the once great Grand Alliance had lost its grandeur, like a bad three-way marriage turned bitter by suspicions, betrayals, and money problems.

Truman had by this time met with the Chinese foreign minister, T. V. Soong, and had finally informed him of the secret Yalta agreements. "There was a long discussion of every point," Undersecretary of State Joseph Grew wrote in his notes of this meeting, "the president making it clear that he was definitely committed to the agreements reached by President Roosevelt." Soong understood that the Chinese would have to make major concessions in order to get the Soviets into the war against Japan, and he told Truman there was no way the Chinese could honor these agreements, about which they were never consulted.

For Truman, an agreement between China and the USSR was imperative, not just because he wanted Soviet commitment to the Pacific war but also because he wanted Stalin to be aligned with the current Chinese government under Chiang Kai-shek, not the rebel Chinese Communists, currently gaining power under Mao Tse-tung in the north. Regarding the concessions to the Soviets, Soong declared that China would prefer to "settle the controversy by military action." The Chinese would fight rather than make these concessions to the Soviets. But both Soong and Truman knew that China had no resources to wage war above and beyond the war it was already fighting. Soong had since left Washington en route to Moscow, in an attempt to negotiate directly with Stalin.

In the New Mexico desert, a construction crew reporting to a Harvard experimental physicist named Kenneth T. Bainbridge was putting the finishing touches on a proving ground, where the test shot was set to go off. After more delay, the atomic bomb test was now scheduled for July 15, just as Truman would be arriving at Potsdam. Truman and his closest aides were awaiting news from New Mexico with great anticipation.

Truman rushed through his final personal arrangements in anticipation of his journey. He saw his dentist, who made a house call to the White House. ("A lot has happened since I saw you last," he told his dentist, who in turn told the president he needed a root canal, and performed the procedure on the spot.) Truman packed his finest suits, formal wear for the evenings, cold weather clothes for the ship cruise across the Atlantic, and hot weather clothes for summer in Berlin. He needed his "high hat, top hat, and hard hat," he joked.

"It'll be a circus sure enough," he wrote Bess. "But we will get it done I hope."

There was no letup in the schedule on July 6, the day Truman and his party were set to leave Washington. At the morning staff meeting, all talk was of the voyage to Europe. Neither Truman nor Jimmy Byrnes had any experience negotiating with the likes of Stalin and Churchill. Eben Ayers admitted in his diary after the morning meeting what many in Washington were feeling: fear that Truman and Byrnes were going to make mistakes at Potsdam, mistakes that the American public, perhaps even future generations, was going to have to pay for. Ayers feared Potsdam would be a "'babes in the wood' affair."

The president's calendar on this day listed no fewer than twenty appointments. He had a budget meeting and a cabinet meeting. He issued three executive orders, most notably an order to create an emergency board to investigate labor strikes at midwestern railroad companies critical to the war effort. Exhausted, he left the White House by motorcade at 9:40 p.m. with members of his party. He made sure to surround himself during his travel with old friends, men who set him at ease: Charlie Ross, Harry Vaughan. He even brought along his old pal Fred Canfil. At

9:50 the party boarded a special train at track 2 in Union Station, bound for the shipyard in Newport News.

Truman had a strong wind at his sails. At the time of his departure, a new Gallup poll set his approval rating at a miraculous 87 percent. Never during any of Franklin Roosevelt's days as president had FDR enjoyed an approval rating that high. America found Truman to be "fair-minded . . . a hard worker . . . a realist who looks at things squarely and seeks good advice," according to the poll. He was "better at handling people than Roosevelt," and he "had no crackpot ideas." Still, no approval ratings could ease Truman's fears. As Robert Nixon wrote of Truman in the *Washington Post*, "The present conference projects him into the world spotlight."

He knew his country was counting on him, and that he would be held accountable. As Judge Sam Rosenman wrote in a memo to the president, "The American people expect you to bring something home to them."

While still on the train, Truman wrote Bess. They had spoken by phone recently, and she had seemed to him rather upset. The stress of living a public life was maddening her, and they had years left to go before it would be over. Their marriage was suffering. "I'm sorry if I've done something to make you unhappy," Harry wrote Bess, sitting in the swaying belly of the president's Pullman car en route to Newport News. "All I've ever tried to do is make you pleased with me and the world. I'm very much afraid I've failed miserably . . . Now I'm on the way to the high executioner."

Churchill had given this Big Three conference an ominous code name: Terminal. The president and his party boarded the USS *Augusta* on the morning of July 7. Truman had not stepped foot in Europe since he was a soldier in 1918. Less than three months had passed since the moon and all the stars had fallen upon him. As he wrote in his diary on July 7, the day the *Augusta* pulled out of port: "How I hate this trip!"

THE *AUGUSTA*'S CAPTAIN JAMES FOSKETT personally escorted Truman to his quarters. The president would stay in the admiral's cabin (which had its own private head), directly across from the captain's cabin, where Jimmy Byrnes was assigned, both cabins one flight up from the ship's main deck. The *Augusta* measured 600¼ feet long, its beam rising 66 feet high. Cruising speed: 32.7 knots. The ship was named for a city in Georgia, but the crew called it "Augie" for short, and it had a distinguished career. It was aboard this ship that Franklin Roosevelt and Winston Churchill met face-to-face for the first time as leaders of their respective countries, in Canada's Placentia Bay on August 9, 1941. Now, with Truman aboard, the *Augusta* followed 1,000 yards behind the light cruiser USS *Philadelphia,* the two ships operating as Task Force 68.

An "Advance Map Room" was set up onboard with a direct communications line to the White House Map Room, so the president could be in constant contact with intelligence sources from all over the world. Truman was given a telephone directory for onboard calls (he was #51), along with instructions for laundry, barber, and tailor. He had a list of the books in the ship's library, and another of the crew members from his home state of Missouri. At lunch the first day at sea, he stood on line in the chief petty officer's mess with his aluminum tray, and when he sat down at a table, the sailors next to him were too nervous to speak. He lightened them up quickly. "Old Harry sat around batting the breeze like he'd known us all his life," recalled one sailor who sat next to Truman.

The ocean voyage would last eight days, and at night the *Augusta* traveled with lights on rather than in blackout, now that German U-boats — the rattlesnakes of the sea, as FDR had called them — were no longer torpedoing ships in the Atlantic. Truman's group fell into a routine. The State Department had put together red-covered tomes full of position papers for Truman to memorize. Similar books were prepared for Roosevelt on the way to Yalta, but FDR never read them. Truman did – thousands of pages. At least once a day he met with Byrnes and Leahy, along with assistants, to firm up proposals that were then prepared for presentation at the upcoming conference. Recalled Chip Bohlen, who was present at many of these meetings: "Truman, a newcomer as a world leader, was understandably somewhat nervous about confronting such awesome figures as Churchill and Stalin . . . During our conferences, Truman spent little time on small talk and jokes. He stuck to business."

Each day Truman received news updates from the Advance Map Room. The first day at sea, a memo arrived detailing Curtis LeMay's latest bombing of Japan: "600 B-29 Superfortresses have dropped nearly 4,000 tons of incendiary and demolition bombs on the main Japanese island of Honshu." Japanese cities such as Shimizu and Kofu were receiving their "first baptism of incendiaries," the firebombs killing indiscriminately. Rumors of peace feelers from the Japanese had led Undersecretary of State Joseph Grew to make a statement from Washington: "Conversations relating to peace have been reported to the Department from various parts of the world, but in no case has an approach been made to this Government, directly or indirectly, by a person who could establish his authority to speak for the Japanese Government, and in no case has an offer of surrender been made."

When Truman was not in conferences, he walked the ship from bow to stern restlessly, followed often by Fred Canfil, as loyal as a dog, and Harry Vaughan, who had a habit of talking too much. ("I don't suppose anyone gives more advice than I do," Vaughan said, "and has less of it used.") Each night at six o'clock a thirty-piece band played a symphonette program, followed by dinner. At eight o'clock a movie was shown in Byrnes's room (the first night featured *The Princess and the Pirate,* starring Bob Hope). Truman slipped out of these movies to play poker in his quarters. One night over a card game, conversation turned to the election in Britain. Churchill believed that his present government would win, but one could not say for sure. At the poker table, newsman Robert Nixon insisted that Churchill was on his way out of office.

"The Conservative government, with Churchill as its head, is going to go out," Nixon insisted. Was he right? The voting had taken place, and it would be days before the count was completed, which meant that, if there was a change in British leadership, it would occur right in the middle of the Potsdam Conference.

The mood aboard the ship was positive, though the pressure was palpable. The two previous Big Three meetings, Tehran and Yalta, had occurred under a veil of secrecy. The entire world knew of this upcoming conference. Meanwhile, the president was eager to hear news of the test shot in New Mexico. Admiral Leahy was still positive the experiment would never work. "This is the biggest fool thing we have ever done," the White House chief of staff insisted. "The bomb will never go off, and I speak as an expert in explosives."

///

On July 14 the *Augusta* steamed past the white cliffs of Dover and into the English Channel. Truman stood atop the bridge focusing his eyes on this breathtaking sight. Seven ships of His Majesty's fleet greeted the president, six destroyers and the HMS *Birmingham* light cruiser, which served as an escort. Aboard each stood rows of hundreds of British sailors saluting Truman, shouting three cheers as he passed.

"Three cheers for Mr. Truman," thousands of sailors roared, "President of the United States!"

The *Augusta* cruised past an army encampment along the shore where thousands of American GIs were awaiting their journeys home, the men climbing over one another trying to get a look at the president. As the ship moved closer to its berth, Truman saw a sea of ecstatic Belgians and Hollanders on the banks of the water — men, women, old and young, shouting with delight and pumping fists in the air. They were a reminder that Truman was the face of the nation that had saved these people from Hitler. He was the face of the nation that was now the hope of rebirth for millions of Europeans.

At Antwerp the *Augusta* was boarded by a welcoming party, notably General Eisenhower himself. Truman walked off the boat at 11:10 a.m. on July 15. The scene was a mesmerizing display of security and logistics. Soldiers began unloading from the *Augusta* 83 suitcases, 1 trunk, 40 small pieces, plus office gear, Map Room equipment, 36 cans of motion picture film, and the president's kitchen equipment, which would follow him to Potsdam. Swarms of military police had been surveilling this terrain for days, and twelve P-47 Thunderbolt fighter planes patrolled the skies. Truman climbed into an armored car, and a motorcade left the port for a forty-five-minute ride to an airfield in Brussels, where transport planes awaited. Secret service and MPs flanked the motorcade, while directly behind the president's car a truck motored with eight machine gunners and eight sharpshooting riflemen.

In Brussels the party took off in three C-47 transport planes and landed some three hours later at Gatow outside Berlin. A dozen officials greeted Truman, including Ambassador Harriman and Secretary of War Stimson, who had arranged travel for himself and his team aboard the USS *Brazil* and had arrived the day before. Though not officially invited, Stimson was to play a key role at Potsdam. The Second Armored "Hell on Wheels" Division performed military honors at the airfield. Truman inspected the guard, as was custom. "Everyone was relieved when this was over," recalled Joseph Davies, who was present. "The Secret Service had been quite nervous about it. When [Truman] walked in front of the line they could not possibly have protected him from a long distance shot."

Then Truman was back in a car for the ten-mile drive to his villa. From inside his car, he could hear explosions in the distance. Russians were still detonating German mines, left over from the war. The explosions were at a safe distance but close enough to rattle the president's nerves. Along this short drive he saw another ominous sight. The airfield at Brussels had been guarded by American and British troops, but here in eastern Germany the roadway was guarded by Russians. Armed frontier guardsmen stood along the entire route at 50- to 100-yard gaps, each a reminder that the president was inside Soviet-occupied territory.

He arrived at his quarters in Babelsberg – a small suburb between Berlin and Potsdam – at approximately 5 p.m., the motorcade lurching to a stop at 2 Kaiserstrasse, a three-story stucco villa on Lake Griebnitz. The lake had served as a popular summer getaway for Berliners before the war, while the villa itself had belonged to a well-known German filmmaker. This filmmaker had been taken by the Soviets – to where, no one knew. "The house as all others was stripped of everything by the Russians," Truman wrote in a diary on this day. "Not even a tin spoon left." The Soviet hosts had hastily refurnished the place with odds and ends, giving it a bizarre feel. "It is comfortable enough," Truman noted, "but what a nightmare it would give an interior decorator." Though the villa was yellow, it quickly became known as "the Little White House."

Truman had a bedroom, an office, and a bathroom, a flight of steps above the ground floor. Windows offered a view of the lake. In a room between his bedroom and his office, the head of the secret service detail, George Drescher, had already unpacked his bags. Byrnes, Leahy, Ross, Vaughan, and Chip Bohlen also took up residence in this house. There were no screens on the windows; mosquitoes would be feasting at night. Additionally, the bathrooms were "wholly inadequate," according to Commander William Rigdon, an assistant naval aide who would be in charge of the president's kitchen.

But at least the Americans knew they were safe. Army engineers had fumigated the place, checked all the electrical wiring, and inspected the foundation for booby traps or bombs. Secret service had assigned code names to each member of the party, in case their communications were intercepted. Truman was Kilting; Leahy was Coffeetree; Byrnes was Iceblink.

In several nearby villas, Washington officials were settling in. A whole American neighborhood had been created here in Babelsberg, the villas marked "State Department" and "Chiefs of Staff" and "Foreign Office." American flags flew from each, and U.S. military police patrolled the main road 24/7. Truman had issued strict orders that no American should "liberate" any items from any of these villas. No souvenirs. Each official was assigned a mess area and times when he could eat, and given information on the locations of bars where Americans could gather, where films would be shown, plus the locations of barbershops and laundry. Each man received a "Safeguard Your Health" memorandum, with instructions to drink water only from "authorized sources," not to enter unauthorized buildings, and to consume only U.S. ration liquor, as "the cleanliness and purity" of foreign liquors were questionable.

To accommodate all these figures, the army had requisitioned an extraordinary amount of materials: 5,000 linen sheets, 50 vacuum cleaners, 20 lawn mowers, 100 bedside lamps, 250 bottle openers, 250 corkscrews, 500 ashtrays, 25 reams of paper, 100 garbage baskets, 20 electric typewriters, and 3,000 rolls of toilet paper. All of Truman's food would be served at his villa, where also his valet would handle his laundry. The army had flown in a physician for the president – Dr. Wallace Graham, who had attended wounded men at the D-day invasion and the Battle of the Bulge and had been wounded himself in the fighting. A Missourian, Dr. Graham would become Truman's physician from this point onward, for the rest of Truman's life.

The president was exhausted from the journey. He had no way of knowing how long his sojourn in Europe would last. That night he cabled Matthew Connelly in the White House, instructing him to deliver the following message to Mrs. Truman: "Safely landed in Berlin. Things in good shape. Margie owes me two letters. Please call Mamma. Lots of love. Signed Harry." Then he went to bed.

He had a lot on his mind. The prime minister would be calling at the Little White House in the morning.

///

At 11 a.m. on July 16, Winston Churchill appeared at Truman's villa with members of his party, including his daughter Mary. Churchill, now seventy years old (nearly a decade older than Truman), was bleary-eyed. He was a night owl. As his daughter mentioned, to make this 11 a.m. appointment, Churchill had awoken earlier than he had in ten years. Truman had already been awake for four and a half hours.

The president was slightly dubious about Churchill, for the prime minister had been at times demanding and irritating in his correspondence. "The difficulties with Churchill are very nearly as exasperating as they are with the Russians," Truman had recently written in a letter to Eleanor Roosevelt. Churchill also enjoyed the patrician upbringing that instantly ingratiated him to Roosevelt – a background of wealth and social stature that Harry Truman lacked completely. Upon their first shake of hands, however, Truman fell for the prime minister.

"I had an instant liking for this man who had done so much for his own country and for the Allied cause," Truman later wrote. "There was something very open and genuine about the way he greeted me."

The pink-cheeked prime minister stood only five feet six, but he possessed a transcendent magnanimity. His life seemed to chart the very course of British history, starting in the military (he had served in Cuba, India, Egypt, and Sudan), then in government (he had been, at different times, secretary of state for war, secretary of state for the colonies, minister of defense, and, since 1940, prime minister). He was an accomplished landscape painter and the author of more than twenty books – histories, memoirs, and biographies.* Though his mother, Lady

---

* "It was great fun writing a book," Churchill once said. "One lived with it. It became a companion." Source: https://www.nationalchurchillmuseum.org/winston-churchill-the-writer.html, last accessed April 6, 2017.

Randolph Churchill, was American-born, Churchill had come to symbolize Britain's resolve. His speeches during the early war years, when the United Kingdom's fate looked bleak at the hands of the Nazis, had inspired the will of the nation to fight, and like FDR, Churchill had a deep understanding of his place in time, the knowledge that his life would be chronicled by authors and warriors forever.

Churchill had arrived in Germany the day before, like Truman, and was staying in a similar villa at 23 Ringstrasse, two blocks away – a six-minute walk. In addition to his daughter, the prime minister had with him his foreign minister, the First Earl of Avon, Anthony Eden, who would be at the prime minister's side during the conference, and Alexander Cadogan, a British foreign affairs expert. With Byrnes present, the group enjoyed a two-hour social visit. Truman told the prime minister that he had prepared an agenda for the conference and asked Churchill if he had as well.

"No," the Briton said. "I don't need one." Truman must have wondered if the prime minister was overconfident. Either way, it was clear that Churchill had long grown accustomed to face-to-face diplomacy at its highest stakes.

By the end of their first meeting, the prime minister came to understand what all believed to be Truman's most noteworthy personal trait: his "obvious power of decision." Truman invited personal friendship, and Churchill was moved. "I felt that here was a man of exceptional character and ability," he wrote of his first impressions of Truman, "with an excellent outlook exactly along the lines of Anglo-American relations as they had developed, simple and direct methods of speech, and a great deal of self-confidence and resolution."

Before leaving, Churchill and Truman "struck a blow for liberty" with tumblers of whiskey. The meeting, all agreed, was wonderful. One of Churchill's entourage, Cadogan, wrote in his diary: "P.M. delighted with Pres."

///

Truman was expecting to meet Stalin in the afternoon but was informed that the Soviet generalissimo was ill, so his arrival would await another day. Stalin, it turned out, was recovering from a mild heart attack. So Truman decided on an unscheduled tour of Berlin. He left the Little White House at 3:40 in an open car with Leahy and Byrnes beside him. The car turned onto the famed Autobahn, and along one side of the highway, the U.S. Second Armored Division was deployed – some eleven hundred jeeps, trucks, and tanks, probably the largest armored division in the world. When the president's car stopped to greet the division's commanding general, Leahy said, "This is the most powerful land force I have ever seen. I do not see how anybody could stop them if they really wanted to go somewhere."

The general responded, "Nobody has stopped them yet!"

Turning toward the city center, Truman saw for the first time what the Allies had done to Berlin. American and British bombers had reduced the city to rubble – piles of it two and three stories high – while the Red Army had sprayed what little bits of buildings were still standing with machine-gun fire. "You could smell the effluvia of the unburied dead," remembered journalist Robert Nixon, who was in a car following Truman's. "It was a ghostly sight." The stink of death, and of feces emanating from shattered buildings that were being used as outdoor toilets, was made more acute by stifling July heat. Through this destruction, Russian bulldozers had cleared a way for cars to travel.

The sight of surviving Berliners left Truman in despair. He described "the long, never-ending procession of old men, women, and children wandering aimlessly along the Autobahn and the country roads carrying, pushing, or pulling what was left of their belongings." There was little access to food, water, or shelter. Here was a woman trying to start a fire so that she could heat soup for her children. Here was a sign amidst the rubble reading NICHT FÜR JUDEN (Not for Jews). At the center of Berlin, the car turned down the Wilhelmstrasse to the remains of Hitler's Reich Chancellery. Truman could now see the shattered balcony where the Nazi leader had so often addressed his brainwashed followers.

"That's what happens," Truman said to Leahy and Byrnes, "when a man overreaches himself. I never saw such destruction. I don't know whether they learned anything from it or not."

Truman had fought in a European war as a younger man and had seen war's devastation. But he had never seen anything like Berlin in July 1945. In contrast to the Great War, World War II was a fully industrialized conflict. The French 75 cannon had given way to swarms of 60,000-pound, four-engine bomber aircraft capable of shredding whole cities. He wrote in a diary entry that night of his impression of Berlin. It had left him philosophical and fearful for the future of mankind.

"I hope for some sort of peace — but I fear that machines are ahead of morals by some centuries and when morals catch up perhaps there'll [be] no reason for any of it. I hope not. But we are only termites on a planet and maybe when we bore too deeply into the planet there'll [be] a reckoning — who knows?"

32

AT THE BOMB TEST SITE IN NEW MEXICO, a desert gunnery range miles from any other sign of civilization, clocks read eight hours earlier than they did in Berlin. As Churchill and Truman were conferring in the Little White House for the first time on July 16, Robert Oppenheimer and General Leslie Groves were in a control bunker ten thousand yards from ground zero.

In the darkness the desert skies had produced a furious squall. Thirty-mile-per-hour winds strafed the bunker, and thunder cracks shook the earth. The first atomic explosion was scheduled for 4 a.m., but the weather threatened everything. There was talk of postponement.

"If we postpone," said Oppenheimer, "I'll never get my people up to pitch again."

Groves was adamant: This was the time. They had to get the Trinity test shot done before Truman sat down at the negotiating table in Potsdam. Besides, each day the war in the Far East continued, more American soldiers died.

Every thirty minutes, Oppenheimer and Groves left their bunker and walked out into the stormy night to discuss the weather. The chief meteorologist, Jack Hubbard, promised that the storm would move on before sunrise. Was he right? Groves had no faith in the weatherman; he found Hubbard to be "obviously confused and badly rattled." The group decided to push forward, postponing ninety minutes until 5:30 a.m. — which was not ideal, as the scientists needed Trinity to go off in darkness for the sake of the high-speed cameras. It had to be done not a minute past 5:30.

Nerves had stretched to the breaking point. "There was an air of excitement at the camp that I did not like," Groves later wrote, "for this was a time when calm deliberation was most essential." He feared that one of these scientists might crack, that nervous collapse or even hysteria was imminent. "The strain had been great on all our people, and it was impossible to predict just when someone might give way under it. There was always the chance, too, that a trained saboteur might be present, either within or without the organization, awaiting an opportunity."

Enrico Fermi, the Italian physicist, worried that the storm could drench the scientists with radioactive rain, post-detonation. "There could be a catastrophe," he warned Oppenheimer. In addition, a last-minute test of the firing mechanism had malfunctioned, and now the team believed there was a good chance Trinity would be a dud. This news had caused Oppenheimer to become highly emotional. Fermi also worried that, if the bomb did work, it could potentially ignite the atmosphere. To lighten the strain, the scientists took bets as to how big the explosion would be — if there would be one at all. Oppenheimer had bet conservatively: 3,000 tons TNT equivalent. Edward Teller — the brilliant Hungarian physicist, who later would become "the father of the hydrogen bomb" — bet the highest: 45,000 tons.

The test site was sixty miles northwest of the tiny village of Alamogordo; the Spanish had referred to this stretch of rattlesnake-infested desert as Jornada del Muerto — historically translated as Journey of the Dead Man, or Journey of Death. The gadget itself hung 100 feet above the ground, inside a tower. The bomb looked like a ball with wires poking out in all directions, like some primordial organism, only it was encased in metal and was the size of a Volkswagen. It was a "Fat Man" implosion-type bomb, using plutonium enriched at the Hanford reactor.

Oppenheimer's team would remember the way he smoked cigarettes and drank black coffee during the early morning hours, unable to mask his anguish. At one point he cracked a book of Baudelaire poems, reading the verse quietly as lightning flashes lit up the night sky. (An aficionado of the written word, Oppenheimer had taken the name of the test shot — Trinity — from a John Donne poem.) "It was raining cats and dogs, lightning and thunder," recalled Los Alamos scientist Isidor Rabi. "[We were] really scared [that] this object there in the tower might be set off accidentally. So you can imagine the strain on Oppenheimer."

Hundreds of scientists were spread out around the test site, which had three bunkers all situated at ten thousand yards. Others had gathered on Compania Hill, a viewing site twenty miles northwest of ground zero. The men were organized into groups according to function: Services, Shock and Blast, Measurements, Meteorology, Spectrographic and

Photographic, Airborne Measurements, and Medical. Each man had dark glasses to protect the eyes. The observers were told to lie down and bury their faces in their arms at the moment of detonation. Few were intending to follow those orders, noted Edward Teller: "We were determined to look the beast in the eye." One of the scientists recalled, "With the darkness and the waiting in the chill of the desert the tension became almost unbearable."

At 5:10 a.m. a Chicago physicist named Sam Allison announced over a loudspeaker from the control center: "It is now zero minus twenty minutes." At zero minus five minutes, the soldiers guarding the tower that held the gadget climbed into jeeps and abandoned their posts, motoring to the safety of the control bunkers. As clocks ticked away the final minutes, everyone present took position. In Oppenheimer's bunker, S-10000, observers watched him. He barely breathed, holding on to a post to steady himself. The shot was set to go off by automatic timer, and it was the job of a scientist named Donald Hornig to monitor it; in the final minute, Hornig would be the only one who could flip a switch to stop Trinity. "My hand was on the switch," he recalled. "I could hear the timer counting . . . three . . . two . . . one . . .

"Now!"

///

"My first impression was one of tremendous light," Groves recorded, "and then as I turned, I saw the now familiar fireball . . . The light had been so much greater than any human had previously experienced."

"All of a sudden, the night turned into day," recalled scientist Joe Hirschfelder, "and it was tremendously bright; the chill turned into warmth; the fireball gradually turned from white to yellow to red as it grew in size and climbed into the sky."

General Thomas Farrell, the army's chief of field operations at Los Alamos: "The lighting effects beggared description. The whole country was lighted by a searing light with the intensity many times that of the midday sun. It was golden, purple, violet, gray, and blue. It lighted every peak, crevasse and ridge of the nearby mountain range with a clarity and beauty that cannot be described but must be seen to be imagined."

The group watched as a mushroom cloud climbed to a height of over ten thousand feet. Farrell approached Groves and said to his boss, "The war is over."

Oppenheimer himself later recalled the moment. "We knew the world would not be the same. A few people laughed, a few people cried. Most people were silent. I remembered the line from the Hindu scripture, the Bhagavad-Gita . . . 'Now I am become death, the destroyer of worlds.'"

Roughly thirty minutes later, General Groves called his contact in Washington, an official from the Interim Committee named George L. Harrison, by phone. One hour after that Groves called in more details. It was Harrison's job to construct a cable to be sent to the secretary of war, now in Germany. Harrison wrote out the words in thinly veiled code with a note of comic relief, and at 9:30 a.m. eastern time he showed this cable to his superiors, who approved it. The cable fired off at 11:15 a.m. Washington time.

In one of history's more macabre ironies, the Trinity shot went off at roughly the moment when Harry Truman and Winston Churchill were striking a blow for liberty, unaware, thousands of miles away at the Little White House in Babelsberg.

///

Truman dined at 8 p.m. that night in his villa, with Ambassador Harriman and Joseph Davies among others. A band from the Second Armored Division played a concert during the dinner. As coffee was being served, one of Truman's aides approached to inform him that the secretary of war and General Marshall were on their way to the Little White House to discuss an important matter. Stimson and Marshall arrived soon afterward to find Truman in his office on the second floor. Jimmy Byrnes was also present. Stimson gave Truman a cable, which had arrived from George L. Harrison in Washington. It read:

> Operated on this morning. Diagnosis not yet complete but results seem satisfactory and already exceed expectations. Local press release necessary as interest extends great distance. Dr. Groves pleased. He returns tomorrow. I will keep you posted.

Truman and Byrnes "were delighted" by the news, Stimson recorded in his diary. The scientists had pulled it off. This was the news they had been waiting for, what must have felt like the answer to every question. The bomb was now in Truman's proverbial hands, which made the former farmer and haberdasher the most powerful man who had ever lived.

The sentence regarding "local press release" signified that the Trinity shot had been so loud, citizens living great distances away had heard the blast and had contacted authorities, and so the army had put out a faux press release to throw off any suspicion. The press release indicated that an unexpected explosion had occurred at the Alamogordo Army Air Base, and that there had been "no loss of life."

Conversation in the Little White House turned to Japan as the secretary of war had more news. Stimson said that a peace feeler had apparently come from Tokyo, to representatives of Stalin's government in Moscow. There was no evidence that the feeler had any substance, but it was encouraging news. Earlier on this day, Stimson had written a memorandum to Truman called "The Conduct of the War with Japan," and it is highly likely that he handed Truman this document during this sit-down. It concerned the ultimatum that Stimson had discussed with the president – a warning to Japan that something deeply destructive was about to happen, in hopes that Japan would surrender.

"It seems to me that we are at the psychological moment to commence our warnings to Japan," Stimson wrote. "Moreover, the recent news of attempted approaches on the part of Japan to Russia, impels me to urge prompt delivery of our warning. I would therefore urge that we formulate a warning to Japan to be delivered during the course of this Conference." If the Japanese then refused to surrender, Stimson concluded, "the full force of our newer weapons should be brought to bear."

Stimson also brought up Russia. The closer Truman moved toward the negotiating table at Potsdam, the more Stimson feared the Soviets' intentions in the Far East. He worried that Stalin aimed to do in the Far East what he was doing in eastern Europe – extend the influence of the USSR and communism. Stimson argued that, in negotiations, the United States should prevent the Soviets from gaining full control of trade ports in the Far East, such as Dairen in Manchuria. He also feared new developments in Korea, and the following sentence presaged a whole new war that would begin before the Truman administration was over: "The Russians, I am also informed, have already trained one or two divisions of Koreans," Stimson wrote. He worried that the Russians would use these military divisions to "influence the setting up of a Soviet dominated local government [in Korea]."

Korea, Stimson concluded, "is the Polish question transplanted to the Far East."

Following this meeting, Truman bounded down the stairs of the Little White House in a conflicted mood. On the first floor, Joseph Davies was still lounging, post-dinner.

"Is everything all right?" Davies asked.

"Yes, fine!" Truman said.

"Over here or back home?"

"Back home. It has taken a great load off my mind." Only later would Truman tell Davies what he was talking about — Trinity, calling it a "terrible success."

///

At noon on July 17, one day after the Trinity shot, a bulletproof limousine pulled up to the Little White House in Babelsberg. It was surrounded by scurrying groups of cold-faced men, wearing ties and bearing guns. The limousine had curtains, so no one could see who was inside. When the car door opened, Stalin appeared. The Man of Steel wore a military tunic, and he was flanked by Molotov and the translator Pavlov. The group was shown into the Little White House, where Truman was sitting behind an oversized wooden desk near a sun-brightened window. "I got to my feet and advanced to meet him," Truman wrote in his diary. "He put out his hand and smiled."

Joseph Stalin was the most mysterious man alive. Few Americans had ever laid eyes on him. None knew where he lived, or with whom, or what his passions were, if any, outside of power politics. It was known, however, that he was born into abject poverty in the province of Georgia, and that he had risen to power during the struggles of the communist revolution, a time when only the most Machiavellian of militants could have survived, let alone flourished. He had taken over the Communist Party in 1922, and this was the foundation of his dictatorship. It was no coincidence that almost all of the powerful Soviets who had risen alongside Stalin — that is, any potential rivals — had since been assassinated, deported, tried, and executed for political crimes, or had simply vanished off the face of the earth. Stalin, meanwhile, had ushered the Soviet Union into the industrial age, as the feared dictator of what was now some 190 million subjects.

Truman was surprised by Stalin's diminutive stature. The sixty-six-year-old Soviet stood only about five feet five inches. His trimmed gray hair was brushed back from his bulging brow, which accentuated his eyes — yellow, as if stained by cigarette smoke. His skin was rugged and pockmarked, and his teeth were cracked and discolored. He wore a mustache gently pointed at the ends, and his smile was remarkably unassuming. Truman was told that Stalin had a deformed arm, but the president saw no evidence of it in person. "What I noticed especially," Truman recorded, "were his eyes, his face, and his expression."

The Russia expert George Kennan, who had spent time with Stalin over the years while working in the Moscow embassy (where he still worked), described the sensation of being in the Soviet's presence: "An unforewarned visitor would never have guessed what depths of calculation, ambition, love of power, jealousy, cruelty, and sly vindictiveness lurked behind this unpretentious façade. I was never in doubt, when visiting him, that I was in the presence of one of the world's most remarkable men — a man great, if you will, primarily in his iniquity: ruthless, cynical, cunning, endlessly dangerous; but for all of this — one of the truly great men of the age."

Stalin apologized for showing up a day late, as his doctor had insisted he travel by train, rather than by air. Truman and Stalin then dove into the agenda for Potsdam. Truman noticed how Stalin looked him directly in the eye when he spoke, and the president spoke "straight from the shoulder," as he put it. Interpreter Chip Bohlen sat by taking notes. Bohlen scribbled the following:

TRUMAN: "I am here to — be yr friend — deal directly yes . . ."
STALIN: "Good — help — work — USSR go along with US."

The conversation turned to the complicated issue of China. Stalin revealed that negotiations with Chinese foreign minister T. V. Soong in Moscow had moved along with little success. These negotiations involved the secret Yalta agreements, the willingness of the Chinese to grant the Soviets access to ports and control of Chinese railroads. The Chinese refused to agree to all the terms. The trouble with the Chinese, Stalin claimed, is that they "don't understand horse trading." But the talks were ongoing, and Stalin had decided to join the war against Japan anyway, he told the president, fixing the date now at August 15.

Truman had come to Potsdam with many goals, but "the most urgent, to my mind," he later wrote, "was to get from Stalin a personal reaffirmation of Russia's entry into the war against Japan, a matter which our military chiefs were most anxious to clinch." Truman had accomplished this goal before the first conference plenary session had begun. He wrote in his diary: "Most of the big points are settled. He'll [Stalin] be in the Jap War on August 15th. Fini Japs when that comes about."

Truman suggested that Stalin and his party stay for lunch. Stalin replied that he could not, but Truman pressed him. "You could if you wanted to," he said.

It was agreed. Colonel Rigdon, in charge of serving lunch, dashed into the kitchen, where Truman's mess staff was working. There was no time to find more opulent fare. Rigdon later recalled, "All I could do was increase the quantities of liver and bacon that I had planned to serve as the main course, and of side dishes."

Lunch was served at 1:40 p.m. Stalin revealed at the table that he did not believe Adolf Hitler was dead. "I think he's loose somewhere," Stalin said — maybe in Argentina or Spain. Stalin praised the wine on the table, so bottles were brought out for his inspection; the wine was from California. Truman later presented a number of bottles to Stalin as a gift. After lunch, the group moved onto a porch for photographs — the leaders posed with smiles on their faces, like old friends — and then the Soviets departed.

That afternoon the president prepared himself for the first plenary meeting at Potsdam. One can only imagine the thoughts moving through his mind as he dressed in his rooms, donning a dark gray double-breasted suit, a white shirt, and a bow tie. He had come to some conclusions about Stalin already. As he wrote in his diary on this day: "I can deal with Stalin. He is honest — but smart as hell."

At 4:40 p.m. Truman left the Little White House with his staff in a motorcade — MPs on motorcycles, secret service in jeeps, with flags flying and sirens blaring. The palace where the conference was to be held was called Cecilienhof, and it was a ten-minute drive. At a gatehouse manned by Russian soldiers, the flags of the three nations flew in the breeze — the Stars and Stripes, the Union Jack, the Hammer and Sickle. When the big iron gate opened, Truman's motorcade moved through winding tree-lined roads manned by green-capped Red Army soldiers with bayoneted rifles. The palace then revealed itself — three stories with a high red tiled roof, with an arch in the center leading into a courtyard, where the main entrances were situated. The palace had been completed in 1917 and contained 176 rooms. Inside the courtyard the Russians had planted a large red star, made out of geraniums. The red flowered star "strikingly informs all that the Russians are the conference host," recorded one of Truman's bodyguards, escorting him on this day.

Each nation's delegation had its own entrance into the palace. Truman and his party walked through their own door, down long hallways to a dark-wood-paneled conference room with high ceilings and a large grid of windows that allowed natural light to flood the room. In the center was a round table surrounded by chairs, with miniature flags of the three nations at the center. There was no water or glasses on the table, but there were ashtrays aplenty. Both Stalin and Churchill and their parties had arrived before Truman. At 5 p.m. the parties assembled and posed for photographs and newsreel cameras. Joseph Davies recalled walking into the conference room with Truman: "As we entered, we were almost blinded by a battery of klieg lights and moving picture cameras. Very shortly thereafter, however, the business was 'on.'"

Fifteen men sat at the negotiating table, five from each nation, and the rest of the advisors sat ringed around them. This table felt familiar to Truman, for it had the aura of a great big poker table. He eyed his opponents. He knew that they hoped to take advantage of him, the inexperienced one, who had been an obscure county judge just ten years earlier, and whose rise seemed still inexplicable. The Big Three leaders had come together to map out the future, but their interests were not the same. At 5:10 p.m., here in this palace — "only a few miles from the war-shattered seat of Nazi power," as Truman put it — the historic Potsdam Conference was called to order.

Part V

Little Boy, Fat Man, and Potsdam

*He had tremendous native courage. He had,
what really gets down to the word, "guts."
He had no fear of anything. He had a
tremendous sense of patriotism and an awe
of the Presidency.*

— Robert Nixon, journalist at
Potsdam, on Harry Truman

My God, what have we done.

—*Enola Gay* copilot Robert A.
Lewis, while staring down at the
Hiroshima mushroom cloud

"WHO IS TO BE THE CHAIRMAN at our conference?" Churchill asked.

The Russian interpreter Pavlov translated Churchill's question for Stalin, who responded, "I propose President Truman of the United States."

Churchill: "The British delegation supports this proposal."

Truman said, "I accept the chairmanship of this Conference."

Potsdam's first agreement was made. The negotiations would never be that easy again. Perhaps Truman did not realize that Stalin had already begun his careful manipulation. Stalin would never offer anything – not even simple graciousness – without asking for something in return, further on down the line.

Sitting at the table from the United States: Truman, with Secretary Byrnes and Admiral Leahy on his right, interpreter Chip Bohlen on his left, and former Moscow ambassador Joseph Davies on the other side of Bohlen. In the background: Ambassador Harriman and various members of the State Department. (The Chiefs of Staff had come to Potsdam, but as military men, they were not in the negotiating chamber.)

From Britain: Prime Minister Churchill, Churchill's election opponent, Clement Attlee of the Labour Party, and Foreign Secretary Anthony Eden, among others.

From the Soviet Union: Generalissimo Stalin, with Molotov on his right, and the translator Pavlov on his left. Also: the fierce negotiator Andrey Vyshinsky – who had served as Stalin's legal mastermind during the Great Purge trials of the 1930s – and the nearly as cunning foreign minister, Andrei Gromyko.

Much of this first meeting was devoted to procedure. Truman had come prepared, and he launched forward with his first point. "One of the most acute problems at present is to set up some kind of mechanism for arranging peace talks," he said. "Without it, Europe's economic development will continue to the detriment of the cause of the Allies and the whole world." He recommended the establishment of a council of foreign ministers from Britain, the United States, the USSR, France, and China. "That is," he said, "the permanent members of the Security Council of the United Nations set up at the San Francisco Conference." This council, Truman said, should play the role of hammering out all the peace treaties for all the belligerents.

As the room filled with smoke, an agenda for the conference began to take shape. The list of questions that needed addressing grew profoundly daunting: the future of Germany and the matter of German reparations, the Polish regime (still clearly Soviet-controlled), the role of China in the peace talks, and the complexity of Italy's role in Europe. (Under Mussolini, Italy had fought with the Nazis at the cost of many Allied soldiers, but had been the first of the Axis to surrender and had recently declared war on Japan just three days earlier, in hopes of joining the UN.) All these issues formed what Churchill called "the tangled problems of Europe — the volcano from which war springs."

Truman's personality emerged early. He wanted efficient talks. He wanted the agenda for the next day's discussions set before today's were over. "I don't want just to discuss," he said, "I want to decide." He wanted the talks to begin at 4 p.m. instead of 5. He also took a moment to voice what everyone in the room was thinking: "I am well aware that I am now substituting for a man whom it is impossible to substitute, the late President Roosevelt. I am glad to serve, even if partially, the memory which you preserve of President Roosevelt."

Before the first meeting was over, the first conflict arose, an omen of what was to come. This fray was over German warships, which were in British possession.

"There is only one other question," Stalin said, as the session neared its end. "Why does Mr. Churchill deny the Russians their share of the German navy?"

"I have no objections," said Churchill. "But since you have asked me this question, here is my answer: This navy should be either sunk or divided."

"Do you want it sunk or divided?" asked Stalin.

"All means of war are terrible things," said Churchill, avoiding the question.

"The navy should be divided," said Stalin. "If Mr. Churchill prefers to sink the navy, he is free to sink his share of it. I have no intention of sinking mine."

"At present, nearly the whole of the German navy is in our hands," said Churchill.

"That's the whole point," Stalin came back. "That's the whole point. That is why we need to decide the question."

Truman ended the session here before any decision on the German fleet was made, after one hour and forty-five minutes of sparring. "Tomorrow," he said, "the sitting is at four o'clock."

With the meeting adjourned, the delegations funneled to an adjoining room where the hosts had prepared an elaborate buffet. As Truman was soon to learn, this was the Russian way of doing things. "The table was set with everything you could think of," he recalled. Goose liver, caviar, every kind of meat one could imagine, along with cheeses of different shapes and colors, and endless wine and vodka.

Minutes after 7 p.m., Truman left the palace in his motorcade. At a checkpoint along the road back to the Little White House, Russian soldiers stopped the president's car for questioning, at which point a Russian lieutenant appeared and berated the soldiers for holding the American president up. Leahy leaned into Truman's ear as the driver put the car in gear. "I'll bet that lieutenant is shot in the morning," he said.

Later that night, at his villa, Truman received Secretary of War Stimson, who came bearing another cryptic communication from Washington regarding the atomic bomb test in New Mexico.

> Doctor has just returned most enthusiastic and confident that the little boy [the bomb being ready for use against Japan] is as husky as his big brother [the Trinity test shot]. The light in his eyes discernible from here [Washington DC] to Highhold [Stimson's private estate on Long Island] and could have heard his screams from here to my farm.

///

Numerous accounts of Potsdam describe Truman in moments of pensive repose at his villa. He was worried. All three delegations understood that, even before the conference began, powerful forces were at work, undermining its success. The Big Three were emerging from the war as victors, but they were entrenched in economic and political instabilities that set their best interests in conflict. Historians would forever debate the cause and effect of these instabilities, and while certain circumstances seem self-evident today, they were not at the time.

The Americans saw themselves as world policemen and moral arbiters. But did their capitalist interests and their suspicion of the Soviets subjugate objective reasoning? Would the inexperience of their new president come into play? Britain — the Gilded Age's greatest power — was a fading flame. Even as the Potsdam Conference began, the Big Three was being called the Big Two and a Half. The Soviets were the most vexing. While their objectives at the negotiating table seemed relatively clear, their motivations were far from it. These motivations would only become more understood through time. The world's only communist nation saw itself as an island in a sea boiling with predators. The story of Russia had been a story of invasions. Through the years, Russia had been attacked by everyone from the Mongols to Napoleon. For centuries, marauding tribes had plundered the land now known as the USSR. In more recent times Russia had fought two wars against invading German armies and had lost a war with Japan, in 1904–1905. Only now after all these generations had the country emerged as a major global power. Stalin saw in every neighboring state a chance to influence the future and create security for the USSR through control of these neighboring governments via secret police, authority over the press, and puppet regimes.

Herein lay the reason why Stalin had committed so much blood to the war and was willing to sacrifice more in the fight with Japan. Stalin would see some twenty-four million of his subjects, military and civilian, die as a result of World War II, millions more than had died from any other nation. (China was second with roughly 20 million military and civilian deaths, while the United States lost about 418,500.) Now the Soviets intended to capitalize on this investment in blood; they believed that this bloodletting entitled them to power and expansion. This thinking informed Stalin's every statement at Potsdam.

Only one thing felt certain: the United States and the Soviet Union were going to enter the second half of the twentieth century as global superpowers of unprecedented strength. George Kennan of the Moscow embassy defined the USSR at this time: "Two hundred million people, united under the strong and purposeful leadership of Moscow and inhabiting one of the major industrial countries of the world, constitute a single force far greater than any other that will be left on the European continent when this war is over; and it would be folly to underestimate their potential – for good or evil."

The negotiations were at hand. Populations and borders had shifted or disappeared during the war, so vast frontiers, such as those along the edges of Poland, the USSR, and Germany, needed to be remapped and millions of peoples potentially moved. New governments in many nations had to be agreed upon, according to principles of government that were themselves not agreed upon. Meanwhile, millions in Europe were starving, the Pacific war was raging, and the Americans had a secret that had the potential to change everything.

///

On the morning after the first Potsdam plenary session, Truman breakfasted with his nephew Sergeant Harry Truman – the son of the president's brother, Vivian. Sergeant Truman had been aboard the *Queen Elizabeth* ready to sail home for America when army officials plucked him up and delivered him to Babelsberg. "They gave him the choice of sailing or coming to see his uncle," Truman wrote Bess. "The nicest looking soldier you can imagine."

At 1:15 p.m. Truman walked the few blocks to Churchill's villa, accompanied by a half dozen officials including Charlie Ross and Harry Vaughan. The president lunched with Churchill alone, however. The prime minister expressed melancholy over the state of the British empire. Britain was deeply scarred by Nazi bombing, and the country was emerging from the European war with a debt of £3 billion. Truman was sympathetic, implying that there would be future economic aid. The United States owed Britain for giving so much to defeating the Third Reich. Truman said, "If you had gone down like France, we might be fighting the Germans on the American coast at the present time. This justifies us in regarding these matters as above the purely financial plane."

Truman brought up the Trinity test, of which Churchill had been informed the day before during a meeting with Secretary of War Stimson. ("The experiment in the New Mexican desert has come off," Stimson had said. "The atomic bomb is a reality.") Churchill referred to Trinity as "world shaking news," though it was not unexpected. Since the early days of the Manhattan Project, Churchill had been a coconspirator with Franklin Roosevelt.* As the bomb became more and more of an American phenomenon, there was certainly jealousy on the part of Churchill. Now FDR was gone, and Truman must have felt to the prime minister like an interloper. Nevertheless, Churchill was thrilled with the news of Trinity, and he had come to immediate conclusions, which he shared with Truman. Churchill was deeply disturbed by the idea of an invasion of Japan. It could cost a million American lives and another half million British, he believed. With the bomb, there was an alternative.

"Now all this nightmare picture had vanished," Churchill later wrote, due to this "supernatural weapon." "In its place was the vision — fair and bright indeed it seemed — of the end of the whole war in one or two violent shocks." From the point of view of both Truman and Churchill, the genius of the bomb was that it could save lives by putting an end to the fighting and giving the Japanese a reason to surrender. "By using this new agency," Churchill believed, "we might not merely destroy cities, but save the lives alike of friend and foe."

Churchill also believed that the Russians were no longer needed in the war against Japan, a question that Byrnes and Stimson and the American chiefs of Staff were now examining from every angle. With the bomb, Churchill believed Stalin's bargaining power with the Japanese war was now gone. But, the prime minister added, the employment of the atomic bomb — without Stalin's knowledge of its existence — would be construed by him as a shocking betrayal. Truman made no commitment on whether the United States favored having the Soviets in the Japanese war, but the president did agree: the time was near to reveal this secret to Stalin.

"I think," Truman told Churchill, "I had best just tell him after one of our meetings that we have an entirely novel form of bomb, something

---

* At a 1943 meeting in Quebec, the United States and Britain had made a pact regarding the bomb. Their agreement listed the following: "We [the U.S. and Britain] will never use this agency against each other," "we will not use it against third parties without each other's consent," and "we will not either of us communicate any information about [the bomb] to third parties except by mutual consent." Source: Articles of Agreement Governing Collaboration Between the Authorities of the USA and the UK in the Matter of Tube Alloys, avalon.law.yale .edu, last accessed January 28, 2017.

quite out of the ordinary, which we think will have decisive effects upon the Japanese will to continue the war."

Churchill agreed.

In his diary, Truman wrote on this day, "Believe Japs will fold before Russia comes in. I am sure they will when Manhattan appears over their homeland."

///

Minutes after 3 p.m., Truman and Byrnes paid a visit to Stalin's villa, with the translator Chip Bohlen in tow. Inside, the Soviets presented the Americans with yet another buffet of delicacies, then Stalin led Truman out onto a balcony overlooking Lake Griebnitz. Toasts were made and diplomatic language was exchanged. There were serious misunderstandings about each leader in the opposing nation, both agreed. Truman suggested Stalin visit the United States, as a means of changing public opinion, in both countries. Stalin made no commitment, but he did admit that it was going to be harder for the Soviets to cooperate with the United States in peacetime, as they had in war.

Stalin brought up a peace feeler from Japan that had arrived via an emissary in Moscow. Chip Bohlen was taking notes of the conversation in Stalin's villa, and he later formulated the following depiction of this moment: "Stalin said that the Soviet Union had received a communication from the Japanese, and he handed to the president a copy of a note from Sato, the Japanese ambassador at Moscow, with a message from the [Japanese] Emperor . . . Stalin inquired of the president whether it was worth while [to] answer this communication. The President replied that he had no respect for the good faith of the Japanese."

Truman, Stalin, Byrnes, and Molotov talked over the issue, concluding that news of this Japanese peace feeler was so vague, it deserved no serious response. Surely, leaders in Tokyo were becoming aware of the Red Army forces amassing along the border of Japanese-occupied Manchuria, and they feared what the Russians were about to do next. If Emperor Hirohito wanted peace, he would make a more formal approach. This discussion was cut short, however. Truman left Stalin's villa with Byrnes and Bohlen, and less than an hour later the delegations were back at the negotiating table.

Truman was in terrific form at the second plenary session, which was called to order minutes after 4 p.m. on July 18. His style was different from his predecessor's. Roosevelt improvised, while Truman stuck to the script. Roosevelt's discourse rambled, but Truman was "crisp and to the point," according to Bohlen, who served as Russian translator to both presidents. "Where Roosevelt was warmly friendly with Churchill and Stalin," Bohlen noted, "Truman was pleasantly distant." At one point during the conversation, Truman scribbled on a piece of paper – "Joe, how am I doing?" – and passed it across the table to Joseph Davies, who wrote back, "You are batting 1000 percent. You are holding your own with the best at this table."

Churchill was not himself, on the other hand. He appeared ill prepared, to the dismay of his delegation, who assumed he had become distracted by the current election count, which could end his term of office in a matter of a few days. This second meeting's major topics were control of Germany and Poland's government. Churchill seized on questions posed and deconstructed them by asking more questions. "What is the meaning of reference to submission of the United Nations?" "What do we mean by Germany?" "Are we going to have uniform control or different practices in the four [occupation] zones?" Truman grew frustrated by the prime minister's verbosity. The president wrote in a diary on this day: "I'm not going to stay around this terrible place all summer just to listen to speeches. I'll go home to the Senate for that."

Stalin, on the other hand, was laconic, friendly, and fiercely protective of his interests. Of all the poker faces Truman had ever stared down, none beat the Man of Steel. "Stalin," Truman concluded, "is as near like Tom Pendergast as any man I know."

Meanwhile, outside the negotiating chamber, the scene at Potsdam had become a beehive of rumor and intrigue. "This whole environment at Berlin is somehow beyond words," Stimson wrote in a letter to his wife. The Russian sector was closed and closely guarded. Stimson described his impression of the Soviets: "There was evident . . . palpable and omnipresent, the atmosphere of dictatorial repression. Nothing in [my] life matched this experience . . . What manner of men were these with whom to build a peace in the atomic age?"

In the American and British sections, the experience was different. "The general atmosphere at Babelsberg between the British and American sectors was that of a community compound," noted one member of the British group, "where people lived in self-contained working units, invited each other to their houses, [and] greeted each other in the street. Absolutely *everyone* was there. It was the last great beano of the war."

In Berlin itself, thousands of journalists from around the globe lounged wherever they could, unable to get access to concrete facts, as they were forbidden from attending the conference. Warriors from three conquering armies rubbed elbows in the streets. Soldiers would describe a psychological darkness in Berlin; it was a city balanced on a razor's edge. Chip Bohlen recalled his one night free at Potsdam, going to the only open nightclub in Berlin: "The hall was filled with soldiers of three armies, most of them intoxicated and all of them heavily armed."

A black market thrived openly in Berlin's streets, with goods and services readily traded. At one point all the eggs in the president's villa disappeared, to the chagrin of Commander William Rigdon, in charge of the pantry. Rigdon inquired among secret service men, who could not solve the mystery but could provide this piece of information: a single egg on the Berlin black market could bring ten dollars. General Arnold wrote in his diary of Berlin's black market: "Jewels, rings traded for bread but principally for canned meat. Trading posts in action with hundreds of people all day long." Women, according to Arnold's diary, were part of this black market's trade. At one point, according to a story told by Truman's driver, Floyd Boring, the president was getting into his car when an army colonel whispered to him: "Listen, I know you're alone over here [without your wife] . . . If you need anything like, you know, I'll be glad to arrange it for you."

Truman responded furiously: "Hold it; don't say anything more. I love my wife, and my wife is my sweetheart. I don't want to do that kind of stuff . . . I don't want you to ever say that again to me."

Truman was all business at Potsdam. The night after the second plenary session, he described his view of the scene in a letter to Bess. He was handling himself all right, he told her.

"Admiral Leahy said he'd never seen an abler job and Byrnes and my fellows seemed to be walking on air. I was so scared I didn't know whether things were going according to Hoyle or not [a reference meaning in accord with the rules]. Anyway, a start has been made and I've gotten what I came for – Stalin goes to war August 15 with no strings on it . . . I'll say that we'll end the war a year sooner now, and think of the kids who won't be killed! That is the important thing."

TRUMAN REACHED HIS BOILING POINT at the third Potsdam sit-down, which began at 4:05 p.m. on July 19. The Big Three leaders sparred over the fate of Franco's government in Spain (Stalin wanted Franco out, while Truman could not allow the United States to get entangled). They argued over the regime in Yugoslavia (Truman and Churchill wanted democratic elections, while Stalin supported Tito's dictatorship). The prime minister and the generalissimo even argued over whether Churchill's jabs at the Soviets over Tito were "complaints" or "accusations." Here is where Truman let loose.

"I am here to discuss world affairs with Soviet and Great Britain governments," he said. "I am not here to sit as a court. That is the work of San Francisco. I want to discuss matters on which the three governments can come to agreement."

Churchill responded, "I thought that this was a matter in which the United States was very interested, particularly in view of the Yalta papers."

"That is true," Truman said. "I want to see the Yalta papers carried out."

Stalin insisted he was right; Tito would stay.

Truman: "Let us drop it."

Churchill: "It is very important."

Truman: "We are dropping it only for the day as we did with Franco."

By the end of the session, Truman was exasperated. He had come to Potsdam to make decisions, but the three leaders could not agree on anything. "On a number of occasions," he later wrote, "I felt like blowing the roof off the palace."

The stakes were rising. Joseph Davies, sitting at the table, summed up the players. Churchill had found a footing and was performing magically. He "portrays the classic tradition and best of England," Davies wrote. "His use of the spoken word is classic." Stalin "has no such graciousness of manner, but he has a dignity and power which startles one every now and then . . . I watched him sitting in his chair, listening, with eyes almost closed. When he speaks, it is tersely. Each sentence is a naked idea, stated in as few words as possible. He clips off ideas like a machine gun."

As for Truman, "He was thrown into this arena without much notice. Several of the delegates, both British and Soviet, have commented upon the quality of this forthright American from Independence, Missouri. They have been impressed by 'his fine head,' the honest look out of his eyes; and his direct simplicity in speaking his mind . . . He brings a refreshing atmosphere to this old Europe."

At the end of this session — the first where "the fur flew," as Davies put it — Churchill's foreign minister, Anthony Eden, declared that they had exhausted the agenda. Churchill said, "It has exhausted me."

By the conference's third day, two critical issues pressed upon the American delegation, behind the scenes. The first regarded the ultimatum to Japan. It was near time to finalize the language, and the future of the war appeared to hinge on a singular matter: whether or not to inform the Japanese that their emperor could remain in power. "The maintenance of the dynasty," Assistant Secretary of War John J. McCloy wrote in a memo to his boss, Henry Stimson. "This point seems to be the most controversial one and one on which there is a split in opinion in the State Department."

Using "Magic" deciphering equipment, American army intelligence had cracked codes and were reading secret Japanese communications. According to an "ultra top secret" memorandum, dated July 17, Japanese foreign minister Togo sent the following sentences in a memo to Ambassador Sato, who was in Moscow and was responsible for the Japanese peace feelers there. "We have been fully aware from the outset that it would be difficult under existing circumstances to strengthen the ties of friendship between Japan and Russia or to make effective use of Russia in ending the war," Togo cabled Sato. "The present situation, however, is such that we have no recourse but to make efforts along those lines."

The communication concluded: "If today, when we are still maintaining our strength, the Anglo-Americans were to have regard for Japan's honor and existence, they could save humanity by bringing the war to an end. If, however, they insist unrelentingly upon unconditional surrender, the Japanese are unanimous in their resolve to wage a thoroughgoing war."

By "Japan's honor and existence," the communication clearly referred to the emperor. If the emperor was permitted to remain in power, the Japanese would bring "the war to an end." If not, the Japanese would continue to kill and be killed. This communiqué noted that Japan was "still maintaining our strength," suggesting to the Americans that the enemy could keep fighting for a long time to come. Years after the war, Truman confirmed that he had read Magic intercepts while at Potsdam, so he knew of these discussions.

Many of the president's top aides, including Stimson and Leahy, agreed that the Allies should drop unconditional surrender. Leahy believed that the Japanese decision to surrender lay in the hands of the emperor, so any statement or action that threatened the emperor would make surrender more difficult for Japan. Even Churchill had come to this conclusion. "I felt that there would be no rigid insistence upon 'unconditional surrender,'" he wrote in his memoirs.

Others disagreed. Byrnes had sought the advice of Cordell Hull, who had been Roosevelt's deeply respected secretary of state for most of the war, and who had resigned due to ill health in 1944. (Hull had been a major force behind the original planning of the United Nations, and would be awarded the Nobel Peace Prize in 1945 for these efforts.) Hull responded that if the Americans agreed to allow the emperor to remain in power, "terrible political repercussions would follow in the United States." Hull noted that he was thinking of how "the general public will doubtless construe" the matter. Byrnes agreed with Hull; he thought the American people would "crucify" the president if he accepted anything less than unconditional surrender. Truman would be responsible for the final decision, but Byrnes had become his most influential advisor.

The second critical issue facing the Anglo-Americans was the USSR's commitment to joining the war against Japan. Now that the United States had the bomb, was Russian participation in the Pacific war necessary? The American and British leaders feared that, with Stalin's soldiers marching into China and Korea and eventually Japan itself, the Red Army would spread the Soviets' totalitarian brand of communism like a disease into the Far East. Byrnes later said, "I cannot speak for others but it was ever present in my mind that it was important that we should have an end to the war before the Russians came in." However, Truman still supported the idea of the Red Army joining the war. As he wrote Bess as late as July 20: "I have to make it perfectly plain to them at least once a day that my first interest is U.S.A., then I want the Jap War won and I want 'em both [the UK and USSR] in it."

Whichever way opinion fell among the American delegation, Stalin was intent on joining the Pacific war. The only way to stop him from pushing his armies east was to end the war before he could do so.

///

Just hours after tempers boiled over at the negotiating table for the first time, the Americans hosted the first of the Potsdam tripartite dinners, at the Little White House. The cold glares of rigorous diplomacy gave way to smiles, some of them genuine. Dinner that night had to be the most elaborate served anywhere in Europe in years: pâté de foie gras, caviar on toast, cream of tomato soup, olives, perch sauté meunière, filet mignon, mushroom gravy, shoestring potatoes, peas and carrots, tomato salad with French dressing, Roca cheese, and vanilla ice cream with chocolate sauce, the ice cream flown in from the USS *Augusta* in Antwerp. The wines included a chilled German white called Niersteiner from 1937; a fine Bordeaux, Mouton d'Armailhac; Champagne, 1934 Pommery; plus coffee, cigars, cigarettes, port, cognac, and vodka.

"Had Churchill on my right, Stalin on my left," Truman wrote Bess. The first toast was to President Roosevelt. They toasted to Churchill, then to Stalin, then Truman wanted to toast both Churchill and Stalin together. "That gives us two drinks," Truman announced, and Stalin replied, "That pays." Churchill even toasted to his political opponent, Clement Attlee, sitting quietly across the table: "I raise my glass to the leader of His Majesty's loyal opposition." Churchill's biting sarcasm was not lost on Attlee, who had thus far said very little at Potsdam.

From the American side, James F. Byrnes made quite an impression. "Jim Byrnes was in unusually good form," recalled one ambassador present. "His stories were good, and told with both Irish and southern charm." Leahy, meanwhile, took some ribbing from the others for his alcohol abstinence.

Truman drank bourbon during the toasts, while Churchill had brandy, and Stalin appeared to be drinking vodka. Even the pianist was toasted. Staff Sergeant Eugene List was a concert musician from Manhattan serving in Berlin with the GI Orchestra when, out of nowhere, he got orders: "Better spruce up. You're playing for the president tonight." List had his pants pressed, shaved out of his army helmet, and jumped into a car, which sped him to the Little White House. He performed brilliantly as the headliner for the show, topping it off with the "Missouri Waltz" for the president. At one point, after List played a piece by the Russian composer Tchaikovsky, Stalin jumped to his feet and shouted in Russian. All nervously awaited the translator Pavlov, who said, "A toast to the pianist!"

At one point Truman asked the crowd, "Where will the next conference be?"

The president suggested Washington, and Churchill threw out London. Stalin responded slyly, "Well, you know there are also palaces in Japan."

It was likely at this dinner where Truman famously introduced his old friend Fred Canfil to Stalin. Canfil had traveled with Truman as part of security detail.

"Marshal Stalin," Truman said to the Soviet dictator, "I want you to meet Marshal Canfil." (Canfil was a U.S. marshal in Kansas City.) Stalin sized up the strange-looking Missourian with the giant head and the ever-present cigarette. After this meeting, Canfil was treated with great respect and deference by all the Soviet delegation.

"The ambassadors and Jim Byrnes said the party was a success," Truman wrote Bess. "I'm sick of the whole business. But we'll bring home the bacon."

The next morning General Eisenhower called on the president at the Little White House, along with General Omar Bradley. After a quick lunch, the group left by open car for the American sector in Berlin. Here again was the odor of death and destruction, and the miserable procession of German citizens in rags, pushing what few belongings they had through the rubble. "You never saw as completely ruined a city," Truman recorded. The scene was quite a contrast from the dinner the night before.

In a courtyard of a building that was formerly the Nazi Air Defense Command – run by Hermann Göring, chief architect of the Luftwaffe – Truman watched as soldiers raised the Stars and Stripes up a flagpole. Honors were accorded by an honor guard from the Forty-First Infantry. This flag now flying over Berlin was the same flag that flew atop the White House at the time of Pearl Harbor and on the day the United States declared war on Nazi Germany. The army had raised this very flag over Rome when that city fell, and over Paris too when the Allies liberated the City of Lights. Truman made some extemporaneous remarks, as the flag rippled in the breeze:

General Eisenhower, officers, and men: This is an historic occasion . . . We are here today to raise the flag of victory over the capital of our greatest adversary . . . Let's not forget that we are fighting for peace and for the welfare of mankind. We are not fighting for conquest. There is not one piece of territory or one thing of monetary nature that we want out of this war. We want peace and prosperity for the world as a whole . . . If we can put this tremendous machine of ours, which has made this victory possible, to work for peace, we could look forward to the greatest age in the history of mankind. That is what we propose to do.

After the ceremony Truman wrote in his diary, "Flag was on the White House when Pearl Harbor happened. Will be raised over Tokyo."

///

Over the next days, fatigue set in. Evening plenary meetings, daytime meetings of the foreign ministers, meetings of an economic subcommittee and the Combined Chiefs of Staff — the negotiations began to wear the delegations down. Britain's chief of Imperial General Staff, Sir Alan Brooke, spoke for all when he wrote in his diary, "It all feels flat and empty. I am feeling very, very tired and worn out."

The complexity of the issues kept agreements out of reach, time and again. The Americans and the British favored welcoming Italy into the UN, but Stalin capitalized, arguing that if so, the Anglo-Americans should also recognize the governments of Romania, Hungary, and Bulgaria — all clearly Sovietized.

Russian troops had amassed on the Turkish border. Turkey was strategically imperative for Stalin, because it controlled the Black Sea straits. Was Turkey to be annihilated by the Red Army?

Stalin clashed bitterly with Churchill and Truman over Poland's western frontier. The Soviets believed that a broad section of eastern Germany should be given to the Poles.[*] As an important source of coal, it was valuable territory. Polish leaders came to Potsdam and argued that

---

[*] At Yalta the Big Three agreed to allow the eastern Polish border to be moved west, so the USSR was given a part of Poland. Thus, at Potsdam, Poland wanted to get some frontier back, at the expense of the Germans.

they were entitled to it, as "an expression of historical justice," since "the Germans had attempted to destroy the Polish population and ruin Polish culture." Truman and Churchill refused to agree to allow Poland's border to be pushed so deeply into Germany. The Polish government had reorganized, but it still was in Soviet control. Pushing the border west meant pushing Stalin's power west.

"There were many other matters on which it was right to confront the Soviet Government," Churchill later wrote, "and also the Poles, who, gulping down immense chunks of German territory, had obviously become their [Russia's] ardent puppets." Besides, Churchill believed that nine million Germans were living in this part of Germany; what would become of them, if it were handed over to Poland?

And what of Germany itself? Churchill and Truman wanted to destroy all hints of Nazism, then rebuild Germany, because only a strong, reunified Germany could provide security in Europe. Stalin disagreed. Twice in the span of his lifetime, his country had fought wars with Germany. A weak Germany was in his best interest.

For all three leaders, economics complicated the negotiations. The UK and the USSR were desperate for money and resources, and both countries were counting on loans from the United States after the war. Truman, on the other hand, needed to protect American taxpayers. Truman now worried that all the ailing countries of Europe — millions and millions of war victims — would be dependent on the United States for food and aid. There would be intense pressure on him to make sure American taxpayers were not about to write what Senator Arthur Vandenberg called "the most colossal blank check in history."

"The United States can not, moreover, pour out its resources without prospective return," Truman argued at the negotiating table. "I will not sanction the continued handing out of funds to nations which should be self-supporting. We want to help these nations to become self-supporting."

Ultimately, the most heated friction between the Americans and the Soviets was ideological. While debating the fates of the governments of Italy, Hungary, Romania, Bulgaria, Turkey, Austria, and other countries, one difference separated the two nations continuously. The United States wanted democratic nations and political stability for the world, for reasons of moral righteousness, peace, and economic gain. There was a quest for balance of power. The Soviets wanted instability, an imbalance of power, for reasons of survival. For the Soviets, strong nations were threats, while weak nations were not. This disparity would form the fabric of the Iron Curtain.

///

Stalin hosted the Russian state dinner on the night of July 21, attempting to outdo the Americans in a contest of decadence. "Started with caviar and vodka . . ." Truman wrote Margie, "then smoked herring, then white fish and vegetables, then venison and vegetables, then duck and chicken and finally two desserts, ice cream and strawberries and a wind-up of sliced watermelon. White wine, red wine, champagne and cognac in liberal quantities." At one point Truman asked the Man of Steel how he could drink so much vodka. Through an interpreter, Stalin said, "Tell the president it is French wine, because since my heart attack I can't drink the way I used to."

Churchill promised he would "get even." So when the prime minister hosted his dinner on July 23, he had the entire British Royal Air Force Orchestra playing. Stalin arrived at Churchill's dinner in a bulletproof limousine with some fifty armed guards, while Truman showed up on foot with Byrnes, Leahy, and three secret service men.

Meanwhile, major story lines of the conference were playing out behind closed doors, away from the plenary meetings and the lavish dinners. "Much is going on here that does not meet the eye," Joseph Davies wrote in his diary.

On July 21, Truman received possibly the most memorable memorandum he would ever read. Stimson arrived at the Little White House at 3:30 p.m., bearing a full description of Trinity from General Groves. "It was an immensely powerful document," Stimson confided in his diary. Groves's memorandum had arrived by a special courier who had traveled thousands of miles on airplanes to put this document in front of the president; it was so explosive, the general refused to cable it overseas due to security reasons. Behind closed doors in the Little White House, Stimson read the document aloud to Truman and Byrnes. It took some time, as it was fourteen pages double-spaced.

At 530, 16 July 1945, in a remote section of the Alamogordo Air Base, New Mexico, the first full scale test was made of the implosion type atomic fission bomb. For the first time in history there was a nuclear explosion. And what an explosion! . . . The test was successful beyond the most optimistic expectations of anyone. Based on the data which it has been possible to work up to date, I estimate the energy generated to be in excess of the equivalent of 15,000 to 20,000 tons of TNT.

The details of Groves's report proved riveting. As Stimson read, he noted that Truman and Byrnes "were immensely pleased." Groves continued in his memo:

For a brief period there was a lighting effect within a radius of 20 miles equal to several suns in midday; a huge ball of fire was formed which lasted for several seconds. This ball mushroomed and rose to a height of over ten thousand feet before it dimmed. The light from the explosion was seen clearly at Albuquerque, Santa Fe, Silver City, El Paso and other points generally to about 180 miles away.

Groves noted that windows were shattered by the blast as far off as 125 miles from ground zero. The steel tower from which the bomb dropped evaporated. The fireball climbed to 41,000 feet, while the mushroom cloud itself contained "huge concentrations of highly radioactive materials." Groves quoted Thomas Farrell, chief of field operations at Los Alamos, regarding the scene at Trinity after the detonation: "As to the present war, there was a feeling that no matter what else might happen, we now had the means to insure its speedy conclusion and save thousands of American lives."

After reading the document, Stimson looked up at the president. Truman was "tremendously pepped up by it," Stimson noted. "He said it gave him an entirely new feeling of confidence."

Stimson then brought Groves's memorandum to Churchill's villa. The prime minister concluded: "Stimson, what was gunpowder? Trivial. What was electricity? Meaningless. The atomic bomb is the second coming of wrath."

JULY 24 THROUGH JULY 26 proved to be the critical days at Potsdam.

In his villa the morning of July 24, the president gave the go-ahead to send the final draft of the ultimatum to Japan — the Potsdam Declaration — to the Map Room at the White House, for forwarding to the ambassador to China, Patrick Hurley, in Chungking. The plan was to have Hurley bring the document to the Chinese generalissimo Chiang Kai-shek and get his approval on the wording, as the ultimatum was to be from all three nations that had declared war on Japan: the United States, Britain, and China. Truman and Churchill had signed off on the document; once Chiang Kai-shek did the same, the ultimatum would be published around the world.

For weeks, the State and War Departments had struggled with the emperor conundrum and the use of the term *unconditional surrender*. Having cracked the Japanese codes, the Americans were continuing to monitor enemy communications. In another intercepted, decoded, and translated Japanese communiqué, Foreign Minister Togo in Tokyo had written the following to the Japanese ambassador in Moscow: "With regard to unconditional surrender . . . we are unable to consent to it under any circumstances whatever. Even if the war drags on and it becomes clear that it will take much more bloodshed, the whole country as one man will pit itself against the enemy in accordance with the Imperial will so long as the enemy demands unconditional surrender."

The ultimatum's final draft *did* employ the term *unconditional surrender*. The draft included the following verbiage, however, which was meant to signify that the emperor would not be imprisoned or killed:

> The Japanese military forces, after being completely disarmed, shall be permitted to return to their homes with the opportunity to lead peaceful and productive lives. *We do not intend that the Japanese shall be enslaved as a race or destroyed as*

a nation [author's italics], but stern justice shall be meted out to all war criminals, including those who have visited cruelties upon our prisoners. The Japanese Government shall remove all obstacles to the revival and strengthening of democratic tendencies among the Japanese people. Freedom of speech, of religion, and of thought, as well as respect for the fundamental human rights shall be established . . . The occupying forces of the Allies shall be withdrawn from Japan as soon as these objectives have been accomplished and there has been established in accordance with the freely expressed will of the Japanese people a peacefully inclined and responsible government.

While the Potsdam Declaration did not use the words *atomic bomb,* it did spell out that "utter destruction" was imminent. It concluded: "We call upon the government of Japan to proclaim now the unconditional surrender of all Japanese armed forces, and to provide proper and adequate assurances of their good faith in such action. The alternative for Japan is prompt and utter destruction."

Moments after the document was sent to the Chinese for approval, Stimson came to the Little White House for a 10:20 a.m. meeting with Truman. Stimson said that he thought it was a mistake to demand unconditional surrender, but that it was now too late. The conversation turned to the Manhattan Project. Truman said that he planned to tell Stalin about the atomic bomb after the plenary meeting later in the day. Stimson then showed Truman the latest top-secret cable revealing dates when the bomb was expected to be ready.

Stimson's visit with Truman on July 24 lasted not longer than an hour. But it was a critical hour for humankind. No piece of paper documents Truman's official decision to drop the atomic bomb on Japan. However, the following day, Truman described this meeting with Stimson in the following words, in his diary:

The weapon is to be used against Japan between now and August 10th. I have told the Sec. of War Mr. Stimson to use it so that military objectives and soldiers and sailors are the target and not women and children. Even if the Japs are savages, ruthless, merciless and fanatic, we as the leader of the world for the common welfare cannot drop this terrible bomb on the old Capital [of Japan] Kyoto or the new [Tokyo]. He & I are in accord. The target will be a purely military one and we will issue a warning statement asking the Japs to surrender and save lives. I'm sure they will not do that, but we will have given them a chance. It is certainly a good thing for the world that Hitler's crowd or Stalin's did not discover this atomic bomb. It seems to be the most terrible thing ever discovered, but it can be made the most useful.

///

At eleven thirty that morning – a short time after Stimson left Truman's villa – Churchill and the British military leaders arrived for a conference of the Combined Chiefs of Staff. The elite British and American military officials offered the prime minister and the president a document spelling out the final strategy to bring the war to an end.

The ground invasion was still considered "the supreme operations in the war against Japan." Although so many officials close to Truman had stated, or would later do so, that the Russians were no longer needed, the final decision of the Combined Chiefs of Staff was to "encourage Russian entry into the war against Japan." The reason was certainly the incertitude of the bomb. Even at this late date, these officials could not be sure the bomb was going to go off. "All of us wanted Russia in the Japanese War," Truman later said. "Had we known what the atomic bomb would do, we'd have never wanted the Bear in the picture." The Combined Chiefs set a goal of ending the war on November 15, 1946 – almost sixteen more months, during which casualties were predicted to be heavy.

Hours later, at 5:15 p.m., Truman called the next plenary session to order, and the bitterest debate yet befell Potsdam. On the agenda: the governments of eastern Europe and the borders of Poland. Stalin pressed to have the governments of Hungary, Bulgaria, Romania, and Finland be regarded the same as Italy. He wanted these governments officially recognized by London and Washington. Truman and Churchill did not view Italy as Soviet-influenced, and thus they were prepared to welcome Italy into the community of nations. The other countries were clearly being governed by Soviet puppet regimes, operating behind the Iron Curtain.

CHURCHILL: "We have been unable to get information, or to have free access to the satellite states [Hungary, Bulgaria, Romania]. As soon as we have proper access to them, and proper governments are set up, we will recognize them — not sooner."

STALIN: "But you have recognized Italy."

TRUMAN: "The other satellite states will be recognized when they meet the same conditions as Italy has met . . . We are asking re-organization of these governments along democratic lines." (All at the table understood what Truman was really saying: that Truman and Churchill would refuse to recognize any govern-ment they believed to be Sovietized.)

STALIN: "The other satellites have democratic governments closer to the people than does Italy."

TRUMAN: "I have made clear we will not recognize these govern-ments until they are reorganized."

Churchill raised Romania as an example. "Our mission in Bucharest has been practically confined," Churchill said. "I am sure the Marshal [Stalin] would be amazed to read the long list of incidents which have occurred."

Stalin responded with rage. "They are all fairy tale[s]."

There would be no agreement. Soviet influence was creeping deep into eastern Europe, and Truman and Churchill could not stop it, unless they chose to use military force.

After the session adjourned, Truman made his move. He instructed his interpreter, Bohlen, not to follow him, then he walked slowly around the conference table toward Stalin and engaged the Soviet leader in a quiet conversation. The time was 7:30 p.m. The Russian interpreter, Pav-lov, translated.

"I casually mentioned to Stalin," Truman later wrote, "that we had a new weapon of unusual destructive force. The Russian Premier showed no special interest. All he said was that he was glad to hear it and hoped we would make 'good use of it against the Japanese.'" From across the room, Bohlen watched Stalin's face closely. "So offhand was Stalin's response," noted Bohlen, "that there was some question in my mind whether the president's message had got through."

Afterward, Churchill approached Truman and asked, "How did it go?"

"He never asked a question," Truman responded.

The deed was done. The Americans and British all assumed that Stalin had no knowledge of the existence of atomic science. As Bohlen later noted, "I should have known better than to underrate the dictator."

As evidence would later show, not only were the Russians avidly spying on the Americans' work in the atomic energy field, they were already working on their own bomb. After the meeting, one of the Russian delegation, Marshal Georgy Zhukov, recalled Stalin and Molotov discussing Truman's admission that night, in hushed tones. Molotov told Stalin it was time to "speed things up." "I realized they were talking about research on the atomic bomb," Zhukov later recalled.

There can be no exact date when the Cold War started. However, as historian Charles L. Mee Jr. has pointed out, the nuclear arms race is a different story: "The Twentieth Century's nuclear arms race began at the Cecilienhof Palace at 7:30 p.m., on July 24, 1945."

///

On the morning of the twenty-fifth, Truman was stunned to learn that Ambassador Hurley in Chungking had not yet received the draft of the Japanese ultimatum. Byrnes ordered an immediate investigation; this communication breakdown was going to get somebody fired. As it turned out, Map Room officials at the White House had apparently handed the document to the navy to send, and unaware of the document's importance, naval officers failed to shoot it out for five hours. Then they sent it through Honolulu, where it was further delayed.

Truman and Byrnes were furious. Any delay with the Potsdam Declaration would delay the use of the bomb and thus the end of the war.

Ambassador Hurley finally cabled Truman and Byrnes that the ultimatum had reached him at 8:35 p.m. Chungking time on July 25, the day *after* the ultimatum was originally sent from Truman's villa. Hurley cabled Truman, "The translation was not finished until after midnight." When the ambassador tried to deliver the ultimatum to Chiang Kai-shek for his approval, the Chinese generalissimo was not at his palace but rather across the Yangtze River in the mountains. Hurley had to go hunting for a ferry to cross the river in the middle of the night.

Later that day, at the Cecilienhof Palace in Potsdam, the Big Three once again sparred at the negotiating table. At the end of this ninth plenary meeting, cameramen charged into the chamber to capture a moment of pathos. Winston Churchill and his political opponent, Clement

Attlee, would be leaving Germany for Britain, where they would learn the results of the election. Churchill and Attlee gathered for formalities with Truman and Stalin. Truman said to the two Britons, "I must say good luck to you both."

"What a pity," Stalin said.

"I hope to be back," Churchill replied.

Stalin looked over at Churchill's opponent, Attlee. Judging from the look on Attlee's face, Stalin said aloud that Attlee appeared in no hurry to fill Churchill's shoes.

As Churchill turned for the exit, Joseph Davies watched him go. "There was a glint of a tear in his eyes," Davies recorded, "but his step was firm and his chin thrust out. He seemed to sense that he had reached the end of the road."

The prime minister was leaving at a low point for the conference. Negotiations had not gone smoothly on this day. The Big Three had clashed once again over eastern Europe, with no progress made. As Truman put it in a letter to Bess, "There are some things we can't agree to. Russia and Poland have gobbled up a big hunk of Germany and want Britain and us to agree. I have flatly refused. We have unalterably opposed the recognition of police governments in the Germany Axis countries [Romania, Bulgaria, and Hungary]. I told Stalin that until we had free access to those countries and our nationals had their property rights restored, so far as we were concerned, there'd never be recognition."

Now Churchill was leaving, and anything major had yet to be accomplished at Potsdam.

After good-byes and formal photographs, Truman motored back to his villa with Joseph Davies. In the car, Truman appeared exhausted. The Potsdam Conference was not going as planned. The gulf between the Soviets and the Americans was growing more vast and ominous. Soon Truman was going to have to return to the United States and face the nation. He would be held accountable, and it was hard to fathom now, motoring in a car from the Cecilienhof Palace, how Congress would react to the Potsdam proceedings. According to Davies's recollections, Truman said during this short car ride that he was thinking of resigning the presidency "if, now, the president is not supported by the Senate and Congress." A keen student of history, Truman was well aware what this would mean to his legacy; no American president had ever resigned.

It was a startling revelation and a window into the president's consciousness at this pivotal moment. Davies replied that this would "bear thinking over."

///

Truman awoke customarily early on July 26. With the British leaders absent, there would be no negotiations. At 8 a.m. he boarded the *Sacred Cow* for a flight to Frankfurt. Among others, he had Harry Vaughan and Fred Canfil with him. Another plane carried Jimmy Byrnes and his staff, while a third flew members of the press covering the president's trip. General Eisenhower greeted Truman at the U.S. Army airfield in Frankfurt, along with an honor guard from the 508th Parachute Infantry.

Army units lined the roadways for thirty straight miles. Truman rode in Eisenhower's armored car with the general, inspecting the troops. At one point he asked a private for his name. "It scared him so badly he couldn't answer," Truman recalled, "but I finally coaxed it out of him." The office of the presidency was a powerful thing indeed. Eisenhower's car steered deeper into the countryside, through quaint villages that had not been bombed. These communities were a reminder that not all Germans were Nazis. There were plenty of Germans who had lived reluctantly through this war and had lost so much — family members, businesses, their very way of life. Eisenhower later remembered a poignant moment from this ride.

"Now, in the car," Eisenhower recalled, "he suddenly turned toward me and said: 'General, there is nothing that you may want that I won't try to help you get. That definitely and specifically includes the presidency in 1948.'"

Eisenhower laughed aloud. "Mr. President," he said with sincerity, "I don't know who will be your opponent for the presidency, but it will not be I."

The group ended up at the Frankfurt headquarters where Eisenhower had organized the military government of the American-occupied zone in Germany. The offices were housed in the building formerly owned by I. G. Farben, the giant chemical company that had mixed many of the poisons used to gas victims in the Nazi death camps.

When Truman arrived back at the Little White House at 7 p.m., two cables awaited him. One was from longtime United States ambassador to Britain John Winant, writing from London. Churchill had been defeated.

The people of Great Britain had elected Clement Attlee their new prime minister. Members of the American delegation were stunned, but not nearly as stunned as Churchill himself. The second cable was from Ambassador Hurley in Chungking. Chiang Kai-shek had agreed to the wording of the ultimatum with one minor change.

At 9:20 p.m. Berlin time on July 26, Charlie Ross handed the Potsdam Declaration out to members of the press, whose job it would now be to spread this document all the way to Tokyo. It demanded "unconditional surrender" from Japan. "We, the president of the United States, the president of the National Government of the Republic of China, and the Prime Minister of Great Britain, representing the hundreds of millions of our countrymen, have conferred and agree that Japan shall be given an opportunity to end this war," it began.

"The time has come for Japan to decide whether she will continue to be controlled by those self-willed militaristic advisers whose unintelligent calculations have brought the Empire of Japan to the threshold of annihilation, or whether she will follow the path of reason."

Ross cabled his assistant, Eben Ayers, in the White House: "The President's wish is that OWI [the Office of War Information] begin getting message to Japanese people in every possible way." Soon airplanes were flying over the mainland of Japan, dropping 600,000 leaflets out the windows. The ultimatum was soon being read over the radio, and news of it appeared on the front pages of newspapers all over the globe, on the morning of July 27.

On the night of the twenty-sixth, Truman tried to relax on the porch of his villa. One member of the delegation saw him there and wrote in his diary: "He looked tired." Truman knew that Stalin was going to be furious. Stalin had never been consulted on the ultimatum. But then the Soviets were not yet at war with Japan, and thus had no authority to make any official demands. Just as the ultimatum was released to the press, Truman had a special messenger walk the Potsdam Declaration over to Molotov in the Russian sector of Babelsberg. The president was sure he would be hearing from the Russians, the next day.

36

VYACHESLAV MOLOTOV showed up at the Little White House for a one-on-one with James Byrnes at 6 p.m. on July 27. Even before Molotov arrived, the stage was set for high conflict. "Important day," Byrnes's assistant, Walter Brown, wrote in his notes. "Either Russia's going to play ball and quit wanting so much or our relations will deteriorate . . . JFB [James F. Byrnes] and the president have been becoming more exasperated with the Russians every day."

Byrnes and Molotov sat down with their interpreters, Bohlen and Pavlov. Molotov appeared furious. Why, he wanted to know, were the Soviets not consulted regarding this ultimatum to Japan? According to Bohlen's minutes of the meeting, "The Secretary [Byrnes] said that we did not consult the Soviet Government since the latter was not at war with Japan and we did not wish to embarrass them. Mr. Molotov replied that he was not authorized to discuss this matter further. He left the implication that Marshal Stalin would revert to it at some time."

The British delegation had not yet returned to Potsdam. Byrnes and Molotov attempted to negotiate alone one of the conference's most bitter disagreements: reparations and the future of Germany. Justice and precedent demanded that the Germans pay the Allies damages. The USSR had suffered more death in this war than any other nation by far, and the Soviets expected to get the lion's share of reparations in return. The money was critical to the Soviet plan for postwar expansion. At Yalta, Roosevelt had accepted a figure of $20 billion as a proposal — as "a basis for negotiations" — of which the USSR would receive half. Now, at Potsdam, the Soviets wanted the $10 billion from Germany. Byrnes tried to explain himself to Molotov. The $20 billion figure was set up *as a basis for discussion.*

"If you say I owe you a million dollars and I say I will discuss it with you," Byrnes said, "that does not mean I am going to write you a check for a million dollars."

"I see," Molotov came back. But he did not; the idea was not sinking in. The Soviets wanted to get paid.

The Americans were wary of the reparations issue, for there was now ample evidence that the USSR had been looting territories that the Red Army had conquered, Germany in particular. The Soviets had been paying themselves already, at the Germans' expense. Truman had appointed Edwin Pauley, a wealthy California oilman, as the U.S. representative on the Allied Reparations Committee. Pauley had been touring Germany and observing the Soviets, at times carrying a 16-millimeter camera surreptitiously. His stories were incredible. He wrote of Red Army men packing "woodworking machines, bakery ovens, textile looms, electric generators, transformers, telephone equipment — countless items, most of which could not be considered war potential, and assuredly not war booty. Yet there they were, moving before my eyes, on their way to the Soviet Union."

Less than one week before the Byrnes-Molotov meeting, two of Pauley's men had witnessed loading platforms in railroad stations in Berlin where "swarms of workmen, mostly men in Russian Army uniforms," were moving "boxes, crates, sacs, bales, drums, boilers, partially-covered machine tools and large pieces of machinery" onto trains bound for the Soviet Union. "Electrical equipment, stamping mills, wood-working machinery, printing presses . . ."

When Byrnes asked Molotov if the Soviet authorities were removing German equipment and materials, even household goods, for transport to the USSR, Molotov did not deny it. "Yes," he said, "this is the case."

As for the $10 billion payout, it was not practical, Byrnes explained to Molotov. Germany was in a shambles; hundreds of thousands were starving, in desperate need of water and shelter. The only way Germany would be able to pay out $10 billion was through loans from the United States, which would likely never be paid back. The American government had made that mistake before, after World War I, and the American people would not stand for it again. Byrnes had come up with a different course of action — "namely, that each country would obtain its reparations from its own zone [of occupation] and would exchange goods between the zones," Byrnes said.

Molotov wanted clarification. Did this mean that each of the four nations now occupying its own zone of Germany "would have a free hand in their own zones [to extract reparations] and would act entirely independently of the others?"

According to the meeting minutes: "The Secretary [Byrnes] said that was true in substance but he had in mind working out arrangements for the exchange of needed products between the zones." The Russian zone grew the most food but had less industry; the British zone had the most manufacturing but would need to import food. The economic complexities would require trade, and meanwhile, each occupying nation could extract reparations from its own zone. Byrnes's plan was an attempt to create a mechanism for a peaceful occupied Germany that would eventually reunify. It sought to avoid future conflict between the United States and the USSR, and thus the dividing of Germany between west and east.

"The Secretary said that he felt that without some such arrangement the difficulties would be insurmountable and would be a continued source of disagreement and trouble between our countries," Bohlen recorded in his notes.

Molotov refused to let go of the issue, repeating that the Americans were breaking a promise made at Yalta over this $10 billion. The meeting ended where it had started, with no agreement. Already, the hope for a peaceful reunification of Germany was slipping away.

///

By the morning of July 28, Truman was suffering emotional exhaustion. He had been away from Washington now for twenty-two days. He was able to call Bess on a transatlantic telephone, but hearing her voice made him "terribly homesick." He wrote his mother and his sister a letter. "Well," the missive began, "here another week has gone and I'm still in this godforsaken country awaiting the return of a new British Prime Minister."

Throughout his journey to Europe, he had followed closely the argument in the Senate over the UN Charter. Early on the twenty-eighth, Truman received word that the Senate was set to vote. Edward Stettinius cabled the president: "The debate on the United Nations Charter has gone smoothly. Approximately forty members of the Senate have spoken during the week. No difficulties have arisen. Every indication now [is] that the Senate will vote on the Charter this afternoon and adjourn tonight."

Hours later Stettinius cabled again to let Truman know that the Senate had ratified the UN Charter. It was a bright moment in a dark time.

Truman gave a statement to Charlie Ross, who cabled it to the White House for release at 6 p.m. Washington time: "It is deeply gratifying that the Senate has ratified the United Nations Charter by a virtually unanimous vote. The action of the Senate substantially advances the cause of world peace." Truman must have thought of Roosevelt on this occasion. The question remained whether the UN would be able to do its job or soon be made obsolete by World War III.

On the same day the Senate ratified the UN Charter, Japan responded officially to the Potsdam Declaration. Tokyo was rejecting it. The Japanese government "does not consider [the Potsdam Declaration] of great importance," Prime Minister Kantarō Suzuki said in a press conference. "We must *mokusatsu* it." When the Foreign Broadcast Intelligence Service translated the word *mokusatsu*, it used the word *ignore*. In reality, the word meant "to kill with silence" — a vague notion. Another report from a Japanese news agency quoted the Japanese reaction to the ultimatum, saying Japan would "prosecute the war of Great East Asia to the bitter end."

The enemy's intentions were made clear by its actions: suicide attacks. On July 29, the day after Tokyo rejected the Potsdam ultimatum, kamikazes swarmed American ships. One plunged into the destroyer USS *Callaghan,* sending it to the bottom of the Pacific with forty-seven men still aboard. (The *Callaghan* would be the last American destroyer sunk in World War II.) "Japs . . . used several planes simultaneously," reported a top-secret military update cabled from Washington to Truman's villa on July 30. The "flimsy" kamikaze planes were built "using wood and fabric with some plywood," the report pointed out. These planes were built for one-way trips, and the Americans could only infer that the enemy intended indeed to fight to the end of its resources and to the last man.

In the days following Tokyo's rejection of the Potsdam Declaration, the American newspapers reported the snub, as well as vivid accounts of the suicide bombings. The *New York Times*'s front page: JAPANESE CABINET WEIGHS ULTIMATUM . . . EMPIRE WILL FIGHT TO THE END.

///

The new prime minister appeared at the Little White House at 9:15 p.m. on July 28. Clement Attlee had the look of an aging university professor

— a bald dome ringed with hair, balanced on thin shoulders, lips curled around an ever-present pipe. He was an Oxford man with a conventional middle-class upbringing who had risen to the ranks of national power in Britain quietly, serving for the last three years as deputy prime minister. Unlike Churchill, Attlee seemed without ego or charisma. The American delegation found it hard to fathom that the British citizenry had elected this man to take charge of His Majesty's government at this critical moment. The Soviets seemed to feel the same way. As Admiral Leahy chronicled, "Although [Churchill] was their antagonist at almost every turn, Stalin and his top advisors appeared to have had a high personal regard for Churchill. There was a noticeable coolness in their attitude after Attlee took over."

Now two of the Big Three leaders were rookies. Like Truman, Attlee was suddenly a figure of international curiosity. Unlike Truman, Attlee had been elected by his people as their leader.

Nevertheless, here was a new prime minister with his hand reached out to Truman. Attlee had brought with him a new foreign secretary, Ernest Bevin, who spoke with a cockney accent and weighed some 250 pounds. With Byrnes and Leahy present, they dug immediately into the confounding problem of finding agreement with the Soviets, on anything. Roughly an hour later, at 10:30 p.m., the Big Three returned to the negotiating table at Cecilienhof Palace and resumed their work. Stalin asked to make a statement.

"The Russian delegation was given a copy of the Anglo-American declaration to the Japanese people," he said. "We think it our duty to keep each other informed." His tone suggested betrayal on the part of the Americans and British, but then he left the issue aside, as if he was holding on to it for when he needed it later. Then Stalin relayed startling news. The Japanese had reached out through diplomatic channels in Moscow again, attempting to get the Soviets to act as an intermediary in peace discussions.

"I received another communication informing me more precisely of the desire of the Emperor to send a peace mission headed by Prince Konoye, who was stated to have great influence in the Palace," Stalin said. "It was indicated that it was the personal desire of the Emperor to avoid further bloodshed. In this document there is nothing new except the emphasis on the Japanese desire to collaborate with the Soviets. Our answer of course will be negative."

The Americans had given the enemy the opportunity to surrender. The Japanese had refused. The peace feeler in Moscow could only mean that the Japanese wanted to negotiate the terms, which would violate the spirit of unconditional surrender. (What seems most interesting about this conversation at Potsdam is not what was said about this peace feeler but what wasn't: Truman had the bomb, and so he did not need to make any concessions; Stalin wanted the war to continue, so he could spread his power into the Far East, on the boot treads of the Red Army.)

Truman responded, "I appreciate very much what the Marshal has said." Then he asked that the conference move ahead to the evening's agenda.

The president knew at this point that the Russians and the Americans had probably come together as far as they could. And the absence of Winston Churchill had deflated the mood in the negotiating chamber. All that was left was to fight out the final issues and sail for home.

///

On the island of Tinian, the 509th was ready to fly. The Little Boy bomb was nearing the end of its journey. Weighing 9,700 pounds, 10 feet long, and 28 inches in diameter, it was the ultimate expression of modernity's defining ambition: to harness power. The bomb was set to usher in a new epoch, and destiny had made Harry Truman its midwife. He awoke in his villa on the morning of Tuesday, July 31, to a cable from the secretary of war, who was already back in Washington. "The time schedule on Groves' project," it read, "is progressing so rapidly that it is essential that statement for release by you be available not later than Wednesday, August 1."

Stimson was referring to a statement from the president that the White House would release to the press after the bomb's detonation, not the release of the bomb itself. Truman turned this cable over and wrote on the back in big black penciled letters: "Suggestion approved. Release when ready but not sooner than August 2. HST." He handed the communiqué to the Advance Map Room's Lieutenant George Elsey, to send back to Washington.

Over the next two days the Big Three hammered away in the Cecilienhof Palace, finalizing any agreements they could. Molotov made a strange request. He wanted the Americans to construct a document formally asking the USSR to join the war against Japan. Truman thought otherwise; instead he formulated a document pointing out the USSR's duty under various agreements to assist in preserving world peace. The Soviets agreed to compromise on German reparations, and the Anglo-Americans agreed to compromise on Poland's western frontier, allowing this border to move deeper into Germany, along the Oder and Neisse Rivers, where it exists today. The Big Three agreed to attempt a revision of the 1936 Montreux Convention, which gave Turkey the sole rights to control sea straits from the Mediterranean to the Black Sea—a victory for Stalin.

Germany would be purged of Nazism, and the occupation would continue according to the zone borders already drawn. (Here the Americans made a mistake, failing to see the consequences of having Berlin deep inside and surrounded by Russian-occupied territory: that the Soviets would in the future blockade the Allies from Berlin. "This was not foreseen at all," recalled the Map Room's Elsey. "It was not foreseen by anybody, at least anybody on the United States–British side. The Russians may have been smart enough to have foreseen the implications.")

Truman had one pet issue he wanted to discuss, the internationalization of certain waterways, which he believed would lubricate trade and political relations in this newly imagined Europe. Stalin refused to even discuss the matter.

"Marshal Stalin," Truman said, "I have accepted a number of compromises during this conference . . . I make a personal request now that you yield on this point." Truman was asking that this issue simply remain a subject of future discussion. Stalin yelled out, "Nyet!" Then he said in English, so there was no doubt: "No, I say no!"

The president and the prime minister refused to acquiesce on Stalin's insistence that the United Nations recognize the puppet regimes of Hungary, Romania, and Bulgaria. And Stalin refused to negotiate any changes in these governments. Thus, at Potsdam, the Eastern Bloc crystallized. As Ambassador Harriman later noted, "There was no way we could have prevented these events in Eastern Europe without going to war against the Russians. A few American officers – and some of the French – talked of doing just that. But I cannot believe that the American people would have stood for it, even if the president had been willing, which he was not."

At the last plenary meeting on August 1, which began at the late hour of 10:30 p.m., all three delegations were prepared to sign off on the final wordings of the Potsdam accords — a contract spelling out the few agreements the three governments had achieved. Even the signing of this contract resulted in contretemps. Stalin felt that he should sign first, as it was his turn following the signings of agreements at the Tehran and Yalta Conferences.

"You can sign any time you want to," Truman said. "I don't care who signs first."

Attlee suggested that the signing go in alphabetical order. "That way," he joked, "I would score over [the Russian delegation's] Marshal Zhukov."

Stalin signed first, followed by Truman, then Attlee.

The clock had just ticked past midnight when Truman said, "I declare the Berlin Conference adjourned — until our next meeting which, I hope, will be at Washington."

"God willing," said Stalin. He added, "The Conference, I believe, can be considered a success."

Truman said, "I want to thank the other Foreign Ministers and all those who have helped us so much in our work."

"I join in the expression of these feelings in respect of our Foreign Ministers," added Attlee.

"I declare the Berlin Conference closed," said Truman.

After a formal good-bye, the president turned and made his way out of the palace with his entourage. He would never see Stalin in person again. Ten years would pass before American and Soviet leaders would meet face-to-face—President Dwight Eisenhower, Soviet Premier Nikolay Bulganin, and Soviet Communist Party Chief Nikita Khrushchev, in Geneva in 1955.

///

Truman took off from Gatow at 8:05 the next morning, bound for Britain, where he would confer with the king of England — "the Limey King," as he wrote Bess. Time would tell how the American public would regard the Potsdam Conference. So much on the agenda had fallen by the wayside. Clearly the Soviets' greatest defeat was the failure of Stalin to force Truman, Churchill, and Attlee to recognize the Sovietized governments of eastern Europe. And the greatest defeat for the Anglo-Americans was their inability to force Stalin to allow democratic elections in these countries.

Of all those who sat at the negotiating table at Potsdam, Admiral Leahy summed up the conference the most eloquently. "My general feeling about the Potsdam Conference was one of frustration. Both Stalin and Truman suffered defeats . . . The Soviet Union emerged at this time as the unquestioned all-powerful influence in Europe . . . One effective factor was a decline of the power of the British Empire . . . With France grappling for a stability that she had not achieved even before the war, and the threat of a civil war hanging over China, it was inescapable that the only two major powers remaining in the world were the Soviet Union and the United States."

A new geopolitical age was being born. Leahy noted, "Potsdam had brought into sharp world focus the struggle of two great ideas – the Anglo-Saxon democratic principles of government and the aggressive and expansionist police-state tactics of Stalinist Russia. It was the beginning of the 'cold war.'" As for the new president, not yet four months after the shock of Roosevelt's death, Leahy concluded, "Truman had stood up to Stalin in a manner calculated to warm the heart of every patriotic American."

Humanity would be left with many questions following Potsdam, questions that could never be answered. Had Truman been too rigid in his negotiations? Would the Cold War have cast its shadow so darkly upon the world if FDR had not died?

"WELCOME TO MY COUNTRY," said King George VI.

Truman stood aboard the battle cruiser HMS *Renown* in the harbor at Plymouth, England, shaking the hand of George VI, just before 1 p.m. on Thursday, August 2. The British were particularly talented with pomp and circumstance, especially when it came to their sovereign – the famously stuttering king of Britain and its commonwealths. The president had come aboard the *Renown* amid full military honors, with bugles blaring and thousands of sailors of both British and American colors standing at attention, their spines as straight as the *Renown*'s mainmast, upon which the American and British flags waved in the breeze.

At lunch with the king, Truman had Leahy and Byrnes flanking him. The king wore an admiral's uniform, while Truman was in civilian clothes. Truman found George VI to be amazingly well informed. During lunch the king brought up the atomic bomb, and in fact, as Byrnes later recalled, "most of our luncheon conversation was devoted to the bomb." The king was excited about the postwar usefulness of atomic energy. Leahy was still sure the bomb was going to be a dud.

"I do not think it will be as effective as is expected," the admiral said. "It sounds like a professor's dream to me!"

The king leaned in and said, "Admiral, would you like to lay a little bet on that?"

After lunch, the royal party visited Truman aboard his ship, the *Augusta,* again with full military honors. An orchestra played the American national anthem and "God Save the King." The king asked Truman to autograph cards for his wife and daughters, which amused Truman terrifically. He signed his name on the cards, one of which went to the king's daughter Elizabeth, later known as Queen Elizabeth II.

Shortly after George VI departed, the *Augusta*'s engines throttled and the president began his journey home, to face the American people.

///

The first night at sea, Truman's party gathered at eight thirty in Secretary Byrnes's cabin for a movie — *Wonder Man,* about a nightclub owner who gets murdered by gangsters and comes back as a ghost to haunt his killers. Truman did not show up for the film. He stayed in his cabin. No further record of his activities on this night survives, but one can imagine him staring at the ceiling of his quarters, exhausted from the strain of his trip, and tense from anticipation of an explosion that was about to change the world.

Truman had told himself in his diary, days earlier, that "military objectives and soldiers and sailors are the target and not women and children." Surely he knew that this bomb, as technologically marvelous as it was, did not have the sentience to separate military individuals from civilians. He could only hope that it would serve its purpose: to end the war, to save lives.

He requested no ceremony upon his return to the United States, for celebration would seem callous in moments of such public agony. He wanted to slip quietly back into the White House, and he worked hard on the trip home. He had flown Judge Sam Rosenman to Potsdam, and Rosenman was now aboard the *Augusta* to work on a speech with Truman. Rosenman recalled, "The President, coming home from Potsdam, pointed out that practically all of his time had been taken up with foreign affairs in which one crisis after another had come his way; and now that he was coming home from the Potsdam Conference he had to give some attention to domestic affairs." The speech they worked on together would come to be known as the 21-point program, policies that would launch the Truman era domestically in the postwar world. Aboard the ship, these policies were formulating in Truman's mind and in Rosenman's pen. Neither could know yet how explosive these twenty-one points would prove to be.

The tumult of postwar reconversion on the home front had already begun. The administration canceled tens of millions of dollars in war contracts in the months of June and July, leaving tens of thousands out of work. Truman's new Treasury secretary, Fred Vinson — just days into his tenure — had begun sending near-panicked memorandums to the president while Truman was at Potsdam. Vinson was predicting coal and food shortages, devastating transportation breakdowns, and labor problems — essentially, economic chaos.

Meanwhile, the world was beginning to digest the Potsdam accords, which were excerpted in newspapers around the globe. Here was a record of the work the Big Three had accomplished. Thus far, the reaction was lukewarm at best, especially in Europe, which faced more economic upheaval than the Americans did. "The Potsdam communique was not greeted with unquestioning enthusiasm over here," CBS's Edward R. Murrow reported from London, his voice piping into millions of American homes. "The comment was restrained. There was a tendency to point out the many matters that were not solved . . . There doesn't seem to be any doubt that President Truman acquitted himself well."

In the Far East, Japan continued to burn. On August 1, Curtis LeMay issued a warning to Japanese citizens in twelve cities to leave their homes and jobs to save their lives, as their cities were top on what was being called in the press LeMay's "death list" — Mito, Fukuyama, Ōtsu, among others. On August 2, the day Truman met with the king of England and then started the transatlantic journey home aboard the *Augusta*, the Twenty-First Bomber Command struck the enemy with what the *New York Times* called "the greatest single aerial strike in world history." Nearly 900 B-29s pounded targets with 6,632 tons of conventional and incendiary bombs. The flames engulfed miles of Japanese cities. "The sight was incredible beyond description," recalled one B-29 crewman. These attacking planes saw no opposition. "They knew we were coming but they didn't do anything about it," said one officer.

As the *Augusta* pushed deeper into the Atlantic, Truman's curiosity over the bomb grew excruciating. Given the secrecy of the mission, he received no updates. He was in the dark. At one point, the *Augusta*'s Advance Map Room cabled the White House inquiring about any news of "the Manhattan Project." White House Map Room operatives responded that they could find no evidence of any such project. The *Augusta* cabled again to say, "Captain Vardaman [a Truman naval aide and close friend] has now indicated matter is so secret he wants no, repeat no, inquiries of any sort made by the Map Room on this project."

Truman did meet with the press aboard the ship, briefing them on the incredible story of the atomic bomb, under the condition that it was still a war secret and nothing could be published. It was an extraordinary leap of faith, to inform reporters of the bomb's existence before knowing what Little Boy's results would be. Merriman Smith of the United Press remembered that Truman "was happy and thankful that we had a weapon in our hands which would speed the end of the war. But he was apprehensive over the development of such a monstrous weapon of destruction."

Truman also answered reporters' questions about Joseph Stalin. The Man of Steel was "an S.O.B.," the president said, while on the boat headed home. "I guess he thinks I'm one too."

///

From his headquarters on Guam in the South Pacific, at 2 p.m. on August 5, Curtis LeMay gave the final go-ahead for the 509th wing to fly the secret mission the following day – August 6. LeMay had been a busy man. His firebombing campaign had laid waste to nearly sixty square miles in and around Tokyo, plus vast sections of Nagoya, Kōbe, Osaka, Yokohama, and Kawasaki. As the official U.S. Army Air Forces history of World War II would later read: "The six most important industrial cities in Japan had been ruined."

Only recently had LeMay learned of the bomb. A special messenger had flown to his headquarters on Guam to brief him on the Manhattan Project. "I didn't know much about this whole thing and didn't ask about it, because it was so hot," LeMay recorded. "Didn't wish to have any more information than it was necessary for me to have." He had orders as to the first bomb's primary target: Hiroshima. According to intelligence sources, Hiroshima was "an Army city . . . a major quartermaster depot" with warehouses full of military supplies – guns and tanks, machine tools, and aircraft parts. "Residential construction is typically Japanese. There are two types of warehouses. The Ujina Port region is congested with both fireproof and combustible warehouses, open stores and open factories." Intelligence sources also found that Hiroshima had no POW camps, so the Americans could be relatively sure they would not be bombing their own men.

LeMay's command had not yet hit Hiroshima. It was a thriving city and a virgin target, with a population of 318,000, according to American intelligence.

On the afternoon of August 5, on the island of Tinian, army officials pushed the Little Boy bomb out of a warehouse at the airfield. A dozen men in short-sleeved tan uniforms gathered around it wearing expressions of concern, wheeling Little Boy on a platform as if it were a patient on a hospital gurney. It was roughly egg-shaped, with a steel shell and a tail poking out the back to guide its trajectory. One of the men working at Tinian that day described it as looking like "an elongated trash can with fins." When it came to the Manhattan Project, everything was experimental. Little Boy employed a different gun mechanism than the one used in the Trinity shot, so there was no certainty that this weapon would go off.

The air base at Tinian was in itself an industrial marvel, and an emblem of American ingenuity. A year earlier, most of this little island was covered in sugarcane. Now the island was home to an airfield howling day and night with heavy flight traffic. "Tinian is a miracle," noted one writer who saw it at the time. "Here, 6,000 miles from San Francisco, the United States armed forces have built the largest airport in the world . . . From the air this island, smaller than Manhattan, looked like a giant aircraft carrier, its deck loaded with bombers." The airport was fully ready. It had been built to serve one purpose above all others: Little Boy. On the afternoon of August 5, army personnel eased the weapon through open bomb bay doors into the belly of a B-29 Superfortress, using a hydraulic lift.

That very afternoon the pilot of this B-29, Paul W. Tibbets, had named the airplane *Enola Gay*, after his mother. Surely Mrs. Tibbets had never dreamed that her legacy would carry such historical import, for the *Enola Gay* was about to become the most infamous military aircraft ever flown. A sign painter had placed the letters of her name beneath the pilot's window, at an angle in foot-high black brushstrokes. The airplane had been built in a factory in Omaha, Nebraska, completed earlier in the year. It would fly as part of a seven-plane task force — all B-29s — including three weather recon aircraft (one over Hiroshima, two over secondary targets), one plane carrying blast measurement equipment, one plane for camera equipment and observation, one spare aircraft, and the delivery machine itself, the *Enola Gay*.

"By dinnertime on the fifth," Tibbets recorded, "all [preparations were] completed. The atom bomb was ready, the planes were gassed and checked. Takeoff was set for [2:45 a.m.]. I tried to nap, but visitors kept me up."

The final briefing for the seven flight crews was at midnight, in a room by the runway where the aircraft would take off. Less than forty-eight hours earlier, the crew members of these ships had learned of the atomic bomb for the first time, the secret behind the mission for which they had been training for months. They were shown aerial photographs of the targets – the primary, Hiroshima, and secondaries, Kokura and Nagasaki. They were told details of the Trinity shot, and while they were supposed to see footage of Trinity, the motion picture machine had broken, and so the visual effects of the bomb remained a mystery to them. They had known that they had been training for something special, but still, they were amazed. "It is like some weird dream," said one crew member, radioman Abe Spitzer of Wendover, Utah, "conceived by one with too vivid an imagination."

During the final briefing, each member was given dark glasses to protect the eyes from the blast, which, they were told, would be like a new sun being born. A weatherman briefed the crew on what to expect – smooth flying – then a chaplain gave a blessing, asking the Almighty Father "to be with those who brave the heights of Thy heaven and who carry the battle to our enemies."

Thousands of miles away aboard the *Augusta* in the Atlantic, at nearly this exact moment, Truman was attending his own church services in the ship's forward mess hall, for it was still August 5 – a Sunday. Truman was the butt of jokes that morning, because he had "overslept" – remaining in bed past five thirty. With Byrnes and the *Augusta*'s skipper, Captain James Foskett, by his side, Truman prayed as the ship's chaplain, Kenneth Perkins, led the group in a hymn:

> Faith of our fathers, we will strive
> To win all nations unto Thee
> And through the truth that comes from God
> Mankind shall then indeed be free.

They sang "Come Thou Almighty King" and "The Old Rugged Cross."

At 2:27 a.m. on Tinian, Tibbets sparked the *Enola Gay*'s four Wright Cyclone engines, and the plane pushed forward onto a runway. He would recall the feeling of the aircraft's yoke in his hands; the plane felt torquey, yearning for flight. The *Enola Gay* had been given the code name Dimples 82. Tibbets called to flight control. The quick conversation as he later remembered it: "Dimples Eight Two to North Tinian Tower. Taxi-out and take-off instructions."

Orders returned: "Dimples Eight Two from North Tinian Tower. Take off to the east on Runway A for Able."

Tibbets was cleared for takeoff. The copilot, Robert Lewis, counted down: "Fifteen seconds to go. Ten seconds. Five seconds. Get ready."

At 2:45 a.m., the *Enola Gay*'s wheels left the ground.

///

By the time Truman sat down to dinner in the *Augusta*'s wardroom with the ship's officers, at six o'clock on the night of August 5, the *Enola Gay* was rendezvousing with two escorts over the island of Iwo Jima at 9,300 feet. In the South Pacific, the sun was just rising on August 6. At 7:30 a.m., William Sterling Parsons – the ordnance expert who had worked on the bomb at Los Alamos beside Robert Oppenheimer, and who was now aboard the *Enola Gay* as the weaponeer – climbed down to the bomb bay and armed Little Boy, pulling out green plugs and replacing them with red ones. Weather was clear, so Tibbets decided to gun for the primary target. "It's Hiroshima," he announced over the intercom, throttling the *Enola Gay* upward to 31,000 feet. The crew slipped on heavy flak suits, and Tibbets reminded them to don their heavy glasses at the moment of detonation.

At 8 p.m. on August 5 aboard the *Augusta,* the evening's film presentation began – *The Thin Man Goes Home,* starring the comic duo William Powell and Myrna Loy. Again, Truman did not attend, according to the ship's log. He might have been playing poker, or staring at the ceiling of his cabin, or perhaps still praying, alone. Around the time the film began, Little Boy's target came into focus. "I see it!" yelled the *Enola Gay*'s bombardier, Thomas Ferebee. The airplane was traveling at 328 miles per hour on automatic pilot at 31,000 feet when Ferebee took aim in his bombsight. Hiroshima lay below. Copilot Robert Lewis was taking notes in a logbook during the mission. Looking down at Hiroshima, he wrote the words "perfectly open target." Ferebee let the bomb loose. "For the next minute," Lewis wrote, "no one knew what to expect."

Tibbets recalled: "I threw off the automatic pilot and hauled *Enola Gay* into the turn. I pulled antiglare goggles over my eyes. I couldn't see through them; I was blind. I threw them to the floor. A bright light filled the plane. The first shock wave hit us."

Copilot Lewis recorded: "There were two very distinct slaps on the ship, then that was all the physical effects we felt. We then turned the ship so we could observe the results and then in front of our eyes was without a doubt the greatest explosion man has ever witnessed ... I am certain the entire crew felt this experience was more than any one human had ever thought possible ... Just how many Japs did we kill? ... If I live a hundred years I'll never quite get these few minutes out of my mind."

In the moment, Lewis was writing in his logbook, scribbling with difficulty since it was dark in the vibrating aircraft. He wrote, "My God, what have we done."

Tibbets recalled: "We turned back to look at Hiroshima. The city was hidden by that awful cloud ... boiling up, mushrooming, terrible and incredibly tall. No one spoke for a moment; then everyone was talking. I remember Lewis pounding my shoulder, saying 'Look at that! Look at that! Look at that!' Tom Ferebee wondered about whether radioactivity would make us all sterile. Lewis said he could taste atomic fission. He said it tasted like lead."

Another member of the flight crew, navigator Theodore "Dutch" Van Kirk, thought to himself in this moment the same thought that would rush through the minds of hundreds of thousands of Allied soldiers in the coming days: "Thank God the war is over and I don't have to get shot at anymore. I can go home."

On the ground, it was 8:15 in the morning. The city was bustling, as forty-five minutes earlier, citizens were alerted with an "all clear" message, that it was safe to go outside. When the bomb detonated, many thousands of citizens of Hiroshima disappeared off the face of the earth, instantly and without a trace. Survivors would remember the flash of light first, followed by a sound that had never been heard by human ears. "We heard a big noise like a 'BOONG!' 'BOONG!' Like that. That was the sound," Tomiko Morimoto, who was thirteen at the time, later recalled. And then, "everything started falling down; all the buildings started flying around all over the place. Then something wet started coming down, like rain. I guess that's what they call black rain. In my child's mind, I thought it was oil. I thought the Americans were going to burn us to death. And we kept running. And fire was coming out right behind us."

Only one person reported to be within a 100-yard radius of Hiroshima's ground zero survived the blast. His name was Goichi Oshima. Ten years later he described what he saw: "A sudden flash, an explosion that defies description, then everything went black. When I came to, the Hiroshima I knew was in ruins."

Aboard the *Augusta,* Truman went to bed that night likely within an hour or two after detonation. At 1 a.m. (now August 6), the ship crossed into a new time zone in the Atlantic and the officers set clocks back one hour. Truman awoke to a beautiful quiet day at sea, the sun bright and warm. The ship's officers shifted to warm-weather uniforms: khaki and gray, with the crew in white, due to the Gulf Stream's temperate breezes. After breakfast, Truman relaxed on the deck and listened to the ship's band play a concert, unaware at this moment that Hiroshima had been all but wiped off the planet.

///

Lunch aboard the *Augusta.* Truman sat down in the aft mess hall at 11:45 a.m. Also at the table: Jimmy Byrnes and members of the ship's crew, George T. Fleming of Thompsonville, Connecticut; Edward F. Place of Woodhaven, New York; Edward Clifford of San Francisco; Tony Torregrossa of Northville, New Jersey; F. C. Roaseau of Bald Knob, Arkansas; and Eino Karvonen of Two Harbors, Minnesota. Minutes before noon – some sixteen hours after the destruction of Hiroshima – Frank Graham, a captain in the navy working in the Advance Map Room, hurried into the mess hall and handed Truman a message. The president looked down and focused his eyes:

> Following info regarding Manhattan received. "Hiroshima bombed visually with only one tenth cover at 052315A. There was no fighter opposition and no flak. Parsons reports 15 minutes after drop as follows: 'Results clear cut and successful in all respects. Visible effects greater than in any test. Conditions normal in airplane following delivery.'"

Truman jumped to his feet and shook hands with the messenger. "Captain," Truman said, "this is the greatest thing in history! Show it to the Secretary of State." Graham handed the message to Byrnes, who read it and belted out the words "Fine! Fine!"

Minutes later Graham returned with another message, this one from Henry Stimson in Washington. Truman read:

To the President
From the Secretary of War

Big bomb dropped on Hiroshima August 5 at 7:15 p.m. Washington time. First reports indicate complete success which
was even more conspicuous than earlier test.

Holding the two messages in his hand, Truman turned to Byrnes and
shouted, "It's time for us to get on home!" Then he signaled to the crowd
in the mess hall to quiet down, banging a piece of silverware against a
glass. The sailors hushed, and Truman announced the news of the atomic
bombing of Hiroshima. The room exploded in applause, feeding off
the president's excitement. With Byrnes at his heels, Truman marched
quickly to the wardroom, where the *Augusta*'s officers were lunching. In
a voice "tense with excitement," according to one man present, Truman
said, "Keep your seats, gentlemen. I have an announcement to make to
you." The officers stared at him with puzzled faces, and Truman continued: "We have just dropped a bomb on Japan which has more power
than 20,000 tons of TNT. It was an overwhelming success."

As applause and whistles filled the wardroom, Truman continued onward, intent on visiting every section of the ship to inform the crew of
the bomb. All over the *Augusta,* the mood in those following afternoon
hours soared among sailors who, for so long, had feared for their lives
and yearned for their homes. The mood could be summed up in a sentence spoken by one of those sailors that afternoon: "I guess I'll go home
sooner now."

///

In Washington, assistant press secretary Eben Ayers gathered reporters
working their usual White House beat. It was roughly 11 a.m. Ayers had
only recently gotten his first inkling of the atomic bomb. A couple of
days earlier he had been toiling in his office with the president's correspondence secretary, Bill Hassett, when an officer from the War Department appeared. This officer was, as Ayers recalled, "somewhat excited
and under some tension as he told us that an important story – a tremendous news story – was due to break within a few days." The story
regarded "a most secret thing . . . a great new bomb or weapon." This officer gave Ayers a statement from President Truman, to be released when

the weapon was used. Security was imperative, Ayers was told. No one was to see this statement until further orders.

Now it was go time. Charlie Ross had cabled from the *Augusta* that it was time to release the president's statement. Ayers had copies of it in his hand, ready for distribution. He called out to the newsmen who had gathered before him.

"I have got here what I think is a darned good story. It's a statement by the president, which starts off this way." Ayers then read aloud the first paragraph: "'Sixteen hours ago an American airplane dropped one bomb on Hiroshima, an important Japanese Army base. That bomb had more power than 20,000 tons of TNT. It had more than two thousand times the blast power of the British "Grand Slam" which is the largest bomb ever yet used in the history of warfare.'"

Ayers continued in his own words: "Now, the statement explains the whole thing. It is an atomic bomb, releasing atomic energy. This is the first time it has ever been done."

One reporter yelled out: "It's a hell of a story!"

///

Aboard the *Augusta*, and in millions of households, Americans gathered around their radios, listening to Truman's statement being read over the airwaves. His statement spoke of "a harnessing of the basic power of the universe . . . We are now prepared to obliterate more rapidly and completely every productive enterprise the Japanese have above ground in any city. We shall destroy their docks, their factories, and their communications. Let there be no mistake; we shall completely destroy Japan's power to make war . . . If they do not now accept our terms they may expect a rain of ruin from the air, the likes of which has never been seen on this earth."

Truman held a press conference on the ship, reading his statement again and answering questions about the greatest wartime secret of all. He brought up the Potsdam Declaration. "Their leaders promptly rejected that ultimatum." He gave ample credit to the secretary of war, Henry Stimson, who had guided the project all the way, from a governmental level. Truman read his statement for newsreel cameras also, speaking soberly into the camera. "The Japanese began the war from the air at Pearl Harbor," he said. "They have been repaid many fold." At the same time, Prime Minister Attlee released a statement, and the War

Department released its own, with an image of the Little Boy bomb and an aerial photograph of Hiroshima — how it appeared before the event. Immediately, American and British news sources began monitoring Japanese radio, where already, cryptic announcements were being made — rail service in and around Hiroshima had been canceled, and the scene in that city was under investigation.

That afternoon a curious scene unfolded aboard the *Augusta*. At three thirty, less than four hours after the president received word of Little Boy, Truman and members of his party attended a boxing program on the ship's deck, with the Gulf Stream's warm breezes swirling their hair. A former New York stage star and current U.S. Navy mailman named Charles Purcell emceed the event. Trusty Fred Canfil acted as a referee as sailors took to the ring and hurled punches at one another. The audience roared with approval; the harder the blows, the louder the crowd cheered. At one point, one of the ring posts fell over and knocked a spectating sailor in the head, injuring him slightly. He was taken off to the ship's infirmary.

Truman sat watching the action, awaiting the *Augusta*'s arrival in Newport News, Virginia, the following afternoon. Surely the words of his atomic bomb statement were still echoing in his head — particularly his closing lines. He understood that the bomb had ushered in not just a new era of humanity's understanding of nature's forces but also a new understanding of humanity's capacity for self-destruction. Maybe the bomb would win the war. But at what cost?

"I shall give further consideration," Truman's statement had ended, "and make further recommendations to the Congress as to how atomic power can become a powerful and forceful influence towards the maintenance of world peace."

38

TRUMAN'S CAR PULLED UP to the White House South Gate a few minutes past II p.m. on August 7. Waiting for him outside in the night was a small group of staffers: Matt Connelly, Eben Ayers, and Bill Hassett. "The president stepped out," recalled Ayers, "looking fit and somewhat tanned from the ship voyage." Truman pumped handshakes, then headed into the White House, where cabinet officials — the new faces of the Truman administration — were waiting to greet him in the Diplomatic Reception Room. The new Treasury secretary, Fred Vinson, was there, along with the new attorney general, Tom Clark, the new secretary of labor, Lewis Schwellenbach, and others. The president was exhausted — the trip had lasted exactly one month and one day almost to the minute — and he desired a cocktail.

"Come on up to the room," he said.

The group followed him to his second-floor study. Truman spotted his piano. He sat down and played a few bars, then he dialed Mrs. Truman to let her know he had gotten home safely (she was leaving Independence to return to Washington the following day). By this time, the drinks were poured.

Staffers and cabinet men were intensely curious about the Russians, and Truman regaled them with stories of Stalin's giant limousine and Molotov's distemper. Someone asked how much drinking had gone on at Potsdam, and Truman wove tales of the epic procession of toasts, particularly at the Russian dinner. Churchill consumed the most alcohol, but there was no excessive drinking, Truman assured everyone.

During the whole of this conversation that night in the White House, the bomb never came up, as the subject was so raw, it seemed inappropriate in this relaxed state to touch upon it. Recalled Ayers many years later: "Now, that may seem strange — it does to me now — but I don't think anybody mentioned it."

Finishing his drink, Truman came to the following conclusion regarding Potsdam: he was happy to be home, and he would be just fine, he told his audience, if he never stepped foot in Europe again.

///

After weeks of inactivity, the West Wing came alive the next morning, August 8. At Truman's 9 a.m. staff meeting, Charlie Ross handed out boxes of Russian cigarettes. The smokes were curious-looking filterless cardboard tubes with a small bit of tobacco wrapped in paper at the end. Now the bomb dominated the discussion. Truman knew that public relations would be key to how the world responded to Hiroshima, and he felt that the pope should be contacted. He had no idea how to get ahold of the Vatican, nor did anyone else present. After the staff meeting, Stimson arrived at the president's office with aerial photographs of Hiroshima, along with further reports of the bomb's wrath.

From the pictures, Hiroshima was unrecognizable as a city. As Stimson recalled in his diary on this day: "[Truman] mentioned the terrible responsibility that such destruction placed upon us here and himself."

As for Japan, it was imperative that the situation be handled just the right way, Stimson said. "When you punish your dog you don't keep souring on him all day after the punishment is over," he said. "If you want to keep his affection, punishment takes care of itself." It was the same with Japan, Stimson figured. "They naturally are a smiling people and we have to get on those terms with them." Easier said than done, both men agreed.

Meanwhile the story of the atomic bomb was just beginning to transfix the world. Over four square miles of Hiroshima was gone, from a single blast. The flash of the bomb was seen 170 miles from ground zero. Aerial photos appeared in newspapers, as did the first reports from within Japan. Tokyo radio reported that "practically all living things, human and animal, were literally seared to death by the tremendous heat and pressure." Crewmen aboard the *Enola Gay* gave their first interviews.

"The crew said, 'My God,' and couldn't believe what had happened," said weaponeer William Parsons. "A mountain of smoke was going up in a mushroom with the stem coming down. At the top was white smoke but up to 1,000 feet from the ground there was swirling, boiling dust." General Carl Spaatz, one of the army air forces' top officials, called the atomic bomb "the most revolutionary development in the history of the world."

Soon after Stimson's departure from Truman's office on the morning of August 8, the president received word from the Moscow embassy that, as of this day, the Russians considered themselves at war with Japan. The Red Army was set to push across the borders of Manchuria. Truman contacted Charlie Ross, who called reporters in from the press gallery for a quick conference. Newspapermen crowded into the Oval Office at 3 p.m., and Leahy and Byrnes also attended.

Someone shouted, "Welcome home!"

"I am glad to be here," Truman said. "The finest place in the world, the United States is!" He smiled for pictures, then said, "Is everybody here?"

"I think they're all in, Mr. President," said Ross. "Yes, they're all in."

"I have only a simple announcement to make," Truman said. "I can't hold a regular press conference today; but this announcement is so important I thought I would call you in." He paused, then said with great emphasis, "Russia has declared war on Japan! That is all!"

The newsmen roared and applauded, then pushed out through the narrow doors as fast as they could.

Truman spent the afternoon catching up. He signed the United Nations Charter on August 8. (On this same day, the Allies signed the London Agreement, which officially set the stage for the war crimes trials at Nuremberg.) He had been gone a long time, and with Bess also absent from the White House, he had bills stacked up on his desk, many for White House groceries. He sat at his desk writing out no fewer than a dozen checks from a special White House account he had opened at Hamilton National Bank. He owed the Metropolitan Poultry Company $5.03, and the General Baking Company $1.44. As he signed these checks, he had no idea that a new attack wave of B-29s was gunning for Japan on this day, with a second atomic bomb.

///

Soviet forces reported at a million strong charged into Japanese-occupied Manchuria on August 8. Ambassador Harriman cabled to inform Truman that he had met with Stalin and Molotov regarding the details. Harriman also informed Truman that he had discussed the bomb with Stalin. The Soviet dictator admitted that his country had already been working on an atomic weapon, but "had not been able to solve" the conundrum of splitting atoms yet. The Soviets did not have a bomb, but it was only a matter of time.

Stalin made his intentions in the Far East all too clear: he was interested in "war trophies." Harriman reported directly to Truman: "[Stalin] indicated that some of the Japanese properties, including the shares of some Japanese enterprises, should be considered as Soviet war trophies in areas occupied by the Red Army." Stalin was going to take possession of everything he could.

Truman had already made up his mind: under no condition would he allow the Soviets to occupy any piece of Japan.

On the day the Soviets attacked Japanese strongholds in Manchuria, another wave of B-29 Superfortresses pounded targets on Japan's mainland. More B-29s flew over Japanese cities dropping leaflets, which rained down on terrified civilian populations. This paper read in part, "America asks that you take immediate heed of what we say on this leaflet. We are in possession of the most destructive explosive ever devised by man . . . We have just begun to use this weapon against your homeland." It asked Japanese citizens to "petition the Emperor to end the war."

Before sunrise in the South Pacific on August 9 (it was still August 8 in Washington), a task force of B-29s took flight to deliver the Fat Man bomb on Japan. Truman was aware that a second bomb would be employed, but he gave no direct order for this mission. There was no button pushed, no paper trail that connects the president directly to Fat Man. William L. Laurence of the *New York Times* was embedded with a crew on this mission.

"We are on our way to bomb the mainland of Japan," he wrote while aboard one of the B-29s that morning.

The weapon was loaded in the belly of *Bockscar,* a Superfortress named after the ship's pilot, Captain Frederick C. Bock of Greenville, Michigan. (Bock did not actually fly the airplane on this mission, however.) Fat Man weighed 10,800 pounds, and utilized the same gun mechanism and fissile material used in the Trinity test shot in New Mexico, so there was little doubt that it would be just as explosive. The weapon was painted mustard yellow and had signatures of members of the crew that had assembled it, along with an acronym on its steel nose: JANCFU, for "Joint Army-Navy-Civilian Fuckup." Laurence reported: "I watched the assembly of this man-made meteor during the past two days, and was among the small group of scientists and Army and Navy representatives privileged to be present at the ritual of its loading in the Superfort last night, against a backdrop of threatening black skies torn open at intervals by great lightning flashes. It is a thing of beauty to behold, this 'gadget.' In its design went millions of man-hours of what is without doubt the most concentrated intellectual effort in history."

The *Bockscar* made three runs over its primary target, Kokura. The citizens of that metropolis had no idea that cloud cover saved tens of thousands of their lives on this morning. The pilot — Major Charles Sweeney of North Quincy, Massachusetts — turned to the secondary target, Nagasaki, arriving over that city at minutes before 11 a.m. local time. The *Bockscar* was at 29,000 feet when it released the bomb. A cameraman captured the blast on film, preserving this dark moment in black-and-white celluloid. There is no sound to the footage, only imagery. The blast looks as if the earth had popped like a balloon and released a belch of smoke from deep within. The mushroom cloud is all that can be seen; there is no picture of the fury below it.

Truman later wrote of Nagasaki, "This second demonstration of the power of the atomic bomb apparently threw Tokyo into a panic, for the next morning [August 10] brought the first indication that the Japanese Empire was ready to surrender."

///

At 7:33 a.m. on August 10 in Japan, monitors recorded the following broadcast over Radio Tokyo:

> The Japanese Government today addressed the following communication to the Swiss and Swedish Governments respectively for transmission to the United States, Great Britain, China, and the Soviet Union . . . The Japanese Government is ready to accept the terms enumerated in the joint declaration which was issued at Potsdam, July 26, 1945, by the Heads of Government of the United States, Great Britain, and China, and later subscribed by the Soviet Government, with the understanding that said declaration does not comprise any demand which prejudices the prerogatives of His Majesty as a sovereign ruler. The Japanese Government hopes sincerely that this understanding is warranted and desires keenly that an explicit indication to that effect will be speedily forthcoming.

By 9 a.m. in Washington, Truman had Byrnes, Leahy, Stimson, and Forrestal in his office to discuss procedure. The president went around the room and asked each man for his opinion. What the Japanese appeared to be offering was *not* unconditional surrender. As so many in the Truman administration had predicted, the fate of the emperor was *the* question that separated war from peace.

Leahy and Stimson had no compunction about allowing the emperor to remain. If anything, he would be useful in engendering peace among the citizenry. Byrnes was less sure; he believed the United States should dictate all the terms. Forrestal brought forth the wisest plan; he suggested a reply in which the Allies could accept Japan's terms, if these terms were spelled out further so that the Potsdam terms could be clearly accomplished. In other words, the emperor could remain *if he surrendered unconditionally.*

Over the next hours Byrnes wrote out a reply while Truman attended to his usual, grueling list of meetings. The president sat uncomfortably through fifteen-minute sessions successively with Congressman Mike Mansfield of Montana, Senator Carl Hayden of Arizona, Senator Warren Magnuson of Washington, and Senator Joseph O'Mahoney of Wyoming. Truman had five-minute blocks scheduled each with the ambassadors of South Africa, El Salvador, Panama, and Guatemala, one after the other. Finally, at 1 p.m., Byrnes appeared with his draft of the reply, which Truman and Leahy tugged on while eating lunch.

The president was nearly a half hour late for a 2 p.m. cabinet meeting. Truman took his now usual place, with his back to the windows looking out over the White House Rose Garden. Byrnes read aloud Japan's full statement (which by now had arrived via diplomatic channels through the Swiss legation). Then he read aloud the draft reply to the Japanese. In the middle of it, he paused. Remembered Secretary of Commerce Henry Wallace, who was sitting at the table: "Byrnes stopped while reading the proposal and laid special emphasis on the top dog commander over [Emperor] Hirohito being an American. They were not going to have any chance for misunderstandings as in Europe." The United States alone would deal with the Japanese. There would be no zones of occupation, no Soviet or British control.

Still, the reply to the Japanese needed approval from Britain, China, and the USSR. Truman interjected to say that the Americans would not negotiate with the Russians on this matter. Stimson said that the Russians were likely to delay in any response to a draft reply to the Japanese, so the Red Army could push as deep into the Far East as possible before surrender was accomplished.

General Groves had communicated to the War Department on this day, saying the next bomb would be ready for delivery after August 17 or 18. But now, in the cabinet meeting, Truman said that he was ordering an end to the atomic bombing. He could not stomach the idea of wiping out another 100,000 people, of killing "all those kids," he said to his cabinet.

As for unconditional surrender, Truman knew there was no way to please everyone. Many Americans wanted the Japanese emperor charged with war crimes and prosecuted to the fullest, as was happening with top Nazi officials. The White House mailroom was clogged with letters from citizens who hoped Truman would follow this course; they wanted to see the emperor executed. Truman had received a missive from Senator Richard Russell, Democrat of Georgia, who asked that the United States continue bombing until the Japanese "beg us to accept unconditional surrender." Russell believed "the vast majority of the American people" thought the emperor "should go," and that "if we do not have available a sufficient number of atomic bombs with which to finish the job immediately, let us carry on with TNT and fire bombs until we can produce them."

(To this, Truman responded: "I certainly regret the necessity of wiping out whole populations because of the 'pigheadedness' of the leaders of a nation and, for your information, I am not going to do it unless it is absolutely necessary . . . My objective is to save as many American lives as possible but I also have a humane feeling for the women and children of Japan.")

The final draft reply to Japan went out through State Department channels that afternoon of August 10 to the embassies in London, Moscow, and Chungking. It did address the issue of the emperor, reading, in part: "From the moment of surrender, the authority of the Emperor and the Japanese Government to rule the state shall be subject to the Supreme Commander of the Allied Powers who will take such steps as he deems proper to effectuate the surrender terms . . . The ultimate form of government of Japan shall, in accordance with the Potsdam Declaration, be established by the freely expressed will of the Japanese people."

The reply attempted to satisfy all those Americans who demanded unconditional surrender, while allowing the Japanese the right to retain their emperor, and thus, for peace to follow.

That night, all of Washington was abuzz. "Rumors flew, switchboards jammed, reporters chain-smoked – and the hottest story in the world, the end of the war – lay tantalizingly just out of reach," recorded one reporter. "Head-men of the government filed in and out of the White House. Hordes of jumpy reporters milled about, waiting tensely for the word that would send them to tell the world that it was all over."

Truman went about his business. Throughout his political career, he had shown a remarkable talent to exude poise during moments of extraordinary excitement and stress – but never more than now. As one reporter noted, he was "the calmest man in town."

///

As the world awaited news of peace, the atomic bomb loomed over the public consciousness. Citizens in every civilized country struggled to understand what the bomb was, how it worked, and what it meant for the future of humanity.

Many were insisting that these unmasked secrets of the universe were destined to change the world for the better. "The real significance [of atomic energy] does not lie in the fact that this new bomb has accomplished an almost incredible feat of destruction," wrote Canada's Munitions Minister C. D. Howe. The "unbelievably large amounts of energy" unlocked by atomic scientists could now be "made available for practical use."

Others were sure that the world was coming to an end. Wrote the Reverend Robert Gannon, a religious leader and president of Fordham University, "Our savage generation cannot be trusted with [atomic science] at all. It is a triumph of research, but unfortunately it is also a superb symbol for the Age of Efficient Chaos."

The most prevalent emotion was awe – amazement that the natural world could possess such furious powers, and that humans had figured out how to harvest them, whether for good or evil. The story of how this came about would rivet generations to come. As Truman himself said in his statement about the bomb: "We have spent more than two billion dollars on the greatest scientific gamble in history – and we have won."

Clark Clifford, a White House lawyer and a rising star in the Truman administration, was in his office when he learned of the first atomic bombing.

"My initial thought upon hearing the news," he wrote, "was as simple as that of most other Americans: the war would be over sooner than we had suspected . . . I knew too little at first to suspect the larger truth: that we had entered an age in which warfare would never be the same – that, in fact, the development of nuclear weapons would turn out to be the most significant event of the century."

On the night of August 10, one day after the atomic bombing of Nagasaki and just hours after the reply to Japan had been sent out to London, Moscow, and Chungking, Prime Minister Attlee and his foreign secretary, Ernest Bevin, agreed to the terms set out in Byrnes's draft to Japan, with minor adjustments. Their communiqué arrived in Washington at 9:48 p.m. Washington time. Churchill also phoned the American embassy in London to express his approval. The following morning, at 7:35, an aide brought Truman China's reply. Chiang Kai-shek also agreed to the wording of the document. Which left only the Soviets.

Byrnes, meanwhile, received two cables from Harriman, who had met with Stalin and Molotov in the Kremlin regarding the matter. Stalin was "skeptical" of the Japanese peace feeler, since it did not meet the terms of unconditional surrender, and "the Soviet forces, therefore, were continuing their advance into Manchuria . . . [Stalin] gave me the definite impression that he was quite willing to have the war continue." Later Harriman cabled Truman again. At 2 a.m. Moscow time, the Soviets agreed to the terms of surrender, under one condition: "The Allied Powers should reach an agreement on the candidacy or candidacies for representation of the Allied High Command to which the Japanese Emperor and the Japanese Government are to be subordinated."

Stalin wanted a Russian general to represent his country in the surrender process, and he wanted his country to share in the occupation of Japan, even though the Soviets had been in the war for less than one week. Harriman informed Stalin that the U.S. government would never agree to such a clause. A "most heated discussion" followed, Harriman recorded, and the Soviets backed down, approving the wording of the response to Japan. On August 11, the United States sent the finalized reply to Japan through the Swiss government. Also on August 11 Truman informed the Allies that General Douglas MacArthur would be the supreme commander over Japan and alone would represent the Allies in the surrender process.

No word arrived from Tokyo the next day – August 12, which marked the four-month anniversary of Roosevelt's death. These four months had stunned the world. The *New York Times* on August 12: "Victory was already assured when President Roosevelt died. Since then two of the mightiest empires of the world have collapsed. History has recorded the decline and fall of empires before, but never with such rapidity. During these four months events that once covered years, even centuries, were consummated in weeks and days . . . Surely the revolutionary changes wrought during this period are such that it is safe to say that a new era in mankind's history is beginning."

But what kind of world would this new era usher in? Even before Japan replied to the new surrender demands of August 11, new threats of war surfaced in the East. In China, communist forces were taking advantage of Japan's collapse. Communist troops under Mao Tse-tung were demanding that Japanese troops surrender to *them*, so that they could acquire the Japanese weapons. Truman's ambassador to China, Patrick Hurley, warned the president that, if this were allowed to occur, a "fratricidal war" in China "will thereby be made certain." Public opinion held that "nothing short of a miracle could prevent the collapse of the government of China," Hurley noted.

China was on the brink of civil war and communist revolution.

Meanwhile the Soviets had other territorial goals in the Far East. On August 11 a State Department official in Moscow, Edwin Pauley, sent a top-secret cable to Truman and Byrnes following troubling conversations he had engaged in with representatives of Stalin's government. "Conclusions I have reached thru [*sic*] discussions . . . lead me to the belief that our forces should occupy quickly as much of the industrial areas of Korea and Manchuria as we can." Truman concurred. The following day the Joint Chiefs of Staff sent General MacArthur orders regarding China and Korea: "The President desires that such advance arrangements as are practicable be made to occupy the Port of Dairen [in China] and a Port in Korea immediately following the surrender of Japan if those ports have not at that time been taken over by Soviet forces."

With Japan's military rule disintegrating, a power vacuum was forming in the Far East. Even before the Japanese surrender, the race was on for control of China and Korea.

On August 12, the four-month anniversary of Roosevelt's death, Edward R. Murrow offered a point of view over CBS Radio regarding the war's end: "Secular history offers few, if any, parallels to the events of the past week. And seldom, if ever, has a war ended leaving the victors with such a sense of uncertainty and fear, with such a realization that the future is obscure and that survival is not assured."

///

At 6:10 p.m. on August 14, in his State Department office, Jimmy Byrnes received a messenger from the Swiss chargé d'affaires, who came bearing the document all the world had been waiting for: Japan's acceptance of the surrender terms. Byrnes moved quickly to the White House to deliver the document to Truman. Bess had returned to Washington, and at seven o'clock that night, when newsmen pushed into Truman's office to hear the announcement, she was in the room. The air felt charged with excitement. This war that had killed tens of millions of soldiers and civilians — the worst catastrophe that had ever struck the human race — was over. Certainly in the minds of all those in the Oval Office, the right side had won.

Klieg lights nearly blinded the president as he stood up from behind his desk, holding a document in his right hand. He had Byrnes and Leahy sitting on his right, and Cordell Hull — FDR's longtime and highly respected secretary of state — sitting on his left, so that Roosevelt would have a presence in the room. Cabinet officials stood in a row directly behind Truman. Newsreel cameras were rolling as he began his statement.

"I have received this afternoon a message from the Japanese Government," Truman said. He paused to say that Charlie Ross would be handing this document out, so there was no need for reporters to be taking notes down word for word. He continued, "In reply to the message forwarded to that Government by the Secretary of State on August 11, I deem this reply a full acceptance of the Potsdam Declaration which specifies the unconditional surrender of Japan."

He went on to announce General MacArthur's role as supreme allied commander over Japan, and that the proclamation of VJ-day would await the signing of the official surrender documents.

When he was done, reporters sprinted out of his office, and the news of Japan's surrender began to spread across the globe.

Truman had no more appointments on August 14. Outside the White House, in Lafayette Square, crowds had long since begun to gather, for the news of surrender had legs. It had already crisscrossed all of Washington and beyond. By the time Truman had finished his press conference to announce the end of the war, the crowd outside the White House gates had reached some 75,000-strong, almost triple the capacity of the baseball stadium where the Washington Nationals played. Police were attempting to maintain order – to no avail. People stood atop their automobiles, while dozens of others honked their car horns. Military officers danced jigs in the streets. A man with a blond woman on his arm, a highball in one hand and a bottle of whiskey in the other, meandered through the throng drunk, while another reveler did the same, wearing a turban made out of ticker tape. From inside the White House, Truman could hear the crowd chanting.

"We want Harry! We want Harry!"

The more time that passed, the larger the crowd grew, and the louder the chanting.

"WE WANT HARRY! WE WANT HARRY!"

The sun had begun to set when Truman appeared on the White House lawn, with Bess. MPs and secret service men sprinted around wildly trying to figure out how to keep the president safe. Truman made a V symbol for victory with his hand, flashing it at the crowd, which responded with deafening roars. Even Bess, as uncomfortable as she had proven to be in the public eye, could not keep the pleasure from illuminating her face. Remembered one man present: "[Truman] was on the White House lawn pumping his arms like an orchestra conductor at tens of thousands of cheering Americans who suddenly had materialized in front of the mansion."

After a few minutes Truman went back inside the White House, so he could call his mother and personally deliver the news: World War II was over. ("That was Harry," ninety-two-year-old Mamma Truman said after hanging up. "Harry's such a wonderful man . . . I knew he'd call.") Then Truman called Eleanor Roosevelt. "I told her," he later recalled, "that in this hour of triumph I wished that it had been President Roosevelt, and not I, who had given the message to our people."

Outside the crowds kept chanting Truman's name, so he went out into the hot August night again and stood on a patio observing, with Bess on his arm. It was, in the words of one reporter present, "the wildest celebration this capital ever saw." At the center of it all were Harry and Bess.

Truman had studied enough history to put this moment in context. The United States had provided soldiers and a great majority of the tools of war that destroyed Nazism and saved Europe. The United States had defeated a Japanese military intent on dominating all of the Far East. In the eyes of the world, this was America's finest hour. Never before had the United States achieved such prestige. What Truman did not know at this moment was this: never would the United States achieve such prestige again.

Epilogue

We can set no bounds to the possibilities of airplanes fly-
ing through the stratosphere dropping atomic bombs on
great cities . . . I understand that the power of the bomb
delivered on Nagasaki may be multiplied many times as
the invention develops. I have so far heard no suggestion
of any possible means of defense . . . If mankind continues
to make the atomic bomb without changing the political
relationships of States, sooner or later these bombs will be
used for mutual annihilation . . . It is clear to me, there-
fore, that, as never before, the responsible statesmen of the
great Powers are faced with decisions vital not merely to
the increase of human happiness but to the very survival
of civilization.

— Prime Minister Clement Attlee to
Harry Truman, September 25, 1945

AT 8 P.M. ON SEPTEMBER 2, 1945, on the starboard deck of the battle-
ship named for the president's home state, the USS *Missouri*, Japanese
officials signed their names to the surrender documents. The scene in
Tokyo Bay was awestriking. A fleet of navy ships lay at anchor, American
flags rippling in the wind. American bombers roared overhead; General Carl Spaatz of the U.S. Army Air Forces had warned that those aircraft were ready to release eight thousand tons of bombs on Japan at the
slightest sign of treachery. General MacArthur stood on the *Missouri*'s
deck monitoring the proceedings, his face so expressionless, he looked

like he was already turning into a bust that would sit in a museum. Once the Japanese officials signed the documents, MacArthur became the supreme ruler of eighty million Japanese subjects. Representing Truman on board the *Missouri* that night was the president's nephew, Seaman First Class John C. Truman.

With peace came all the adversity that Truman anticipated, and a whole lot more. As one biographer, Robert J. Donovan, put it many years ago, "For President Truman the postwar period did not simply arrive — it broke about his head with thunder, lightning, hail, rain, sleet, dead cats, howls, tantrums, and palpitations of panic." The president dug in. The now famous thirteen-inch-long sign appeared on his desk, a gift from his friend Fred Canfil, who had seen a sign like it in an Oklahoma reformatory. It read, THE BUCK STOPS HERE!

Four days after Japan signed the surrender documents, on the one-month anniversary of Hiroshima, Truman delivered to Congress the twenty-one-point program that he had worked on with Judge Sam Rosenman aboard the USS *Augusta,* on his way home from Potsdam. In it, he outlined his domestic strategy for postwar America — hyper-fast reconversion to a peacetime economy, unemployment and labor programs, anti-inflation policy, investment in housing, small business, and farming, aid for veterans, and more. Many in Congress still hoped that Truman would prove more conservative than Roosevelt. From these twenty-one points, Truman showed that he would not. Republicans in Congress reacted negatively. In the 1946 midterm elections, Republicans seized control of the House and Senate for the first time since 1928, and from this point on, the man from Missouri found himself treading in a political shark tank.

In the Far East, China and Korea were spinning out of control. In Korea, American and Soviet military commanders agreed to allow the Japanese south of the 38th parallel to surrender to U.S. forces, and north of the 38th parallel to the Red Army. Less than five weeks after Japan's surrender, a U.S. Army commander in Korea compared the situation in that country to "a powder keg ready to explode on application of a spark." A civil war in Korea was inevitable. (Today the 38th parallel roughly demarcates the border between North and South Korea.) Before the end of 1946, China too was locked in a full-blown civil war, also between Communist and non-Communist regimes.

Throughout eastern Europe, the Soviets continued to consolidate power and spread influence. Hungary, Bulgaria, Romania, Poland, Czechoslovakia

— all these nations became firmly Sovietized. By 1949, the Soviet zone of occupation in Germany had closed off its borders, becoming its own communist country commonly known as East Germany. That same year, the Soviets successfully tested their own nuclear weapon.

The long period of runaway inflation and economic paralysis that many feared would strike the United States following the war never did. Still, Truman was criticized for his tax policy ("High Tax Harry"), for labor strife, and for his groundbreaking support of civil rights, which did not sit well with many Americans.

For the rest of his time in office, historic challenges faced the presidency. Today he is remembered for the Truman Doctrine and the Marshall Plan, programs that hurled billions of dollars at European countries in an attempt to keep emerging democratic regimes from falling to communism. Truman's recognition of Israel in 1948 made him the first world leader to embrace the new nation. His administration is remembered for the Berlin Airlift following the Soviet blockade, for the founding of the CIA and the Atomic Energy Commission, and for his role among others in the founding of NATO. He is remembered for firing General Douglas MacArthur in 1951 — which set off a firestorm in Washington — and for his role in creating the modern Department of Defense.

In 1950, in a combined effort with the United Nations, Truman sent troops into Korea to fight Soviet-backed communist forces. The Cold War was no longer a war of posturing and paranoia. Like the "Phony War" of World War II, the Cold War became a real war of death and destruction. Truman was criticized for failing to get consent from Congress, which never declared war. This criticism only heightened when American forces failed to rid the Korean peninsula of communism.

Truman faced reelection in 1948, against Thomas Dewey of New York. His popularity ratings had plummeted by this time, but as in his 1940 Senate campaign, he surprised everyone, perhaps even himself, by declaring his candidacy and his resolve to win. As in his 1940 Senate campaign, he was given almost no chance at victory. Newspapers and polls unanimously predicted a landslide, but he came out victorious. Perhaps only the presidential election of 2016 surpasses 1948 as the biggest upset in American electioneering history. Truman's victory moved his daughter, Margaret, to pronounce, "Harry S. Truman was no 'accidental President,'" for now he had been elected by the American people.

Still, among all those historic chapters, Truman is remembered first

and foremost for his decision to employ atomic weapons — Little Boy
and Fat Man, the only two nuclear bombs ever used against human targets. More than seventy years later, this decision remains almost certainly the most controversial that any president has ever made.

///

How many human beings did the two atomic bombs kill? It is impossible
to say, and that alone inspires a sense of the weapons' capacity to anni-
hilate. The United States Department of Energy has estimated the number at 200,000, maybe more, over a five-year span, "as cancer and other
long-term effects took hold." And that is just for the Hiroshima bomb.

Since August 1945, the atomic bombings have pit moralists against
one another. Critics tend to argue with theories, leaving only questions
rather than answers. Was the bomb used for political purposes? Was it a
power play against the Soviets? Did the Americans race to use it to stop
the Soviets from charging farther into the Far East? How deeply did racism toward the Japanese play into the decision? Would Japan have surrendered without the use of the bomb? And if so, when, and after how
many more lives lost? To use a colloquialism, the answers to these questions depend on whom you ask.

General Eisenhower argued against dropping the bomb, in conversations with the president prior to August 1945. There is no record of Admiral Leahy's opposition prior to Hiroshima, but after the war Leahy
wrote: "It is my opinion that the use of this barbarous weapon at Hiroshima and Nagasaki was of no material assistance in our war against
Japan. The Japanese were already defeated and ready to surrender because of the effective blockade and the successful bombing with conventional weapons . . . My own feeling was that in being the first to use
it, we had adopted an ethical standard common to the barbarians of the
Dark Ages. I was taught not to make war in that fashion, and wars cannot be won by destroying women and children."

Leahy's argument is dubious. Why was it wrong to kill with atomic
bombs, when the Americans had been firebombing civilian neighborhoods in Japan for months? (After the war, regarding these firebombing
missions, Curtis LeMay wrote, "I suppose if I had lost the war, I would
have been tried as a war criminal . . . But all war is immoral, and if you
let that bother you, you're not a good soldier.")

The fact remains, almost every advisor to Truman recommended the bomb's use at the time. Noted Henry Stimson, as he looked back two years later in 1947: "The face of war is the face of death . . . The decision to use the atomic bomb was a decision that brought death to over a hundred thousand Japanese. No explanation can change that fact and I do not wish to gloss it over. But this deliberate, premeditated destruction was our least abhorrent choice."

George Marshall, the most respected military mind of his era, later wrote: "I regarded the dropping of the bomb as of great importance and felt that it would end the war possibly better than anything else, which it did, and I think that all the claims about the bombings afterward were rather silly."

Churchill provided another point of view in his writings after the war: "The historic fact remains, and must be judged in the after time, that the decision whether or not to use the atomic bomb to compel the surrender of Japan was never even an issue. There was unanimous, automatic, unquestioned agreement around our table; nor did I ever hear the slightest suggestion that we should do otherwise."

Eleanor Roosevelt supported Truman's use of the bomb, and this author has never heard the argument that FDR would have decided against its employment.

Every person who advised Truman on the matter saw this decision from a different point of view. As for Truman himself, there remains no evidence that he used the bomb for any political reason. He measured the lives that would be lost in a ground invasion of Japan and did the math: "It occurred to me that a quarter of a million of the flower of our young manhood were worth a couple of Japanese cities, and I still think they were and are."

This author agrees with historians Stephen Ambrose and Douglas Brinkley, who wrote in their book *Rise to Globalism:* "The simplest explanation is perhaps the most convincing. The bomb was there. Japan was not surrendering. Few in the government thought seriously about not using it. To drop it as soon as it was ready seemed natural, the obvious thing to do. As Truman later put it, 'The final decision of where and when to use the atomic bomb was up to me. Let there be no mistake about it. I regarded the bomb as a military weapon and never had any doubt that it should be used.'"

Truman left office amid miserable approval ratings in January 1953, as Eisenhower began his term. The American economy was booming, but global instability, the spread of communism, fear of the nuclear arms race, the Korean War, bipartisan bickering, all of it cast a dark shadow on Truman's administration at its denouement.

The day Harry and Bess moved out of the White House, he turned around at the door and waved good-bye to staff members. He had served as president for seven years, nine months, and eight days. He hesitated one last moment before leaving "the Great White Jail," then repeated a joke he often told. He said, "You know, many times in my despair at the White House, I've always wondered whether the nation and the world would have been much better off if Harry Truman, instead of being President of the United States, had played piano at a bawdy house." "Then," recalled a photographer who was there that day, "he turned around and left."

Through the years, historians have revived Truman's approval ratings. In 2015 one *Boston Globe* writer noted, "Harry S. Truman is now considered one of our most successful presidents, rating in the top 10 in every historical survey." Ironically, Truman's greatest strength came from what was perceived, on April 12, 1945, as his greatest weakness: his ordinariness. As Jonathan Daniels wrote of Truman, "Americans felt leaderless when Roosevelt died. Truman taught them, as one of them, that their greatness lies in themselves."

Harry S. Truman died twenty years after leaving office, the day after Christmas in 1972, at age eighty-eight. Bess Truman followed ten years later, and they are buried next to each other in a courtyard of the Harry S. Truman Library & Museum in Independence, Missouri. At the time of Truman's death, he was well aware that his legacy was still embattled. While he was president, he kept a quotation of Abraham Lincoln in a leather portfolio on his desk. It read, "I do the very best I know how — the very best I can; and I mean to keep doing so to the end. If the end brings me out all right, what is said against me won't amount to anything. If the end brings me out wrong, ten angels swearing I was right won't make any difference."

Acknowledgments

Completing a book of 160,000 words feels like shepherding 160,000 beloved kittens across a busy highway. I owe a great deal of gratitude to a lot of people. First, I would like to thank the archivists at the research institutions where I visited, most notably the Harry S. Truman Library & Museum in Independence, Missouri; the National Archives in College Park, Maryland; the Library of Congress in Washington, DC; the FDR Presidential Library & Museum in Hyde Park, New York; and the Manuscripts & Archives at Yale University in New Haven, Connecticut.

Particular gratitude goes to Greg Bradsher at the National Archives, Randy Sowell at the Truman Library, and Professor Jon Taylor at the University of Central Missouri, a wonderful historian and writer whose close read of my manuscript truly helped me get it to the finish line. A special thank-you goes to Lisa Sullivan and the Harry S. Truman Library Institute for a small grant to help in research expenses. (At no time did Ms. Sullivan or anyone from the institute ask to see any part of my manuscript before publication.) My hope is that all of these figures who helped me along the way find value in this book.

This is my third book with the same editor, publisher, and agent, and that is truly a special thing. My endless gratitude goes to Susan Canavan at Houghton Mifflin Harcourt and Scott Waxman at the Waxman Leavell Literary Agency. Your belief in me has changed the course of my life, and I will never forget it. Thank you also to everyone at Houghton Mifflin Harcourt and the Waxman Leavell agency for all your hard work. Megan Wilson at HMH is a great talent, as is editor Margaret Wimberger, whose careful reads and help shaping my endnotes were invaluable. Endless thank-yous to all of you.

As I wrote in the acknowledgments for my previous book, my wife, Michelle, is a great force behind everything we do together as a team. Without her, I would still be on page one, not of this manuscript but of everything in my life. Thank you, Michelle! Thank you also to Clayton

Baime and Audrey Baime. You are the lights of your parents' lives. Keep growing and being all you can be. Remember that every day is a blessing and should be savored. Remember every day how much you are loved, and that with this love comes responsibility.

My father, David Baime (to whom this book is dedicated), and my mother, Denise Baime, read numerous drafts of this manuscript. Both would have made terrific editors. Thank you for always being there, and I hope that this book can be an apology for all I put you through when I was a kid.

I would like to thank my family, whom I can never repay for all their love, understanding, and kindness through the years: Abby Baime, Susan Baime, my Aunt Karen and Uncle Ken Segal (who have always treated me as one of their own), the late Bill Green and the late Mildred Leventhal, my "outlaws" Connie and the late Bill Burdick, Jack and Margo Ezell, my many wonderful cousins and friends of the Crystal/Sabel/Segal clan, and the GG's Ken and Edna Wheeldon. I would also like to thank so many people in the publishing and movie business who have guided me along the way. These figures include (in no particular order) Jimmy Jellinek, Chris Napolitano, Bob Love, Dave Itzkoff, Adam Thompson, Sam Walker, Lee Froehlich, Steve Randall, Mike Guy, James Kaminsky, Ken Gross, Lucas Foster, Alex Young, Greg Veesor, Scott Alexander, Steven Kotler, Richard Stratton, Amy Grace Loyd, Jon Marcus, John H. Richardson, and so many others. I am so grateful to have had the chance to work with you, and I hope to do so again.

To paraphrase Geoffrey Chaucer, go little book!

Notes

Note on Research and Perspective

This book is about the legacy of Harry Truman, but all books have legacies of their own. I think and hope that people who have read many books about Truman will find in this one the following conclusion, which I think sets this book apart in the canon of Truman literature: *President Truman did not simply step onto the moving FDR train during his World War II presidency. In fact, he was a far greater agency of change during these four months than other writers have suggested.*

History is in itself a kind of myth. It morphs through time as new ideas and evidence come to light. The dynamics of research can change with the onset of new technologies, which can make certain documentation more important in the eyes of historical chroniclers than others. And then there are the perspectives of storytellers, who can move legacies and place them firmly where they have never been before. As Aldous Huxley once wrote, "The charm of history and its enigmatic lesson consist in the fact that, from age to age, nothing changes and yet everything is completely different." During my three years of research, I relied as much as possible on primary sources and the direct perspectives of as many participants in these events as I could. I wanted the creative process to be akin to recording music on vintage instruments, to make it sound like a thing of the past. Diaries, original documentation, minutes from meetings, official cables — these became beacons in the search for truth. Certainly there were times when I did use secondary sources, but in these instances I tried to use books written by people present in the rooms during the events and conversations I have depicted, such as Harry S. Truman, Margaret Truman, Winston Churchill, James F. Byrnes, Jonathan Daniels, Chip Bohlen, and others.

Truman wrote in his book *Mr. Citizen,* "It is my opinion that the only accurate source of information on which to make a proper historical assessment of the performances of past Presidents is in the presidential files." For this reason, I spent weeks at the Truman Library in Independence, Missouri, and many more at home accessing files available digitally through the library's website. In addition, I used the personal papers of other figures, including, but not limited to, Franklin Roosevelt, Henry Stimson, Henry Morgenthau, Curtis LeMay, General Leslie Groves, Admiral William Leahy, Joseph Davies, Bess Truman, Margaret Truman, Mary Jane Truman, Eben Ayers, James Aylward, James Pendergast, Fred Canfil, Matthew Connelly, Jonathan Daniels, Robert Hannegan, Verne Chaney, Victor Messall, Reathel Odum, Joseph Grew, Edwin Pauley, Harry Vaughan, Tom Evans, General Hap Arnold, George Elsey, Dean Acheson, Agnes Wolf, Rufus Burrus, Alonzo Fields, Hugh Fulton, Spencer Salisbury, Edward Jacobson, Edward McKim, Samuel Rosenman, Harold Smith, Monrad Wallgren, Rose Conway, and others. I examined the papers of Truman's doctor, Wallace Graham, and the diaries of the dentist who made White House house calls in 1945, Bruce Forsyth.

There were moments during this research when I saw the words "new accession" in the finding aids for manuscript collections. These were exciting moments, for they offered up documents that were not available to the major Truman biographers of a generation ago. The many dozens of oral histories available at the Truman archives also proved invaluable.

In the end, my goal was to produce a book that Harry Truman would have found factual. Whether or not this is the case, I can never know, but it was the standard that I set for myself.

I've used the following abbreviations for frequently cited series and subseries from the Truman Library:

FBPAP: Family, Business, and Personal Affairs Papers
FCF: Family Correspondence File
LNF: Longhand Notes File
MRF: Map Room File, 1945
OF: Official File, 1945–1953
PCF: Press Conference File
PPF: President's Personal File, 1945–1953
PRF: White House Press Release Files, 1945–1953
PSF: President's Secretary's Files, 1945–1953
SMOF: Staff Member and Office Files
WHCF: White House Central Files, 1945–1953

Also note: Oral histories can be found at https://www.trumanlibrary.org/oralhist/oralhis.htm.

Introduction

PAGE

ix *a* Washington Post *poll ranked him:* "New Ranking of U.S. Presidents Puts
Lincoln at No. 1, Obama at 18," *Washington Post,* February 16, 2015.
"*The Romans must have felt*": Doris Kearns Goodwin, *No Ordinary Time:
Franklin & Eleanor Roosevelt; The Home Front in World War II* (New York:
Simon & Schuster, 1994), p. 606.
"*Perhaps not since the dawn*": Diary of Joseph Davies, April 19, 1945, Joseph
Edward Davies Papers, box 1:16, Manuscript Division, Library of Congress,
Washington, DC.

x "*by accident*": Truman speaking in the introductory film at Harry S. Truman
National Historic Site visitor center, Independence, Missouri.
"*Here was a man who*": Oral history interview, Robert G. Nixon, p. 159,
Truman Library.
"*Here was a guy*": Oral history interview, Harry H. Vaughan, p. 52, Truman
Library.
"*All the world is asking*": "Truman: A Plain Genial Man Who Likes to Listen,"
Chicago Daily Tribune, August 14, 1945.
"*the deadliest campaign*": Bill Sloan, *The Ultimate Battle: Okinawa 1945 – The
Last Epic Struggle of World War II* (New York: Simon & Schuster Paperbacks,
2008), p. 5.
"*The four months that have*": "The Past Four Months: Unequalled in History,"
New York Times, August 12, 1945.

Timeline

xiv "*No! No!*": "Cries No! No! As Partisan Shoot Him, Girl Friend," *Washington
Post,* April 30, 1945.

xv "*as soon as possible*": Selected Documents on the Topic of the Atomic Bomb,
box 1, Franklin D. Roosevelt Presidential Library, Hyde Park, NY.

xvi "*The alternative for Japan*": The Potsdam Declaration, http://afe.easia
.columbia.edu/ps/japan/potsdam.pdf.

Chapter 1

3 "*the whole weight of the moon*": "The Whole Weight of the Moon and Stars,"
Daily Boston Globe, May 3, 1945.
"*a transfer of power*": Harry S. Truman, *Mr. Citizen* (New York: Bernard Geis
Associates, 1960), p. 9.
"*He's the man who cracks*": William M. Rigdon, *White House Sailor* (New York:
Doubleday, 1962), p. 188.
"*Mozart, Beethoven*": "It is not noise. It is music," Harry Truman's Record
Albums, Harry S. Truman National Historic Site, National Park Service,
https://www.nps.gov/hstr/learn/historyculture/truman-record-collection.htm.

4 *The Trumans' bank account :* Financial records, Bess W. Truman Papers,
   Financial Affairs File, box 9, Truman Library.
   "regular Army marching speed": John Hersey, "Mr. President — Quite a Head
   of Steam," Profiles, *New Yorker,* April 7, 1951.
   "You had to get up early": Oral history interview, James J. Rowley, p. 23,
   Truman Library.
   "Look at that thing": Hersey, "Mr. President."

5 *"I used to get down here":* Harry S. Truman to Mary Jane Truman and Martha
   Ellen Truman, April 11, 1945, FBPAP:FCF, box 19, Truman Papers.
   "I imagine Spot is getting": Harry S. Truman to May Wallace, April 12, 1945,
   letter quoted on Harry S. Truman National Historic Site, National Park
   Service, https://home.nps.gov/hstr/learn/historyculture/upload/Wallace%20
   Homes%20Site%20Bulletin.pdf.
   "They are a contrary outfit": Truman to James M. Pendergast, April 12, 1945,
   James M. Pendergast Papers, box 1, Truman Library.

6 *"with all the brisk eagerness":* Allen Drury, *A Senate Journal: 1943–1945* (New
   York: McGraw-Hill, 1963), p. 409.
   "Don't you think we ought": Oral history interview, Edward D. McKim, p. 121,
   Truman Library.

7 *"duty" to witness the camp's:* Dwight D. Eisenhower, *Crusade in Europe* (New
   York: Avon, 1952), p. 451.
   "The things I saw beggar": Dwight D. Eisenhower to General George C.
   Marshall, cable, at "Ohrdruf," United States Holocaust Memorial Museum,
   https://www.ushmm.org/wlc/en/article.php?ModuleId=10006131.
   "the stories of Nazi brutality": Eisenhower, *Crusade in Europe*, p. 451.

8 *"furious ground fighting":* "Yanks Regain Kakazu Peak on Okinawa,"
   Washington Post, April 12, 1945.
   "Total roof area damaged": Twenty-First Bomber Command operations
   report, Curtis E. LeMay Papers, box 28, Manuscript Division, Library of
   Congress, Washington, DC.
   "My idea of what was humanly": Curtis E. LeMay with MacKinlay Kantor,
   Mission with LeMay: My Story (New York: Doubleday, 1965),
   p. 353.

9 *The city had changed:* Descriptions of Washington, DC, come from William
   L. O'Neill, *A Democracy at War: America's Fight at Home & Abroad in World
   War II* (Cambridge, MA: Harvard University Press, 1993); Richard Lingeman,
   Don't You Know There's a War On? The American Home Front 1941–1945 (New
   York: Thunder's Mouth, 1970); and A. J. Baime, *The Arsenal of Democracy:
   FDR, Detroit, and an Epic Quest to Arm an America at War* (Boston: Houghton
   Mifflin Harcourt, 2014).
   "If you want a friend": Walter John Raymond, *Dictionary of Politics: Selected
   American and Foreign Political and Legal Terms* (Lawrenceville, VA: Brunswick,
   1973), p. 225.
   "District (not exceeding ten . . .)": United States Constitution, https://www
   .archives.gov/founding-docs/constitution-transcript.
   "It abounds in phonies": Jonathan Daniels, *Frontier on the Potomac* (New York:
   Macmillan, 1946), p. 7.

10 *"I've never known any President":* Arthur M. Schlesinger Jr., "F.D.R. as

President," Don Congdon, ed., *The Thirties: A Time to Remember* (New York: Simon & Schuster, 1962), p. 431.

"It is one of the episodes": George E. Allen, *Presidents Who Have Known Me* (New York: Simon & Schuster, 1960), p. 120.

2 percent of Democratic voters: "7 Out of 10 Democrats Favor Wallace," *Washington Post,* July 19, 1944.

"I knew almost nothing": William D. Leahy, *I Was There: The Personal Story of the Chief of Staff to Presidents Roosevelt and Truman Based on His Notes and Diaries Made at the Time* (New York: Whittlesey House, 1950), p. 248.

"Truman [was] still unknown": "Bricker, Truman Still Unknown to Millions Despite Fanfare," *Washington Post,* November 3, 1944.

11 *"In the scheme of American":* Allen, *Presidents,* p. 137.

"a graveyard of politicians": Ibid.

"The Vice President has not": Luther Huston, "The Vice President Talks of His New Job," *New York Times Magazine,* January 21, 1945.

"political Eunuch": Truman to Hugh P. Williamson, April 5, 1945, letter pictured on Christie's auction house website, christies.com, last accessed January 11, 2017.

"Study history": Huston, "Vice President Talks."

"Anything can happen": "Lauren Bacall Aids Show for Services," *Washington Post,* February 11, 1945.

12 *"Don't say that":* "Truman Has Job That He Didn't Want," *Hartford Courant,* April 16, 1945.

"I'm afraid you're right": McKim oral history, p. 106.

"He knew that": Oral history interview, Harry Easley, p. 99, Truman Library.

"We saw Harry Truman come in": Drury, *Senate Journal,* p. 106 and 410.

13 *"I feel somewhat hesitant":* Congressional Record, April 12, 1945.

"Dear Mamma and Mary": H. S. Truman to M. J. Truman and M. E. Truman, April 12, 1945, FBPAP:FCF, box 19, Truman Papers.

"You know," Drury said: Drury, *Senate Journal,* p. 410.

Chapter 2

14 *"Oh no, no":* Bernard Asbell, *When F.D.R. Died* (New York: Signet, 1961), p. 17.

15 *"God-awful":* A. J. Baime, *The Arsenal of Democracy: FDR, Detroit, and an Epic Quest to Arm an America at War* (Boston: Houghton Mifflin Harcourt, 2014), p. 251.

"I was terribly shocked": Henry Morgenthau diaries, April 11, 1945, Franklin D. Roosevelt Library, http://www.fdrlibrary.marist.edu/_resources/images/morg/mpd18.pdf.

16 *"Oh, I don't feel any too good":* Asbell, *When F.D.R. Died,* p. 18.

"The purge was everywhere": Charles E. Bohlen, *Witness to History: 1929–1969* (New York: W. W. Norton, 1973), p. 43.

17 *"Never — neither then nor at any":* George F. Kennan, *Memoirs: 1925–1950* (Boston: Atlantic Monthly Press, 1967), p. 57.

"In the opinion of this Government": John Lewis Gaddis, *The United States and*

the Origins of the Cold War: 1941–1947 (New York: Columbia University Press, 1972), p. 4.

"If Hitler invaded Hell": Winston S. Churchill, *The Second World War*, vol. 3, *The Grand Alliance* (New York: Rosetta, 2002), p. 331.

"Stalin's aim is to spread": Gaddis, *Origins of the Cold War,* p. 54.

"I just have a hunch": Ibid., p. 64.

18 *"The far reaching decisions"*: Franklin D. Roosevelt to Joseph Stalin, February 23, 1945, Franklin D. Roosevelt, Papers as President: Map Room Papers, http://www.fdrlibrary.marist.edu/archives/collections/franklin/?p=collections/findingaid&id=511&q=&rootcontentid=144934#id144934.

"in about one month": Herbert Feis, *From Trust to Terror: The Onset of the Cold War, 1945–1950* (New York: W. W. Norton, 1970), p. 25.

"I am outraged": W. Averell Harriman to Roosevelt, March 14, 1945, Franklin D. Roosevelt, Papers as President: Map Room Papers, http://www.fdrlibrary.marist.edu/archives/collections/franklin/?p=collections/findingaid&id=511&q=&rootcontentid=144934#id144934.

"At present, all entry": Churchill to Roosevelt, March 16, 1945, ibid.

19 *"I feel certain that"*: Harriman to Roosevelt, April 3, 1945, ibid.

"I cannot conceal": Roosevelt to Stalin, March 29, 1945, ibid.

"Matters on the Polish question": Stalin to Roosevelt, April 7, 1945, ibid.

"It may be assumed": Stalin to Roosevelt, April 3, 1945, ibid.

"I have received with astonishment": Roosevelt to Stalin, April 4, 1945, ibid.

20 *"There must not, in any event"*: Roosevelt to Stalin, April 11, 1945, ibid.

"Averell [Harriman] is right": Joseph E. Persico, *Roosevelt's Centurions: FDR and the Commanders He Led to Win World War II* (New York: Random House, 2013), p. 498.

"We really believed": Robert E. Sherwood, *Roosevelt and Hopkins: An Intimate History* (New York: Harper & Brothers, 1948), p. 870.

"The two months that had passed": Winston S. Churchill, *The Second World War,* vol. 6, *Triumph and Tragedy* (New York: Rosetta, 2002), p. 510.

21 *"A typical State Department"*: Asbell, *When F.D.R. Died,* p. 39.

"Here's where I make law": Ibid.

22 *"May I respectfully suggest"*: Harriman to Roosevelt, April 12, 1945, Franklin D. Roosevelt, Papers as President: Map Room Papers, http://www.fdrlibrary.marist.edu/archives/collections/franklin/?p=collections/findingaid&id=511&q=&rootcontentid=144934#id144934.

"I do not wish to": Roosevelt to Harriman, April 12, 1945, ibid. Also: Michael Dobbs, *Six Months in 1945: From World War to Cold War* (New York: Alfred A. Knopf, 2012), p. 158.

"Now we've got just about": Interview with Elizabeth Shoumatoff, in "Roosevelt Jovial Before Collapse," *New York Times,* April 16, 1945.

"I have a terrific headache": Asbell, *When F.D.R. Died,* p. 42.

"Ask the Secret Service": Ibid., p. 43.

Chapter 3

23 *"It was a stricken":* Michael Reilly, *Reilly of the White House* (New York: Simon & Schuster, 1947), p. 232.

Pulse: 104: The specifics of Dr. Bruenn's examination and procedure are from Bernard Asbell, *When F.D.R. Died* (New York: Signet, 1961), pp. 45–46.

"Dr. Bruenn told me it was": Transcript of press conference with Ross McIntire, April 12, 1945, Eben A. Ayers Papers, box 10, Truman Library.

24 *"The President was* in extremis*":* Asbell, *When F.D.R. Died,* p. 48.

"Dr. Bruenn told me things": McIntire press conference.

"[I] asked her to come": Transcript of press conference with Stephen Early, April 12, 1945, Ayers Papers, box 10.

"I got into the car": Doris Kearns Goodwin, *No Ordinary Time: Franklin & Eleanor Roosevelt; The Home Front in World War II* (New York: Simon & Schuster, 1994), p. 603.

"gold-plated office": Harry S. Truman to Mary Jane Truman and Martha Ellen Truman, April 11, 1945, April 12, 1945, FBPAP:FCF, box 19, Truman Papers.

25 *"Sam wanted me":* Ibid., April 16, 1945.

"I guess some fellahs": Alfred Steinberg, *Sam Rayburn: A Biography* (New York: Hawthorn, 1975), p. 195.

"This is the VP": David McCullough, *Truman* (New York: Touchstone, 1993), p. 341.

"as quickly and quietly": H. S. Truman to M. J. Truman and M. E. Truman, April 16, 1945.

"He is kind of a pale": Steinberg, *Sam Rayburn,* p. 225.

"Jesus Christ and General Jackson": Ibid.

"[I] told my office force": H. S. Truman to M. J. Truman and M. E. Truman, April 16, 1945.

26 *"in almost nothing flat":* Ibid.

"Harry," she said, "the president": Ibid.

The lightning has struck!: Various forms of this quote have been attributed to Truman in numerous sources, for example, Richard Rhodes, *The Making of the Atomic Bomb* (New York: Touchstone, 1986), p. 614.

"I was fighting off tears": Memoirs by Harry S. Truman: 1945; Year of Decisions (New York: Konecky & Konecky, 1955), p. 5.

"It was the only time in my life": H. S. Truman to M. J. Truman and M. E. Truman, April 16, 1945.

"Is there anything I can do": Truman, *Memoirs,* p. 5.

"I want to see you": Oral history interview, James J. Rowley, p. 15, Truman Library.

"During the drive": Oral history interview, Robert G. Nixon, p. 109, Truman Library.

27 *"It is my sad duty":* Ibid., p.110

"Everything was completely": The Diaries of Edward R. Stettinius, Jr., 1943–1946, eds. Thomas M. Campbell and George C. Herring (New York: New Viewpoints, 1975), p. 313.

"I told her as soon as": H. S. Truman to M. J. Truman and M. E. Truman, April 16, 1945.

28 *"I have a flash for you"*: Asbell, *When F.D.R. Died*, p. 79.
"From then on there was": Robert H. Ferrell, ed., *Truman in the White House: The Diary of Eben A. Ayers* (Columbia: University of Missouri Press, 1991), p. 8.
"In an odd, tight voice": Margaret Truman, *Bess W. Truman* (New York: Macmillan, 1986), pp. 249–50.

29 FLASH WASHN — FDR DEAD: Anecdote and dialogue from Asbell, *When F.D.R. Died*, pp. 80–85.

30 *"Her face was a study"*: Diary of Joseph E. Davies, April 12, 1945, Joseph Edward Davies Papers, box 1:16, Manuscript Division, Library of Congress, Washington, DC.
"In the long Cabinet Room": Jonathan Daniels, *Frontier on the Potomac* (New York: Macmillan, 1946), p. 10.
"The Cabinet was assembling": Davies diary, April 12, 1945.
"It is my sad duty to report": James Forrestal, *The Forrestal Diaries*, ed. Walter Millis (New York: Viking, 1951), p. 42.
"I want every one of you": Henry Morgenthau diaries, April 12, 1945, Franklin D. Roosevelt Presidential Library, http://www.fdrlibrary.marist.edu/_resources/images/morg/mpd19.pdf.
"Mr. Truman, I will do": Ibid.

31 *"He spoke very warmly"*: Diary of Henry L. Stimson, April 12, 1945, Stimson Papers, series 2, box 172, Yale University Library.
"sad and a little frightened": Daniels, *Frontier on the Potomac*, p. 11.
"I told him that he had": Campbell and Herring, *Diaries of Edward R. Stettinius*, p. 315.

32 *"I, Harry Shipp Truman"*: Truman, *Bess W. Truman*, p. 252.
"In that moment of actual": Jonathan Daniels, *The Man of Independence* (Port Washington, NY: Kennikat, 1971), p. 27.
"Mr. President, will you come": Oral history interview, Eben A. Ayers, p. 8, Truman Library.

33 *"The world may be sure"*: Statement by the President After Taking the Oath of Office, April 12, 1945, https://trumanlibrary.org/publicpapers/index.php?pid=1.
"about a most urgent matter": Truman, *Memoirs*, p. 10.
"He wanted me to know": Ibid.
"That was all he felt free": Ibid.
"I was very much shocked": Diary of Harry S. Truman, April 12, 1945, PSF, Truman Papers.

34 *"The President has left"*: Daniels, *Frontier on the Potomac*, p. 12.

Chapter 4

35 *"It finally crushed him"*: Robert E. Sherwood, *Roosevelt and Hopkins: An Intimate History* (New York: Harper & Brothers, 1948), p. 880.
"Good God!": Cabell Phillips, *The Truman Presidency: The History of a Triumphant Succession* (London: Collier-Macmillan, 1966), p. 1.
"I realize," he told listeners: Radio broadcast, April 12, 1945, transcript in Tom L. Evans Papers, box 5, Truman Library.

"The gravest question-mark": Diary of Arthur H. Vandenberg, excerpted in Arthur H. Vandenberg, Jr., ed., *The Private Papers of Senator Vandenberg* (Boston: Houghton Mifflin, 1952), p. 165.

"He seemed deeply moved": W. Averell Harriman to White House, cable, quoted in W. Averell Harriman and Elie Abel, *Special Envoy to Churchill and Stalin 1941–1946* (New York: Random House, 1975), p. 440.

36 *"We have the miracle"*: Albert Speer, *Inside the Third Reich* (New York: Avon, 1975), p. 586.

"as if I had been struck": Winston S. Churchill, *The Second World War*, vol. 6, *Triumph and Tragedy* (New York: Bantam, 1953), p. 403.

"We pondered over the effect": Dwight D. Eisenhower, "Crusade in Europe," *Life*, December 13, 1948.

"We talked for nearly": H. W. Brands, *The General vs. the President: MacArthur and Truman at the Brink of Nuclear War* (New York: Penguin, 2016), Kindle edition.

"It seems very unfortunate": David McCullough, *Truman* (New York: Touchstone, 1993), p. 350.

"As long as he lived": Oral history interview, Mary Jane Truman, pp. 1–2, Truman Library.

37 *"Mother is terribly, terribly"*: "Truman's Mother," *Pittsburgh Press*, April 13, 1945.

"Roosevelt was a great": Kai Bird and Martin J. Sherwin, *American Prometheus: The Triumph and Tragedy of J. Robert Oppenheimer* (New York: Vintage, 2005), p. 290.

"He did not say much to us": Margaret Truman, *Bess W. Truman* (New York: Macmillan, 1986), p. 252.

"Be good, Harry": Ibid., p. 253.

38 *he awoke to find his wife*: Ibid.

"Who the hell is Harry": Jonathan Daniels, *The Man of Independence* (Port Washington, NY: Kennikat, 1971), p. 111.

Chapter 5

41 *"We would hunt birds'"*: *Memoirs by Harry S. Truman: 1945; Year of Decisions* (New York: Konecky & Konecky, 1955), p. 114.

42 *"You know," said a Grandview*: Oral history interview, Stephen S. Slaughter, p. 34, Truman Library.

"light-foot Baptist": Harry S. Truman to Bess W. Wallace, March 19, 1911, FBPAP:FCF, box 1, Truman Papers.

"Rebel Democrats": See Meyer Berger, "Mother Truman – Portrait of a Rebel," *New York Times*, June 23, 1946.

"No one could make remarks": "Truman Memoirs: Part 2," *Life*, October 3, 1955.

"He was one of the hardest": Sound recording of Truman interview, MP2002-21, Screen Gems Collection, Truman Library.

"flat eyeballs": "A President Grows Up," Truman Library, https://www.truman library.org/whistlestop/fastfacts/ffearly.htm.

"It was very unusual": Oral history interview, Mize Peters, p. 11, Truman
Library.

43 *"a new consciousness"*: Willa Cather, *O Pioneers!* (New York: Penguin Classics,
1989), p. vii.

"There were quite a few saloons": Oral history interview, Mary Jane Truman,
p. 35, Truman Library.

"Work Mules for Sale!": Mary Jane Truman Papers, box 1, Truman
Library.

"When I was about six": Longhand note, May 14, 1934, Pickwick Papers,
PSF:LNF, Truman Papers.

"the most popular man": Henry P. Chiles quoted in "Truman Places: 608 North
Delaware," https://www.trumanlibrary.org/places/in12.htm.

44 *"was never popular"*: Alonzo L. Hamby, *Man of the People: A Life of Harry
S. Truman* (New York: Oxford University Press, 1995), p. 3.

"At one time," according to: Oral history interview, Mary Ethel Noland, p. 56,
Truman Library.

"He ended up being": M. J. Truman oral history, p. 3.

"In reading the lives of great": Longhand note, May 14, 1934, Pickwick Papers,
PSF:LNF, Truman Papers.

"History showed me that": Truman, *Memoirs*, p. 120.

45 *"If I succeeded in"*: Longhand note, May 14, 1934.

On August 23, 1898: M. J. Truman Papers, box 1.

"He didn't get to play": Oral history interview, Mrs. W.L.C. Palmer, p. 17,
Truman Library.

"a very, very genteel": Oral history interview, Pansy Perkins and Pauline Sims,
p. 5, Truman Library.

46 *"Well, don't I get one"*: Robert H. Ferrell, *Harry S. Truman: A Life* (Columbia:
University of Missouri Press, 1994), p. 188.

Chapter 6

47 *"My father's finances became"*: Longhand note, May 14, 1934, Pickwick Papers,
PSF:LNF, Truman Papers.

"It took all I received": Ibid.

"I became very familiar": *Memoirs by Harry S. Truman: 1945; Year of Decisions*
(New York: Konecky & Konecky, 1955), p. 123.

"J. A. Truman & Son": Margaret Truman, *Bess W. Truman* (New York:
Macmillan, 1986), p. 34.

Truman family's 1910 tax return: Mary Jane Truman Papers, box 2, Truman
Library.

"I have memorized a whole": Harry S. Truman to Bess W. Wallace, August 18,
1914, FBPAP:FCF, box 3, Truman Papers.

48 *"We are living on bread"*: Truman to Wallace, June 16, 1911, FBPAP:FCF, box 1.

"Aunt Ella": Truman, *Bess W. Truman*, p. 30.

49 *"It seems to me"*: Truman to Wallace, July 1, 1912, FBPAP:FCF, box 2.

"It is a family failing": Truman to Wallace, June 22, 1911, FBPAP:FCF, box 1.

"He thought I was about": Longhand note, Pickwick Papers, May 14, 1934, PSF: LNF.

"Politics is all he ever": Truman to Wallace, August 6, 1912, FBPAP:FCF, box 2.

"I have been tossed upon": Jon Meacham, *American Lion: Andrew Jackson in the White House* (New York: Random House, 2009), p. xvii.

"If Andrew Jackson can be President": Ibid., p. 20.

50 *"Nobody talks anything but"*: Truman to Wallace, November 5, 1912, FBPAP: FCF, box 2.

"Politics sure is the ruination": Truman to Wallace, August 19, 1913, FBPAP:FCF, box 2.

51 *"Mrs. Wallace wasn't a bit"*: David McCullough, *Truman* (New York: Touchstone, 1993), pp. 91–92.

"I had been sitting": Jonathan Daniels, *The Man of Independence* (Port Washington, NY: Kennikat, 1971), p. 74.

"I am convinced": Truman to Wallace, February 4, 1916, FBPAP:FCF, box 3.

"My money is in now": Truman to Wallace, March 5, 1916, FBPAP:FCF, box 3.

52 *"My ship's going to come in"*: Truman to Wallace, October 29, 1913, FBPAP:FCF, box 3.

"How would you like": Longhand note, May 14, 1934, Pickwick Papers, PSF:LNF.

"Queen of the Waves": "Lusitania's Great Size and Speed," *Washington Post*, May 8, 1915.

"The country was horrified": A. Scott Berg, *Wilson* (New York: G. P. Putnam's Sons, 2013), p. 362.

"I am simply on needle points": Truman to Wallace, November 16, 1916, FBPAP:FCF, box 4.

53 *"My luck should surely"*: Truman to Wallace, January 23, 1917, FBPAP:FCF, box 4.

"[Germany] is firing upon our": "Germany's Acts of War," *New York Times*, March 19, 1917.

"I advise that the Congress": Woodrow Wilson, *The War Message of President Woodrow Wilson Delivered to the Congress* (San Francisco: A. M. Robertson, 1917), p. 8.

"I was stirred in heart": Longhand note, May 1931, PSF:LNF.

"The difference between a bold": George E. Allen, *Presidents Who Have Known Me* (New York: Simon & Schuster, 1960), p. 90.

"farmer, oil": FBPAP: Military File, box 33, Truman Papers.

54 *"I don't think it would be"*: Truman to Wallace, July 14, 1917, FBPAP:FCF, box 4.

Chapter 7

55 *"Dust in my teeth"*: Truman to Wallace, October 19, 1917, FBPAP:FCF, box 4.

"It was the coldest": Oral history interview, Floyd T. Ricketts, pp. 4–5, Truman Library.

"a fine Jewish boy": Longhand note, May 14, 1934, Pickwick Papers, PSF:LNF, Truman Papers.

56 *"It is eleven o'clock"*: Harry S. Truman to Bess W. Wallace, March 29, 1918, FBPAP:FCF, box 5, Truman Papers.

"Dear Harry, May this photograph": Margaret Truman, *Bess W. Truman* (New York: Macmillan, 1986), p. 283.

"There we were watching": David McCullough, *Truman* (New York: Touchstone, 1993), p. 111.

"trying to drink": Truman to Wallace, April 14, 1918, FBPAP:FCF, box 5.

"The country is very pretty": Truman to Wallace, April 23, 1918, FBPAP:FCF, box 5.

57 *"I think of Battery D"*: Oral history interview, Harry E. Murphy, p. 30, Truman Library.

"Most of the young fellows": Ricketts oral history, pp. 3–4.

"He took command of the battery": Oral history interview, Edward D. McKim, p. 4, Truman Library.

"I didn't come over here": Jonathan Daniels, *The Man of Independence* (Port Washington, NY: Kennikat, 1971), p. 95.

"He let us know he was": McKim oral history, p. 16.

"I am a Battery commander": Truman to Wallace, July 14, 1918, FBPAP:FCF, box 5.

58 *"I have my doubts"*: Truman to Wallace, July 31, 1918, FBPAP:FCF, box 5.

"The roads [that led]": Unpublished memoirs of Battery D soldier Verne Chaney, Verne E. Chaney Papers, Truman Library.

"we pulled over the crest": Ibid.

"It was our first taste of war": Ricketts oral history, p. 10.

"Then all hell broke loose": Chaney memoirs.

"My battery became panic-stricken": *Memoirs by Harry S. Truman: 1945; Year of Decisions* (New York: Konecky & Konecky, 1955), p. 129.

"The first sergeant got": Oral history interview, Walter B. Menefee, p. 8, Truman Library.

59 *"gasping like a catfish"*: McCullough, *Truman,* p. 122.

"I would make an effort": Chaney memoirs.

"The fireworks started": Oral history interview, McKinley Wooden, p. 42, Truman Library.

"I saw bodies without heads": Chaney memoirs.

60 *"plumb crazy"*: Truman to Wallace, September 15, 1918, FBPAP:FCF, box 5.

"The rest of us would look like": Oral history interview, Harry H. Vaughan, p. 6, Truman Library.

"The great drive has": Truman to Wallace, October 6, 1918, FBPAP:FCF, box 5.

"The silence that followed": Truman, *Memoirs,* p. 131.

"Vive President Wilson!": Ibid.

"You may invite the entire": Wallace to Truman, March 16, 1919, FBPAP:FCF, box 6.

"You've just never seen": McCullough, *Truman,* p. 144.

61 *"Well, now, Mrs. Truman"*: Oral history interview, Ted Marks, p. 28, Truman Library.

"The Wallaces . . . rather ignored": Oral history interview, Edgar C. Faris Jr., p. 112, Truman Library.

"I finally decided to sell": Longhand note, May 14, 1934, Pickwick Papers, PSF:LNF, Truman Papers.

Chapter 8

62 SHIRTS, COLLARS, HOSIERY: From the myriad of photographs of the store online.
    the lease called for $350: Court papers, lawsuit against Truman and Jacobson, FBPAP: General File, box 28, Truman Papers.
    "Twelfth Street was in": "Collars and Cuffs," Talk of the Town, *New Yorker,* September 1, 1945.
    "I am still paying": Longhand note, May 14, 1934, Pickwick Papers, PSF:LNF, Truman Papers.

63 *"How'd you like to be"*: Jonathan Daniels, *The Man of Independence* (Port Washington, NY: Kennikat, 1971), p. 109.
    "Funny thing": "Collars and Cuffs."
    "I never will forget": Oral history interview, Edgar G. Hinde, p. 45, Truman Library.
    "He kind of stammered": Oral history interview, Henry P. Chiles, p. 36, Truman Library.
    "The purse strings": Lyle W. Dorsett, *The Pendergast Machine* (Lincoln: University of Nebraska Press, 1968), p. 55.

64 *"It's a very simple thing"*: Marquis Childs, "Campaign," *The Thirties: A Time to Remember,* ed. Don Congdon (New York: Simon & Schuster, 1962), p. 434.

65 *"Certainly Mike and Tom"*: Robert H. Ferrell, ed., *Dear Bess: The Letters from Harry to Bess Truman, 1910–1959* (New York: W. W. Norton, 1983), p. 304.
    "I won the dirtiest": Truman interview notes, Jonathan Daniels Papers, box 1, Truman Library.
    "Morning, Judge": Oral history interview, A. Layle Childers, Harry S. Truman National Historic Site, National Park Service, https://www.nps.gov/hstr/learn /historyculture/upload/childers_interview.pdf.
    "Old Tom Pendergast wanted": Oral history interview, Harry H. Vaughan, p. 12, Truman Library.

66 *"as if I were the president"*: Jon Taylor, *Harry Truman's Independence: The Center of the World* (Charleston, SC: History Press, 2013), n.p.
    "to live up to my good mother's": Longhand note, Pickwick Papers, PSF:LNF.
    "Everybody thought Mr. Truman": Oral history interview, Mize Peters, pp. 28–29, Truman Library.
    "This sweet associate of mine": Longhand note, n.d., Pickwick Papers, PSF:LNF, Truman Papers.

67 *"We never had to do"*: Oral history interview, Nathan Thomas Veatch, pp. 79–80, Truman Library.
    "If I were to choose the five": Oral history interview, Dixie Pollard, p. 4, Truman Library.
    "Mr. Truman had a natural": Oral history interview, Oscar L. Chapman, pp. 837–38, Truman Library.

"extraordinarily efficient": Truman interview notes, Daniels Papers.

68 *(there were 70,950):* Dixon Wecter, "From Riches to Rags," *The Thirties: A Time to Remember,* ed. Don Congdon (New York: Simon & Schuster, 1962), p. 30.

"I am firm in my belief": Ibid.

"The fundamental business": Herbert Hoover, Statement on the National Business and Economic Situation, American Presidency Project, http://www.presidency.ucsb.edu/ws/?pid=21979.

"one of the most uncontrollable": "Market Checks Fresh Drop to Deeper Depths," *Christian Science Monitor,* October 29, 1929.

"pretty hard on head": Harry S. Truman to Bess W. Truman, May 11, 1933, FBPAP:FCF, box 8, Truman Papers.

"The finances of the county": H. S. Truman to B. W. Truman, February 12, 1931, FBPAP:FCF, box 7.

69 *"outbreaks of gunplay":* "Two Killed in Missouri Vote Rioting," *Washington Post,* March 28, 1934.

"The manager gave me": H. S. Truman to B. W. Truman, April 28, 1933, FBPAP:FCF, box 7.

"Since childhood at my": Longhand note, n.d., Pickwick Papers, PSF:LNF, Truman Papers.

70 *"We've spent $7,000,000":* Ibid.

"I wonder if I did": Ibid.

"Maybe I can put": Ibid.

"The only thing we have to fear": Footage of Franklin Roosevelt's first inaugural speech, https://www.youtube.com/watch?v=7nSgMWW-8o8.

"No power on earth": Milton Meltzer, *Never to Forget: The Jews of the Holocaust* (1976, reprint New York: HarperCollins, 1991), p. 18.

71 *"the Mussolini of Missouri":* "Pendergast Machine Dominates Missouri," *Washington Post,* August 14, 1934; and "The Big Fellow," *Washington Post,* September 18, 1936.

"He was an able clear thinker": "Jackson Democratic Club," Truman Library, https://www.trumanlibrary.org/places/kc8a.htm.

"If you don't have a candidate": Oral history interview, James P. Aylward, pp. 62–64, Truman Library.

Chapter 9

72 *"Judge," Aylward said:* Oral history interview, James P. Aylward, pp. 65–67, Truman Library.

"one of the most fascinating": Lyle W. Dorsett, *The Pendergast Machine* (Lincoln: University of Nebraska Press, 1968), p. 112.

"Tomorrow I am to make": Longhand note, May 14, 1934, Pickwick Papers, PSF:LNF, Truman Papers.

73 *"Two words are all any":* Interview notes, Jonathan Daniels Papers, box 1, Truman Library.

"For this bellhop": David McCullough, *Truman* (New York: Touchstone, 1993), p. 208.

74 *"Truman is little known"*: "Jim Reed May Run as an Independent," *New York Times*, May 20, 1934.
   "I'll tell you we had": Aylward oral history, pp. 75–76.
   "the swarthy, right-hand man": "Political Gang Chieftain Slain," *Washington Post*, July 11, 1934.
   "If anything happens": McCullough, *Truman*, p. 207.
   "Boss Pendergast's Errand Boy": Marquis Childs, "Unpromising Freshman of 1934," *St. Louis Post-Dispatch*, November 11, 1942.
   "County Judge Truman is": Ibid.
   "He pulled Jackson County": Oral history interview, Mrs. W.L.C. Palmer, p. 40, Truman Library.

75 *"What's a senator?"*: Margaret Truman, "I Don't Want to Go to Washington," *Detroit Free Press*, November 30, 1956.
   "wailing dramatically": Margaret Truman, *Harry S. Truman* (New York: William Morrow, 1973), p. 89.
   "undoubtedly the poorest": Jonathan Daniels, *The Man of Independence* (Port Washington, NY: Kennikat, 1971), p. 176.
   "Men," Garner said: Aylward oral history, p. 118.
   "the teeming galleries were hushed": "Senate Begins New Session in Solemn Mood," *Chicago Daily Tribune*, January 4, 1935.

76 *"the Senator from Pendergast"*: Robert H. Ferrell, *Harry S. Truman: A Life* (Columbia: University of Missouri Press, 1994), p. 188.
   "If you had seen Harry": Childs, "Unpromising Freshman."
   "not considered brilliant": "New Faces in the Senate," *Washington Post*, November 12, 1934.
   "Don't start out with": *Memoirs by Harry S. Truman: 1945; Year of Decisions* (New York: Konecky & Konecky, 1955), p. 144.
   "Sen. Thomas Truman": FDR daily calendar, February 14, 1935, Franklin D. Roosevelt Presidential Library, http://www.fdrlibrary.marist.edu/daybyday /daylog/february-14th-1935/.
   "No one who hasn't had": Donald M. Nelson, *Arsenal of Democracy* (New York: Harcourt Brace, 1946), p. 14.
   "I was practically tongue-tied": Truman, *Harry S. Truman*, p. 91.

77 *"That man was there earlier"*: Oral history interview, Edgar C. Faris Jr., p. 71, Truman Library.
   "the average man for a happier": Truman speech, n.d., FBPAP, box 28, Truman Papers.

78 *"Kind of hard . . . to attend"*: Harry S. Truman to Bess W. Truman, June 22, 1935, FBPAP:FCF, box 8, Truman Papers.
   "She would drop paper clips": Oral history interview, Reathel Odum, p. 21, Truman Library.
   "There's a driving force": H. S. Truman to B. W. Truman, June 22, 1935.
   "arranging a compromise": "Pendergast, Jailed Boss, Poor Guesser on Horses," *Daily Boston Globe*, May 28, 1939.

79 *"Pendergast has been a good"*: Truman Didn't Seek Presidency – It Came," *Washington Post*, April 16, 1945.
   "The terrible things done": H. S. Truman to B. W. Truman, October 1, 1935, FBPAP:FCF, box 8.

"Never before or since": Truman, *Harry S. Truman*, p. 117.

"I feel as if my four years": Ibid.

"There is nothing more pitiful": Oral history interview, George Tames, p. 37, Truman Library.

"Everybody keeps telling me": Truman, *Harry S. Truman*, p. 118.

Chapter 10

80 *"scared stiff"*: Norman Beasley, *Knudsen: A Biography* (New York: McGraw-Hill, 1947), p. 164.

"Airplanes! Airplanes!": Ibid.

"aerial attacks, stupendous": "The Meaning of 'Blitzkrieg,'" *New York Times*, April 5, 1940.

81 *"little chance of renomination"*: "Pendergast Term Called 'Too Light,'" *New York Times*, May 24, 1939.

"I'll beat the hell": "Stark to Run for Truman's Seat in Senate," *Washington Post*, June 24, 1939.

"Harry, I don't think": Jonathan Daniels, *The Man of Independence* (Port Washington, NY: Kennikat, 1971), p. 198.

"He had very little backing": Oral history interview, John W. Snyder, pp. 64–65, Truman Library.

"I'm going to file": Daniels, *Man of Independence*, pp. 198–99.

"The Senator will not": Snyder oral history, pp. 60–62.

"We didn't give him": Oral history interview, A. J. Granoff, p. 86, Truman Library.

82 *"I had a bank balance"*: Margaret Truman, *Harry S. Truman* (New York: William Morrow, 1973), p. 124.

"An effort should be made": Campaign update no. 1, Victor R. Messall Papers, box 10, Truman Library.

"At 16, I was able to feel": Truman, *Harry S. Truman*, pp. 127–28.

"I believe in the brotherhood": Truman speech, Messall Papers, box 10.

"I think that was the all-time": Oral history interview, Harry H. Vaughan, p. 32, Truman Library.

"a dead cock in the pit": Alonzo L. Hamby, *Man of the People: A Life of Harry S. Truman* (New York: Oxford University Press, 1995), p. 235.

"Without fraudulent votes": Excerpt of article quoted in letter to editor, *Kansas City Star*, June 25, 1940, Messall Papers, box 11, Truman Library.

"Truman is through": Truman, *Harry S. Truman*, p. 123.

83 *"The President asks me"*: Stephen Early to R. H. Wadlow, chairman of Truman Labor Reception Committee, July 30, 1940, PPF, file 6337, Franklin D. Roosevelt Papers, Franklin D. Roosevelt Presidential Library, Hyde Park, NY.

"owes his place to the notorious": "Embarrassing the President?," *Christian Science Monitor*, August 2, 1940.

"I'm going to bed": Truman, *Harry S. Truman*, p. 133.

"This is Dave Berenstein": Ibid.

84 *"I thought Wheeler"*: Harry S. Truman to Bess W. Truman, August 10, 1940,
FBPAP:FCF, box 11, Truman Papers.
"fateful," for it was: Truman, *Harry S. Truman*, p. 138.
"I am introducing": Harry S. Truman, speech on the Senate floor,
Congressional Record, February 10, 1940.
"Guns, planes, ships": Franklin D. Roosevelt, "The Great Arsenal of
Democracy," *American Rhetoric: The Top 100 Speeches*, http://www.american
rhetoric.com/speeches/fdrarsenalofdemocracy.html.

85 *"probably signifies the entry"*: Truman, *Congressional Record*, February 10, 1940.
"aircraft factories in San Diego": Ibid.

86 *"Come in," Truman said:* Oral history interview, Matthew J. Connelly, pp. 2–3,
Truman Library.
"a big fat fellow": Daniels, *Man of Independence*, p. 224.
"a man who could look": Oral history interview, Wilbur D. Sparks, p. 106,
Truman Library.
"There is no substitute": *Memoirs by Harry S. Truman: 1945; Year of Decisions*
(New York: Konecky & Konecky, 1955), p. 168.
"If our plans for military": "Billions Waste on Arms Charged," *Chicago Tribune*,
August 15, 1941.
"Hugh was a brilliant": Oral history interview, Robert L. Irvin, p. 39, Truman
Library.

87 *"It was very widely seized"*: Connelly oral history, p. 21.
"This is Roy Webb": Truman's account of his day on December 7, 1941,
from H. S. Truman to Mary Ethel Noland, December 14, 1941, Mary Ethel
Noland Papers, box 1, Truman Library. Dialogue is from "How the President
Remembers Pearl Harbor," *Los Angeles Times*, December 2, 1951.

88 *"Vice President . . . Mr. Speaker"*: Franklin D. Roosevelt, Day of Infamy speech,
https://www.youtube.com/watch?v=8bmYwEFWLI.g.
"To thousands": "Truman Report Wins Author Popularity," *Washington Post*,
March 8, 1942.

89 *"My committee has had"*: Truman, *Harry S. Truman*, p. 144.
"He's so damn afraid": H. S. Truman to B. W. Truman, December 21, 1941,
FBPAP:FCF, box 12.
"He had tremendous personal": Irvin oral history, p. 59.
"had served as watchdog": "Billion-Dollar Watchdog," *Time*, March 8, 1943.

Chapter 11

91 *"beating too fast"*: Physician notes, April 19, 1943, Truman Papers, https://
www.trumanlibrary.org/whistlestop/study_collections/militarypersonnelfile
/display/index.php?documentid=RG407nlhst-359&documentVersion=both.
126/86: Ibid.
"He works under a great deal": Ibid.
"I just always had": Oral history interview, Shirley Key Hehmeyer, p. 29,
Truman Library.

92 *"Dad has been through"*: Bess W. Truman to Margaret Truman, n.d., Bess W. Truman Papers, box 88, Truman Library.

"Something's going on": Oral history interview, Matthew J. Connelly, p. 75, Truman Library.

SECRETARY OF WAR: *"Hello"*: Transcript from Henry Lewis Stimson Papers, microfilm roll 127, Yale University Library.

93 *"the lunatic fringe"*: Thomas H. Ferrell, *Choosing Truman: The Democratic Convention of 1944* (Columbia: University of Missouri Press, 1994), p. 33.

only one in fifty Democratic voters: "Wallace Gets 4–1 Indorsement [*sic*] in Gallup Poll," *Boston Globe,* July 19, 1944.

94 *"You are not nominating"*: Jonathan Daniels, *The Man of Independence* (Port Washington, NY: Kennikat, 1971), p. 237.

"Truman will nominate": Tom Connally, as told to Alfred Steinberg, *My Name Is Tom Connally* (New York: Thomas W. Crowell, 1954), p. 268.

"the 'White House' has decided": Allen Drury, *A Senate Journal: 1943–1945* (New York: McGraw-Hill, 1963), p. 210.

95 *"in charge of that war"*: Ferrell, *Choosing Truman,* p. 7.

"I hardly know Truman": Ibid.

96 *"Now, Bob"*: Conversation according to Edwin Pauley, who was in the room, oral history interview, Edwin W. Pauley, p. 20, Truman Library.

"Boys, I guess it's Truman": Ferrell, *Choosing Truman,* p. 102, footnote 28.

"Truman just dropped into": Jonathan Daniels, "How Truman Got to Be President," *Look,* August 1, 1950.

"Roosevelt was ducking": Pauley oral history, p. 23.

"Harry," said Hannegan: Daniels, "How Truman Got to Be President."

97 *"I'm looking at the other"*: Ferrell, *Choosing Truman,* p. 53.

"What are you doing": Oral history interview, Tom L. Evans, p. 434, Truman Library.

"Well, I don't want to drag": Ibid., pp. 335–35a.

99 *"Dear Bob [Hannegan]"*: Ferrell, *Choosing Truman,* p. 81.

"I have been associated with": "Wallace Left to Delegates by Roosevelt," *New York Times,* July 18, 1944.

100 *The* Washington Post *was saying:* Ibid.

Wallace was "out": "Capital Sees Wallace 'Out' as Nominee," *Los Angeles Times,* July 13, 1944.

"prominently in the advance": "Wallace Left to Delegates."

"Frank, go all out": Ferrell, *Presidential Leadership: From Woodrow Wilson to Harry S. Truman* (Columbia: University of Missouri Press), p. 124.

Chapter 12

101 *"In the room was a number"*: Oral history interview, Tom L. Evans, p. 355, Truman Library.

"Whenever Roosevelt used": Memoirs by Harry S. Truman: 1945; Year of Decisions (New York: Konecky & Konecky, 1955), p. 192.

"Bob," Roosevelt said: Ibid.

"Well, I just think": Evans oral history, p. 356.

102 *"I'll do it":* Ibid.

"I've just told the president": Ibid.

"one who is endowed": Democratic National Convention newsreel, https://www.youtube.com/watch?v=xfbUYkLm67k.

103 *"You seem to be":* Conversation from "President Favors Truman, Douglas," *New York Times,* July 21, 1944.

"We want Wallace!": DNC newsreel.

"To say the place became": Oral history interview, Edwin W. Pauley, p. 30, Truman Library.

"bedlam broke out": Oral history interview, Neale Roach, p. 24, Truman Library online.

"Stop that organ!": Ibid., p. 25.

104 *"By the authority":* Pauley oral history, p. 33.

"high pitch of excitement": "Second Place Race Sets Session Afire," *New York Times,* July 22, 1944.

HITLER EXECUTES PLOTTERS!: "Hitler Executes Plotters!" *Chicago Tribune,* July 21, 1944.

"extemporaneously": "Second Place Race."

"all the qualities": Ibid.

105 *"I reveled in the pandemonium":* Margaret Truman, *Bess W. Truman* (New York: Macmillan, 1986), p. 230.

"Mother was barely able": Ibid.

"There being 1,176": DNC newsreel.

"Will the next Vice President": Thomas H. Ferrell, *Choosing Truman: The Democratic Convention of 1944* (Columbia: University of Missouri Press, 1994), p. 89.

"By golly," he said: Ibid.

"help shorten the war": DNC newsreel.

"I don't know what else": Margaret Truman, *Harry S. Truman* (New York: William Morrow, 1973), p. 182.

106 *"We were blinded":* Truman, *Bess W. Truman,* p. 231.

"Are we going to have to": Ibid.

"Few people can hate": Allen Drury, *A Senate Journal: 1943–1945* (New York: McGraw-Hill, 1963), p. 219.

"How does it feel": Conversation from "Truman Campaign Up to President," *New York Times,* July 22, 1944.

"I never have and I never": "Bess Truman Leaves Politics to Her Husband," *Chicago Daily Tribune,* July 22, 1944.

Chapter 13

107 *"It was obvious sincerity":* Oral history interview, Walter Hehmeyer, p. 84, Truman Library.

"This is the kind of man": Ibid.

"the Missouri Compromise": Drew Pearson, "Washington Merry-Go-Round," July 28, 1944, *Washington Post*.

"He is no great campaigner": "Missouri Compromise," *Christian Science Monitor*, July 22, 1944.

"Poor Harry Truman": David McCullough, *Truman* (New York: Touchstone, 1993), p. 320.

"I would rather have": "Mrs. Truman, 91, Wanted Son to Stay in Senate," *Chicago Daily Tribune*, July 22, 1944.

"He did not want it": "Truman's Mother Prefers Son in Senate Post," *Atlanta Constitution*, July 22, 1944.

108 *"You'd have thought I was"*: Harry S. Truman to Bess W. Truman, August 18, 1944, FBPAP:FCF, box 14, Truman Papers.

"One of us has to stay": Margaret Truman, *Harry S. Truman* (New York: William Morrow, 1973), p. 186.

"the flash light newspaper": Harry S. Truman to Margaret Truman, August 18, 1944, reprinted in ibid., pp. 184–85.

"You know," Truman said: Oral history interview, Harry H. Vaughan, p. 77, Truman Library.

"What do I know about politics?": Oral history interview, Matthew Connelly, p. 102, Truman Library.

"Nobody knew whether or not": Oral history interview, Edward D. McKim, p. 117, Truman Library.

109 *"His voice is good but"*: Allen Drury, *A Senate Journal: 1943–1945* (New York: McGraw-Hill, 1963), p. 246.

"one of the most amazing": "Truman's Story That of Average American Citizen," *Boston Daily Globe*, July 23, 1944.

"There will be no time": "Truman Tells Voters to Shun Inexperience," *Washington Post*, September 1, 1944.

"Payroll Bess": "Bess Truman Is Dead at 97," *New York Times*, October 18, 1982.

"Meet Truman, Pendergast's": "Meet Truman, Pendergast's Oiler of Roads," *Chicago Daily Tribune*, September 13, 1944.

"Truman Reign in County": "Truman Reign in County an Epic of Waste," *Chicago Daily Tribune*, September 14, 1944.

110 *"Jonathan was worried"*: George E. Allen, *Presidents Who Have Known Me* (New York: Simon & Schuster, 1960), p. 145.

"It shook the whole universe": Oral history interview, Tom L. Evans, p. 412, Truman Library.

"We are unalterably opposed": Jonathan Daniels, *The Man of Independence* (Port Washington, NY: Kennikat, 1971), p. 126.

"Ask yourself if you want": "Truman Welcomed by His Home Town," *New York Times*, November 5, 1944.

"Everybody around here": "Truman Plays Paderewski as Missouri Slips," *Boston Daily Globe*, November 8, 1944.

"Wow," Truman said: Ibid.

111 *"[Truman] told me that the last"*: Oral history interview, Harry Easley, pp. 98–99, Truman Library.

"Hon. Harry S. Truman": Franklin D. Roosevelt to Truman, November 8, 1944,

PPF:6337, Franklin D. Roosevelt Papers, Franklin D. Roosevelt Presidential Library, Hyde Park, NY.

The Marine Band played: "Program of the Ceremonies Attending the Inauguration," Alonzo Fields Papers, box 1, Truman Library.

112 *"We have learned to be":* "Roosevelt's Inaugural Address Text," *Washington Post,* January 21, 1945.

"I suddenly found myself": Truman, *Harry S. Truman,* p. 195.

"Jimmy, I can't take this": Doris Kearns Goodwin, *No Ordinary Time: Franklin & Eleanor Roosevelt; The Home Front in World War II* (New York: Simon & Schuster, 1994), p. 573.

"Now you behave yourself": "Truman Memoirs: Part 3," *Life,* October 10, 1955.

113 *"I've got some bad news":* Conversation from oral history interview, Matthew J. Connelly, p. 117, Truman Library.

114 *"Do the suicides mean":* "Timeline: The War in the Pacific," on website for *Victory in the Pacific,* WGBH *American Experience,* PBS, http://www.pbs.org /wgbh/americanexperience/features/timeline/victory/%3Fflavour%3Dmobile.

"We now have ample proof": Robert J. Donovan, *Conflict and Crisis: The Presidency of Harry S. Truman, 1945–1948* (Columbia: University of Missouri Press, 1977), p. 12.

"He never regarded the new": Oral history interview, Thomas C. Blaisdell, p. 63, Truman Library.

"I was custodian": William M. Rigdon, *White House Sailor* (Garden City, NY: Doubleday, 1962), p. 183.

"The second office": Jon Meacham, *Thomas Jefferson: The Art of Power* (New York: Random House, 2013), p. 305.

Chapter 14

117 *"Come on in, Tony":* Truman, President's Memorandum, April 13, 1945, Eben A. Ayers Papers, box 10, Truman Library. Also: "Truman Says He'll Miss Visits by 'Buddies,'" *Washington Post,* April 14, 1945.

"You know, if I could": "Truman Says He'll Miss Visits."

"My," Truman said, smiling: "Party Lines Yield as New President Consults Leaders," *Atlanta Constitution,* April 14, 1945.

"No, nothing beyond what": Ibid.

118 *"Men stood mob-thick":* Jonathan Daniels, *Frontier on the Potomac* (New York: Macmillan, 1946), p. 25.

"It was an amazing day": Oral history interview, Jonathan Daniels, p. 58, Truman Library.

"as if he were testing": Jonathan Daniels, *The Man of Independence* (Port Washington, NY: Kennikat, 1971), p. 27.

"They were confused": Oral history interview, Matthew J. Connelly, p. 127, Truman Library.

"I had no idea": Oral history interview, Eben A. Ayers, p. 10, Truman Library.

"I was frightened to death": Oral history interview, Reathel Odum, p. 44, Truman Library.

119 *"Well, Mr. President," McKim said, "it doesn't":* Conversation from oral history interview, Edward D. McKim, p. 125, Truman Library.

"No man ever came": "The Task of President Truman," *Los Angeles Times,* April 14, 1945.

"almost superhuman task": "President Truman," *Wall Street Journal,* April 13, 1945.

"Riding to work this morning": Diary of Arthur Vandenberg, excerpted in Arthur Vandenberg, Jr., ed., *The Private Papers of Senator Vandenberg* (Boston: Houghton Mifflin, 1952), p. 167.

"No Alexander, or Caesar": "Remarks of Mr. Justice Jackson," April 13, 1945, PPF, box 8, Truman Papers.

120 *the latest War Department figures:* "U.S. Army Casualties," "U.S. Navy Casualties" [includes Marines and Coast Guard], April 14, 1945, figures as of March 31, 1945, Henry Lewis Stimson Papers, microfilm reel 112, Yale University Library.

"Every single man, woman, and child": Franklin D. Roosevelt, "The Great Arsenal of Democracy," "*American Rhetoric: The Top 100 Speeches,* http://www .americanrhetoric.com/speeches/fdrarsenalofdemocracy.html.

In one factory, situated: Much of this paragraph from A. J. Baime, *The Arsenal of Democracy: FDR, Detroit, and an Epic Quest to Arm an America at War* (Boston: Houghton Mifflin Harcourt, 2014).

"the country of machines": Ibid., p. 257.

121 *"I have seen a great many":* Ed Cray, *General of the Army: George C. Marshall, Soldier and Statesman* (New York: Cooper Square, 2000), foreword.

"One cannot yet see": Henry H. Adams, *Witness to Power: The Life of Fleet Admiral William D. Leahy* (Annapolis, MD: Naval Institute Press, 1985), p. 280.

"Take as long as you want": The Diaries of Edward R. Stettinius, Jr., 1943–1946, eds. Thomas M. Campbell and George C. Herring (New York: New Viewpoints, 1975), p. 317.

"I have decided that": Ibid.

122 *"Do you wish me to take":* Ibid., p. 318.

"They were brief": Memoirs by Harry S. Truman: 1945; Year of Decisions (New York: Konecky & Konecky, 1955), p. 17.

"favorable": Diary of Henry L. Stimson, April 13, 1945, Henry Lewis Stimson Papers, Yale University Library.

123 *"bush leaguer":* Adams, *Witness to Power,* p. 282.

"I want you to do the same": Conversation from William D. Leahy, *I Was There: The Personal Story of the Chief of Staff to Presidents Roosevelt and Truman Based on His Notes and Diaries Made at the Time* (New York: Whittlesey House, 1950), pp. 347–48.

At exactly 12:15 p.m.: Presidential Movement Logs, box 1, Records of the U.S. Secret Service, Truman Library.

"Biffle's Tavern": Description of this meeting in Truman, President's Memorandum, April 13, 1945.

124 *"It shattered all tradition":* Vandenberg, *Private Papers,* p. 167.

"It means that the days": Ibid.

"[A] president who didn't have": Harry S. Truman, Speech on Presidential Power, May 8, 1954, printed in *The Power of the Presidency: Concepts*

and Controversy, ed. Robert S. Hirschfield (New Brunswick, NJ: Aldine Transaction, 2012), p. 118.

"Our swan song": Vandenberg, *Private Papers,* p. 167.

"I am coming and prepare for it": Truman, President's Memorandum, April 13, 1945.

"terrible job": David McCullough, *Truman* (New York: Touchstone, 1993), p. 353.

"I'm not big enough": Robert J. Donovan, *Conflict and Crisis: The Presidency of Harry S. Truman, 1945–1948* (Columbia: University of Missouri Press, 1977), p. 15.

"Well, isn't this nice": Conversation from Allen Drury, *A Senate Journal: 1943–1945* (New York: McGraw-Hill, 1963), p. 413.

125 *"We had called him Harry":* Oral history interview, Jack L. Bell, p. 34, Truman Library.

"I don't know if any of you fellows": "President Asks Aid, Prayers from Nation," *Daily Boston Globe,* April 14, 1945.

"If newspapermen ever pray": "New President's First Day on Job Is Crowded One," *Chicago Tribune,* April 14, 1945.

"If I can be of service": Francis X. Winters, *Remember Hiroshima: Was It Just?* (London: Taylor & Francis/Ashgate, 2009), p. 173.

"everything under the sun": Truman, President's Memorandum, April 13, 1945.

126 *"practically jumped down":* Margaret Truman, *Harry S. Truman* (New York: William Morrow, 1973), p. 218.

"With great solemnity": Truman, *Memoirs,* p. 11.

"the bomb might well put us": Ibid., p. 87.

"deteriorated": Campbell and Herring, *Diaries of Edward R. Stettinius,* p. 318.

"I had not met Truman": Charles E. Bohlen, *Witness to History: 1929–1969* (New York: W. W. Norton, 1973), p. 212.

127 *"For the Soviets," Bohlen:* Ibid., p. 188.

"He gave me the impression": Description of this meeting in Truman, President's Memorandum, April 13, 1945. Quotes from Campbell and Herring, *Diaries of Edward R. Stettinius,* p. 318.

"In speaking of President Roosevelt": W. Averell Harriman to Harry S. Truman, April 13, 1945, SMOF:MRF, box 1, Truman Papers.

128 *"There are . . . urgent problems":* Harry S. Truman to Winston S. Churchill, April 13, 1945, SMOF:MRF, box 2, Truman Papers.

Chapter 15

129 *"We have an army":* Diary of Margaret Truman, April 13, 1945, Margaret Truman Papers, box 13, Truman Library.

"There was no escaping": *Memoirs by Harry S. Truman: 1945; Year of Decisions* (New York: Konecky & Konecky, 1955), p. 11.

"bring [Truman] up-to-date": "Memorandum to Mr. Connelly," April 13, 1945, PSF, box 164, Truman Papers.

"The British long for security": "Special Information for the President," April 13, 1945, PSF, box 164, Truman Papers.

130 *"from time to time put forward"*: Ibid.

"A problem of urgent importance": Ibid.

"The plain story is this": Truman, *Memoirs*, p. 23.

131 *"create democratic institutions"*: "Crimea Conference, 1945, Report Signed at Yalta February 11, 1945," text at Library of Congress website, https://www.loc .gov/law/help/us-treaties/bevans/m-ust00003-1005.pdf.

"There are literally thousands": John Lewis Gaddis, *The United States and the Origins of the Cold War, 1941–1947* (New York: Columbia University Press, 1972), p. 139.

"We Americans are not": Ibid., p. 140.

"I doubt that there have been": Oral history interview, Jonathan Daniels, p. 57, Truman Library.

132 *"There is a feeling of"*: Robert H. Ferrell, ed., *Truman in the White House: The Diary of Eben A. Ayers* (Columbia: University of Missouri Press, 1991), p. 11.

"I don't think you ought": Truman, *Memoirs*, p. 23.

"Harry, you forget who": Oral history interview, John W. Snyder, p. 164, Truman Library.

"Did he make that": Truman, *Memoirs*, p. 23.

133 *"I think I admired Mr. Roosevelt"*: Conversation from the diary of Henry Morgenthau, Jr., April 14, 1945, Franklin D. Roosevelt Presidential Library, http://www.fdrlibrary.marist.edu/_resources/images/morg/mpd19.pdf.

"Truman has a mind of his own": Ibid.

134 *"I'm sure this modest man"*: Robert E. Sherwood, *Roosevelt and Hopkins: An Intimate History* (New York: Harper & Brothers, 1948), p. 881.

"Old and young were crying": Truman diary, April 13, 1945, PSF, box 68, Truman Papers.

"Now, the real politicking": Margaret Truman, *Harry S. Truman* (New York: William Morrow, 1973), p. 224.

135 *he prayed that he would be:* Truman, *Memoirs*, p. 37.

tears were rolling from: "Mrs. Truman in Tears," *New York Times*, April 17, 1945.

"Dad was terribly nervous": Truman, *Harry S. Truman*, p. 224.

"Just a minute, Harry": Ibid.

"Mr. Speaker": First speech as president, Harry Truman, https://www .youtube.com/watch?v=yEbkO9aov-M.

136 *Secret service logged:* Presidential Movement Logs, box 1, Records of the U.S. Secret Service, Truman Library.

"Personal and Secret from": Truman to Averell Harriman, April 16, 1945, MRF, box 2, Truman Papers.

137 *"You're impugning the loyalty"*: W. Averell Harriman and Elie Abel, *Special Envoy to Churchill and Stalin 1941–1946* (New York: Random House, 1975), p. 446.

"The President has left": Jonathan Daniels, *Frontier on the Hudson* (New York: Macmillan, 1946), p. 12.

"Little did you think": Rufus B. Burrus to Harry S. Truman, April 13, 1945, Rufus B. Burrus Papers, box 20, Truman Library.

"You are a good man, Harry": C. D. Hicks to Truman, April 13, 1945,
WHCF:PPF, box 479, Truman Papers.

"You know that I am not": Eddie Jacobson to Truman, May 10, 1945,
WHCF:PPF, box 185, Truman Papers.

138 *"I have had the most momentous"*: Harry S. Truman to Martha Ellen
Truman and Mary Jane Truman, April 16, 1945, FBPAP:FCF, box 19,
Truman Papers.

Chapter 16

139 *"Being President is like"*: Harry S. Truman, "The Truman Memoirs," *Life*,
January 23, 1956.

"It takes about 17 hours": *Decision: The Conflicts of Harry S. Truman*, Motion
Picture Collection, Truman Library.

"This limousine-infested Capital": "Truman Walks to Work – Breaking Another
Precedent," newspaper clipping, Victor R. Messall Papers, box 7, Truman
Library.

"Good luck, Harry!": "Truman Starts Another Week at Furious Pace," *Chicago
Daily Tribune*, April 20, 1945.

140 *"capacity for drink"*: Diary of Eben A. Ayers, May 4, 1945, excerpted in
Robert H. Ferrell, ed., *Truman in the White House: The Diary of Eben A. Ayers*
(Columbia: University of Missouri Press, 1991), p. 18.

"I don't like the son-of-a-bitch": Ibid., p. 17.

official meetings schedule: Truman daily calendar, April 17, 1945, https://www
.trumanlibrary.org/calendar/main.php?currYear=1945&currMonth=4&curr
Day=17.

"slowly and with feeling": Notes on meeting with S. J. Wolf, B-File, referring to
"That Dream Will Come True," *New York Times Sunday Magazine*, July 15, 1945,
B-File, Truman Papers.

141 *"Good morning"*: Transcript of press conference, April 17, 1945, PSF:PCF, box
51, Truman Papers.

"We all knew that Roosevelt": Oral history interview, Robert G. Nixon, p. 152,
Truman Library.

"The first thing I want": Transcript of press conference, April 17, 1945.

142 *"His first press conferences"*: Oral history interview, Jonathan Daniels, p. 77,
Truman Library.

"modern noise": "It is not noise. It is music," Harry Truman's Record Albums,
Harry S. Truman National Historic Site, National Park Service, https://www
.nps.gov/hstr/learn/historyculture/truman-record-collection.htm.

Madame Tussauds of London: Office of War Information, memorandum re:
Madame Tussauds, May 10, 1945, Truman Papers, https://www.trumanlibrary
.org/whistlestop/trumanfile/truman-tussaud.htm.

"If Harry Truman can be President": Program transcript, *Truman*, WGBH
American Experience, PBS.org, www.pbs.org/wgbh/americanexperience
/features/. . . /truman-transcript/.

"Mr. and Mrs. Truman lived so": "Dear Washington," *Washington Times-Herald*, clipping, n.d., Victor R. Messall Papers, box 7, Truman Library.

"He brings to the White House": "Truman's Record Shows Practical Prudent Man," *New York Times*, April 15, 1945.

143 *"seen a good deal of [Truman]"*: Joseph C. Grew to Cecil Lyon, May 2, 1945, quoted in a footnote to Department of State memorandum of conversation, May 19, 1945, Official File, box 1928, Truman Papers.

"When I saw him today": John Lewis Gaddis, *The United States and the Origins of the Cold War, 1941–1947* (New York: Columbia University Press, 1972), p. 199.

"Personally," Leahy wrote: William D. Leahy, *I Was There: The Personal Story of the Chief of Staff to Presidents Roosevelt and Truman Based on His Notes and Diaries Made at the Time* (New York: Whittlesey House, 1950), p. 349.

"How do you spell your name?": Transcript of this press conference, April 17, 1945, Matthew Connelly Papers, Truman Library.

"Back to school and photographers": Diary of Margaret Truman, April 17, 1945, Margaret Truman Papers, box 13, Truman Library.

144 *"Few citizens of the capital"*: "Bess Truman Insists Upon Being Herself," *Washington Post*, April 29, 1945.

"My first thought was that": "Truman's Home Town Trusts Him as a Leader," *Atlanta Constitution*, April 15, 1945.

"If he'd have been voted in": "Truman's Mother 'Not Really Glad,'" *Chicago Daily Tribune*, April 17, 1945.

"I told them that my family": Harry S. Truman to Martha Ellen Truman and Mary Jane Truman, April 18, 1945, FBPAP:FCF, box 19, Truman Library.

"Everywhere one hears the remark": "Man from Missouri," *Fortune*, July 1945.

"Few Presidents in history": Diary of Allen Drury, Allen Drury, *A Senate Journal: 1943–1945* (New York: McGraw-Hill, 1963), p. 417.

145 *"Harry Truman is a man of"*: Quoted in Margaret Truman, *Harry S. Truman* (New York: William Morrow, 1973), p. 221.

"He shared so many moments": Margaret Truman, *Bess W. Truman* (New York: Macmillan, 1986), p. 288.

"She was not sure he could": Ibid.

Chapter 17

146 *"large numbers of enemy aircraft"*: "Jap Suicide Flyers Sink Destroyer at Okinawa," *Los Angeles Times*, April 13, 1945.

"but never so extensively": John Lardner, "A Reporter on Okinawa," *New Yorker*, May 19, 1945.

"a branch of hysteria": Ibid.

147 *"We saw great clouds of black"*: "B-29's Set Great Tokyo Fires," *New York Times*, April 14, 1945.

Soon after this mission: "Could Wipe Out Jap Industry, B-29 Head Says," *Washington Post*, April 15, 1945.

"You go ahead and get": Curtis E. LeMay with MacKinlay Kantor, *Mission with LeMay: My Story* (New York: Doubleday, 1965), p. 347.

148 *"Our attempts to bomb precision"*: Curtis E. LeMay to General H. H. Arnold, April 5, 1945, Curtis E. LeMay Papers, box 11, Manuscript Division, Library of Congress, Washington, DC.

"It was against this background": "Analysis of Incendiary Phase of Operations," March 9–19, 1945, Headquarters XXI Bomber Command, LeMay Papers, box 37.

"the ruthless bombing from the air": Franklin D. Roosevelt, "Appeal to Russia and Finland to Stop Bombing Civilians," December 1, 1939, http://www.presidency.ucsb.edu/ws/?pid=15845.

"inhuman barbarism": Ibid.

"home industries carried on": "Analysis of Incendiary Phase," LeMay Papers.

149 *"The bombs from a single"*: Ibid.

"I'm sweating this one": St. Clair McKelway, "A Reporter with the B-29s," *New Yorker,* June 23, 1945.

"I was a machine": LeMay and Kantor, *Mission with LeMay,* p. 218.

"A quick glance at the map": Arnold to LeMay, April 18, 1945, LeMay Papers, box 11.

150 *"Anything you have seen"*: "Allies Free 39,000 in Nazi Horror Camp," *Christian Science Monitor,* April 20, 1945.

"There were children": "2d Army Frees 29,000 in Nazi Horror Camp," *Chicago Daily Tribune,* April 19, 1945.

"And now, let me tell you": Edward R. Murrow, *In Search of Light: The Broadcasts of Edward R. Murrow, 1938–1961* (New York: Alfred A. Knopf, 1967), pp. 90–95.

151 *"There is complete economic"*: McCloy's report is excerpted in *Memoirs by Harry S. Truman: 1945; Year of Decisions* (New York: Konecky & Konecky, 1955), pp. 102–4.

"without drastic action": Memorandum for the president: "Review of Food Supply," April 16, 1945, PSF, box 104, Truman Papers.

152 *"Why should we not cross"*: Winston S. Churchill to Dwight D. Eisenhower, March 31, 1945, reprinted in Winston S. Churchill, *The Second World War,* vol. 6, *Triumph and Tragedy* (New York: Bantam, 1962), p. 397.

"raise grave and formidable": Churchill to Franklin D. Roosevelt, April 1, 1945, reprinted in ibid., p. 399.

Eisenhower chose to halt: Covered extensively in Dwight D. Eisenhower, *Crusade in Europe* (New York: Avon, 1952). For a concise version, see "Why Eisenhower Halted at the Elbe," *Christian Science Monitor,* April 10, 1995.

"The armies had outrun": Henry L. Stimson and McGeorge Bundy, *On Active Service in Peace and War* (New York: Harper & Brothers, 1948), p. 566.

"In this atmosphere of disturbance": McCloy's report, pp. 102–4.

153 *"Mr. Secretary"*: Conversation from Henry Morgenthau, Jr., diaries, April 20, 1945, Franklin D. Roosevelt Presidential Library, http://www.fdrlibrary.marist.edu/_resources/images/morg/mpd19.pdf.

fiscal year spending for 1945: Memorandum for the president, "Financing the War," PSF, box 139, Truman Papers.

"public authority must be": John Maynard Keynes, "An Open Letter to President Roosevelt," December 16, 1933, http://la.utexas.edu/users/hcleaver /368/368KeynesOpenLetFDRtable.pdf.

155 *"The quickest Cabinet meeting"*: Diary of Henry L. Stimson, April 20, 1945, Henry Lewis Stimson Papers, Yale University Library.

"He was very vigorous": *The Price of Vision: The Diary of Henry A. Wallace 1942–1946*, ed. John Morton Blum (Boston: Houghton Mifflin, 1973), p. 437.

"a fine man, good looking": Descriptions of cabinet members from Harry S. Truman to Jonathan Daniels, February 26, 1950 (unsent), published in *Off the Record: The Private Papers of Harry S. Truman*, ed. Robert H. Ferrell (Columbia: University of Missouri Press, 1980), p. 174.

156 *"Matt," Truman barked:* Conversation from oral history interview, Matthew J. Connelly, p. 174, Truman Library.

157 *"Miss Tillie, who do you think"*: Ibid., p. 175.

"Boy, what a man": Ibid., p. 176.

"Charlie and I graduated": Transcript of press conference, April 20, 1945, PSF:PCF, box 51, Truman Papers.

"Chief Counsel for the United States": Executive Order no. 9547, May 2, 1945, https://www.trumanlibrary.org/executiveorders/index.php?pid=734.

"Dear Mamma + Mary": Harry S. Truman to Martha Ellen Truman and Mary Jane Truman, April 21, 1945, FBPAP:FCF, box 19, Truman Papers.

158 *"legal sheets"*: Oral history interview, Roberta Barrows, p. 50, Truman Library.

"I had to know their background": Ibid., p. 51.

"They are all major": Oral history interview, Edward D. McKim, p. 176, Truman Library.

"We have interests in": Edward R. Stettinius to Truman, April 18, 1945, PSF, box 161, Truman Papers.

"We want no Gestapo": Longhand note, May 12, 1945, PSF:LNF, box 283, Truman Papers.

159 *"Hitler was the one"*: A. J. Baime, *The Arsenal of Democracy: FDR, Detroit, and an Epic Quest to Arm an America at War* (Boston: Houghton Mifflin Harcourt, 2014), p. 174.

"Would you comment": "Truman Stands by Pro-Negro Senate Record," *Chicago Defender*, April 28, 1945.

Margaret had nine cavities: Diary of Bruce Forsyth, White House dentist, Bruce D. Forsyth Papers, box 1, Truman Library.

"We all wanted to see Harry": "Time Out for Cronies," *Washington Star*, April 19, 1945, Fred Canfil Papers, box 3, Truman Library.

"I was saying goodbye to": Quotes in Doris Kearns Goodwin, *No Ordinary Time: Franklin & Eleanor Roosevlet: The Home Front in World War II* (New York: Simon & Schuster Paperbacks, 1994), p. 618.

160 *"The expression on Mother's face"*: Margaret Truman, *Bess W. Truman* (New York: Macmillan, 1986), p. 260.

Chapter 18

162 *"I want you to go over"*: W. Averell Harriman and Elie Abel, *Special Envoy to Churchill and Stalin 1941–1946* (New York: Random House, 1975), p. 3.
"[Harriman] recognized no interests": George F. Kennan, *Memoirs: 1925–1950* (Boston: Atlantic Monthly Press, 1967), pp. 232–34.

163 *"The Soviet Union had two"*: Memorandum of conversation, April 20, 1945, PSF, box 164, Truman Papers.
"a barbarian invasion": Ibid.
"And anyway," he said: David McCullough, *Truman* (New York: Touchstone, 1993), p. 371.
"[Truman] added that he intended": April 20, 1945, memorandum of conversation.

164 *"I gained great respect"*: Harriman and Abel, *Special Envoy*, p. 3.
"It would be a blessing": John Lewis Gaddis, *The United States and the Origins of the Cold War, 1941–1947* (New York: Columbia University Press, 1972), p. 159.
"GPU guys": Oral history interview, Elbridge Durbrow, p. 39, Truman Papers.
"I followed them around": Ibid.
"Real name is Skriabin": Department of State memorandum, "Molotov, Vyacheslav Mikhailovich: Biographical Sketch," April 20, 1945, PSF, box 164, Truman Papers.
"He has always carried out": Ibid.

165 *"the greatest admiration for"*: Department of State, memorandum of conversation, April 22, 1945, PSF, box 164, Truman Papers.
"It was now clear that": Memorandum of meeting at the White House, "2:00 PM, April 23," PSF, box 164, Truman Papers.
"It was now or never": Harriman and Abel, *Special Envoy*, p. 452.

166 *"The United States government could"*: Memorandum of conversation, April 23, 1945, PSF, box 164, Truman Papers.
"How I enjoyed translating": Charles E. Bohlen, *Witness to History: 1929–1969* (New York: W. W. Norton, 1973), p. 213.
"That will be all": Ibid.
"I have never been talked to": Harriman and Abel, *Special Envoy*, p. 453.
"a head-on collision": Diary of Henry L. Stimson, April 23, 1945, Henry Lewis Stimson Papers, Yale University Library.
"I did regret that Truman": Harriman and Abel, *Special Envoy*, p. 453.

167 *"I gave it to him straight"*: Diary of Joseph E. Davies, April 30, 1945, Joseph Edward Davies Papers, box 16, Manuscript Division, Library of Congress, Washington, DC.
"It would be too bad": Davies diary, April 30, 1945.

Chapter 19

168 *"There was little"*: Robert H. Ferrell, ed., *Truman in the White House: The Diary of Eben A. Ayers* (Columbia: University of Missouri Press, 1991), p. 14.

"as soon as possible on": Diary of Henry L. Stimson, April 24, 1945, Henry
Lewis Stimson Papers, Yale University Library.
Through a second door: Leslie L. Groves, report of meeting with the president,
April 25, 1945, Atomic Bomb Collection, box 1, Truman Library.
"Within four months we shall": Memorandum discussed with the president,
April 25, 1945, Stimson Papers.
"An atom is made up of": Memorandum for the secretary of war, April 23, 1945,
National Security Archives online, http://nsarchive.gwu.edu/NSAEBB
/NSAEBB162/3a.pdf.
169 *Manhattan District Project:* Ibid.
"The successful development": Ibid.
"the element uranium may be": Albert Einstein to Franklin D. Roosevelt,
August 2, 1939, Significant Documents Collection, box 1, Franklin D.
Roosevelt Presidential Library.
"Probably no other scientist": Arthur Holly Compton, *Atomic Quest: A Personal
Narrative* (New York: Oxford University Press, 1956), p. 30.
"Alex," Roosevelt said: Godfrey Hodgson, *The Colonel: The Life and Wars of
Henry Stimson 1867–1950* (New York: Alfred A. Knopf, 1990), p. 288.
"This needs action": Ibid.
170 *"Vannevar Bush came in"*: Stimson diary, November 6, 1941.
"I would spend so much": Forrest C. Pogue, *George C. Marshall: Statesman
1945–1959* (New York: Viking, 1987), p. 11.
"The laboratory will be": Leslie L. Groves to J. Robert Oppenheimer, February
25, 1943, Leslie L. Groves Papers, box 36, Manuscript Division, Library of
Congress, Washington, DC.
171 *"My two great loves"*: Kai Bird and Martin J. Sherwin, *American Prometheus:
The Triumph and Tragedy of J. Robert Oppenheimer* (New York: Vintage, 2005),
caption in photo insert.
"While I felt that the possibility": Leslie M. Groves, *Now It Can Be Told: The Story
of the Manhattan Project* (New York: Da Capo, 1962), p. 69.
"Never in history has anyone": Ibid., p. 72.
172 *"tube alloys"*: Numerous cables, such as Winston S. Churchill to Franklin D.
Roosevelt, March 20, 1943, Atomic Bomb File, box 1, Franklin D. Roosevelt
Presidential Library.
"with the scientists' prediction": James F. Byrnes, *Speaking Frankly* (New York:
Harper & Brothers, 1947), p. 257.
"By next summer this will": Vannevar Bush and James B. Conant to Henry L.
Stimson, cover letter to memorandum, "Salient Points Concerning Future
International Handling of Subject of Atomic Bombs," September 30, 1944,
National Archives. Also quoted in Amir D. Aczel, *Uranium Wars: The Scientific
Rivalry That Created the Nuclear Age* (New York: St. Martin's Griffin, 2009),
p. 204.
"We were up against some": Stimson diary, March 5, 1945.
173 *"intended by one fell, drastic"*: "Huge Reprisal Blow Threatened by Nazis," *New
York Times,* December 4, 1943.
"sold the president a lemon": Stimson diary, March 15, 1945.
"I understand that the expenditures": James F. Byrnes, memorandum for the

president, March 2, 1945, Selected Documents on the Topic of the Atomic Bomb, box 1, Franklin D. Roosevelt Presidential Library.

"within four months": Henry L. Stimson, memorandum discussed with the president, April 25, 1945, Stimson Papers.

174 *"A great deal of emphasis"*: Groves, report of April 25, 1945.

"be eventually at the mercy": April 25, 1945, memorandum, Stimson Papers.

"Is that you, Mr. President?": Transcript of conversation, April 25, 1945, William D. Leahy Papers, Records of the Joint Chiefs of Staff, box 6, National Archives, College Park, MD. Also: *Memoirs by Harry S. Truman: 1945; Year of Decisions* (New York: Konecky & Konecky, 1955), pp. 89–94.

"I think he [Himmler]": Ibid.

175 *"The conference began in"*: *New Yorker*, Talk of the Town, May 5, 1945.

176 *"I'm counting on you"*: *The Diaries of Edward R. Stettinius, Jr., 1943–1946*, eds. Thomas M. Campbell and George C. Herring (New York: New Viewpoints, 1975), p. 322.

"great humanitarian": Harry S. Truman, Address to the United Nations Conference in San Francisco, April 25, 1945, American Presidency Project, http://www.presidency.ucsb.edu/ws/?pid=12391.

"You members of this Conference": Ibid.

"It would be a relatively": Diary excerpted in Arthur Vandenberg, Jr., ed., *The Private Papers of Senator Vandenberg* (Boston: Houghton Mifflin, 1952), p. 156.

Chapter 20

178 *"Put it there"*: "Put It There," *Chicago Daily Tribune*, April 28, 1945.

"This is the Red Army": "Hitler's Redoubt Invaded," *Chicago Daily Tribune*, April 28, 1945.

"looked more like a giant": "Juncture of Two Allied Armies on Elbe River Bisects Germany," *Christian Science Monitor*, April 27, 1945.

179 *"The last faint, desperate"*: Statement by the President Announcing the Junction of Anglo-American and Soviet Forces in Germany, April 27, 1945, https://www.trumanlibrary.org/publicpapers/viewpapers.php?pid=19

"No! No!": "Cries No! No! As Partisan Shoot Him, Girl Friend," *Washington Post*, April 30, 1945.

"The brains which took Fascist": Ibid.

"understand the meaning of": Statement by the President on the Surrender of German Forces in Italy, May 2, 1945, https://www.trumanlibrary.org/public papers/viewpapers.php?pid=27.

"Hitler died at noon today": "Hitler Dead, Reports Insist," *Daily Boston Globe*, April 30, 1945.

180 *"The words were the comments"*: Jonathan Daniels, *Frontier on the Potomac* (New York: Macmillan, 1946), p. 25.

"Mr. President, would you care": Transcript of press conference, May 2, 1945, PSF:PCF, box 51, Truman Papers.

"Any person guilty": Press release, April 23, 1945, PSF, box 68, Truman Papers.

181 *"All resistance collapsed":* Dwight D. Eisenhower, *Crusade in Europe* (New York: Avon, 1952), p. 458.
　　more than 50 percent of children: Food for the Liberated Countries, address by Herbert Hoover, May 9, 1945, Henry Lewis Stimson Papers, microfilm reel 112, Yale University Library.
　　A third of children in Belgium: Ibid.
　　"It is now 11:59": Ibid.
　　"The needs of the liberated": White House press release re: report of Judge Samuel Rosenman, May 22, 1945, PSF, box 197, Truman Papers.
182 *"I fear terrible things":* Winston S. Churchill to Harry S. Truman, May 11, 1945, Naval Aide to the President File, box 7, Truman Papers.
　　"stick to my guns": Transcript of phone conversation in *The Diaries of Edward R. Stettinius, Jr., 1943–1946,* eds. Thomas M. Campbell and George C. Herring (New York: New Viewpoints, 1975), p. 339.
　　"It is precedent": Ibid.
　　"Stick to your guns": Ibid.
183 *"A serious shadow fell":* Diary excerpted in Arthur Vandenberg, Jr., *The Private Papers of Senator Vandenberg* (Boston: Houghton Mifflin, 1952), p. 185.
　　"Bohlen," Masaryk said: Charles E. Bohlen, *Witness to History: 1929–1969* (New York: W. W. Norton, 1973), p. 214.

Chapter 21

184 *A bill for $419.45:* Bill to National Park Service from Woodward & Lathrop, Washington, DC, Financial Affairs File, box 9, Bess W. Truman Papers, Truman Library.
　　"Cranks are just as likely": Ira Smith with Joe Alex Morris, *Dear Mr. President: The Story of Fifty Years in the White House Mail Room* (New York: Julian Messner, 1949), p. 217.
185 *the president's salary was:* Untitled document on president's salary and White House budget, Eben A. Ayers Papers, box 24, Truman Library.
　　"Visiting the White House in person": Margaret Truman, *The President's House: A First Daughter Shares the History and Secrets of the World's Most Famous Home* (New York: Ballantine, 2003), p. 7.
　　"Everything seems larger": Ibid., p. 10.
　　"dark, clunky furniture": Ibid., p. 212.
186 *"At 0241 hours this morning":* Supreme Headquarters, Allied Expeditionary Force, Rheims, France [Eisenhower's office], to War Department, Washington, DC, cable, May 7, 1945, William D. Leahy Papers, Records of the United States Joint Chiefs of Staff, box 5, record group 218, National Archives, College Park, MD.
　　"What is the use of me": Transcript of telephone conversation, May 7, 1945, ibid.
187 *"I have agreed with the London":* Statement by the President on the Timing of the Announcement of the German Surrender, May 7, 1945, https://www.trumanlibrary.org/publicpapers/viewpapers.php?pid=32.

"I am sixty-one this morning": Harry S. Truman to Martha Ellen Truman and Mary Jane Truman, May 8, 1945, FBPAP:FCF, box 19, Truman Papers.

"You're forty years old!": Transcript of press conference, May 8, 1945, PSF:PCF, box 51, Truman Papers.

188 *"Our victory is but half-won"*: Broadcast to the American People Announcing the Surrender of Germany, May 8, 1945, Audio Collection, Truman Library online, https://www.trumanlibrary.org/ww2/veday.htm.

"I can almost hear": Steve Neal, ed., *Eleanor and Harry: The Correspondence of Eleanor Roosevelt and Harry S. Truman* (New York: Citadel, 2002), p. 25.

189 *"at half-pace"*: "V-E Day Celebrations in the Nation Are Sporadic," *Wall Street Journal*, May 9, 1945.

"There are no words": Edward R. Murrow, *In Search of Light: The Broadcasts of Edward R. Murrow, 1938–1961* (New York: Alfred A. Knopf, 1967), p. 97.

"Our nation," Murrow said: Ibid.

"Things have moved at a terrific": H. S. Truman to M. E. Truman and M. J. Truman, May 8, 1945.

190 *"supervise, regulate, and control"*: Notes of an informal meeting of the Interim Committee (meeting minutes), May 8, 1945, Atomic Bomb Collection, Truman Library.

"Gentlemen, it is our": D. M. Giangreco and Kathryn Moore, *Dear Harry: Truman's Mailroom, 1945–1953* (Mechanicsburg, PA: Stackpole, 1999), p. 282.

191 *"Hiroshima is the largest"*: Notes on initial meeting of Target Committee (meeting minutes), April 27, 1945, National Security Archive online, http://nsarchive.gwu.edu/NSAEBB/NSAEBB162/4.pdf.

"thoroughly frightened": James F. Byrnes, *All in One Lifetime* (London: Museum, 1960), p. 283.

192 *"We saw, of course, what everybody"*: Transcript of conference, Special Committee of the Senate and House of Representatives Which Investigated Atrocities in Germany, May 9, 1945, Henry L. Stimson file, box 2, National Archives, College Park, MD.

"It seems to me that matters": Winston S. Churchill to Harry L. Truman, May 6, 1945, Naval Aide to the President File, box 7, Truman Papers.

193 *"I am unable to understand"*: Truman to Joseph Stalin, May 16, 1945, MRF, box 2, Truman Papers.

"using one excuse or another": Memorandum for the president, "The Current Situation in Bulgaria," May 3, 1945, William D. Leahy Papers, Records of the United States Joint Chiefs of Staff, box 1, record group 218, National Archives, College Park, MD.

"excludes the possibility": Stalin to Churchill, forwarded to Truman, reprinted in a memorandum for the secretary of state, May 9, 1945, SMOF: Naval Aide to the President Files, box 7, Truman Papers.

"There should now be no valid": Truman to Churchill, May 9, 1945, SMOF:MRF, box 1, Truman Papers.

194 *"Mr. President,"* he cabled: Churchill to Truman, May 12, 1945, SMOF: Naval Aide to the President File, box 7, Truman Papers.

Chapter 22

195 *"Oh, fiddlesticks!"*: Conversation from "President Spends Quiet Day with His 92-Year-Old Mother," *Washington Evening Star,* May 12, 1945; "Mother Visits Truman; Goes by Air at 92," *Chicago Daily Tribune,* May 12, 1945.
"wreathed in smiles": Ibid.
"She's certainly a grand old": "Truman's Mother Flies to Capital," *New York Times,* May 12, 1945.

196 *"Mamma," Truman said:* "Mother Truman – Portrait of a Rebel," *New York Times,* June 23, 1946.
"When he was a boy, Harry": Ibid.
"She is a dear little old": Diary of Joseph E. Davies, May 13, 1945, Joseph Edward Davies Papers, box 16, Manuscript Division, Library of Congress, Washington, DC.
"Isn't he a Yankee?": Margaret Truman, *Harry S. Truman* (New York: William Morrow, 1973), p. 245.
"Nothing they can say about me": Harry S. Truman to Martha Ellen Truman and Mary Jane Truman, June 19, 1945, FBPAP:FCF, box 19, Truman Papers.
"It is a terrible": H. S. Truman to M. E. Truman and M. J. Truman, April 29, 1945, FBPAP:FCF, box 19, Truman Papers.

198 ALWAYS DO RIGHT!: William E. Leuchtenburg, *The American President: From Teddy Roosevelt to Bill Clinton* (New York: Oxford University Press, 2015), p. 321.
"deliberately organized – or disorganized": Robert Dallek, *Franklin D. Roosevelt and American Foreign Policy, 1932–1945* (New York: Oxford University Press, 1995), p. 29.
"You have no idea": Oral history interview, Roberta Barrows, p. 56, Truman Library.
"By the way," Truman said: Oral history interview, Floyd M. Boring, p. 8, Truman Library.

199 *"Now look, I know you"*: Barrows oral history, p. 67.
"matching combinations of socks": Robert H. Ferrell, ed., *Truman in the White House: The Diary of Eben A. Ayers* (Columbia: University of Missouri Press, 1991), p. 24.
"That would have been too bad": Schwellenbach quoted in Henry A. Wallace diary, *The Price of Vision: The Diary of Henry A. Wallace, 1942–1946,* ed. John Morton Blum (Boston: Houghton Mifflin, 1973), p. 478.
"Just a few days after Truman": Oral history interview, Robert G. Nixon, p. 349, Truman Library.

200 *"You know, I'm almost"*: H. S. Truman to Bess W. Truman, August 12, 1946, FBPAP:FCF, box 15, Truman Papers.
"Kentucky bourbon": "Books of the Times: Memoirs of a (Maybe the) Washington Insider," *New York Times,* May 13, 1991.
"guarded his chips as though": Clark Clifford with Richard Holbrooke, *Counsel to the President: A Memoir* (New York: Random House, 1991), p. 70.
"Harry Vaughan was as out of place": Oral history interview, Walter Hehmeyer, p. 74, Truman Library.
"Potomac fever": Truman, *Harry S. Truman,* p. 215.

"Mrs. Roosevelt is no longer": Steve Neal, ed., *Eleanor and Harry: The Correspondence of Eleanor Roosevelt and Harry S. Truman* (New York: Citadel, 2002), p. 23.

"I just can't have him": Oral history interview, Harry Easley, pp. 111–12, Truman Library.

"Truman brought in a bunch": Nixon oral history, p. 170.

"How can I bring big": Ibid.

201   *"The more we see and hear"*: "The Truman Poise," *Dallas Times Herald,* June 1, 1945.

"I had to learn to say": Margaret Truman, *The President's House: A First Daughter Shares the History and Secrets of the World's Most Famous Home* (New York: Ballantine, 2003), p. 233.

Dozens of women: "Tea at the White House," May 24, 1945, guest list, SMOF: White House Social Office Files, box 25, Truman Papers.

"Now stop it": Margot Ford McMillen and Heather Roberson, *Into the Spotlight: Four Missouri Women* (Columbia: University of Missouri Press, 2004), p. 124.

"The imperious dowager": Michael Beschloss, "Harry Truman's Formidable Mother-in-Law," *New York Times,* May 8, 2014.

202   *"meals so gray"*: "The First Kitchen," *New Yorker,* November 22, 2010.

"Now that's the way": David McCullough, *Truman* (New York: Touchstone, 1993), p. 386.

"challenged the [farm] bloc": "Truman Sets a Pattern for a Term as President," *New York Times,* May 6, 1945.

"At the savage intersection": Clifford and Holbrooke, *Counsel to the President,* p. vii.

Chapter 23

203   *"the government of any country"*: Transcript of the Lend-Lease Act (1941), https://www.ourdocuments.gov/doc.php?doc=71&page=transcript.

"Give us the tools and we": Winston S. Churchill, Give Us the Tools speech, https://www.ourdocuments.gov/doc.php?doc=71&page=transcript.

"the most unsordid act": Charles More, *Britain in the Twentieth Century* (New York: Routledge, 2007), p. 130.

"one minute or $1 into": John Lewis Gaddis, *The United States and the Origins of the Cold War, 1941–1947* (New York: Columbia University Press, 1972), p. 179.

"Deliveries of supplies under": Memorandum for the president, May 11, 1945, PSF, box 164, Truman Papers.

204   *"Other lend-lease supplies"*: Ibid.

the United States had sent 593,259: War Shipping Administration, memorandum for the president, May 12, 1945, PSF, box 164, Truman Papers.

"There can be no post-war": Gaddis, *Origins of the Cold War,* p. 196.

"He . . . seemed eager to make": *The Price of Vision: The Diary of Henry A. Wallace 1942–1946,* ed. John Morton Blum (Boston: Houghton Mifflin, 1973), p. 437.

"You could go into [Truman's] office": Robert J. Donovan, *Conflict and Crisis: The Presidency of Harry S. Truman, 1945–1948* (Columbia: University of Missouri Press, 1977), p. 24.

205 *"Tell the son of a bitch":* Ken Hechler, *Working with Truman: A Personal Memoir of the White House Years* (Columbia: University of Missouri Press, 1982), p. 53.

Yugoslavian forces had hung: Department of State, memorandum of conversation with the president, May 10, 1945, WHCF:OF, file 1928, Truman Papers.

"no less dictatorial": Memorandum for the president, William J. Donovan, April 30, 1945, Rose A. Conway Papers, box 9, Truman Library.

"In foreign affairs, as in": Ibid.

"The issue, therefore, is hardly": Ibid.

"You are no doubt receiving": Harry S. Truman to Winston S. Churchill, May 11, 1945, MRF, box 2, Truman Papers.

206 *"has all the rights to hold":* Ambassador in Yugoslavia, cable to secretary of state, May 18, 1945, William D. Leahy Papers, Records of the United States Joint Chiefs of Staff, box 12, record group 218, National Archives, College Park, MD.

"many Italians of all classes": Department of State, memorandum for the president, "Current Foreign Developments," May 15, 1945, PSF, box 164, Truman Papers.

"The Yugoslavs are making": Ibid.

"I am unable and unwilling": Harry S. Truman to Winston S. Churchill, May 14, 1945, SMOF:MRF, box 2, Truman Papers.

"We had another explosive": Memoirs by Harry S. Truman: 1945; Year of Decisions (New York: Konecky & Konecky, 1955), p. 243.

207 *"Any country seeking to attack": The Diaries of Edward R. Stettinius, Jr., 1943–1946,* eds. Thomas M. Campbell and George C. Herring (New York: New Viewpoints, 1975), p. 354.

"The idea of a Germany": George F. Kennan, *Memoirs: 1925–1950* (Boston: Atlantic Monthly, 1967), p. 258.

208 *"Sources declare that the Communist":* OSS, memorandum to the president, May 18, 1945, Rose A. Conway Papers, box 9.

"[Dr. Soong] discussed at some length": Department of State, memorandum of conversation, May 14, 1945, WHCF:OF, file 1928, Truman Papers.

209 *"A future war with Soviet":* Gar Alperovitz, *The Decision to Use the Atomic Bomb* (New York: Vintage, 1995), p. 139.

"much disturbed": Diary of Joseph E. Davies, May 13, 1945, Joseph Edward Davies Papers, box 16, Manuscript Division, Library of Congress, Washington, DC.

"these damn sheets": Ibid.

"The rapid and serious deterioration": Joseph E. Davies to Truman, May 12, 1945, unsent, Davies Papers, box 16.

"The situation today": Ibid.

210 *"Ambassador Harriman said that":* Department of State, memorandum of conversation, May 15, 1945, WHCF:OF, file 1928, Truman Library.

"He said that their": Diary of James Forrestal, May 14, 1945, *The Forrestal Diaries,* ed. Walter Millis (New York: Viking, 1951), p. 57.

"All agree," he informed: Henry L. Stimson to Harry S. Truman, May 16, 1945,

included in diary of Henry L. Stimson, Henry Lewis Stimson Papers, Yale University Library.

"*A solution must be found*": Ibid.

211 "*All of this is a tough*": Ibid.

"*The longer the meeting [is] delayed*": Department of State, May 15, 1945, memorandum of conversation.

"*We shall probably hold more*": Stimson to Truman, May 16, 1945, included in Stimson diary.

"*Over any such tangled wave*": Ibid., May 15, 1945.

"*it seems a terrible thing*": Ibid.

"*It seems to me that*": Churchill to Truman, May 21, 1945, Naval Aide to the President File, box 7, Truman Papers.

212 "*When he's talking to some*": Jon Meacham, *Franklin and Winston: An Intimate Portrait of an Epic Friendship* (New York: Random House, 2003), p. 80.

"*the purity of St. Francis*": Alfred Steinberg, *Sam Rayburn: A Biography* (New York: Hawthorn, 1975), p. 140.

"*looked like death*": Robert E. Sherwood, *Roosevelt and Hopkins: An Intimate History* (New York: Harper & Brothers, 1948), p. 881.

"*The skin of his face*": Ibid.

"*I asked him to go to Stalin*": Robert H. Ferrell, ed., *Off the Record: The Private Papers of Harry S. Truman* (Columbia: University of Missouri Press, 1980), p. 31.

"*make it clear to Uncle Joe*": Ibid.

213 "*Hopkins was the first Western*": W. Averell Harriman and Elie Abel, *Special Envoy to Churchill and Stalin, 1941–1946* (New York: Random House, 1975), p. 268.

"*He wanted me to go to London*": Davies diary, May 21, 1945, Davies Papers, box 17.

"*He told me then of the atomic bomb*": Ibid.

"*Hopkins and Davies left simultaneously*": Ferrell, *Off the Record*, p. 32.

Chapter 24

214 "*unreal, light as fantastic glass*": Michael S. Sherry, *The Rise of American Air Power: The Creation of Armageddon* (New Haven: Yale University Press, 1987), p. 274.

"*The sheer number of bombs*": Robert Guillain, *I Saw Tokyo Burning: An Eyewitness Narrative from Pearl Harbor to Hiroshima* (Garden City, NY: Doubleday, 1981), p. 210.

"*The last of old Tokyo's*": Ibid., p. 211.

215 "*We plastered the as-yet-unburned*": Curtis E. LeMay with MacKinlay Kantor, *Mission with LeMay: My Story* (New York: Doubleday, 1965), p. 373.

"*I feel that the destruction*": Ibid.

FILLING "GOOP BOMBS": "Filling 'Goop Bombs' That Are Frying Japan Like Mixing Cake Dough," *Boston Globe*, July 1, 1945.

"*The M-69s*": "Behind the World War II Fire Bombing Attack of Tokyo," *Time*, March 9, 2015.

"I told him I was anxious": Henry L. Stimson diary, June 6, 1945, Henry Lewis Stimson Papers, Yale University Library.

216 *"yellow bastards," "yellow monkeys"*: See John W. Dower, *War Without Mercy: Race & Power in the Pacific War* (New York: Pantheon, 1986).

"Japanese atrocities marked fall": "Japanese Atrocities Marked Fall of Nanking from Chinese Command," *New York Times*, January 9, 1938.

"racial menace": Dower, p. 7.

"The best psychological warfare": William D. Leahy, *I Was There: The Personal Story of the Chief of Staff to Presidents Roosevelt and Truman Based on His Notes and Diaries Made at the Time* (New York: Whittlesey House, 1950), p. 72.

217 *"Apparently, the atrocities"*: Diary of Henry H. Arnold, John W. Huston, ed., *American Airpower Comes of Age: General Henry H. "Hap" Arnold's World War II Diaries* (Maxwell Air Force Base, AL: Air University Press, 2002), pp. 332–33.

"Apply full and unremitting pressure": Leslie M. Groves, *Now It Can Be Told: The Story of the Manhattan Project* (New York: Da Capo, 1962), p. 263.

218 *"The Japanese are a fanatical"*: Diary of Joseph C. Grew, May 28, 1945, WHCF:OF, file 1926, Truman Papers.

"If some indication can now": Ibid.

219 *"The Emperor Hirohito was Japan"*: "The God-Emperor," *Time*, May 21, 1945. Also quoted in Michael Sherry, *The Rise of American Air Power*, p. 303.

"The Japanese campaign involves": Stimson diary, May 15, 1945.

Chapter 25

220 *"all the prerogatives"*: Memorandum for the president, "Visit of Iraqi Regent," May 25, 1945, PSF, box 158, Truman Papers.

"Your Royal Highness": Memorandum, "Covering the Procedure to be Followed for the Visit of the Regent of Iraq," May 28, 1945, SMOF: White House Social Office Files, box 25, Truman Papers.

221 *"If such rights are given to us"*: "Visit of Iraqi Regent" memo.

"Iraq is extremely rich in oil": Ibid.

"Our real interest in the Middle East": Ibid.

"The Arabs, not only in Palestine": Ibid.

"no decision affecting the basic": Franklin D. Roosevelt to Prince Abdul Ilah, April 12, 1945, PSF, box 158, Truman Papers.

222 *"It was truly a magnificent"*: Margaret Truman, *The President's House: A First Daughter Shares the History and Secrets of the World's Most Famous Home* (New York: Ballantine, 2003), p. 95.

"I want to say to the Regent": Informal Remarks of the President, May 29, 1945, PSF, box 190, Truman Papers.

"He told us in the morning": Robert H. Ferrell, ed., *Truman in the White House: The Diary of Eben A. Ayers* (Columbia: University of Missouri Press, 1991), p. 34.

223 *"I'm one American who didn't"*: Ibid., p. 29.

"There are letters addressed": Ibid., p. 32.

"A Convalescent Taxpayer": A Convalescent taxpayer to Harry Truman, June 2, 1945, file unknown, Truman Papers.

"Whole Nation Reflects Era": "Whole Nation Reflects Era of Good Feeling Inspired by President," *Washington Post*, July 8, 1945.

"There is one thing about President": "Talk of the Town," *New Yorker*, April 28, 1945.

An overwhelming majority: "Presidential Timber in 1948?" *Washington Post*, May 16, 1945.

"Although President Truman stepped": "Poll Finds Majority Gives Truman Approval," *Los Angeles Times*, May 11, 1945.

224 *"He is capable and"*: Ayers diary, Ferrell, *Truman in the White House*, p. 31.

"I have some Cabinet changes I want": Transcript of press conference, May 23, 1945, PSF, box 51, Truman Papers.

"I don't give a damn": Ayers diary, Ferrell, *Truman in the White House*, p. 33.

225 *"[Stalin] said that if the United States"*: Robert Sherwood, *Roosevelt and Hopkins: An Intimate History* (New York: Harper & Brothers, 1948), p. 894.

"If the refusal to continue": Ibid.

"I am distressed to have": Winston S. Churchill to Harry S. Truman, May 28, 1945, SMOF: Naval Aide to the President Files, box 7, Truman Papers.

"This cut the pipeline": Oral history of Robert G. Nixon, p. 167, Truman Library.

"Daughter was in": Longhand note, June 1, 1945, PSF:LNF, box 283, Truman Papers.

226 *"It is the extraordinary isolation"*: Emmet John Hughes, *The Living Presidency: The Resources and Dilemmas of the American Presidential Office* (New York: Coward, McCann & Geoghegan, 1973), p. 26.

"The White House becomes especially": Truman, *The President's House*, p. 14.

"I shall be very glad to meet": Churchill to Truman, May 29, 1945, Naval Aide to the President Files, Box 7, Truman Papers.

227 *"I have no objections against"*: Joseph Stalin to Harry S. Truman, May 30, 1945, SMOF: Naval Aide to the President Files, box 9, Truman Papers.

"I will gladly come to Berlin": Churchill to Truman, June 1, 1945, SMOF: Naval Aide to the President Files, box 8, Truman Papers.

"Nothing really important": Ibid.

Chapter 26

231 *"It looks as though Stalin"*: Harry Hopkins to Harry S. Truman, May 30, 1945, SMOF:MRF, box 1, Truman Papers.

"Harry Hopkins has just sent me": Winston S. Churchill to Truman, June 1, 1945, Naval Aide to the President Files, box 8, Truman Papers.

"If this is true": Robert H. Ferrell, ed., *Truman in the White House: The Diary of Eben A. Ayers* (Columbia: University of Missouri Press, 1991), p. 39.

232 *"plans for bringing about unconditional"*: Special Message to the Congress on Winning the War with Japan, June 1, 1945, https://www.trumanlibrary.org /publicpapers/viewpapers.php?pid=52.

"I always get those dirty": Harry S. Truman to Martha Ellen Truman and Mary Jane Truman, June 16, 1945, FBPAP:FCF, box 19, Truman Papers.

233 *"Can you imagine a fat pig"*: Ibid.

"Their [the British] unanimous view": Memorandum for the president, "War Criminals," April 19, 1945, Samuel I. Rosenman Papers, box 10, Truman Library.

"Its size *and* character*"*: Henry Stimson, quoted in Richard Rhodes, *The Making of the Atomic Bomb* (New York: Touchstone, 1986), p. 642.

234 *"He thought these weapons might"*: Memorandum of conversation with General Marshall, May 29, 1945, Henry L. Stimson Papers, box 12, National Archives, College Park, MD.

"Every effort should be made": Ibid.

"[Marshall] spoke of the type of gas": Ibid.

235 *"Every feature of his body"*: Kai Bird and Martin J. Sherwin, *American Prometheus: The Triumph and Tragedy of J. Robert Oppenheimer* (New York: Vintage, 2005), p. 29.

"the granddaddy of today's": Ernest O. Lawrence and the Cyclotron, R&D Accomplishments, U.S. Department of Energy website, https://www.osti.gov /accomplishments/lawrence.html.

"this project should not": Notes of meeting of the Interim Committee, May 31, 1945, Truman Library, https://www.trumanlibrary.org/whistlestop/study _collections/bomb/large/documents/index.php?documentdate=1945-05-31 &documentid=39&pagenumber=1.

"This discovery might be compared": Ibid.

"a scientific certainty": Ibid.

"tremendous": Ibid.

"The basic endeavors": Ibid.

236 *"Stalin would ask to be"*: Ibid.

"should seek to make a profound": Ibid.

"a foregone conclusion that": Arthur Holly Compton, *Atomic Quest: A Personal Narrative* (New York: Oxford University Press, 1956), p. 238.

"While recognizing that the final": Notes of meeting of the Interim Committee, June 1, 1945, Truman Library, https://www.trumanlibrary.org /whistlestop/study_collections/bomb/large/documents/index.php?document date=1945-06-01&documentid=40&pagenumber=1.

237 *"Leonard," Truman uttered:* Oral history interview, J. Leonard Reinsch, p. 61, Truman Library.

"This is a lonesome place": H. S. Truman to B. W. Truman, June 3, 1945, FBPAP:FCF, box 14, Truman Papers.

"I'm always so lonesome": Longhand note, Harry Truman, June 1, 1945, PSF:LNF, box 283. Note: This document is dated June 1, but in it Truman discusses going to church, which, according to his daily calendar, made the date June 3, a Sunday.

"Don't think over six people": Ibid.

238 *"rather dull," he wrote:* Ibid.

"It came as something": Drew Pearson, "Washington Merry-Go-Round," *Washington Post,* June 11, 1945.

"You evidently are just finding": H. S. Truman to Margaret Truman, June 11, 1945, FBPAP:FCF, box 18, Truman Papers.

239 *"the Great White Jail"*: "Harry Truman and the Potsdam Conference," Truman Library, https://www.trumanlibrary.org/teacher/potsdam.htm.

"I'm just a prisoner": "Town Talk," *Washington Post*, June 5, 1945.
"you son of a bitch": Clark Clifford with Richard Holbrooke, *Counsel to the President: A Memoir* (New York: Random House, 1991), p. 72.
"He loved these wild games": Oral history interview, Robert G. Nixon, p. 270, Truman Library.
"Have been going through some": Longhand note, June 1, 1945.
"I'm a damn fool I guess": Ibid.

Chapter 27

240 *"Stalin overruled Molotov"*: Harry H. Hopkins to Harry L. Truman, telegram, June 6, 1945, SMOF:MRF, box 1, Truman Papers.
241 *"I was fully in sympathy"*: Diary of Henry L. Stimson, June 6, 1945, Henry Lewis Stimson Papers, Yale University Library.
"Those French ought to be": Diary of Eben A. Ayers, Robert H. Ferrell, ed., *Truman in the White House: The Diary of Eben A. Ayers* (Columbia: University of Missouri Press, 1991), p. 37.
"the almost unbelievable threat": Joseph C. Grew to Ambassador Caffery in France (to forward a letter from Truman to de Gaulle), June 6, 1945, Foreign Relations of the United States, Department of State, https://history.state.gov/historicaldocuments/frus1945v04/d699.
"General DeGaulle agrees to": Allied Headquarters, Caserta, Italy, to War Department, June 10, 1945, William D. Leahy Papers, Records of the United States Joint Chiefs of Staff, box 12, record group 218, National Archives, College Park, MD.
"Mr. President," he said: Memorandum of conversation, Cabinet Meeting, June 8, 1945, WHCF:OF, box 1928, Truman Papers.
242 *"Tell me," Truman asked:* Diary of Joseph E. Davies, June 4, 1945, Joseph Edward Davies Papers, box 17, Manuscript Division, Library of Congress, Washington, DC.
"chemical soup": Ibid., May 26, 1945.
"was not a 'smooth' session": Ibid.
"Great, you did a splendid job": Ibid.
"To the great American Envoy": Ibid.
243 *"He was completely fed up"*: Joseph E. Davies, "Full Report to Truman on Mission to Churchill," June 12, 1945, Davies Papers, box 17.
"even more bitter towards": Ibid.
"communist propagandists and leaders": Ibid.
"As I listened to his denunciation": Davies diary, May 26, 1945, Davies Papers, box 17.
"Europe would be prostrate": "Davies, "Report to Truman on Mission to Churchill."
"Perhaps it would fall to a very": William D. Leahy, *I Was There: The Personal Story of the Chief of Staff to Presidents Roosevelt and Truman Based on His Notes and Diaries Made at the Time* (New York: Whittlesey House, 1950), p. 379.
"A great man, but first, last": Ibid.

244 *"[She] had an extraordinary"*: Charles E. Bohlen, *Witness to History: 1929–1969* (New York: W. W. Norton, 1973), p. 221.

"Two months ago," Hopkins began: Minutes of Stalin-Hopkins meeting, May 26, 1945, Robert E. Sherwood, *Roosevelt and Hopkins: An Intimate History* (New York: Harper & Brothers, 1948), p. 888.

"felt a certain alarm": Ibid., May 27, 1945, p. 893.

"properly deployed": Hopkins to Truman, May 29, 1945, SMOF:MRF, box 1, Truman Papers.

245 *"must have a good reason"*: Ibid.

"Japan is doomed and the Japanese": Hopkins to Truman, May 30, 1945, SMOF:MRF, box 1, Truman Papers.

"The Marshal expects that Russia": Ibid.

"He stated categorically": Hopkins to Truman, May 29, 1945.

246 *"a battery of photographers greeted"*: Davies diary, June 13, 1945, box 17.

"This was an extraordinary": Sherwood, *Roosevelt and Hopkins*, p. 916.

Chapter 28

247 *"I sit here in this old house"*: Harry S. Truman to Bess W. Truman, June 12, 1945, FBPAP:FCF, box 14, Truman Papers.

"Just two months ago today": Ibid.

"It was nice to talk": H. S. Truman to B. W. Truman, June 15, 1945, FBPAP:FCF, box 14.

"His family is gone": Steve Neal, ed., *Eleanor and Harry: The Correspondence of Eleanor Roosevelt and Harry S. Truman* (New York: Citadel, 2002), p. 22.

The total program for the new: Press release, "President Requests $39 Billion Military Budget for War Department," June 11, 1945, PSF, box 197, Truman Papers.

"The supply lines to feed": Statement by the President on the Continued Need for Food, June 2, 1945, Truman Library, https://www.trumanlibrary.org/public papers/index.php?pid=56&st=&sti=.

248 *"Took Ross, Snyder and Rosenman"*: Longhand note, June 5, 1945, PSF:LNF, box 283, Truman Papers.

"has answered by actions": "Truman Steers Back from Rule by New Dealers," *Chicago Daily Tribune*, May 28, 1945.

"The President has to look out": Harry S. Truman, Address at Memorial Hall in Buffalo, October 9, 1952, PSF, box 28, Truman Library.

249 *"practically identical"*: Minutes of Meeting Held at the White House on 18 June 1945, Truman Papers, https://www.trumanlibrary.org/whistlestop/study _collections/bomb/large/documents/pdfs/21.pdf.

"the only course to pursue": Ibid.

"Our estimates are that our": Ibid.

"It is a grim fact": Ibid.

"every individual moving": Ibid.

250 *"vitalize the Chinese"*: Minutes of Meeting, 18 June 1945.

"submerged class": Ibid.

"would result only in making": Ibid.

"We gave up unconditional surrender": John Lewis Gaddis, *The United States and the Origins of the Cold War, 1941–1947* (New York: Columbia University Press, 1972), p. 10.

251 *"Truman was always a good"*: William D. Leahy, *I Was There: The Personal Story of the Chief of Staff to Presidents Roosevelt and Truman Based on His Notes and Diaries Made at the Time* (New York: Whittlesey House, 1950), p. 385.

"McCloy, you didn't express": This conversation is from McCloy's recollections, quoted at length in Len Giovannitti and Fred Freed, *The Decision to Drop the Bomb* (New York: Coward-McCann, 1965), p. 136.

252 *"We were told that it"*: Transcript of testimony by J. Robert Oppenheimer, April 12, 1954, United States Atomic Energy Commission (Washington, DC: Government Printing Office, 1954).

"Almost everyone knew that": Gerard DeGroot, *The Bomb: A History of Hell on Earth* (London: Pimlico, 2005), p. 42.

253 *"We feel compelled to take"*: Franck Report, excerpted in Barton J. Bernstein and Allen J. Matusow, eds., *The Truman Administration: A Documentary History* (New York: Harper Colophon, 1966), p. 11.

"a nuclear armament race": Ibid., p. 12.

"large accumulations of poison gas": Ibid.

"a demonstration of the new weapon": Ibid., p. 13.

"The opinions of our scientific": "Recommendations on the Immediate Use of Nuclear Weapons," June 17, 1945, National Security Archive online, http://nsarchive.gwu.edu/NSAEBB/NSAEBB162/19.pdf.

254 *"definitely the biggest crowd"*: "Hero's Welcome: Million Out to See 'Ike' in the Capital," *Atlanta Constitution,* June 19, 1945.

"greatest ovation in 25 years": "Congress Accords Ike Its Greatest Ovation in 25 Years," *Washington News,* June 19, 1945.

"looked nervous and embarrassed": Diary of Allen Drury, June 18, 1945, *A Senate Journal: 1943–1945* (New York: McGraw-Hill, 1963), p. 449.

"a real man": Harry S. Truman to Martha Ellen Truman and Mary Jane Truman, June 16, 1945, WHCF:PPF, box 19, Truman Papers.

"Eisenhower's party was": Harry S. Truman to Bess W. Truman, June 19, 1945, WHCF:PPF, box 14.

255 *"Okinawa: It is officially stated"*: Captain Vardaman to the president, June 19, 1945, SMOF: Naval Aide to the President Files, box 16, Truman Papers.

"The strength of will-power": Winston S. Churchill to Truman, June 21, 1945, SMOF:MRF, box 8, Truman Papers.

Chapter 29

256 *"I didn't know you could get up"*: "President Flies Non-Stop to West," *New York Times,* June 20, 1945.

"Harry Truman has now been": Drew Pearson, "Washington Merry-Go-Round," *Washington Post,* June 19, 1945.

257 *"It sure is swell for you"*: Ibid.
"a human lane up the main": "President Ends Air Trip to Northwest," *Los Angeles Times,* June 20, 1945.

258 *"The whole countryside seemed"*: *The Diaries of Edward R. Stettinius, Jr., 1943–1946,* eds. Thomas B. Campbell and George C. Herring (New York: New Viewpoints, 1975), p. 402.
"The whole city was all keyed": Oral history interview, Henry Reiff, p. 83, Truman Library.
"world organization with police": Ian Buruma, *Year Zero: A History of 1945* (New York: Penguin, 2013), p. 309.
"It's what we stand for": "Truman Acclaimed on Arrival by Air to Close Parley," *New York Times,* June 26, 1945.
"Well, you certainly have done": Conversation from Campbell and Herring, *Diaries of Edward R. Stettinius,* pp. 403–4.

259 *"The Charter of the United Nations"*: Address in San Francisco at the Closing Session of the United Nations Conference, June 26, 1945, Truman Library, https://www.trumanlibrary.org/publicpapers/viewpapers.php?pid=73.

260 *"to find a way to end war!"*: Statement by Harry S. Truman at the San Francisco conference, https://www.youtube.com/watch?v=TCOvCemH8AQ.
FINDER! DO NOT OPEN: Stephen C. Schlesinger, *Act of Creation: The Founding of the United Nations* (New York: Perseus, 2003), p. 257.
"By jove, look who's here": "Truman Tells Home Folks His Job Is Winning Peace," *New York Times,* June 28, 1945.
WELCOME HOME, HARRY!: "Truman Realizes Ambition of Filling Home-Town Hall," *Washington Post,* June 28, 1945.

261 *"Hello Harry!"*: "Home Folks," *Christian Science Monitor,* June 28, 1945.
"the things that had happened": "Truman Realizes Ambition."
"That gives you a rent free": Harry S. Truman to Martha Ellen Truman and Mary Jane Truman, June 16, 1945, FBPAP:FCF, box 19, Truman Papers.
"Gentlemen, and ladies": Transcript of press conference, June 27, 1945, PSF, box 51, Truman Papers.

262 *"Is it Mr. Byrnes, Mr. President?"*: Ibid.
"This is the most wonderful": "Truman Realizes Ambition."
"Time and again, I have tried": Ibid.
"I arrived at the White House": Ibid.
"The first one is to win": "Our World Role," *New York Times,* July 1, 1945.

263 *Missouri did not practice:* See "The State of Missouri," *Fortune,* July 1945.
"It looks to us": "Truman's Hometown Is 'Smalltown, USA,'" *New York Times,* July 1, 1945.

264 *"Hello there, Eddie"*: "Praise Makes Him Swell Up, Truman Says," *Washington Post,* June 29, 1945.
"I want some shirts": Ibid.
"If it had been left to your": Margaret Truman, *Bess W. Truman* (New York: Macmillan, 1986), p. 298.
"Mother had flatly refused": Ibid., p. 266.
"Take a few more of us": Ibid.

265 *"The choice before the Senate"*: Address Before the Senate Urging Ratification

of the Charter of the United Nations, July 2, 1945, Truman papers, https://www.trumanlibrary.org/publicpapers/viewpapers.php?pid=76.

266   *"I don't think you know Jimmy"*: Oral history interview, Samuel I. Rosenman, p. 25, Truman Library.

     "It just shows how cruel": Diary excerpted in Arthur Vandenberg, Jr., ed., *The Private Papers of Senator Vandenberg* (Boston: Houghton Mifflin, 1952), p. 225.

     "My, but he has a keen mind": Longhand note, July 7, 1945, PSF:LNF, box 283, Truman Papers.

Chapter 30

267   *"I sure dread this trip worse"*: Harry S. Truman to Bess W. Truman, July 12, 1945, FBPAP:FCF, box 14, Truman Papers.

     "All attempts to secure": Supreme Headquarters, Allied Expeditionary Force to War Department, cable, June 20, 1945, William D. Leahy Papers, Records of the United States Joint Chiefs of Staff, box 10, record group 218, National Archives, College Park, MD.

     "No explanation can be given": General Floyd Parks to War Department, cable, ibid., box 6.

268   *"in order that full continuity"*: Winston S. Churchill to Truman, June 14, 1945, SMOF: Naval Aide to the President Files, box 8, Truman Papers.

     "There isn't any doubt": "Why Jimmy Byrnes Is Now So Close to the President," *Daily Boston Globe,* July 30, 1945.

269   *"just taking a little something"*: Transcript of press conference, July 5, 1945, PSF, box 51, Truman Papers.

     "a good letter opener": Ibid.

     "I have a successor in mind": Ibid.

     "now actually going on": Memorandum for the president, "Proposed Program for Japan," July 2, 1945, Henry L. Stimson Papers, box 23, National Archives, College Park, MD.

     "There is reason to believe": Ibid.

     "Japan has no allies": Ibid.

270   *"On grounds of secrecy the bomb"*: Henry L. Stimson, "The Decision to Use the Atomic Bomb," *Harper's,* February 1947.

     "overwhelming character of the force": "Proposed Program for Japan" memorandum.

     "the inevitability and completeness": Ibid.

     "substantially add to the chances": Ibid.

     "that we were busy": Diary of Henry L. Stimson, July 3, 1945, Stimson Papers.

     "with the purpose of having": Ibid.

271   *"Yes," Truman answered*: Diary of Henry L. Stimson, July 2, 1945, Stimson Papers.

     "There was a long discussion": Department of State, memorandum of conversation, re: China, June 9, 1945, WHCF:OF, box 1928, Truman Papers.

     "settle the controversy": William D. Leahy, *I Was There: The Personal Story of the*

Chief of Staff to Presidents Roosevelt and Truman Based on His Notes and Diaries Made at the Time (New York: Whittlesey House, 1950), p. 381.

272 *"A lot has happened since"*: Diary of Bruce Forsyth, July 3, 1945, Bruce Forsyth Papers, box 1, Truman Library.

"high hat, top hat": Harry S. Truman to Martha Ellen Truman and Mary Jane Truman, July 3, 1945, FBPAP:FCF, box 19, Truman Papers.

"It'll be a circus sure enough": H. S. Truman to B. W. Truman, July 3, 1945, FBPAP:FCF, box 14.

"'babes in the wood' affair": Diary of Eben A. Ayers, Robert Ferrell, ed., *Truman in the White House: The Diary of Eben Ayers* (Columbia: University of Missouri Press, 1991), p. 5.

273 *"fair-minded . . . a hard worker"*: "Truman Wins Plaudits of Big Majority," Public Opinion News Service, July 1–2, 1945.

"The present conference projects": "President Truman Gains Popularity and Prestige Overseas," *Washington Post*, July 22, 1945.

"The American people expect": Samuel I. Rosenman, John W. Snyder, and George E. Allen, memorandum to the president, July 6, 1945, Foreign Relations of the United States: Diplomatic Papers, the Conference of Berlin (the Potsdam Conference), 1945, vol. 1, doc. 192, Office of the Historian, Department of State, https://history.state.gov/historicaldocuments/frus1945Berlinv01/d192.

"I'm sorry if I've done something": H. S. Truman to B. W. Truman, July 6, 1945, FBPAP:FCF, box 14.

"How I hate this trip!": Longhand note, July 7, 1945, PSF:LNF, box 283, Truman Papers.

Chapter 31

274 *he was #51*: USS *Augusta* Corrected Telephone Directory, PSF, box 141, Truman Papers.

"Old Harry sat around batting": "Cousin Harry," *New Yorker*, November 24, 1945.

275 *"Truman, a newcomer"*: Charles E. Bohlen, *Witness to History: 1929–1969* (New York: W. W. Norton, 1973), p. 226.

"600 B-29 Superfortresses": USS Augusta: "Morning Press," July 7, 1945, PSF, box 141, Truman Papers.

"first baptism of incendiaries": Ibid.

"Conversations relating to peace": Press release, Statement by Acting Secretary of State Joseph C. Grew, July 10, 1945, PSF, box 197, Truman Papers.

"I don't suppose anyone gives": "Maj. Gen. Harry Vaughan, Aide to President Truman, Dies at 87," *Washington Post*, May 22, 1981.

"The Conservative government": Oral history interview, Robert G. Nixon, p. 265, Truman Library.

276 *"This is the biggest fool thing"*: *Memoirs by Harry S. Truman: 1945; Year of Decisions* (New York: Konecky & Konecky, 1955), p. 11.

"Three cheers for Mr. Truman": Log of the President's Trip to Berlin

Conference, July 7, 1945, Truman Library. Note: Much of the detail from Truman's movements during the Potsdam trip comes from this official log. *83 suitcases, 1 trunk:* Harry H. Vaughan, James K. Vardaman, and George C. Drescher to James J. Rowley (Secret Service), July 12, 1945, SMOF: Naval Aide to the President Files, box 5, Truman Papers.

277 *"Everyone was relieved when":* Diary of Joseph E. Davies, July 15, 1945, Joseph Edward Davies Papers, box 18, Manuscript Division, Library of Congress, Washington, DC.
"It is comfortable enough": Ibid.

278 *"wholly inadequate":* Log of the President's Trip, July 15, 1945.
Truman was Kilting: Top Secret Code Name for Places and Passengers, June 27, 1945, William D. Leahy Papers, Records of the United States Joint Chiefs of Staff, box 10, record group 218, National Archives, College Park, MD.
"Safeguard Your Health": Conference Bulletin Number 1, Davies Papers, box 18.

279 *"Safely landed in Berlin":* White House Map Room to Matthew J. Connelly, July 15, 1945, SMOF: Naval Aide to the President Files, box 5, Truman Papers.
"The difficulties with Churchill": Harry S. Truman to Eleanor Roosevelt, May 10, 1945, Steve Neal, ed., *Eleanor and Harry: The Correspondence of Eleanor Roosevelt and Harry S. Truman* (New York: Citadel, 2002), p. 27.
"I had an instant liking": Truman, *Memoirs,* p. 340.

280 *"No," the Briton said:* Ibid.
"obvious power of decision": Robert J. Donovan, *Conflict and Crisis: The Presidency of Harry S. Truman, 1945–1948* (Columbia: University of Missouri Press, 1977), p. 73.
"I felt that here was a man": Winston S. Churchill, *The Second World War,* vol. 6, *Triumph and Tragedy* (New York: Bantam, 1962), p. 541.
"P.M. delighted with Pres.": Charles L. Mee Jr., *Meeting at Potsdam* (New York: Franklin Square, 1975), p. 59.

281 *"This is the most powerful":* William D. Leahy, *I Was There: The Personal Story of the Chief of Staff to Presidents Roosevelt and Truman Based on His Notes and Diaries Made at the Time* (New York: Whittlesey House, 1950), p. 395.
"You could smell the effluvia": Oral history interview, Robert G. Nixon, p. 297, Truman Library.
"the long, never-ending procession": Truman, *Memoirs,* p. 341.
"That's what happens": Ibid.

282 *"I hope for some sort of peace":* Longhand note, July 16, 1945, Truman Papers, https://www.trumanlibrary.org/whistlestop/study_collections/bomb/large /documents/index.php?documentdate=1945-07-16&documentid=1& pagenumber=1. Also: http://nsarchive.gwu.edu/NSAEBB/NSAEBB162/38.pdf.

Chapter 32

283 *"If we postpone":* Kai Bird and Martin J. Sherwin, *American Prometheus: The Triumph and Tragedy of J. Robert Oppenheimer* (New York: Vintage, 2005), p. 307.
"obviously confused and badly": Ibid.

"There was an air of excitement": Leslie M. Groves, *Now It Can Be Told: The Story of the Manhattan Project* (New York: Da Capo, 1962), p. 291.

284 *"The strain had been great"*: Ibid., p. 293.

"There could be a catastrophe": Bird and Sherwin, *American Prometheus*, p. 306.

"It was raining cats and dogs": Richard Rhodes, *The Making of the Atomic Bomb* (New York: Touchstone, 1986), p. 666.

285 *"We were determined to look"*: Ibid., p. 668.

"With the darkness and the waiting": Ibid.

"It is now zero minus twenty": Peter Goodchild, *Edward Teller: The Real Dr. Strangelove* (Cambridge, MA: Harvard University Press, 2004), p. 105.

"My hand was on the switch": Rhodes, *Making of the Atomic Bomb*, p. 670.

"My first impression was one of tremendous": Groves, *Now It Can Be Told*, p. 296.

"All of a sudden, the night": Lawrence Badash, J. O. Hirschfelder, and H. P. Broida, *Reminiscences of Los Alamos 1943–1945* (Boston: D. Reidel, 1980), p. 76.

"The lighting effects beggared": Memorandum for the secretary of war, July 18, 1945, General Leslie R. Groves, Truman Papers, https://www.trumanlibrary.org/whistlestop/study_collections/bomb/large/documents/index.php?documentid=2&pagenumber=1.

"The war is over": Groves, *Now It Can Be Told*, p. 298.

286 *"We knew the world would not"*: Interview with J. Robert Oppenheimer, https://www.youtube.com/watch?v=QBYyUi-Nkts.

"Operated on this morning": Acting chairman of the Interim Committee (Harrison) to secretary of war (Stimson), July 16, 1945, Foreign Relations of the United States: Diplomatic Papers, https://history.state.gov/historicaldocuments/frus1945Berlinv02/d1303.

287 *"no loss of life"*: The press release appears in Vincent C. Jones, *United States Army in World War II: Special Studies: Manhattan* (Washington, DC: Center of Military History, 2007), p. 517.

"The Conduct of the War with Japan": Memorandum for the president, "The Conduct of the War with Japan," July 16, 1945, Henry L. Stimson Papers, Yale University Library.

"It seems to me that we are": Ibid.

"The Russians, I am also informed": Memorandum for the President, "Trusteeship for Korea," July 16, 1945, Henry L. Stimson to Truman, https://history.state.gov/historicaldocuments/frus1945Berlinv02/f732.

"is the Polish question transplanted": Ibid.

288 *"Is everything all right?"*: Diary of Joseph E. Davies, July 16, 1945, Joseph Edward Davies Papers, box 18, Manuscript Division, Library of Congress, Washington, DC.

"I got to my feet and advanced": Longhand note, July 17, 1945, Truman Papers, https://history.state.gov/historicaldocuments/frus1945Berlinv02/d1303.

289 *"What I noticed especially"*: *Memoirs by Harry S. Truman: 1945; Year of Decisions* (New York: Konecky & Konecky, 1955), p. 342.

"An unforewarned visitor would": George F. Kennan, *Memoirs: 1925–1950* (Boston: Atlantic Monthly Press, 1967), pp. 279–80.

"straight from the shoulder": Truman, *Memoirs*, p. 341.

"I am here to — be yr friend": Bohlen notes, Truman-Stalin meeting, July 17,

1945, Foreign Relations: Diplomatic Papers, https://history.state.gov/histori-caldocuments/frus1945Berlinvo2/d710a-5.

"don't understand horse trading": Ibid.

"the most urgent, to my mind": Truman, *Memoirs,* p. 411.

290 *"Most of the big points"*: Longhand note, July 17, 1945.

"You could if you wanted to": Truman, *Memoirs,* p. 341.

"All I could do was increase": William M. Rigdon, *White House Sailor* (New York: Doubleday, 1962), p. 197.

"I think he's loose somewhere": Sound recording of Truman interview, MP2002-309, Screen Gems Collection, Truman Library.

"I can deal with Stalin": Longhand note, July 17, 1945.

291 *"strikingly informs all that"*: Richard Beckman, unpublished memoir, Richard Beckman Papers, box 1, Truman Library.

"As we entered, we were almost blinded": "Potsdam and the Conference Facilities," diary of Joseph E. Davies, July 19, 1945, Davies Papers.

"only a few miles from the war-shattered": Harry S. Truman, "Cold War Starts at Potsdam," *Life,* October 17, 1945.

Chapter 33

295 *"Who is to be the chairman"*: Meeting minutes, Potsdam First Plenary Session, George Modelski and Sylvia Modelski, eds., *Documenting Global Leadership* (New York: Palgrave Macmillan, 1988), p. 393.

"One of the most acute problems": Ibid.

296 *"That is," he said, "the permanent"*: Ibid.

"I don't want just to discuss": Ben Cohen, meeting minutes, Potsdam First Plenary Meeting, July 17, 1945, Foreign Relations of the United States: Diplomatic Papers, Conference of Berlin, https://history.state.gov/historicaldocuments /frus1945Berlinvo2/d710a-10.

"I am well aware that": Modelski and Modelski, *Documenting Global Leadership,* p. 393.

"There is only one other question": Ibid., p. 401.

297 *"The table was set with everything"*: Memoirs by Harry S. Truman: 1945; Year of Decisions (New York: Konecky & Konecky, 1955), p. 350.

"I'll bet that lieutenant": Ibid., p. 351.

"Doctor has just returned": Charles L. Mee Jr., *Meeting at Potsdam* (New York: Franklin Square, 1975), pp. 82–83.

298 *"Two hundred million people"*: George F. Kennan, *Memoirs: 1925–1950* (Boston: Atlantic Monthly Press, 1967), p. 226.

299 *"They gave him the choice"*: Harry S. Truman to Bess W. Truman, July 18, 1945, FBPAP:FCF, box 14, Truman Papers.

"If you had gone down like France": Winston S. Churchill, *The Second World War,* vol. 6, *Triumph and Tragedy* (New York: Bantam, 1962), pp. 539–40.

"The experiment in the New Mexican": Ibid., p. 544.

300 *"world shaking news"*: Ibid.

"Now all this nightmare picture": Ibid., p. 545.

"By using this new agency": Ibid., p. 546.

"I think," Truman told Churchill: Ibid., p. 547.

301 *"Believe Japs will fold"*: Longhand note, July 18, 1945, Truman Papers, https://www.trumanlibrary.org/whistlestop/study_collections/bomb/large/documents/index.php?documentid=63&pagenumber=2.

"Stalin said that the Soviet Union": "HST Let Stalin Stall Tokyo," *Boston Globe*, August 23, 1960.

302 *"crisp and to the point"*: Charles E. Bohlen, *Witness to History: 1929–1969* (New York: W. W. Norton, 1973), p. 228.

"Joe, how am I doing?": Diary of Joseph E. Davies, July 18, 1945, Joseph Edward Davies Papers, box 18, Manuscript Division, Library of Congress, Washington, DC .

"What is the meaning of reference": Ben Cohen, meeting minutes, Potsdam Second Plenary Meeting, July 18, 1945, *Foreign Relations: Diplomatic Papers, Conference of Berlin,* https://history.state.gov/historicaldocuments/frus-1945Berlinv02/d710a-19.

"I'm not going to stay around": Longhand note, July 18, 1945.

"Stalin," Truman concluded: Jonathan Daniels, *The Man of Independence* (Port Washington, NY: Kennikat, 1950), p. 278.

"This whole environment at Berlin": Henry L. Stimson to "My Darling" (Mrs. Stimson), July 18, 1945, Henry Lewis Stimson Papers, Yale University Library.

"There was evident . . . palpable": Henry L. Stimson and McGeorge Bundy, *On Active Service in Peace and War* (New York: Harper & Brothers, 1948), p. 638.

303 *"The hall was filled with soldiers"*: Bohlen, *Witness to History,* p. 228.

"Jewels, rings traded for bread": John W. Huston, ed., *American Airpower Comes of Age: General Henry H. "Hap" Arnold's World War II Diaries* (Maxwell Air Force Base, AL: Air University Press, 2002), p. 376.

"Listen, I know you're alone": Conversation from oral history interview, Floyd M. Boring, p. 16, Truman Library.

"Admiral Leahy said he'd never": H. S. Truman to B. W. Truman, July 18, 1945, FBPAP:FCF, box 14, Truman Papers.

Chapter 34

304 *"complaints" or "accusations"*: Ben Cohen, meeting minutes, Potsdam Third Plenary Meeting, July 19, 1945, Foreign Relations of the United States: Diplomatic Papers, Conference of Berlin, https://history.state.gov/historicaldocuments/frus1945Berlinv02/d710a-29.

"I am here to discuss world": Ibid.

"On a number of occasions": *Memoirs by Harry S. Truman: 1945; Year of Decisions* (New York: Konecky & Konecky, 1955), p. 369.

"portrays the classic tradition": Joseph E. Davies, "The Chiefs of State" at Potsdam, July 19, 1945, Joseph Edward Davies Papers, box 18, Manuscript Division, Library of Congress, Washington, DC.

"has no such graciousness": Ibid.

305 *"He was thrown into this arena"*: Ibid.

"the fur flew": Diary of Joseph E. Davies, July 19, 1945, Davies Papers, box 18.

"It has exhausted me": Ibid.

"The maintenance of the dynasty": Robert P. Newman, *Truman and the Hiroshima Cult* (East Lansing: Michigan State University Press, 1995), p. 68.

"We have been fully aware": "Magic" Diplomatic Summary, July 17, 1945, National Security Archive, http://nsarchive.gwu.edu/NSAEBB/NSAEBB162/33.pdf.

"If today, when we are still": Ibid.

306 *"I felt that there would be no"*: Winston S. Churchill, *The Second World War*, vol. 6, *Triumph and Tragedy* (New York: Bantam, 1953), p. 548.

"terrible political repercussions": Joseph C. Grew, forwarding Cordell Hull note to James F. Byrnes, July 16, 1945, SMOF: Naval Aide to the President Files, box 6, National Archives, College Park, MD.

"crucify": Robert J. Donovan, *Conflict and Crisis: The Presidency of Harry S. Truman, 1945–1948* (Columbia: University of Missouri Press, 1977), p. 99.

"I cannot speak for others but": Len Giovannitti and Fred Freed, *The Decision to Drop the Bomb* (New York: Coward-McCann, 1965), p. 187.

"I have to make it perfectly plain": Harry S. Truman to Bess W. Truman, July 20, 1945, FBPAP:FCF, box 14, Truman Papers.

307 *"Had Churchill on my right"*: Ibid.

"That gives us two drinks": "Dinner at the Little White House," Davies diary, July 20, 1945.

"I raise my glass to the leader": Ibid.

"Jim Byrnes was in unusually": Ibid.

"Better spruce up": "Potsdam Conference," *New Yorker*, December 29, 1945.

308 *"A toast to the pianist!"*: Ibid.

"Well, you know there are": Ibid.

"Marshal Stalin," Truman said: Margaret Truman, *Harry S. Truman* (New York: William Morrow, 1973), p. 281.

"The ambassadors and Jim": H. S. Truman to B. W. Truman, July 20, 1945, FBPAP:FCF, box 14, Truman Papers.

"You never saw as completely": Ibid.

309 *"General Eisenhower, officers, and men"*: Informal Remarks of the President at the Raising of the Stars and Stripes . . . , July 20, 1945, PSF, box 197, Truman Papers.

"Flag was on the White House": Longhand note, July 20, 1945, National Security Archive, http://nsarchive.gwu.edu/NSAEBB/NSAEBB162/38.pdf.

"It all feels flat and empty": Charles L. Mee Jr., *Meeting at Potsdam* (New York: Franklin Square, 1975), p. 167.

310 *"an expression of historical"*: "Summary of the Views Expressed by the Polish Delegation to the Meeting of Foreign Ministers, July 24, 1945," SMOF: Naval Aide to the President Files, box 4, Truman Library.

"There were many other matters": Churchill, *Triumph and Tragedy*, p. 574.

"the most colossal blank check": John Lewis Gaddis, *The United States and the Origins of the Cold War, 1941–1947* (New York: Columbia University Press, 1972), p. 152.

"*The United States can not, moreover*": Ben Cohen, meeting minutes, Potsdam Fourth Plenary Meeting, July 20, 1945, Foreign Relations: Diplomatic Papers, Conference of Berlin, https://history.state.gov/historicaldocuments/frus1945 Berlinv02/d710a-44.

311 "*Started with caviar and vodka*": H. S. Truman to Margaret Truman, July 22, 1945, FBPAP:FCF, box 18, Truman Papers.

"*Tell the president it is French*": Harry S. Truman, "Cold War Starts at Potsdam," *Life,* October 17, 1945.

"*get even*": William D. Leahy, *I Was There: The Personal Story of the Chief of Staff to Presidents Roosevelt and Truman Based on His Notes and Diaries at the Time* (New York: Whittlesey House, 1950), p. 412.

"*Much is going on here that*": Davies diary, July 20, 1945, Davies Papers, box 18.

"*It was an immensely powerful*": Diary of Henry L. Stimson, July 21, 1945, Henry Lewis Stimson Papers, Yale University Library.

"*At 530, 16 July 1945, in a remote*": Leslie R. Groves, memorandum for the secretary of war, July 18, 1945, Truman Papers, https://www.trumanlibrary.org /whistlestop/study_collections/bomb/large/documents/index.php?document id=2&pagenumber=1.

312 "*were immensely pleased*": Stimson diary, July 21, 1945.

"*huge concentrations of highly*": Ibid.

"*As to the present war, there was*": Ibid.

"*tremendously pepped up*": Stimson diary, July 21, 1945.

"*Stimson, what was gunpowder?*": Herbert Feis, *The Atomic Bomb and the End of World War II* (Princeton, NJ: Princeton University Press, 1966), p. 87.

Chapter 35

313 "*With regard to unconditional*": "Magic" Diplomatic Summary, July 22, 1945, National Security Archive, http://nsarchive.gwu.edu/NSAEBB/NSAEBB162 /40.pdf.

"*The Japanese military forces*": "Potsdam Declaration," July 26, 1945, Birth of the Constitution of Japan, National Diet Library, http://www.ndl.go.jp /constitution/e/etc/co6.html.

314 "*utter destruction*": Ibid.

"*We call upon the government*": Ibid.

"*The weapon is to be used*": Longhand note, July 25, 1945, Truman Papers, https://www.trumanlibrary.org/flip_books/index.php?tldate=1945-07-25& groupid=3702&titleid=&pagenumber=1&collectionid=ihow.

315 "*the supreme operations in the war*": Document no. 1381, Combined Chiefs of Staff to Truman and Churchill, July 24, 1945, https://history.state.gov/historical documents/frus1945Berlinv02/d1381.

"*encourage Russian entry into*": Ibid.

"*All of us wanted Russia*": Harry S. Truman to Bess W. Truman, March 3, 1948, represented in Margaret Truman, *Harry S. Truman* (New York: William Morrow, 1973), p. 35.

316 "*We have been unable*": This conversation from Ben Cohen, meeting min-

utes, Potsdam Eighth Plenary Meeting, July 24, 1945, Foreign Relations of the United States: Diplomatic Papers, Conference of Berlin, https://history.state .gov/historicaldocuments/frus1945Berlinvo2/d710a-94.

"*I casually mentioned to Stalin*": *Memoirs by Harry S. Truman: 1945; Year of Decisions* (New York: Konecky & Konecky, 1955), p. 416.

"*So offhand was Stalin's response*": Charles E. Bohlen, *Witness to History: 1929– 1969* (New York: W. W. Norton, 1973), p. 237.

"*How did it go?*": Winston S. Churchill, *The Second World War*, vol. 6, *Triumph and Tragedy* (New York: Bantam, 1962), p. 573.

317 "*I should have known*": Bohlen, *Witness to History*, p. 237.

"*speed things up*": Charles L. Mee Jr., *Meeting at Potsdam* (New York: Franklin Square, 1975), p. 174.

"*The translation was not finished*": Truman, *Memoirs*, p. 390.

318 "*I must say good luck*": Diary of Joseph E. Davies, July 25, 1945, Joseph Edward Davies Papers, box 19, Manuscript Division, Library of Congress, Washington, DC.

"*What a pity*": Conversation from Truman, *Memoirs*, p. 389.

"*There was a glint of a tear*": Davies diary, July 25, 1945.

"*There are some things*": H. S. Truman to B. W. Truman, July 25, 1945, FBPAP:FCF, box 15, Truman Papers.

"*if, now, the president is not*": Ibid.

319 "*bear thinking over*": Davies diary, July 5, 1945.

"*It scared him so badly*": H. S. Truman to B. W. Truman, July 27, 1945, FBPAP:FCF, box 15.

"*Now, in the car*": Dwight D. Eisenhower, *Crusade in Europe* (New York: Avon, 1952), p. 489.

"*Mr. President,*" *he said*: Ibid.

320 "*We, the president of the United*": "Potsdam Declaration."

"*The President's wish is*": Charles G. Ross to Eben A. Ayers, July 27, 1945, SMOF: Naval Aide to the President Files, box 5, Truman Library.

"*He looked tired*": Davies diary, July 27, 1945.

Chapter 36

321 "*Important day*": Diary of Walter Brown, July 27, 1945, National Security Archives, https://nsarchive.gwu.edu/nukevault/ebb525-The-Atomic-Bomb -and-the-End-of-World-War-II/documents/049.pdf

as "*a basis for negotiations*": John Lewis Gaddis, *The United States and the Origins of the Cold War, 1941–1947* (New York: Columbia University Press, 1972), p. 129.

"*If you say I owe you a million*": Walter Brown, minutes of Byrnes-Molotov meeting, July 27, 1945, https://nsarchive.gwu.edu/nukevault/ebb525-The -Atomic-Bomb-and-the-End-of-World-War-II/documents/049.pdf.

322 "*woodworking machines, bakery ovens*": Diary of Edwin W. Pauley, n.d., "Potsdam," Edwin W. Pauley Papers, box 18, Truman Library.

"*swarms of workmen*": Lucien Gulick and J. Howard Marshall, memorandum,

"Russian Machinery Removals from Berlin," July 25, 1945, SMOF: Naval Aide to the President Files, box 4, Truman Library.

"Yes," he said, "this is the case": James F. Byrnes, *Speaking Frankly* (New York: Harper & Brothers, 1947), p. 83.

"namely, that each country": Charles Bohlen, minutes of Byrnes-Molotov meeting, July 27, 1945, Foreign Relations of the United States: Diplomatic Papers, Conference of Berlin, https://history.state.gov/historicaldocuments/frus1945 Berlinv02/d710a-126.

"would have a free hand": Ibid.

323 *"The Secretary [Byrnes] said that was":* Ibid.

"The Secretary said that he felt": Bohlen minutes of Byrnes-Molotov meeting.

"terribly homesick": Harry S. Truman to Bess W. Truman, July 29, 1945, FBPAP:FCF, box 15, Truman Papers.

"Well," the missive began: H. S. Truman to Martha Ellen Truman and Mary Jane Truman, July 28, 1945, FBPAP:FCF, box 19, Truman Papers.

"The debate on the United Nations": Edward R. Stettinius to Truman and James F. Byrnes, July 28, 1945, SMOF: Naval Aide to the President Files, box 6.

324 *"It is deeply gratifying that":* Charles G. Ross to Eben A. Ayers, July 28, 1945, SMOF: Naval Aide to the President Files, box 5.

"does not consider": Charles L. Mee Jr., *Meeting at Potsdam* (New York: Franklin Square, 1975), p. 174.

"prosecute the war of Great East": "Japanese Cabinet Weighs Ultimatum," *New York Times,* July 28, 1945.

"Japs . . . used several planes": Map Room to Advance Map Room, July 30, 1945, SMOF: Naval Aide to the President Files, box 6.

JAPANESE CABINET WEIGHS ULTIMATUM: "Japanese Cabinet Weighs."

325 *"Although [Churchill] was their antagonist":* William D. Leahy, *I Was There: The Personal Story of the Chief of Staff to Presidents Roosevelt and Truman Based on His Notes and Diaries Made at the Time* (New York: Whittlesey House, 1950), p. 419.

"The Russian delegation was given": Ben Cohen, meeting minutes, Potsdam Tenth Plenary Meeting, July 28, 1945, Foreign Relations: Diplomatic Papers, Conference of Berlin, https://history.state.gov/historicaldocuments/frus1945 Berlinv02/d710a-131.

"I received another communication": Ibid.

326 *"I appreciate very much":* Ibid.

"The time schedule on Groves' project": Henry L. Stimson to Truman, July 30, 1945, Truman Papers, https://www.trumanlibrary.org/oralhist/arnimage1.htm.

"Suggestion approved. Release when": Longhand note on back of Stimson to Truman cable, July 30, 1945, Ibid.

327 *"This was not foreseen at all":* Oral history interview, George M. Elsey, p. 350, Truman Libary.

"Marshal Stalin," Truman said: Robert J. Donovan, *Conflict and Crisis: The Presidency of Harry S. Truman, 1945–1948* (Columbia: University of Missouri Press, 1977), p. 88.

"There was no way we could": W. Averell Harriman and Elie Abel, *Special Envoy to Churchill and Stalin 1941–1946* (New York: Random House, 1975), p. 479.

328 *"You can sign any time you want"*: Memoirs by Harry S. Truman: *1945; Year of Decisions* (New York: Konecky & Konecky, 1955), p. 410.

"I declare the Berlin Conference": Conversation from Mee, *Meeting at Potsdam*, pp. 222–23.

"the Limey King": H. S. Truman to B. W. Truman, July 31, 1945, FBPAP:FCF, box 15.

329 *"My general feeling"*: Leahy, *I Was There*, p. 426.

"Potsdam had brought": Ibid., p. 429.

"Truman had stood up": Ibid., p. 427.

Chapter 37

330 *"Welcome to my country"*: Log of the President's Trip to Berlin Conference, August 2, 1945, Truman Library.

"most of our luncheon conversation": James F. Byrnes, *Speaking Frankly* (New York: Harper & Brothers, 1947), p. 263.

"I do not think it will be": William D. Leahy, *I Was There: The Personal Story of the Chief of Staff to Presidents Roosevelt and Truman Based on His Notes and Diaries Made at the Time* (New York: McGraw-Hill, 1950), p. 431.

"Admiral, would you like": Ibid.

331 *"military objectives and soldiers"*: Longhand note, July 25, 1945, Truman Papers, https://www.trumanlibrary.org/flip_books/index.php?tldate=1945-07-25&group id=3702&titleid=&pagenumber=1&collectionid=ihow.

"The President, coming home from": Oral history interview, Samuel I. Rosenman, pp. 57–58, Truman Library.

332 *"The Potsdam communique"*: Edward R. Murrow, *In Search of Light: The Broadcasts of Edward R. Murrow, 1938–1961* (New York: Alfred A. Knopf, 1967), p. 100.

LeMay issued a warning: "12 Japanese Cities Get B-29 Warnings," *New York Times*, August 1, 1945.

"death list": "150-Mile Train of 800 B-29s Strikes with 6000 Tons," *Washington Post*, August 2, 1945.

"the greatest single aerial strike": "World Peak Blow," *New York Times*, August 2, 1945.

"The sight was incredible": "Japs Hit by Mightiest of All Air Raids," *Monroe Evening Times*, Monroe, Wisconsin, August 2, 1945.

"the Manhattan Project": Communications to the Map Room, August 3, 1945, SMOF: Naval Aide to the President Files, box 5, Truman Library.

"Captain Vardaman": Ibid., August 4, 1945.

"was happy and thankful": David McCullough, *Truman* (New York: Touchstone, 1993), pp. 453–54.

333 *"an S.O.B."*: John Lewis Gaddis, *The United States and the Origins of the Cold War, 1941–1947* (New York: Columbia University Press, 1972), p. 243.

"The six most important industrial": W. F. Craven and J. L. Cate, eds., *The Army Air Forces in World War II*, vol. 5, *The Pacific: Matterhorn to Nagasaki* (Washington, DC: Office of Air Force History, 1983), p. 642.

"I didn't know much about this": Curtis E. LeMay with MacKinlay Kantor, *Mission with LeMay: My Story* (New York: Doubleday, 1965), p. 379.

"an Army city . . . a major": Memorandum, "Hiroshima," PSF, box 195, Truman Papers.

334 *"an elongated trash can"*: Richard Rhodes, *The Making of the Atomic Bomb* (New York: Touchstone, 1986), p. 701.

"Tinian is a miracle": Michael D. Gordin, *Five Days in August: How World War II Became a Nuclear War* (Princeton, NJ: Princeton University Press, 2007), p. 60.

"By dinnertime on the fifth": Rhodes, *Making of the Atomic Bomb,* p. 704.

335 *"It is like some weird dream"*: Ibid., p. 700.

"to be with those who brave": Ibid.

"Faith of our fathers, we will strive": "President Prays, Sings on Augusta," *Atlanta Constitution,* August 6, 1945.

"Dimples Eight Two to North": Paul W. Tibbets, "How to Drop an Atom Bomb," *Saturday Evening Post,* June 8, 1946.

336 *"Fifteen seconds to go"*: Rhodes, *Making of the Atomic Bomb,* p. 705.

"It's Hiroshima": Hiroshima and Nagasaki Bombing Timeline, Atomic Heritage Foundation, http://www.atomicheritage.org/history/hiroshima-and-nagasaki-bombing-timeline.

"I see it!": Rhodes, *Making of the Atomic Bomb,* p. 709.

"For the next minute": "Hiroshima Bomb Log Sold for $350,000," BBC News, http://news.bbc.co.uk/2/hi/americas/1898263.stm.

"I threw off the automatic": Tibbets, "How to Drop an Atom Bomb."

"There were two very distinct": "Hiroshima A-Bomb Log Nets $37,000," *New York Times,* November 24, 1971.

337 *"We turned back to look"*: "Bombings of Hiroshima and Nagasaki – 1945," online article, Atomic Heritage Foundation, http://www.atomicheritage.org/history/bombings-hiroshima-and-nagasaki-1945.

"Thank God the war is over": Rhodes, *Making of the Atomic Bomb,* p. 711.

"We heard a big noise like": "Hiroshima Survivor Recalls Day Atomic Bomb Was Dropped," VOA News, October 30, 2009. Also: Email and telephone correspondence with Ms. Morimoto West.

338 *"A sudden flash, an explosion"*: "A-Bombed Hiroshima – Today and 'That Day' in 1945," *Washington Post,* August 2, 1955.

Also at the table: Log of the President's Trip to Berlin Conference, July 7, 1945, Truman Library.

"Following info regarding Manhattan": Cominch & CNO to William D. Leahy, August 6, 1945, SMOF: Naval Aide to the President Files, box 6, Truman Papers.

"Captain," Truman said: Log of the President's Trip, July 7, 1945. Also Margaret Truman, *Harry S. Truman* (New York: William Morrow, 1973), p. 282.

"Fine! Fine!": Cynthia C. Kelly, ed., *Manhattan Project: The Birth of the Atomic Bomb in the Words of Its Creators, Eyewitnesses, and Historians* (New York: Black Dog & Leventhal, 2007), p. 331.

339 *"To the President"*: Henry L. Stimson to Truman, n.d., SMOF: Naval Aide to the President Files, box 6.

"It's time for us to get": Log of the President's Trip, July 7, 1945.

"tense with excitement": "Truman Tells Warship Crew," *Los Angeles Times,* August 7, 1945.

"Keep your seats, gentlemen": Ibid.

"I guess I'll go home": "Truman Dramatically Announces Successful Use of Atomic Bomb," *Hartford Courant,* August 7, 1945.

"somewhat excited and under some": Diary of Eben A. Ayers, n.d., Eben A. Ayers Papers, box 6, Truman Library.

340 *"I have got here what I think"*: Transcript of Eben A. Ayers press conference, August 6, 1945, Ayers Papers, box 6.

" 'Sixteen hours ago an American' ": Ibid.

"Now, the statement explains": Ibid.

"It's a hell of a story!": Ibid.

"a harnessing of the basic power": Statement by the President of the United States, August 6, 1945, Truman Library, https://www.trumanlibrary.org/publicpapers/viewpapers.php?pid=100.

"Their leaders promptly rejected": Statement by the President, August 6, 1945.

"The Japanese began the war": Ibid.

341 *"I shall give further consideration"*: Ibid.

Chapter 38

342 *"The president stepped out"*: Robert Ferrell, ed., *Truman in the White House: The Diary of Eben A. Ayers* (Columbia: University of Missouri Press, 1991), p. 58.

"Come on up to the room": Oral history interview, Eben A. Ayers, p. 54, Truman Library.

"Now, that may seem strange": Ibid.

343 *"[Truman] mentioned the terrible"*: Diary of Henry L. Stimson, August 8, 1945, Henry Lewis Stimson Papers, Yale University Library.

"When you punish your dog": Ibid.

"practically all living things": "Russia Attacks Japan, Second Atomic Bombing!," *Los Angeles Times,* August 9, 1945.

"The crew said, 'My God' ": "One Atomizer Erases 60% of Jap City," *Daily Boston Globe,* August 8, 1945.

344 *"the most revolutionary"*: "Atom Bomb Crew's Story!" *Chicago Daily Tribune,* August 8, 1945.

"Welcome home!": Conversation from transcript of Truman press conference, PSF:PCF, box 51, Truman Papers.

He owed the Metropolitan Poultry: Truman bank records, Bess W. Truman Papers, box 9, Truman Library.

"had not been able to solve": W. Averell Harriman to Harry S. Truman and James F. Byrnes, August 9, 1945, SMOF:MRF, box 1.

345 *"war trophies"*: *Memoirs by Harry S. Truman: 1945; Year of Decisions* (New York: Honecky & Honecky, 1955), p. 424.

"America asks that you take": "Pall Rising 20,000 Feet," *Los Angeles Times,* August 10, 1945.

"We are on our way to bomb": William L. Laurence, "Atomic Bombing of Nagasaki Told by Flight Member," *New York Times,* September 9, 1945.

"Joint Army-Navy-Civilian": Alex Wellerstein, "Nagasaki: The Last Bomb," *New Yorker,* August 7, 2015.

"I watched the assembly": Laurence, "Atomic Bombing."

346 *"This second demonstration"*: Truman, *Memoirs,* p. 426.

"The Japanese Government today": Ibid., p. 427.

347 *"Byrnes stopped while reading"*: *The Price of Vision: The Diary of Henry A. Wallace 1942–1946,* ed. John Morton Blum (Boston: Houghton Mifflin, 1973), p. 474.

348 *"all those kids"*: Blum, *Diary of Henry A. Wallace,* p. 474.

"beg us to accept unconditional": Richard B. Russell Jr. to Truman, August 7, 1945, Decision to Drop the Atomic Bomb Research File, Truman Library.

"I certainly regret the necessity": Truman to Russell, August 9, 1945, ibid.

"From the moment of surrender": Directive to the Supreme Commander for the Allied Armies, PSF, box 159, Truman Papers.

349 *"Rumors flew, switchboards jammed"*: "Truman Calmest Man in Capital as World Awaits," *Daily Boston Globe,* August 11, 1945.

"the calmest man in town": Ibid.

"The real significance": "Canadians' Work on Weapon Told," *New York Times,* August 7, 1945.

"Our savage generation cannot": "What the Atomic Bomb Means – a Digest of Opinion," *New York Times,* August 12, 1945.

"We have spent more than": Statement by the President of the United States, August 6, 1945, Truman Papers, https://www.trumanlibrary.org/publicpapers /viewpapers.php?pid=100.

350 *"My initial thought upon"*: Clark Clifford with Richard Holbrooke, *Counsel to the President: A Memoir* (New York: Random House, 1991), p. 57.

"skeptical": W. Averell Harriman to James F. Byrnes, August 11, 1945, Foreign Relations of the United States: Diplomatic Papers, https://history.state.gov /historicaldocuments/frus1945v06/d409.

"the Soviet forces, therefore": Ibid.

"The Allied Powers should reach": Harriman to Byrnes, cable 2, August 11, 1945, quoted in Truman, *Memoirs,* p. 430.

"most heated discussion": Ibid., p.431

351 *"Victory was already assured"*: "The Past Four Months: Unequalled in History," *New York Times,* August 12, 1945.

"fratricidal war": Truman, *Memoirs,* p. 434.

"nothing short of a miracle": Patrick Hurley to Harry S. Truman, September 12, 1945, SMOF:MRF, box 1, Truman Papers.

"Conclusions I have reached": Edwin W. Pauley to Truman, August 10, 1945, Foreign Relations: Diplomatic Papers, https://history.state.gov/historical documents/frus1945v07/d118.

"The President desires that such": Joint Chiefs of Staff to Douglas MacArthur and Chester W. Nimitz, cable, August 11, 1945, William D. Leahy Papers,

Records of the United States Joint Chiefs of Staff, box 9, record group 218, National Archives, College Park, MD.

"Secular history offers few": Edward R. Murrow, *In Search of Light: The Broadcasts of Edward R. Murrow, 1938–1961* (New York: Alfred A. Knopf, 1967), p. 102.

352 *"I have received this afternoon"*: Transcript of Truman press conference, August 14, 1945, Truman Library, https://www.trumanlibrary.org/publicpapers/view papers.php?pid=107.

353 *"We want Harry!"*: "Truman Replies to Shouts of Crowd, 'We Want Harry,'" *Christian Science Monitor,* August 15, 1945.

"[Truman] was on the White House": "Truman Leads Cheering Throngs in Capital's Wildest Celebration," *Atlanta Constitution,* August 15, 1945.

"Harry's such a wonderful man": David McCullough, *Truman* (New York: Touchstone, 1993), p. 462.

"I told her," he later recalled: Truman, *Memoirs,* p. 438.

"the wildest celebration": "Truman Leads Cheering Throngs."

Epilogue

355 *"We can set no bounds"*: Clement R. Attlee to Harry S. Truman, September 25, 1945, Albert M. Cornelius Papers, box 1, Franklin D. Roosevelt Presidential Library.

356 *"For President Truman the postwar"*: Robert J. Donovan, *Conflict and Crisis: The Presidency of Harry S. Truman, 1945–1948* (Columbia: University of Missouri Press, 1977), p. 107.

THE BUCK STOPS HERE!: "The Buck Stops Here Desk Sign," Truman Library, https://www.trumanlibrary.org/buckstop.htm.

"a powder keg ready to explode": Commander in Chief Army Air Forces Advance Tokyo Japan to War Department, cable, September 18, 1945, William D. Leahy Papers, Records of the United States Joint Chiefs of Staff, box 9, record group 218, National Archives, College Park, MD.

357 *"Harry S. Truman was no 'accidental'"*: Margaret Truman, *Harry S. Truman* (New York: William Morrow, 1973), p. 43.

358 *"as cancer and other long-term"*: "The Manhattan Project: an Interactive History: The Atomic Bombing of Hiroshima," United States Department of Energy, https://www.osti.gov/opennet/manhattan-project-history/Events/1945/hiroshima.htm.

"It is my opinion that the use": William D. Leahy, *I Was There: The Personal Story of the Chief of Staff to Presidents Roosevelt and Truman Based on His Notes and Diaries Made at the Time* (New York: Whittlesey House, 1950), p. 441.

"all war is immoral": Richard Rhodes, *Dark Sun: The Making of the Hydrogen Bomb* (New York: Simon & Schuster Paperbacks, 1995), pp. 21–22.

359 *"The face of war is the face of"*: Henry L. Stimson, "The Decision to Use the Atomic Bomb," *Harper's,* February 1947.

"I regarded the dropping": George C. Marshall, transcript of interview,

February 11, 1957, Marshall Foundation, http://marshallfoundation.org
/library/wp-content/uploads/sites/16/2014/05/Marshall_Interview_Tape14.pdf.
"The historic fact remains": Winston S. Churchill, *The Second World War*, vol. 6,
Triumph and Tragedy (New York: Bantam, 1962), p. 546.
"It occurred to me": James Carroll, *House of War: The Pentagon and the
Disastrous Rise of American Power* (Boston: Houghton Mifflin, 2006), p. 44.
"The simplest explanation": Stephen Ambrose and Douglas Brinkley, *Rise to
Globalism: American Foreign Policy Since 1938* (New York: Penguin, 2011), p. 48.

360   *"You know, many times"*: Oral history interview, George Tames, pp. 39–40,
Truman Library.
"Then," recalled a photographer: Ibid.
"Harry S. Truman is now": "Obama's Legacy Will Be Like Truman's," *Boston
Globe*, February 18, 2015.
"Americans felt leaderless": Jonathan Daniels, *The Man of Independence* (Port
Washington, NY: Kennikat, 1971), p. 19.
"I do the very best I know how": "Good Men at Work," *Life*, February 5, 1951.

Index